The Magnificent
Max Baer

The Magnificent Max Baer

The Life of the Heavyweight Champion and Film Star

COLLEEN AYCOCK
with DAVID W. WALLACE

McFarland & Company, Inc., Publishers
Jefferson, North Carolina

ALSO OF INTEREST
BY COLLEEN AYCOCK AND MARK SCOTT
AND FROM MCFARLAND

Tex Rickard: Boxing's Greatest Promoter (2012);
The First Black Boxing Champions: Essays on Fighters of the 1800s to the 1920s (edited, 2011);
Joe Gans: A Biography of the First African American World Boxing Champion (2008)

Unless otherwise noted, all photographs are from Colleen Aycock's collection.

LIBRARY OF CONGRESS CATALOGUING-IN-PUBLICATION DATA

Names: Aycock, Colleen, author.
Title: The magnificent Max Baer : the life of the heavyweight champion and film star / Colleen Aycock, with David W. Wallace.
Description: Jefferson, North Carolina : McFarland & Company, Inc., Publishers, 2018 | Includes bibliographical references and index.
Identifiers: LCCN 2018030976 | ISBN 9781476671611 (softcover : acid free paper) ∞
Subjects: LCSH: Baer, Max, 1909–1959. | Boxers (Sports)—United States—Biography. | Jewish boxers—United States—Biography. | Actors—United States—Biography.
Classification: LCC GV1132.B3 A93 2018 | DDC 796.83092 [B]—dc23
LC record available at https://lccn.loc.gov/2018030976

BRITISH LIBRARY CATALOGUING DATA ARE AVAILABLE

ISBN (print) 978-1-4766-7161-1
ISBN (ebook) 978-1-4766-3290-2

© 2018 Colleen Aycock. All rights reserved

No part of this book may be reproduced or transmitted in any form or by any means, electronic or mechanical, including photocopying or recording, or by any information storage and retrieval system, without permission in writing from the publisher.

Front cover: Publicity photograph of Max Baer, 1935

Printed in the United States of America

*McFarland & Company, Inc., Publishers
Box 611, Jefferson, North Carolina 28640*

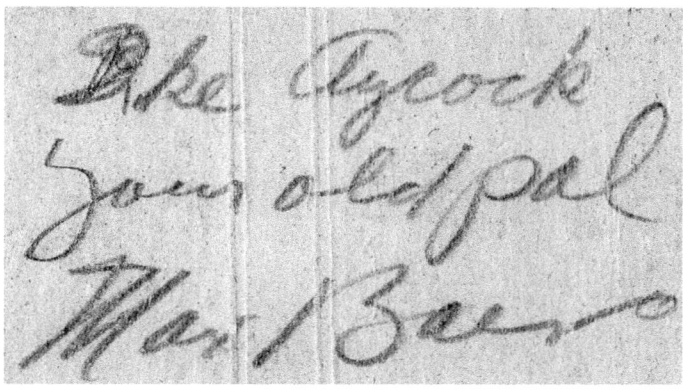

This book is dedicated to my father,
Norman "Ike" Aycock,
one of Max Baer's sparring partners.
The inscription above is from the box Max gave him
that held the pair of gloves they used in the ring.

Table of Contents

Acknowledgments	ix
Preface	1
ONE • The Butcher Boys, 1831 to 1929	5
TWO • Livermore Larruper Kills Campbell, 1930	18
THREE • New York Meets Lochinvar, 1930, 1931	32
FOUR • Pied Piper's Road Back to Contender, 1931	53
FIVE • Elimination Battles of 1932	65
SIX • Battle of the Two Maxes, 1933	80
SEVEN • The Heavyweight Championship, Carnera, 1934	97
EIGHT • Championship Year, 1934 to 1935	113
NINE • Clown Prince Loses Crown to Braddock, 1935	126
TEN • Former Champion Meets Louis, 1935	150
ELEVEN • Madcap Exhibition Tour, 1936	166
TWELVE • Baer Storms England, Farr and Foord, 1937, 1938	178
THIRTEEN • No Clowning for Nova, 1939	197
FOURTEEN • The Screwball Championship, Galento, 1940	214
FIFTEEN • The Magnificent's Last Fights, 1940–1941	228
SIXTEEN • You're in the Army Now! 1942 to 1945	241
SEVENTEEN • Glamour Boy in Hollywood, 1933 to 1958	251
EIGHTEEN • Maximilian's Last Act	270
Postscript	279
Appendix: Ring Record	280
Chapter Notes	284
Bibliography	301
Index	303

Acknowledgments

The book is, of course, dedicated to my father, former Depression-era professional boxer C. Norman "Ike" Aycock, who taught me that hard work and determination would give me a competitive edge in both sport and life.

This biography has been an Aycock-Wallace family project. My husband, Dave Wallace, has been there from the outset, with his computer help for the dissertation 35 years ago; with travel and photographs for all of the projects written for Texas, the U.S. Capitol Historical Society and Statuary Hall; and the same for all boxing books co-authored with Mark Scott. For this project, Dave was even more instrumental in channeling the work to completion: locating, extracting, and feeding me important research materials. We worked side-by-side, taking very few days off, for nine intense months. I want to thank my brother, Bobby Aycock, for the gloves and for locating Dad's scrapbook, which held a wealth of detail from the pages of boxing and golf history. I want to thank my two sons Jason Wallace and Neil Wallace for addressing my questions about court hearings and medicine, respectively. Mom has finally called in her IOUs.

I am indebted to Judge William Pettite, longtime friend of Max Baer's manager, Ancil Hoffman. For Mr. Pettite's many personal Baer, Hoffman and Dempsey stories and documents, and for our many conversations—from February 11, 2014, to the present—I am grateful. His exchanges with Ancil Hoffman, his meetings with Buddy Baer, and his early family ties to Nevada history give personal insight to the life and times written about in this book. Thank you, Melinda Peak, Baer descendant, for her discussion of the Baer sisters and other family stories.

I want to thank authors of the following acclaimed books: Tony Gee, *Up to Scratch: Bareknuckle Fighting and the Champions of the Prize-ring*, for his knowledge of British and early boxing history; Michael DeLisa, *Cinderella Man: The James J. Braddock Story*, for his research on the Braddock-Baer story; Mike Silver, *The Arc of Boxing*, for his broad knowledge of the sport and Max Baer in context; and Harry Boonin, *Never Tell a Boy Not to Fight*, for his help on early Jewish boxers and managers. All four authors contributed documents and offered valuable comments.

If it were not for the help of boxing collector David Bergin, this book would have sorely lacked for photographs and hidden gems of articles I might have missed. I want to thank Dan Cuoco, former president of IBRO and current publisher of its quarterly journal, for his help locating documents and photos, and for entertaining such necessary requests as, "May I interrupt your work again, and have you score this fight for me?" Thanks to other experts who entertained similar requests.

Special thanks to research librarians Alexander Guibert, Center for Sacramento History, and his work on the radio collections of Max Baer; Sandy Irwin, director of the Durango Public Library for her work locating documents of the 1918 influenza epidemic in Colorado; Ms. Coi Drummon-Gehrig, Digital Image Collection administrator of the Denver Public Library, with special help from the Western History Department; and Margaret Schlankey, head of Reference Services, Dolph Briscoe Center for American History, University of Texas, for pulling documents from the *New York Journal American* morgue files and granting me the necessary study time at the LBJ Library amidst the security detail of a visit from five living U.S. presidents. It was quite amusing to see my well-traveled, book-packed vehicle cordoned off and parked next to the immaculately pristine, and very large, presidential motorcade. Such is the work and privilege of a boxing historian.

Preface

Max Baer was one of the most colorful boxers in ring history, a bright light on the drab face of the Great Depression in the 1930s.

Initially, he was known as a killer in the ring, with a knockout overhand right that when connected with a chin or temple could put an opponent to sleep, sadly permanently. In addition, Max had an iron chin, one of the greatest in history, as witnessed by Max Schmeling and Joe Louis. And not since Dempsey-Willard had there been a title match like Baer-Carnera, in which the contender dropped the heavyweight champion to the canvas so many times with such ferociousness. That battle would be enshrined in two boxing films starring Baer, bookending his movie career: *The Prizefighter and the Lady*, made in 1933 before the actual battle, and *The Harder They Fall*, reprised in 1956 with Humphrey Bogart.

When the young star won the world heavyweight title in 1934, he was expected to keep it for ten years, and was projected to be one of the greatest fighters of all time. He held it for only 364 days. The upset was astounding, so much so that many sportswriters of the day refused to believe his first title defense was aboveboard. Then, after Max worked his way back to another title shot, he gave it away to his brother Buddy. Everyone predicted what Max Baer *could* do, but no one could predict what he *would* do.

Max entered the boxing profession in Oakland, California, in 1929, from the same industrial foundry yards where manager Jack Kearns had picked up Jack Dempsey, a little more than a decade earlier. With promoter Tex Rickard's death in 1929, his monopoly on big fights evaporated, destabilizing championship boxing. Promoters rushed in to fill the void, creating turmoil in match selections and uncertainty in the results.

The 1930s began with awkward, indecisive wins and questionable decisions. At the beginning of the decade, the heavyweight crown was lost on a foul, then won on a decision. Max Schmeling won the title on a foul (when Jack Sharkey was ahead on points) in 1930. In the rematch of 1932, Jack Sharkey won by a controversial split decision. In the eyes of the public, neither fighter had truly won the heavyweight crown.

Never before was it quite so obvious to the public that the heavyweight title, and challengers to the title, were determined by referees, state commissioners, promoters, lawsuits, even the mob. Managers and promoters were all competing, or colluding, with one another for boxers and matches. There were so many former champions trying to regain their crowns and income during the 1930s that they made for an entire category of title contenders, making it difficult for the next tier of boxers to break into the ranks. During 1936, Jack Sharkey, Max Schmeling, Primo Carnera, Max Baer, and contender Joe Louis were all staging some kind of comeback on some kind of exhibition tour.

Complicating the matter was the international element. Not since 1906 (with Tommy Burns) had the heavyweight title of gloved boxing been owned by a non–American. From 1928 to 1935, the crown transferred from American to German (Schmeling) to American (Sharkey) to Italian (Carnera) to American (Baer). Westbrook Pegler described it as the "Era of Wonderful Madness." And Max Baer was at the center of this madness.

Baer was particularly heartening in that he became the first real hope for a hard-hitting, Dempsey-like champion. And to satisfy the desire of the fans, Jack Dempsey did return to the spotlight. He came back, in the second phase of his boxing career, to promote fights. Of all the champions and contenders in the ring, Dempsey was most connected with Max Baer. He became his promoter, trainer, and mentor. Max said that the best things boxing gave him were his two real friends: Jack Dempsey and Ancil Hoffman. Max and Ancil had one of the closest relationships of any boxer and manager in the sport, sharing the road, finances, residence, movies, lawyers and accountants for decades, until Max's untimely death.

Before Max Baer, the prize ring was not a place for laughter. It was a hard business. But after the death of opponent Frankie Campbell, Max tried to make it a nicer, better place. Whenever Max was introduced in the ring with other ring stars, he was always given the loudest cheers. He loved his audiences as much as they loved him.

In the year 1940, there were only a few days when Max was absent from the news, and that was five years after he lost the title. Sportswriters were compelled to follow him because they never knew what he would do in the ring or out. His personality came with built-in copy; some said it even "oozed" with it. Max remained newsworthy his entire life. Research for this work covered ten-thousand pieces of published information about him.

Some considered Baer an incorrigible egotist, but he explained it as confidence. Boxing gave him the courage to follow his instincts in the ring, on stage, and in life. He was a masterful emcee and a fluent and graceful entertainer. His ever-happy charm chased away the gloom. He wore colorful clothes. He drove fancy cars. Even before he won the championship, he had three of the finest cars money could buy. He succeeded in two sets of elimination battles during the decade, won the heavyweight title, and after he was dethroned, he won over international audiences. At the end of his career, fans worshipped him like a martyr.

Although Max's tastes were expensive, he was never afraid of being poor. He felt he could always return to the meat block in the butcher business.

Two heavyweight boxers stood out in the decade of the 1930s: Max Baer in the first half and Joe Louis in the second half. The two would meet exactly in the middle—in 1935. Not until the economy had bottomed out and begun its climb back did the heavyweight title regain its promise in the person of Joe Louis. At the end of the decade, 1940, Louis would be champion, and Baer the number-one contender.

Max Baer's life and title reign were short, if not provocative, fostering many questions. Did he have one of the most powerful punches of all time? Was he a womanizer? Was he Jewish? Was he a quitter? Was he the brash rogue who failed to train, and thus, who deserved to lose his world title to James J. Braddock? Was he connected to the mob? And what was to be made of the surprising losses that seemed to mar his achievement in the history books?

Historians have addressed these questions variously over time. In 1934, Baer's initial life story was published in the inaugural edition of *Jack Dempsey's Fight Magazine* in an article by Jack Kafoed. Seven years later in 1941, Nat Fleischer, editor of *The Ring* magazine, wrote a short biography, *Max Baer: The Glamour Boy of the Ring*, capturing Baer's rise from boxing star to cultural icon.

Only a few magazine articles were written after his death in 1959. Forty-five years later, in 2005, a shower of books and a movie appeared about the Cinderella Man, James J. Braddock, marking the centennial of Braddock's birth. Max Baer's story fell into the background of the story of the unlikely contender (Braddock) who came out of the shadowy slums of the Depression to beat the glittery movie star (Baer) who seemed more intent on dancing than fighting. The books published in 2005 about the fairy-tale story of the down-and-out, non-ranked non-contender who beat the champion were Jim Hague's *Braddock: The Rise of the Cinderella Man*; and two books with the same title, *Cinderella Man*, one by Michael DeLisa, subtitled *The James J. Braddock Story*, and the other by Jeremy Schaap, subtitled *James J. Braddock, Max Baer, and the Greatest Upset in Boxing History*.

Max Baer's winning battle with Max Schmeling in 1933 was overshadowed in 1936 and 1938 by Max Schmeling's bouts with Joe Louis. David Margolick's book, *Beyond Glory: Joe Louis vs. Max Schmeling, and a World on the Brink*, was also published in 2005, which also saw the release of the movie *Cinderella Man*, directed by Ron Howard. Well-known screen personalities selected for the starring roles were Russell Crowe, who played Braddock; Renée Zellweger, who played Mae Braddock; and Paul Giamatti, who played manager Joe Gould. Few recognized the star Craig Bierko, who played Max Baer, and no follower of boxing recognized the villainous character the actor portrayed. Max Baer Jr. said of the movie that the only thing Ron Howard got right about his father was his name.

After a decade as a background story, interest in Baer re-emerged in 2016 with a Judaic focus. Two books were published in 2016: *Max Baer and Barney Ross: Jewish Heroes of Boxing*, by Jeffrey Sussman, who identified Max as a Jewish boxer; and *Stars in the Ring: Jewish Champions in the Golden Age of Boxing*, by Mike Silver, who clarified that while Max was not a Jewish boxer, he was, nevertheless, a hero to the Jews.

Each new biographical focus has produced more questions for researchers, such as: Did Max Baer consider himself Jewish? Why did he wear the Star of David on his trunks for his fight with Max Schmeling but not for Tony Galento? What explained Baer's poor title showing against James Braddock? How did he move from the ring stage to the movie stage, and what other boxers did he take with him to that stage? How did his presence in films help to develop the docudrama or the boxing film genre? And what did he do in service to the military during World War II? These are just some of the questions regarding Max Baer's colorful, mercurial, and very full life that this book addresses.

So, amidst all the varied and sometimes confusing stories about Max Baer, why am I so interested in the boxer-soldier-movie star? There are several reasons. First of all, Baer was more complex than his many labels suggest. He was more than "killer," "playboy" or "clown." Secondly, my feelings about the man are deeply rooted in my own family history. I know what life is like for the professional always on the road, mastering his trade, competing for titles, satisfying sponsors and other public demands. Although Max loved his family, he spent more time on the road than at home. He literally died on the road. My brother was a PGA touring golf pro who also died close to the age Max died. The long haul for any touring professional is gritty, and takes its toll on the body and family. My father also faced that toll. He was one of Max Baer's many sparring partners, and he eventually died from dementia-pugilistica. Yet the stories my father told me and the opinions he held of Max were very different from those reflected in a movie that my father never lived to see.

Finally, sixty years after Baer's death, it's time to take a look at what we know about the man and put it all together in a comprehensive biography that includes his boxing, movie, and military careers. With the amazing story of Max Baer, intersecting as it did with the former champion Jack Dempsey, the movies, and World War II, we pick up the marvelous and always surprising link in the chain of ring history.

ONE

The Butcher Boys, 1831 to 1929

Sportswriters working the streets and sporting venues during the Great Depression developed a writing style as tough and gritty as the hardscrabble lives they covered. It mattered little if the facts of their stories were exaggerated or underreported as long as they captured the imagination and sold papers. The language was often demeaning, harsh, sexist, and racist. Sportswriter Ernest Barcella said that Buddy predicted a knockout of Joe Louis in six rounds or less, while Louis "Don't say nuthin'. He just keeps on punching and dreaming—of Southern fried chicken."[1] Bill Corum called Tommy Farr a toothless old pit bull, or worse yet, an old washerwoman after a brisk day at the ironing board. In the vernacular of the game, one Cauliflower Market Reporter said that Ancil Hoffman had bet 20 G's on his boy to put the crusher on Comiskey.[2] The style was alliterative, metaphoric, sardonic and snappy at a time when "Sports" was the largest special section of the mainstream mass-media: the newspaper.

Stories had to be memorable. Shufflin' Sam predicted that Max Baer would take Tony Galento like Grant took Richmond. A *New York Times* reporter said of Max's giant brother Buddy that he had the body of an Ajax, but the fighting heart of a field mouse. He noted that four field mice wrote in to protest. Bill Corum predicted of the Baer-Nova fight that Nova would beat Baer, "because anyone who wants to can."[3] Corum compared Max to a powerful automobile with no starter. Henry McLemore said of Baer in his battle with Louis that Max was like a turtle: "He crawled in his shell and waited for the worst to happen." And of the "Cinderella Man" title fight with James Braddock, director Ron Howard might not have been so eager to make a movie seventy years after the fact had he read McLemore's version of the bout: "For 15 rounds Maxie and Jimmy went through a routine that was a cross between a Viennese waltz without music and two elderly butterfly collectors gathering specimens."[4]

Some believed Max Baer needed no exaggeration because he was just that good. Grantland Rice, considered the grandfather of sportswriters, claimed that Max Baer "might have been one of the best fighters of all time. He certainly had all the physical equipment needed."[5] Dr. Vincent Nardiello, physical examiner of many of the heavyweights through Sugar Ray Robinson, commented: "I've never seen a mass of muscles to compare with Baer's. Baer had the most remarkable physical equipment I ever saw. He should have been heavyweight champion for years."[6] In addition to the physical assets, Paul Zimmerman wrote, "We have always felt that this giant of a man possessed probably more physical assets and an active mind to go with them than any boxer ever took into the ring. He was endowed with power and speed and cunning."[7]

During a professional career that spanned the entire decade of the 1930s, from 1929 to 1941, the Californian was considered one of the most colorful characters in the Golden Age of Heavyweights. His many ring names supported this. Sportswriters strived to one-up the famous name-coining Damon Runyon when assigning unique tags to the Livermore Larruper. Labels like the "Pied Piper of Punch," the "Lothario of the Ring," the "Magnificent Screwball," "Madcap Maxie," the "Roaming Romeo of the Ring," the "Heart Buster of the Beezer Breakers," the "Clouting Clown," the "Clown Prince of Fistiana," the "Pagliacci of Swing," or the "Livermore Loon," all combined Baer's unorthodox fighting style with his flamboyant personality. Even the pun on his name, "Max-a-million," pointed to the limitless wise-cracks Max brought to the otherwise deadly-serious game. He was a natural entertainer, an "Adonis" and a "Glamour Boy" for the women, and a killer in the ring. With the perfect body and the striking ability of a Hercules, it was his first moniker, the "Butcher Boy," that evoked his ranch-to-ring reputation and defined the source of his signature sledgehammer, right-hand chop.

Even before Baer stepped into a boxing ring, he had inherited his harshest moniker from a family line of butchers. Max's paternal grandfather, Achill Baer, was a master butcher in the early days of the Western frontier. According to Max's brother Buddy, their grandfather was "a French Jew from Alsace-Lorraine who migrated to America as a youth."[8] Achill (born in 1831) cut and packed meat at the termination point of the Western cattle trail where the Union Pacific railroad came to Cheyenne, in the Wyoming Territory, in 1867. Achill and his wife Frances Fischel, twenty years younger (born in 1851), had two girls born in Cheyenne: Matilda and Minnie. Jacob (Max Baer's father) and his six brothers were born after the family left the rugged frontier town.

It has been mentioned in several family stories that Achill named his sons for the tribes of Israel. However, only one of those names represented a leader of the twelve Hebrew tribes—Benjamin, for which the origin of the name is questionable in that Benjamin's middle name was Franklin. The other brothers were: Charles, Edward, Jacob, Marx M. (namesake for Max), Joseph (who died at age 16), and Phillip (who died before his first birthday).

By the 1890s, the Achill Baer family had relocated to Elyria, Colorado, a large stockyard area along the railroad, three miles south of Denver's city center. There Achill established a meat market and served as town magistrate. Because boxing was illegal in Denver, the sport took up residence in Elyria, with many famed early boxers plying their trade in the suburb. The city was annexed by Denver in 1904. Son Jake Baer became magistrate after Achill's death, and son Ben took the job after Jake. They were all big, physical men. Papa Achill died in 1900, Mama Fanny in 1925, daughter Tillie in 1903, son Charles in 1918, and son Joseph in 1925. All were buried in the historic Riverside Cemetery in Elyria-Swansea, Denver.

Max Baer's father Jacob or "Jake" Baer was born in Red Jacket, Michigan (Calumet today) on October 12, 1875. Jacob also became a master butcher and stayed in the meat-packing business throughout his working life. By 1900, he was foreman of the Platte Valley Packing Company in Elyria. He was so fast with his hands that he won numerous meat-trimming contests, indicating not only his strength and skill but also his competitive nature that he transferred to his two boys.

After son Max won the heavyweight boxing title in 1934, Jake "reminded Baer the younger that he was not the first but the second world champion in the family … that in 1902 he had taken the meat dressing title from World Champion Muldoon at the Chicago Stockyards."[9] Buddy also explained how in 1910 his father won a medal for dressing

Three-Mile House, a roadhouse and saloon in Elyria (Denver), Colorado, that provided a back room for boxing. Jacob Baer and other notables boxed there in the late 1890s when Achill Baer was sheriff (courtesy Denver Public Library, Western History Collection).

a 1400-pound steer in three minutes and thirty-seven seconds in Denver: "Dressed it so there was an American flag on its back." The process involved "opening the steer, removing the insides, splitting him and turning back the hide."[10] Buddy said, "He could take one side of hide off a steer with three swipes of a six-inch knife."[11]

In addition to his meatpacking skills, Jacob Baer was also an accomplished boxer, earning a competitive title. The obituary of former boxer Pat Kennedy of Denver (1876–1945) mentioned that Kennedy fought and defeated Jake Baer, "one-time champion prizefighter of the west and father of Max Baer," in 1897 at the "Three Mile House," the local road house in Elyria.[12] Records indicated that Jacob was a sparring partner to Tom Sharkey, and son Buddy mentioned that his father had gone twenty-two rounds with Jim Jeffries.[13] But Jacob's mother was not as proud as the Baer menfolk of having a male heir who was a "boxer," a tough label in the day when some considered it to be one rung above professional criminal. According to a family story, when Jacob's mother discovered her son prizefighting, she threw all his boxing equipment down the well and that ended his career.

John Lardner interviewed Jake in 1934, and reported that when Jake was in Denver, "He trained Sharkey, Ben Yanger, Young Corbett, Bob Armstrong, George Dixon, and Kid Broad."[14] Jacob's reputation as a ring man was evident in a wire sent to him by Thomas Beaudry, head of the Piggly-Wiggly grocery store chain, when son Buddy was born. The wire stated, "Congratulations on the new white hope." Buddy was born in 1915, during the last year of the reign of Jack Johnson, the first African American World Heavyweight

Champion. True to the prediction, Buddy grew up to fight the second great black Heavyweight Champion, Joe Louis, "as a white hope."[15]

Omaha, Nebraska, and Kansas City, Missouri, were other Western trail drive and railroad destinations where butchers could find ready work. Jacob Baer first moved out of his father's Denver home to relocate to Kansas City in 1904. Soon after, he joined his brothers Charles and Edward in Omaha, where he worked for the Cudahy Packing Company. Jacob rented a room with the John H. Bales family and soon after married the Bales' daughter Dora, December 24, 1904. Brother Ed served as Jacob's best man. Jacob was 29, and Dora was 26. Both John Bales and Jacob Baer worked for the Swift meatpacking company at the time.

Born in South Omaha were Jacob and Dora's first two children: Frances "Fanny" May, born October 23, 1905, and named for Jacob's mother, and Maximilian "Max" Adelbert, born a chubby 9½ pounds on February 11, 1909, named for Jacob's brother. By 1910, the Jacob Baer family was reported in the federal Census as renting a ranch with brother Edward in Douglas, Nebraska, sixty miles south of Omaha. Both Edward and Jacob were registered in the Omaha City Directory as working for the Higgins Packing Company, which indicated that they were operating a stockyard in Douglas for the packing company in Omaha.

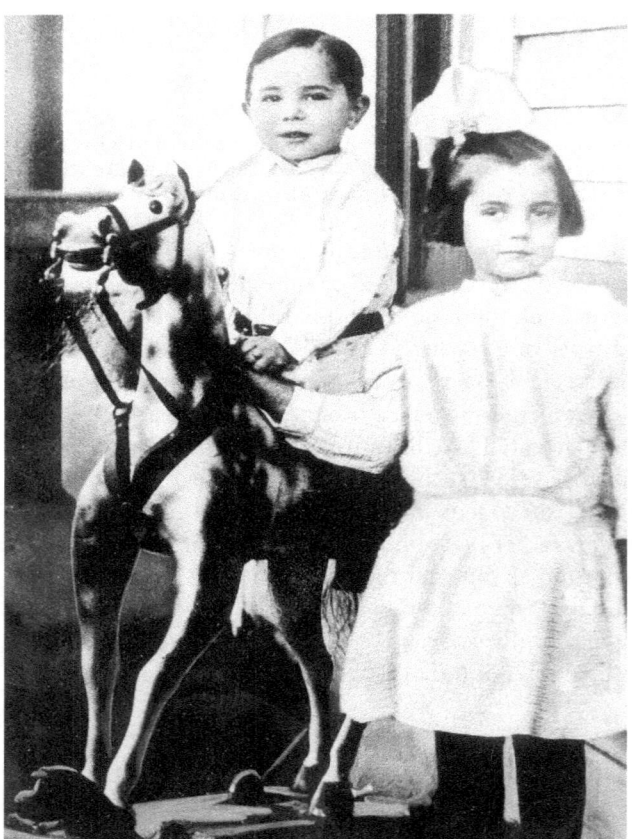

Left: Max Adelbert on rocking horse, four years younger than his eldest sister Fanny May. Both were born in South Omaha, Nebraska. *Right:* Max Baer, age 6, in Koehler, New Mexico.

Two years later, the Jacob Baer family left Nebraska for Denver, where two more children were born: Bernice Jeanette, July 13, 1911, and Jacob Henry Jr., "Buddy," June 11, 1915.

Shortly after Buddy's birth in 1915, Jacob Baer was sent to the mining town of Koehler, New Mexico, to supervise the slaughterhouse operation there. Koehler was a company railroad and coal-mining town established in 1906, sixteen miles southwest of Raton.[16] Koehler Junction, three miles west of town, was the endpoint for the New Mexico cattle trails; and with the convergence of the rail line, Koehler became the largest packing plant outside of Denver. The town eventually grew to a population of 1800, with 158 company homes, three boarding houses, and numerous bathhouses before it was abandoned and became another of the many Western ghost towns.[17] Buddy recalled being told that during their time in Koehler his sister Frances was sent to a boarding school in Denver. No mention was made of Max's schooling. It is possible that at age six or seven, he went to the two-story school in town for the year the family resided in Koehler. Jacob moved the family back to Denver before locating a job in Southern Colorado where his brother Edward worked.

By June 1916, Jacob was successfully supervising the Durango Packing Plant owned by the Graden Mercantile Company. The operation processed meat from the San Juan Basin, a 7,500-square-mile area in the Southwest near the Four Corners region, with the majority of the land in northwestern New Mexico. Jacob also shipped cattle to Denver. Max accompanied his father on one of these trips to Denver.

But in September of 1918, more Americans were needed overseas. On September 12, the Baer brothers joined the many others who registered for the military draft for World War I. Suddenly, in October, Colorado was hit hard by the influenza epidemic of 1918, called the Spanish Flu, but which may have originated in the United States. (The H1N1 virus, also referred to as Swine Flu, had jumped from hogs to the hog farmers and was spread by soldiers.) First afflicted was Charles Baer, who was living in Denver. He died on October 15, leaving wife Margaret and young daughters Della and Esther. (His family was eventually buried together in Riverside Cemetery at Denver.)

The virus spread quickly. Hundreds died throughout Colorado. Schools were closed for six months or longer, homes were quarantined, and public funerals were prohibited. Cities ran out of doctors and coffins. Newspapers published death lists. In Durango, Ed Baer came down with the flu and was sick for only a week before he died on November 5. He was 38. All members of the two Baer families (Ed's wife Mayme and brother Jacob's family) were listed in the *Durango Democrat* on November 6, 1918, as being "critically ill." Max was nine and Buddy three. Jacob had suddenly lost his two closest brothers, and had almost lost his own life, along with members of his family. It must have been a terrifying experience for the nine-year-old. (The pandemic would hit Americans again in 2009. Studies have shown the virus to affect the muscles and walls of the heart, which may have played a long-term role in the early deaths of these Baer family members who already may have been genetically predisposed to heart disease.) The young Max Baer only narrowly escaped death at this time.

It was in the frontier town of Durango that Max heard about Jack Dempsey. In 1919, in Toledo, Ohio, Dempsey reinvigorated the fight business with his world title win over Jess Willard. Coloradans were proud of their connection with "the Manassa Mauler," a tag commemorating his birthplace, a small town in Southern Colorado, ten miles north of the New Mexico state line. Dempsey fought many of his early battles in Durango, in the Gem Theater and in various saloons. Like Max Baer, his father, and others, such as the Chicago "Packinghouse Pride" Battling Nelson, Jack Dempsey was known as a "knockerout" with a sledgehammer blow. Max would follow in this tradition, and in less than a decade, he would be connected with Jack Dempsey.

Jacob Baer had never owned property or an automobile. But in 1923, he had saved enough money to buy a car and move his family from Colorado to California, to another cattle area. Driving during the day over rutted wagon roads and pitching a tent at night was a challenging adventure for the six-member family. In the middle of the trip, an axle broke and the car had to be towed to a gasoline stop in northern Arizona, where the family remained camped until a replacement part could be built. The car was repaired, and with water bags strapped to the front grill, they drove 125 miles over the desert to Needles, California, where they were again stopped. A city roadblock was set up for the filming of a Tom Mix "Western" movie.[18] The glamour and excitement of meeting the movie star likely planted the acting seed in Max's impressionable young mind. Much later, when the two would meet again in Hollywood, Max discovered that Tom Mix kept a boxing gym at his studio office.

After arriving in California, the Baer family stayed with Dora's relatives near Oakland. In the next few years, Jacob easily gained employment in the slaughterhouse business in the various cities of Hayward, Galt, and Livermore, all in the same general area among the thousands of acres of cattle country east of the San Francisco Bay.[19] In 1928, Jacob Baer leased a hog ranch in Galt for his own meatpacking business before buying the Twin Oaks ranch, 30 miles south of Oakland in the Livermore foothills. It was at this time that Augie Silva, a young Portuguese emigrant, one year younger than Max, came to work for Jacob on the Livermore ranch. Augie was so endearing that the Baers adopted him as a son.

Jacob Baer was a large, brawny man of six feet. Both sons resembled him in stature in their later lives. As a teen, Max was tall, broad-shouldered, and lean. His strength and endurance were conditioned by hauling heavy slabs of meat over his right shoulder, herding cattle, and slinging an ax. At age 18, he stood 6 feet and almost 2 inches, had a 44-inch chest, and weighed 190 pounds. Arthur Daley said his shoulders were so wide that he instinctively went through a doorway sideways. His waist seemed as slim as a girl's at 32 inches.[20] Papa Baer told the story about his son's determined work ethic: "Sometimes he worked from 4 o'clock in the morning until 9 or 10 at night. He killed pigs and delivered them from the ranch. One time he dug a gravel pit for 16 hours."[21] He was a strong and obedient son.

The dark, curly-headed Max was always very genial, with a sparkle in his eyes and a boyish smile that revealed his dimpled cheeks. He was shy but personable with the cowboys and enjoyed their witty banter. He said he didn't really go in for sports, although he played a little baseball—but didn't like it. Tried football in school—"too rough."[22] Having missed part of elementary school, Max was probably ill-prepared for higher education. He dropped out of high school to help his father with work on the ranch.

The one physical virtue that Max carried throughout his ring career was no exaggeration: "He was powerful enough to slay an ox with his bare fists."[23] His punch could fell a steer or kill a man.[24] Actually, it wasn't an ox or a steer that Baer slew with his bare fist; "it was a hog," corrected Oakland reporter Dave Hope. He told the story about the time young Max went to the Schenone ranch to pick up a big, strong, angry hog. Three ranch hands tried to put the unwilling animal into the back of a pickup truck, but the pig struggled away. Max came up and "dropped a roundhouse right behind the ear, and the hog subsided."[25]

Several stories circulated about Max's early life as a defender of maidenly honor, but they were not true. One explained how Max had to whack a cowboy for offending his date as the couple walked out of a dance hall. Max said emphatically, "I didn't know how to dance until after I was twenty. I didn't take a girl to that dance. The truth is I never had up to then, kissed a girl, held a girl's hand or escorted any girl around. I was afraid of them—and that's the truth."[26] The only girls he knew were his sisters, and they were *his* protectors.

He admitted that as a child he had been a big "sissy." "I never struck a blow with my fist until I was nineteen. My older sister Frances saved me from getting beaten up by rough boys slapping me around.... I'm not kidding. That's the truth. Few people have lived in more actual fear of death than I lived in fear of physical suffering."[27] Baer's mother had also instilled in him a fear of mussing his clothes. (Such concern may have given him a desire for nice clothes, which he bought regularly as soon as he had money.) But when young, he was truly shy and introverted, and avoided any kind of trouble, admitting that he was the "yellowest" kid in America.

Another story often told about Baer was that he decked a man for accusing him of stealing a bottle of wine outside a dance hall. Baer was mortified by that story, which made him sound like a thief and the aggressor. But the story Max told about the incident would explain his natural tendency and lifelong reaction to a punch (perceived to be pure "craziness") when working the ring.

The truth was that Max went to the weekend dance with a group of guys who stayed outside the dance hall. No one had a date or went inside. A traveling painter had stopped in Livermore to work on a church steeple and decided to go to the dance with a local girl. The painter forgot to lock his truck, and Baer's friends stole the workman's jug of wine. Baer wanted everyone to know that he never drank and had nothing to do with the offense.

When the painter came out of the dance hall, someone tattled. All the boys skedaddled and left Max standing there too frightened to run. He just smiled, which infuriated the painter. Baer said his legs wouldn't move, "my teeth chattered and my heart nearly knocked my ribs loose."[28] The six-foot, two-hundred-pound painter charged over and decked him flush on the chin.

Too scared to fight back, Max just stood there with a big ol' grin on his face and laughed. It was a life-changing moment when he realized it didn't hurt to get hit. He said the event explained why, in so many of his professional fights when he got tagged with a hard punch, he would just laugh or smile. Max said, "I never laughed that way before— never grinned like that—until that punch landed. It's a habit. I grin and don't know I'm doing it."[29] The painter looked at him like he was crazy. Baer reached down to the ground with his right and came up with his fist to hit the man on the chin. Max missed and hit him somewhere behind the ear. The punch knocked the man to the ground. Max stood there laughing. "I grinned—and have no remembrance of that."[30] Later, his pals told him about the incident and his crazy grin. For nineteen years he had been a coward. At that moment, he knew he could be a fighter.

With the power to kill a brute creature with one massive, accurate hit, it wasn't much of a leap for the young Baer to realize he could use those skills and his strong right hand to deck an opponent with one accurate blow to the chin. He certainly had the confidence now. The next day Max went back to Livermore, paid twenty-five dollars for a heavy canvas bag, and carried it to the ranch. He liked to tell the story of having pitched a prize ring behind the pigpen in order to challenge local farm boys, boasting like John L. Sullivan that he could "knock all those guys cockeyed."[31] In fact, his first KO was with one of the ranch hands.[32]

Eventually, he told his father he was finished with ranching and was going to Oakland to become a fighter and make big money like Dempsey and Tunney. His father tried to talk him out of it because, as he said, he used to "play around in the days of the old-timers like Fitzsimmons, and knew how few became really great fighters."[33] Nevertheless, Jake decided to let his son take lessons at the Imperial Club in Oakland.

The "Butcher Boy" became Max's identifying moniker when he hit the gyms thirty miles northwest of Livermore. The ring name was used throughout his career, even late in his career when he was called the "Ex-Butcher Boy." In 1940, Henry McLemore said, in a statement reminiscent of something from his father's career, "Give the California butcher boy a chunk of undressed beef and he'll cut you a mess of tenderloins, T-bones, and porterhouses all in under a minute."[34]

Max rented a room in East Oakland and took a job at the Lorimer foundry as a menial laborer.[35] The foundry made diesel engines for ships and other large commercial equipment. Owner John W. Lorimer emigrated from Scotland, settled in San Francisco, and became associated with the Hercules Gas Engine Company. During World War I his firm joined another gas engine company to form Atlas Imperial, which developed the airless injection system for industrial diesel engines. With his sons, he formed the Lorimer Diesel Engine Company, where Baer worked for three dollars a day (one source said four) when he was "discovered" by the owner's son, J. Hamilton Lorimer.[36] It was said that after he became famous, Baer was discovered by "18,000 people who all claim the credit."[37]

"Ham" Lorimer, also called "the Millionaire Kid," saw Baer at work lugging not one but multiple flywheels, weighing a hundred pounds each, over his right shoulder like a side of meat. It was a struggle for a man to carry one flywheel for the large engines. Lorimer asked if Max needed help. "No," he replied. "More flywheels."[38]

During lunch breaks, Max challenged men to trade punches. Evenings and weekends he spent along Oakland's Franklin Street. Broadway was city center. Franklin, one street parallel, was a place of seedy taverns and boxing gyms. For someone used to the slop of a pigsty and the blood of a slaughterhouse, the wooden floor of a boxing gym, soaked as it was in human blood, sweat, and spit, was a step up. There he could train and fraternize with the professional fight boys. Long before becoming a "lady's man," Max Baer was a true "man's man," always comfortable in a gathering of male companions where he could regale his "pals" with stories and jokes. (He called his friends "pal" throughout his life.) Although he would later become associated with Hollywood ingénues and movie moguls, he would always feel more comfortable in the company of men, children, and the "down-and-outers."

By 1928, when he was nineteen, Max had found a second home in the boxing gym, enjoying the father-like, more experienced fighters such as H.A. "Spider" Griffin. Griff was around when lightweight Joe Gans first came to San Francisco and fought on the same card as heavyweight Jim Jeffries. The old-time boxers were generous to a fault. Griff spoke reverentially of the "incomparable Joe Gans ... listening patiently to the championship aspirations of a kid fighter." He told stories of Jimmy Britt, "pitching handfuls of coins to the sheet hustlers [newsies], and getting belligerent if any others tried to pick them up."[39] Griff gave Max Baer some of his earliest lessons in the art and humanity of boxing.

In addition to the glamorous lore, Baer was attracted to the money associated with the professional sport. Before the stock market crash and during the Roaring Twenties, jobs seemed plentiful. There was always a buck to be made somewhere if a man failed to make it in the fight game. In a period of only eight years since 1919, heavyweight titleholder Jack Dempsey had earned approximately two-and-a-half million dollars, a sum that excluded his film royalties.[40] Max was confident he could excel in the fistic business that earned Dempsey his first million. If not, he could always fall back on the meat business working with his father.

During the 1920s, boxing was a road to fame and fortune. But after the stock market crash of 1929, million-dollar gates evaporated. For some promoters it was often a gamble to see if the income exceeded expenses. The top six professional boxing matches of the 1930s drew two-and-a-half times less than the top six boxing gates during the 1920s. Other professional sports suffered as well. Professional golf, by comparison, did not attract winning purses like boxing. The aggregate field in 1930 was $39,000. Professional golfer Gene Sarazen collected $10,000 of that in 1930, but in 1931 when the economy tightened, Sarazen came in second in prize-winnings with $2850 for the year.[41]

By 1931, baseball managers were re-evaluating contracts. The better players in 1931 were going for about $40,000, although Babe Ruth's contract was twice that amount. His salary would drop by $5000 the next year. Most big-league baseball players were happy to have an annual contract in the $10,000 range.[42] Popular boxers could make half that on a good night, depending on how much money their managers took in cuts and expenses.

If the starry-eyed, ambitious Baer was going to be the next Dempsey in the fight game, he needed to attract a good manager. Initially, Max thought boxing pal Ray Pelkey would step forward. Pelkey was an Oakland middleweight who fought some interesting opponents in front of Oakland fans (Kid Norfolk, Allentown Joe Gans, Leo Lomski). Pelkey had a total of 124 battles under his belt beginning in 1918.[43] Max liked to spar with Pelkey and tease him by holding out his jaw. Whenever Pelkey connected, he found that Baer could take a good punch. He hinted that he would launch Baer in a boxing career, but the promise never materialized.[44]

Many of the first-generation gloved boxers became trainers, managers, and referees when their fighting days were over. The no-nonsense lightweight Jack Blackburn, who battled at the turn of the century, became Joe Louis's trainer during the 1930s. Al Lippe also started boxing the same year as Joe Gans in 1891. Later, he turned manager and promoted Gans for a short time toward the end of Gans's career when he was looking for fights in the Philly area.[45] Lippe had gone to San Francisco hoping to find new talent.

There wasn't much Lippe hadn't seen or turned down in the fight game. Damon Runyon told the story of when Lippe received a telegram from some greenhorn, wannabe fight promoter in some unknown place out West in 1906. The unknown made an offer for a Labor Day fight for Lippe's charge, Abe Attell. The manager threw the telegram in the trash. Later, Lippe happened to be talking to Sam Harris of Baltimore and asked if he knew a guy by the name of Tex Rickard in some place called Goldfield, Nevada. Harris told him he never heard of the guy, but he had also received an offer from the man for his boxer, Terry McGovern, a telegram he also threw away. As it turned out, both managers had trashed offers from Tex Rickard, who staged the "Fight of the Century" between Joe Gans and Battling Nelson. Both managers had snubbed the man who became the biggest fight promoter of the first half of the twentieth century.[46]

Lippe said he had probably managed over 1000 boxers in his day, and when he saw young Max Baer, he recognized his raw talent and took him on as a protégé.

But Baer needed more than an experienced trainer or manager. He needed someone with big money to sponsor him. Thus entered J. Hamilton Lorimer from the diesel engine foundry. Ham had money to spend, and he liked to spend it in the fight game. Lorimer told a reporter that when Baer approached him, he didn't want to make any investment that wouldn't pay a good royalty. Initially, he thought Baer was too good-looking and not serious enough to make it among the dime-a-dozen, hard-core scrappers in the boxing world.[47] But Baer had the charisma and talent to move him to act and, eventually, to drive Ham crazy.

So father Baer signed a contract for his underage son with team Lippe and Lorimer to start Max's professional boxing career. Max was matched with both newcomers and seasoned veterans. From May 1929, when he entered the ring at the age of twenty, to May 1930, the 6'2½" battler with an 81-inch reach fought twenty-two times, winning twenty and losing only two fights by disqualification.

California had been a state known to be legally friendly to boxing. Baer's first fight was promoted by Louie Parente, a promoter from the "old school" fight scene in San Francisco. Parente had learned the craft when working for promoters "Sunny" Jim Coffroth and Ed Graney out of Colma, ten miles south of San Francisco.

In 1906, when California's rules for local fight clubs were expanded to allow ten-round bouts instead of only four, Parente left Coffroth and obtained his own permit to promote prizefights. When Sam Langford came to San Francisco in 1918 and 1919, and Harry Wills in 1919 and 1920, they both worked with Parente. Parente would promote fights for Dempsey, whom he spotted at his gym. So, too, was Parente credited for promoting Max Baer. (Parente would go broke after Baer left California for bigger fights.)

In his first battle, Baer was paired with a former Alaskan heavyweight, "Chief Caribou." What little we know of the boxer was told by "Scoop" Beal for the *Times Standard*, who said that the Chief "slugged through rounds and rounds of gore at the old Broadway Arena in Eureka, California."[48] In Max's debut, Baer knocked the Chief out in the second round. Baer was paid $35, from which he had to give $10 to his manager. Six months later, Baer gave the Chief a rematch and overpowered him by TKO in the first round. The Chief's record did not improve.

In the late 1920s through the mid–1930s, fights ranged in duration from four, six, to ten rounds. Title bouts were fifteen. Baer's first four fights were all "four-rounders" held in Stockton, California.

Soon Baer acquired noted trainer Bob McAllister, who left retirement to train heavyweights. McAllister was an experienced middleweight-to-light heavyweight from San Francisco who fought both contenders and champions in his 41-bout career from 1913 to 1919. He fought future champion Jack Dempsey in 1917, Battling Levinsky and Mike Gibbons (both in the old Madison Square Garden), Gunboat Smith, Mike McTigue, and Fighting Billy Murray, Middleweight Pacific Coast Champion. During World War I, he served as boxing instructor at Camp Funston, Kansas. After the war, he went into the real estate business, and as a hobby began teaching boxing in Stockton, where he took on Max Baer as trainer.

Max in Oakland gym in 1929.

Baer proved to be a crowd-pleasing, aggressive fighter from the sound of the bell until the end. Fighting at 195, he ended all of his four-round fights with ax-landing knockouts. Max kayoed Sailor Leeds in under two minutes in Stockton, and the same for Tillie Taverna, who was a semi-final fighter around San Francisco with a knockout blow of his own.

By his fifth fight, July 24, 1929, Baer found himself back in Oakland as a replacement for the popular Jack Linkhorn, who had developed a case of blood poisoning. His opponent was Benny Hill, a "seasoned" heavyweight from Fresno, California, with 41 fights under his belt. Hill may have been considered a "washed up" fighter when he met Baer, but the Hayward newspaper had only this to say about Max: "We don't know anything about Baer so won't make any predictions."[49]

The next day, the Hayward paper knew something about Max, stating: "Baer trounced [Hill] in 4 rounds—Floored him for a nine count in the first round, and almost finished him in the fourth.... He can hit and absorb punishment and with a little seasoning, he should go far."[50] Baer agreed to a rematch with Hill one week later when, again, Baer won on points. Now fans "clamored" for a fight between Max Baer and Jack Linkhorn. It was said that neither trainer McAllister for Baer nor Kid Hats Parker for Linkhorn wanted a match for fear of putting a loss on their man's record. There was no use pairing them, the *Oakland Tribune* lamented on August 5, "while there are Benny Hills to be battered around."

It was in August, after only a handful of four-round fights, that Baer moved up to six-round fights and was identified by place, as "McAllister's young heavyweight from Livermore."[51] In a night of seven heavyweight bouts, publicized as the battle of the big men at the Arcadia Pavilion in Oakland, Jack Linkhorn met Benny Hill. Baer met African American Al "Red" Ledford who, like Baer, had also beaten Chief Caribou in four rounds. It was their second meeting. And early in the second round, Baer landed a knockout blow on Ledford's chin. The reporter from Livermore was still not impressed: Al Ledford of Sacramento "is a terrific hitter, while Baer is a clever lad, a bit lazy perhaps, but promising for all that."[52] The fight business would not last for Caribou and Ledford. Ledford called it quits after a total of 15 recorded fights and Caribou, 13 (after losing 12).

Max headlined a charity bout in his hometown of Livermore on September 1, 1929, and was promoted as "the most sensational heavyweight developed in the bay district in recent years." He demonstrated his skills in a fight against Joe Simoni (McAllister's other heavyweight).[53] Funds raised from the event went to the American Legion. This event would be the first of Baer's many charitable involvements. He would have another in his hometown before the year was out.

For his next fight, still very early in his career, Max lost his head in anger and was given a foul, but not before giving his opponent a fighting notice. Jack McCarthy met Baer on Louis Parente's card at the Arcadia Pavilion in Oakland. (The Oakland paper used the name Pat McCarthy in the text.) Although McCarthy had a twenty-pound weight advantage, Baer had him down in the first round from a series of strong rights. In the second, McCarthy was down for a seven count and tried to quit, but was saved by the bell. In the third, Baer had him on the ropes when again McCarthy tried to quit. McCarthy turned his back on Baer, and Max hit him with a kidney punch. Baer then backed away and motioned him to come forward. When McCarthy refused, Baer grabbed him by the waist and slammed him to the floor, whereupon referee Billy Snailham raised McCarthy's hand and gave him the decision by foul.

Some reporters were not at all shocked. The hard-nosed Russ Allen said, "Some of the gallery gods thought [Baer] fouled Jack McCarthy. He probably did but Jack deserved it. Baer was trying to make a fight of it. And oh, yes, Max is fighting Frank Rejenski [Rudzenski] six rounds." That was all that was said about Max's next fight.[54] (Max could not remember this opponent's name and called him "Rutabaga.")

Meanwhile, Baer plowed through the pool of local talent, adding up KO wins against Alex Rowe, whom Max knocked out in less than a minute, and Tillie Taverna, who hit like a mule and who was the favorite going into the match. Baer had Taverna down for a nine-count in the first round and down for good using his powerful right in the second. Between those two matches, Max decisioned Natie Brown. It was only Brown's second fight, but the bout went the full six rounds.

Outweighed by twenty pounds in his next bout, Max met Chet Shandel, who had lost only twice in his previous twenty-two bouts. Shandel hit Baer with three hard rights before Baer kayoed him in the second. Excluding the DQ, 1929 had been a brilliant start for Max Baer.

Nationally, heavyweight boxing had faced a lull in 1929, after Gene Tunney left the ring. But December 1929 was shaping up to be an exciting month, with many internationally famous boxers making their way to America. Italian Primo Carnera was in Paris getting ready for his return bout with W.L. "Young" Stribling of Macon, Georgia. Several good heavyweights were signed to battle in New York: Otto Von Porst, Norwegian from Chicago, and English champion Phil Scott, with Jack Dempsey refereeing his first bout in New York. Leading contender Jack Sharkey was in New York, and Max Schmeling was on a boat heading there. Even Argentine Victorio Campolo was hoping for a match in the Big Apple.

Back in Los Angeles, heavyweight Les Kennedy had gone through all the worthy Californians and was looking for good out-of-state talent. On December 31, New Year's Eve at the Olympic Auditorium, Kennedy defeated Jack "the Golden Boy" DeMave of New Jersey. Although DeMave had previously lost twice to Young Stribling, the battles had given him notoriety with a world contender. Thus, Les Kennedy's win over DeMave put the man from Long Beach on a track approaching the higher ranks of the heavyweight division: new meat for the lions of California.

Two

Livermore Larruper Kills Campbell, 1930

By the end of 1929, Max Baer would have his first encounter with the underworld of boxing. The Livermore Larruper would spend much of 1930 testifying before the boxing commission, a governor's committee, and a grand jury. He would be fined, would cause a death in the ring, would lose the house he bought for his parents, and ultimately lose his boxing license, bringing a quick end to a stellar start in California. It was not a good year.

Max was scheduled for two matches in December of 1929: Chet Shandel on the 4th and Tony "Kid Shine" de la Fuente, originally from Prescott, Arizona, on the 30th, both at the Arcadia Pavilion in Oakland. Baer floored Shandel in the second round. But before his bout with Fuente, Baer was approached by gamblers who offered him $2000 to take a fall.

Baer "refused to listen" to their offer and told trainer Bob McAllister that he was going to stop the experienced Fuente at the first opportunity. In the first minute of the first round, Baer "dropped a right-hander on Tony's neck and Fuente covered up. With both gloves jammed against his chin, Fuente's stomach was wide open, but Baer kept pounding the gloves and eventually Tony went down."[1] It was noted that this was the first time in local boxing history that a fighter had been knocked out with a "punch on a glove." Fuentes took the full count. Baer was now mentioned nationally in that both of these December fights were reported across the wires by the Associated Press. Unfortunately, both of his next fights in January would be subjected to official inquiry.

On January 15, 1930, in the Arcadia Pavilion in Oakland, Baer fought Milton "Tiny" Abbott, "the Redwood Giant," a 230-pound, 6'8" (one source said 6'7") giant lumberjack from Fieldbrook, California, near Eureka. Abbott outweighed him by twenty-seven pounds. Baer lost by disqualification when he hit Abbott as the giant was being counted out in the third round. Baer was fined $100. In the rematch on January 29, Baer won in the sixth. Baer's trainer Mike McAllister was so disgusted by Baer's lack of performance in the match that he told the seconds that Baer could have stopped the "big palooka" at any minute. Instead, it appeared that Max had carried Abbott for five rounds before knocking him out.[2]

Baer appeared before the Boxing Commission on February 4, on the charge that he had "carried" his opponent. He would be called again in an investigation into racketeering that continued through November.

It appeared that Baer was offered a $3500 automobile to carry Tiny Abbott. Max told a governor's committee that the week before the second Abbott bout, politician August R. "Gus" Oliva invited him to dinner with an offer. "He told me Abbott was a set-up, and that nobody stood to make any money on the fight unless Abbott came up for the fifth round. He said if Tiny was still on his feet in that round, we could make several thousand dollars." He also said that Oliva "came into his dressing-room before his first fight with Tiny Abbott and offered him an expensive automobile to let his 'opponent' stay five rounds."[3] Baer's manager Al Lippe denied Baer's story. When asked by the committee if his manager repudiated his story because he was paid to do so, Baer replied that "it looked kind of funny because Louis suddenly bought a lot of clothes and seemed to have a great deal of money." "Anyway," Baer told the investigators, "I've learned my lesson. It's quite a jump from pitching hay to this here business, you know. I can't keep up with these here racketeer fellows."[4]

What made Baer and those fights seem all the more suspect was that he was seen driving a new L-29 Chord automobile. Manager Lorimer was able to provide a sales receipt, proving that he was the one who had bought and given Max the expensive car.

By February 11, 1930, Max had come of age and could sign his own legal contracts. Ham Lorimer celebrated Max's twenty-first birthday by signing him to a five-year contract (without Lippe) on February 12. The car gave the appearance of a lavish signing bonus. Twenty-three years after the fact, Max joked, self-deprecatingly, that originally Lorimer offered him a contract that said "I was to get 66⅔ percent, and my manager was to get 33⅓ percent. I wouldn't sign it until they changed it to at least 50–50."[5] That year when he was cash-strapped and couldn't fight, Max sold so many pieces of his share of his contract that the pieces added up to more than one-hundred percent. These contract foibles would be costly, as he would discover eventually in court.

On February 27, 1930, Baer was fined $500 and suspended for two months by the California Athletic Commission for involvement in the Abbott affair. Baer discharged trainer McAllister and did not fight again until April.

To further exasperate the commission, promoters wanted to bring Primo Carnera to California. The commissioners were suspicious. Fearing a fixed fight or one arranged against an inferior, they said that Carnera's opponent had to be "qualified" and not some "push-over." Carnera had fought what appeared to be fourteen "slap downs" in fights that looked "to be in the bag," since many of his opponents had given up without being hit.[6]

Carnera's California representative, promoter Frank Churchill, tried unsuccessfully in April 1930 to arrange a fight in Los Angeles. Lou Parente heard of Carnera's interest and proposed a fight in San Francisco with Max Baer, Leon "Bomba" Chevalier, Chet Shandel or Tiny Abbott, all fighters some believed could be manipulated.[7] Carnera refused to fight the hard-punching Max Baer, Parente's first choice. The events from this point forward, continuing through Baer's fight with Frankie Campbell until Max and Primo met for the championship, would provide the material for the acclaimed movie starring Humphrey Bogart, *The Harder They Fall*, in 1956. The movie would detail what Baer and Carnera had to face during their tenures in the ring. It would be a public wake-up call to the paralyzing effects of racketeering on boxing.

In the movie, the Argentine's crooked manager Benko declares: "We'll kick 'em off in California."[8] Luckily for Baer, Carnera's California "kick-off" wasn't with him. Boxer Leon Chevalier, who had also battled Tony de la Fuente, eagerly saw the ten-round fight with Carnera as an opportunity for instant fame.

Chevalier's April 14, 1930, bout with Carnera ended badly for everyone. Mrs. Chevalier said that her husband was offered $900 to have the fight "in the bag," but he decided to fight instead of going down. During the bout, Carnera looked bewildered when Chevalier did not take the dive. Instead, Chevalier put all of his 225 pounds behind his punches. To prevent him from winning, Chevalier said that between rounds someone rubbed his face with "an eye-burning liquid" and his "nostrils and mouth were filled with pepper and grease."[9] Finally, when he did not go down, an "unauthorized" second "found in" Chevalier's corner threw in the towel in the sixth round. The man throwing in the towel for Chevalier was actually Bob Perry, a member of Carnera's team.

Commissioner Charles F. Traung attended the fight and began an immediate investigation. Chevalier testified that a "bald-headed fellow in my corner told me if I didn't go down in the next round that he would kill me!"[10] (In the movie, the Chevalier character is killed in the shower after the fight for not following directions.) After the investigation, the commission decided: "Carnera will not box in California again." "Indefinite suspension" was given to five of Carnera's managerial staff, along with Chevalier's two seconds.[11] The California suspension would have repercussions for Carnera in New York.

Since a fight with Carnera didn't materialize for Max, he was matched with Jack Stewart, April 9. Baer hurt his hand in the first round after dropping Stewart twice with long, looping lefts. Stewart came back in the second and Baer knocked him down again twice, after which referee Toby Irwin stopped the fight. The bout didn't rock the news. (In fact, it was a slow week everywhere. On April 18, 1930, the BBC reported, "There was no news today."[12])

On April 22, 1930, in his first fight outside the bay area, Max earned a ten-round decision over Ernie Owens in Los Angeles. The victory was not as impressive as Baer's arrival to the famous Olympic Auditorium. The Cord L-29 pulled up, a chauffeur opened the door, and out stepped Max Baer, dressed in proper English sporting attire, with beret cap and pants tucked neatly into his argyle socks. It was then that sportswriters knew they were not dealing with an ordinary pug. Baer was acquiring expensive tastes and an aptitude for publicity. These tastes would soon stress manager Ham Lorimer to his limit.

The fight with Owens drew an unexpected $30,000 gate. Fighting was fairly even until the eighth and ninth rounds, when Baer put Ernie on the floor four times. Owens had never been put down, which made the fight exciting. Baer's take was $2500 and Owens's $189, for reasons not fully explained in the news.[13]

By May 7, 1930, Max had completed his first year of battle and was taking on more challenging talent and expecting greater rewards. Some thought Max was losing the interest of his fans. The *Hayward Review* published one of the most extensive reviews to date with a description of Baer that was not flattering:

> Max Baer scowled, laughed, frowned and cursed for several rounds before settling down to business and knocking out Tom Toner, lanky Irish heavyweight, in the sixth round at the Oakland auditorium last night. And in victory Baer merely intensified the dislike of fans that is growing with every fight. Max looked far from the potential champion he is said to be. His judgment of distance was bad. He swung wild and when he took a few down below, he plainly indicated that the going was too rough. When he became thoroughly aroused he proceeded to fight with the ferocity of a wildcat and it was not long before Toner succumbed to a blast of hefty lefts and rights. Toner was down for a long count immediately preceding the wallops that dumped him for the final. Until the knockout Tom was holding his own, displaying a clever boxing ability and doing some infighting that had Maxie doubled up and complaining.[14]

Famous for his own shenanigans in the boxing business, promoter Jack Kearns, former manager of Jack Dempsey, was still going strong. It spoke volumes about Baer's

"Ham" Lorimer (Baer's first manager) with Max and chauffeur in Los Angeles in his controversial Cord L-29 automobile.

potential to have managers like Kearns in the audience for the Baer-Toner fight. Kearns had started his sports career on the West Coast. He was currently managing Mickey Walker. Kearns was in town for the express purpose of convincing Baer to take him on as manager, especially since Lorimer had let it be known that he wanted to sell Baer's contract. Baer had been living "higher on the hog" than his boxing means provided, becoming an expensive hobby for Lorimer.

After only his first year as manager, J. Hamilton Lorimer was tired of Baer and was willing to sell the four years left on his five-year contract "cheap" to anyone, except Jack Kearns. The rebuff sent Kearns back to New York empty-handed. After receiving several promising offers, Lorimer changed his mind. Word was that Baer might be worth the hassle.

Baer's next fight, on May 28, 1930, made the news as a result of his opponent's love interest. The good-looking Jack Linkhorn was a boxer predicted "to be one of the greatest drawing cards of the decade."[15] Sportswriters believed the bout with Baer could go either way. Kid Parker, "Linky's" manager, said the bout would not go more than four rounds. Ham Lorimer predicted Baer would win in four. It was noted that Linkhorn had to take a streetcar and carry his own duffle full of boxing gear while Baer was driving a $4000 automobile.[16] Since the average cost of a new car was $650, public sympathy was clearly with Linkhorn.

Max Baer (left) squares up with Jack Linkhorn (right), May 28, 1930.

After taking some stiff hits in the breadbasket, Max floored Linkhorn three times before knocking him cold in the first round of ten. Reporter Bob Shand stated that Linkhorn "forgot to duck" three times before 900 Modesto fans. "Baer hits too hard for the average heavyweight and he also hits too fast," said Shand.[17]

Max visited Linkhorn in his dressing room and offered his sympathy. "It was either you or I," he said, "and I was lucky enough to get in the punch. You are a game kid, Jack, and I'm for you. I sure hated to hit you the last time but it is all in the game." Linkhorn told the press, "Max beat me fairly and squarely. Only one of us could win and Baer was the lucky one."[18] Attendance was almost 10,000 and the gate for the fight came to $15,700. Linkhorn's take was 20 percent and Baer's 35 percent after taxes. Linkhorn had been loudly touted as an up-and-coming fighter, so much so that after his loss to Baer, Linkhorn's fiancée Frances Maher attempted suicide by drinking poison. The suicide attempt brought additional undesirable attention to boxing.

After the Linkhorn bout, Max and manager Lorimer said they were headed to New York to see the Sharkey-Schmeling championship bout on June 21, 1930. This trip may not have occurred because Max fought again on June 25, leaving little time to return from the East by train.

Lorimer decided to put Baer to the test. On June 3, he announced that Baer was ready for Frankie Campbell, considered the Heavyweight Champion of the Pacific Coast. "Baer and Campbell are the outstanding heavyweights in the West," he said, "and we might as well settle the question of supremacy right now."[19] The matchmaking for this bout created a multitude of problems for Baer. Ancil Hoffman of Sacramento, had been promoting fights in San Francisco and believed he could land the big fight. Parente believed he had promotional rights on Baer.

With two promoters working on the match, Baer was so confident of being signed that he went out and purchased (on credit) for his parents a $35,000 palatial home in the most expensive part of Oakland: 215 St. James Drive in the Piedmont Hills suburb. The family sold the hog farm and moved into the luxury home. In addition, Max purchased $10,000 worth of furniture, and a $6000 16-cylinder Cadillac for them. And while these might have been "obligations," it must have taken some amount of cash to put these items on account. The prescient reporter Bob Shand said, "He is banking on winning the heavyweight championship of the world. He is a man of destiny and nothing worries him."[20]

Max was banking on the Frankie Campbell fight, but Campbell's managers had little interest in Baer because they were trying to score a match with Paulino Uzcudun. Frankie Campbell was governed by a "syndicate" of managers who all had their hands in his cashbox in Los Angeles. Parente failed to secure the Campbell fight. Ancil Hoffman had not given up and was still working to land the fight.

During this lean time, Baer never saw lack of money as an impediment. He sold part of his contract to the Jacklich brothers for $13,000. In exchange for the cash, they would get fifteen percent of all of his future earnings.

After two months, when Jacob and Dora realized that Max had not been making payments on the expensive home, they moved to a modest dwelling in San Leandro where they remained for the rest of their lives.

Lou Parente announced that he was making two bouts for Max in June. On June 11, Baer was matched with "Buck" Weaver, a twenty-one-year-old "farmer lad" from Oklahoma City (some sources reported that he was from Medicine Lodge, Kansas). The farmer stood 6 feet 5½ inches, weighed 225 pounds, and "had quite a number of fights during 1929," with "a number of KOs to his credit."[21] In the first round, Baer hit him on the chin with a left hook, and Buck went down for a brief count. Then Baer hit him with a right that sent him to the canvas, and seasoned referee Toby Irwin counted him out.

For the June 25 program slot, Parente hoped to get Frankie Campbell to come to San Francisco. But Campbell ducked the proposal (probably for lack of sufficient money in Parente's offer to satisfy his gambler handlers). Word leaked to the papers that Campbell was avoiding Baer. Without Campbell, Parente had to settle for a return bout in Oakland with Ernie Owens. Baer had won their first contest in Los Angeles only a few weeks earlier, and Owens wanted to even the score. Baer needed the money. In the rematch, Baer knocked down Owens three times in the fourth round and again in the fifth, which finished the bout. Most importantly, Bob Shand noted that Max "proves he can 'Stand the Gaff' [spear] as he takes Owen's best blows."[22] The Northern California sensation was now being compared to a young Jack Dempsey.

By 1930, Max Baer was the most recognizable man on the streets of Oakland and was beginning to feel more confident with the girls. He had given boxing lessons to pretty Elvy Sjoberg, secretary for the California Highway Patrol of Alameda County. Max, good friends with the local squad, had volunteered to fight a charity benefit for the traffic officers at the Livermore Rodeo on July 5. He frequently stopped by to check with Elvy on the important plans. At the rodeo, Max would get to see the bucking horse named in his honor. Jack Millerick named the toughest of his wild bucking horses "Max Baer"—it was a huge animal with the "light of death in his eye and a wicked twisting, jolting buck that sends cowboys spinning off his back just like the Livermore Leveler drops the sluggers in the ring."[23]

On July 5, at the rodeo, the big news was announced to the crowd: Max Baer would battle Frankie Campbell. Ancil Hoffman had apparently offered enough money to land the fight at baseball's Recreation Park in San Francisco for either August 25 or September 1.

Baer's July calendar was soon filled: he would fight Les Kennedy, the man Campbell had fought and beaten on May 12.

The Kennedy fight would be another of Baer's unusual affairs. Before the fight, Max was favored two-to-one in the betting odds. But by the time of the match, the odds had shifted to about even. Those betting early on Baer believed that he would kayo his opponent promptly, and those betting on Kennedy believed that he would win on points if the fight went the full ten rounds. Actually, Baer had only gone the ten-round limit once previously, and he had won that fight on points.

Even at this early stage of Baer's career, some followers questioned whether Baer might not be able to sustain his tremendous power over ten rounds. Many thought that he had not been tested seriously, since he usually kayoed his opponents in the early rounds. It is also interesting to note that at this point in his career, Baer had never lost a fight on points.[24] Kennedy had lost to Frankie Campbell, the fighter Max had been chasing. So this was a must-win bout for Baer.

Referee for the July 15, 1930, bout at the Los Angeles Olympic Auditorium was Lieut. Jack Kennedy.[25] Early in the first round, Baer wasted no time in going after his opponent. But after the first round, Les Kennedy was the aggressor. He sank right hands deep into Baer's body that had him doubled up in the third, fourth, and seventh rounds. Max complained to the referee that a blow was low. Kennedy also seemed to be able to land damaging body and head shots on Baer at will. Max seemed lost after the seventh.

Baer's loss to Kennedy was like an earthquake to Northern Californians. The editor of the hometown *Livermore Journal* lamented two days later that it appeared Baer was not fighting his usual game. Every fighter has an off day, but the editor noted that Baer's change in style was puzzling. Here was an orthodox, stand-up fighter who, in this fight, switched back and forth between a crouch and an upright position. Baer's style made no sense, so the writer concluded that maybe Jack Dempsey was now giving private lessons. However, Baer's endurance throughout the fight was noted. He was able to take all that Kennedy had to give without being knocked off his feet.

Many from his hometown area seemed to think Baer deserved the loss, that it was probably good for him in that it "will take all the cockiness out of his head. He will probably learn that he has to box as well as hit if he expects to reach the top or even stay in the second rate class." Maybe "Maxie was getting a little bit too confident. Some of the boys believe he is 'snooty,' but he really does not mean to act that way. He is just a big kid yanked practically overnight from a foundry to the top of the heavyweight division and driving his own 16-cylinder car instead of the other fellow's truck."[26]

Baer boldly responded to the attacks, "Give me a chance, that's all I say. Rome wasn't built in a day. Neither can I become a boxer overnight. I haven't got any alibis for my licking. I don't want any alibis. I was hurt several times by punches to the stomach but I don't think it is fair to intimate that I lack courage. I have as much heart as any other man. Sure he hurt my stomach but I took them, didn't I? And I kept coming, didn't I?"[27]

Boxing Commissioner Charley Traung had been at the fight to judge for himself if it had been an honest one. He had heard beforehand that something about the fight was not right. He remarked afterward, "Baer struck me as a man who was facing too much experience."[28] Baer was guaranteed a rematch.

Back in Livermore, patrons of the California Theater were eager to see the official motion picture of the World's Heavyweight Championship between Jack Sharkey and Max Schmeling. The film took a month to get from New York to California. Technology had added sound to film footage, so attendees could now hear the two boxers address the crowd and hear the blows as they landed in battle. It was exciting stuff, even if a German had won the most important title in boxing. Little did they know that in only three

Left to right: Tom E. Lennon, manager for Christner, unknown trainer, KO Christner, the Akron Giant, Referee Toby Irwin, Max Baer, Ham Lorimer, Baer's manager, and trainer Tillie Herman, August 11, 1930.

years, one of their own would be in the ring with the famous German. Schmeling's win by DQ would toss the heavyweight division into utter mayhem for the next year, with every contender wanting a chance at the title.

After losing the promotional battle over Frankie Campbell to Ancil Hoffman, Louis Parente quickly signed Baer to meet "KO" Christner on August 11. Before meeting Christner in a ten-round main event at the Oakland ballpark, Baer worked daily with Dempsey's former trainer, Tillie Herman. Herman was in town looking for fights, and it turned out that Baer was always looking for sparring partners, and in this case good advice from a sage boxer. The tips would be helpful for the Christner bout, and in reality the Campbell fight.

Christner, the giant from Akron, Ohio, had only been knocked out once in his career (by Primo Carnera), but that didn't worry Max. Max floored him three times in round one with a left hook. Twice Christner took a nine count and was saved by the bell the third time. He was still groggy at the start of round two when Max finished him off with a barrage of lefts and rights. "The ring shook as Christner landed flat on his back."[29]

After twenty-six professional fights in a period of only one year and three months, Max Baer was considered at the top of his fighting game, even after losing to Les Kennedy. Frankie Campbell, along with everyone else, believed he could beat Baer because he had beaten Kennedy at Wrigley Field in Los Angeles by KO in the fourth round. Baer had won only one round in ten with Kennedy in his fight. But one thing was certain: Max Baer needed Campbell's West Coast title to move into the higher ranks.

Frankie Campbell, August 25, 1930, San Francisco

Frankie Campbell was a San Francisco native who, at age twenty-six, had been fighting on and off for six years. His fighting name seemed an appropriate Scottish equivalent of his real name, Francesco Camilli. His crouched position and dodge-and-weave style earned him the ring name, the "Italian Jack Dempsey." He had tried to leave boxing due to unsavory management siphoning off much of his earnings. After two losses and a draw at the end of 1926, Campbell decided to try his hand at baseball. His brother Dolph Camilli was a star first baseman with the Sacramento Coast League team before moving to the majors as first baseman for the Brooklyn Dodgers. Frankie shifted around various baseball teams and eventually tried out for the San Francisco Seals as a third baseman. While talented in both sports, Frankie found he could make more money in the prize ring, and he returned in 1928 for a series of fights in Los Angeles under manager Cal Working and trainer Larry Morrison.

Two years later, when he met Baer, he needed the money that a big fight could draw. Campbell had a wife and a nine-month-old infant to support.

The fight pitted an East Bay slugger against a San Francisco slugger. Both Campbell and Baer were said to be the best heavyweight punchers since Dempsey. This fight was expected to be the best San Francisco fight since Dempsey beat Gunboat Smith thirteen years prior. Surely, predicted proud fans, the winner of the match would become the next world heavyweight champion. To accommodate the large crowd, the baseball field at Recreation Park was selected as the venue.

Campbell was viewed as the veteran with a record of thirteen knockouts in his recent bouts. Baer, on the other hand, had only been fighting for a little over a year, but had scored nineteen knockouts in twenty-six fights. Campbell was 5'10" and was expected to weigh in at 185. Baer had 4½ inches on him and an additional ten pounds. But the day of the fight, Campbell only weighed 179, a fact that worried commissioners. Nevertheless, the fight went on, and fifteen thousand fans (among them Jack Dempsey, Jack Kearns, and Jim Jeffries) showed up to see two of California's finest athletes bludgeon it out for ten scheduled rounds, only to witness a tragedy.

It was the first time reporter Robert Edgren, later to become a California Athletic Commissioner, saw either of the two fighters in action. He compared Campbell to Tom Sharkey, shorter and stockier than his opponent. He compared Baer to Bob Fitzsimmons, but with even broader shoulders and forty additional pounds. He said Campbell generally carried the attack, rushing Baer into the ropes with sheer energy.

In the first round, Campbell came out the aggressor, slamming Baer with body punches. Baer returned the volleys, and with a looping right hand to the chin, he dropped Campbell. Wisely, Campbell took a count of nine before rising, unhurt.

In the second round, Campbell came out again landing body punches. During the toe-to-toe combat, Campbell may have pushed or knocked Baer to the wet canvas. Referee Toby Irwin did not call it a knockdown, but waved Campbell to his corner. Campbell stepped over Baer's legs while retreating when, suddenly, Baer leaped up and followed him. As Campbell looked back and realized Baer was coming for him, Baer landed a hard blow to Campbell's jaw. He seemed to be knocked cold, but managed to catch and hold himself upright with his right arm hanging onto the ropes. The referee appeared ready to stop the fight, but Campbell got to his feet and was ready to continue when the bell rang. Campbell walked by Edgren on the way to his corner. Edgren said he was laughing. However, at his corner Campbell was heard telling Tom Maloney, his cornerman, that something felt like it had snapped in the back of his head.

Campbell went out for the third and fourth rounds, which were an exchange of blows much like in the previous rounds, with Campbell going for the body and Baer landing long rights and lefts to the head.

Then came the fatal fifth round. Baer held Campbell off with his long left. Then he hit Campbell with a hard left and right to the head, knocking him into the corner. Robert Edgren said he was sitting close enough to the ring to see that Campbell was out, that his head was down on his chest and his eyes were closed. But Baer, hovering over him, may not have seen that. Campbell collapsed in a sitting position on the ropes. With hands hanging at his sides, he was defenseless under the hail of Baer's savage blows that landed so fast, perhaps a dozen in seconds, that he was knocked from side to side. Unconscious, Campbell slipped to the floor. Referee Irwin stepped between them and raised Baer's hand in victory, without the formality of a count.

Edgren would never forget what Max had done to Frankie Campbell that night. Edgren said that he had never seen "a champion yet so brainless that he didn't know when he had a fight won, and know enough to hold his hand. Baer has 'everything'— except a brain."[30]

When Campbell's cornermen were unable to revive him, Baer and his seconds, Frankie Burns and Ray Carlen, carried Campbell to the center of the ring. For more than fifteen minutes a physician attempted to bring the boxer back to consciousness, but finally Campbell was taken to St. Joseph's Hospital, where brain specialists were called in.

Frankie Campbell never rallied. One paper said that he was hemorrhaging from his ears and both eyes, and that if he had lived, he would have been blind in one or both

Frankie "Campbell" Camilli, died at age 26, on Aug. 26, 1930, the day after his fight with Max Baer (courtesy Mike Silver).

eyes. Max Baer and manager Ham Lorimer arrived at the hospital the next day at 9:00 a.m. Frankie Campbell died at 11:45 a.m., the result of complications from concussions to the brain, or from what was called a "double cerebral hemorrhage." Newspapers reported that his brain had been snapped from the supporting tissue and was floating in his skull. (Although not a medically sound assessment, readers got the point.[31])

In tears, Baer was one of the first to approach Mrs. Campbell to express his sorrow. Mrs. Campbell replied, "I don't blame you. You couldn't help it. Both of you went into the ring to fight. It might have been you, you know."[32] She must have truly reached into Max's heart and felt a grief as deeply felt as her own because she was one of the few people outside Max's immediate friends and family who understood what he was experiencing. He vowed to do whatever he could to help the Campbell family.

Everyone was criticized for the death: boxers, trainers, managers, promoters, commissioners, and legislators. Baer was criticized for the merciless beating. The name "Butcher Boy" was not lost on the press. There was even talk of lynching the boxer. Police Chief William J. Quinn arrested Baer for manslaughter. Ham Lorimer was nowhere to be found, so promoter Ancil Hoffman posted bail from Baer's full $10,000 earnings from the fight, the highest ever set at the time in California for a manslaughter charge. Everyone connected with staging the fight was ordered to the Hall of Justice for questioning. When asked why he didn't let up the barrage of blows, Baer explained that his determination to win "caused him to make certain Campbell was actually 'out' before withholding his blows."[33] It all happened so quickly. Baer needed this win, and he responded instinctively with what he was trained to do. But that instinct would never be the same again.

Referee Toby Irwin was criticized for not stopping the fight sooner. He explained that because he was moving from one to another corner, his view was obscured by the action.

The state's boxing commissioners came under fire because Campbell had been San Francisco's second death in the prize ring within a week. Johnny Anderson, a 19-year-old lightweight, had died from head injuries in a fight with "Red" Ruehl, and the public was angry.

There had been too many ring deaths, and 1930 had been the deadliest. During that year, 37 men died worldwide from their injuries in the ring—the second largest number in the history of gloved boxing, since the 1890s. Only one year saw more deaths: 1932, when the number reached 39. From 1920 through 1939, 445 men died from boxing, an average of 21 per year, all in the name of sport; and the public was outraged.[34]

Several newspapers reprinted or highlighted excerpts from the editorial written by Allan T. Baum, sportswriter for Hearst's *San Francisco Examiner*:

> Why not tell the TRUTH? Would poor unfortunate Frankie Campbell have done to Max Baer, in the matter of slugging, what Baer did to Campbell, if he had the chance? The answer is YES.
>
> In view of the fact that the terrific and final beating that Campbell took was all in the space of a few seconds, would any competent referee have stopped the bout in view of the conditions? The answer is NO. Who is to blame then for this latest of tragedies connected with the so-called boxing game? Max Baer, the 21-year-old boy? The answer is NO ... the LAW is to blame, nothing else. The law and the modern idea of boxing.
>
> Put two clever BOXERS together in the smallest arena in San Francisco and the place wouldn't be half filled. The promoters would hesitate to make such a match. But two sluggers, two "killers," two men with little or no class as boxers, such as Baer and Campbell, that's different. The largest indoor arena in the city isn't big enough. It takes the ball park to accommodate more than 15,000 fight fans.
>
> The most popular man connected with Fistiana today, active or retired, is Jack Dempsey. Why?

Because he was a "KILLER," a slugger and NOT a boxer. There you have it all in a nutshell. The public wants them that way. The public sneers at a good boxer. Boxing is legal within the laws of California.... In other words, the fight was a legalized homicide.[35]

The headline death in the ring brought national attention to both victim and victor. The twenty-one-year-old was horrified at what had happened, and he would never recover. Had it not been for this ring tragedy, Dan Parker said in the *New York Mirror*, his "killer instinct would have made Baer [the] Greatest."[36]

After the fight, both Baer and his manager Ham Lorimer lost their boxing permits and were banned from the ring indefinitely by the California State Boxing Commission.

A San Francisco grand jury took up the matter on September 25, but no indictment was made. Subsequent investigations did eventually expose the unpleasant underbelly of the "boxing racket," where certain individuals who financed the business were able to take advantage of the boxers. Managers were known to exact a large toll from their boxers' earnings to cover expenses. Promoters took their tax for publicity. Venue managers took their fees for location. Sometimes very little was left for the boxers.

William Hornblower, attorney and state assemblyman, was hired by promoter Ancil Hoffman to help Elsie Campbell with her finances. The attorney revealed that from Frankie Campbell's total "extensive" earnings, very little remained after racketeers took their toll: a $750 car, a $1500 lot and $1800 in cash. The $9000 Campbell was to earn from the Baer fight was being held by Ancil Hoffman for Mrs. Campbell's benefit. Her lawyer figured that Frankie had made at least $30,000 in the past year. Even considering a manager's cut, living and training expenses, he estimated a good $10,000 ought to have remained.

The lawyer asked Carroll Working, Campbell's manager of record, where Campbell's money had gone. He reported, "It went into the build-up campaign for Frankie in Los Angeles for advertising, for getting him good fights, for getting to the top."[37] But Working could not or would not identify who received the money for any of these expenses. When the attorney asked to see the books, Working said that he didn't keep any books, "that Frankie and he had a perfect understanding on that matter, and that Frankie knew and agreed to all expenditures in the build-up campaign."[38] Hornblower announced that he would follow the money from the Baer fight, and that Campbell's managers, Working and Tom "Greaseball" Maloney (Campbell's main second in his corner) would have to fight him in court to get their hands on any of it.

Baer appeared before Judge A.J. Fritz on October 1, as a follow-up to his initial appearance before the grand jury. In addition to the charges made against participants in the Baer-Campbell fight, questions were also asked concerning "influencing decisions" in the "fight racket." Baer admitted that he was offered a bribe by August "Gus" Oliva in the January fight with Abbott to carry him.

On October 28, 1930, Commissioner Traung reinstated Baer's license, believing in his innocence. In November, Baer was back in court in Los Angeles facing a county grand jury convened to discuss possible charges against Gus Oliva, "sporting type" and restaurant owner. Baer had testified that it was Oliva who offered him a "big, shiny automobile" if he would let Tiny Abbott have a good showing with him. But Oliva testified that he was the one who witnessed Lippe offering Baer the bribe.

After the grand jury investigation, California Governor C.C. Young reconvened his committee to investigate "prize fight fixing." The committee had been digging into the "fight racket," going back four years into the Pancho Villa–Jim McLarnin fight, after which Villa died of a suspicious "tooth infection." One of the athletic commissioners was asked to investigate the physician who examined Villa before the fight. When asked about Max Baer "as a square fighter," Commissioner Joseph Genshlea (Commission Secretary) said, "Baer is a hard fighter." In the Frankie Campbell bout, he said Baer "observed all the rules," but was probably open to criticism for "lack of sportsmanship." On the subject of referees, Genshlea said "smart and honest referees" would put prize-fight gamblers out of business, suggesting that the problem was not only a matter of fight fixing with the managers and boxers, but also with the referees.[39]

Ancil Hoffman was questioned about Baer's affiliations. Hoffman said, "Baer has been careless in his associates," but he assured the committee that he was now in control of Max's affairs. He said Baer made last year a total of $51,000 and "threw it all away." He said Max bought two cars, a home for his parents, and "49 pairs of silk socks at one crack."[40]

Athletic Commissioner Charles Traung was called to testify about the threats against his life. He stated that both he and his wife had received violent telephone and mail threats from an "anonymous group" prior to his testimony on fight fixing. He told the committee that on one occasion his wife had been called to the phone and informed, "The next time you see your husband he'll be on a slab at the morgue."[41]

When the state's committee members asked Traung his reasons for reinstating Max Baer's license after the Baer-Abbott fiasco, he said that he "believed Baer was not responsible for the asserted attempts to 'fix' the bout, and he had reinstated him for that reason." Concerning the Campbell fatality, he said Max wanted to stage a benefit for their sake.[42]

While Baer vowed to do whatever he could to help the Campbell family, a charity benefit did not materialize. Baer, who had been a boxing staple in Oakland, was now a controversial figure and remained absent from the ring. During this time, he let his valuable California boxing license lapse, a license that Commissioner Traung had reinstated against popular sentiment. With a new year and a new commission when Max reapplied, a license would be refused because he was seen as "too much of the 'killer' type."[43]

Max Baer was finished with boxing.

But others were not finished with him. Promoter Hoffman saw potential dollar signs in Baer's future elsewhere, especially in New York, where boxing fans had heard of the Butcher Boy's killer reputation.

Three

New York Meets Lochinvar, 1930, 1931

Like Jack Dempsey earlier, Max Baer needed to leave his home in the West and go east if he wanted to make a name for himself in the higher ranks of boxing. New York writer Damon Runyon famously coined Baer's ring name, "Lochinvar," calling him the "Larruping Lochinvar out of the West," after Sir Walter Scott's romantic hero. Scott's epic ballad *Marmion*, originally published in 1833, was still popular in the 1930s. Fans of Baer cleverly identified the handsome, brave, and impetuous young Californian with the Scottish knight, introduced in Canto XII, who arrived unannounced at the wedding feast:

> O, young Lochinvar is come out of the west,
> Through all the wide Border his steed was the best;
> And save his good broadsword he weapons had none,
> He rode all unarm'd, and he rode all alone.
> So faithful in love, and so dauntless in war,
> There never was knight like the young Lochinvar.[1]

With Baer's impressive string of victories in his first year of battle, his admirers would herald, "There never was a knight like the young Lochinvar." And with his conquests in California finished, like the Scottish knight, Baer needed to "come out of the west" to accomplish braver and more heroic feats before he arrived at the wedding feast.

But as a result of Frankie Campbell's death, this brave knight, as physically accomplished as he was in the ring, was an emotional wreck. His sleep was interrupted by nightmares. During the day, his mind wandered back to visions of Campbell lying unresponsive on the canvas. It was a personal battle he would fight for the rest of his life. For months after the death, Baer was tied up in hearings, court appearances, and other matters that affected his peace of mind, his boxing life, and his pocketbook. He was quite sure that he didn't want to fight another round, and he couldn't in California, absent a license.

But promoter Ancil Hoffman had plans for the disenchanted boxer. Immediately after Campbell's death, Hoffman paid for Baer's bail and legal defense and took a wreck of a boxer and offered the cash-strapped pug $5000 for 16⅔ percent of his contract. Baer owned 66⅔ percent and Lorimer owned the balance. Additionally, Hoffman paid Lorimer $10,000 to take over the active management of Baer for six months. These transactions would keep both Hoffman and Baer in court as defendants against Lorimer for the next five years.[2]

Ancil Hoffman had been linked to boxing for over thirty years. He was born in 1884

Ancil Hoffman (right), promoter of the Baer-Campbell match, provided bail money for Max and successfully marketed him in New York, October 29, 1930 (courtesy David Bergin).

in Quincy, Illinois. He migrated with his father, first to Oklahoma for a year to manage a mercantile or "trading post" on an Indian reservation, and then on to Sacramento, where his father became a grocer. Ancil had a stepmother who never encouraged him to attend school, so he dropped out of elementary school at the age of 8. According to his good friend, Judge William Pettite, Ancil went to work at a blue-collar saloon washing out spittoons and cleaning the floors.[3]

Ancil took an interest in boxing and started as a flyweight, at 105 pounds. As he grew into his full height (never more than shoulder-height to Max), he moved up to lightweight and fought in bars in the California communities of Elk Grove, Perkins, Florin, and Sacramento in the Old Pavilion arena at Sixth and M Streets. Eventually, he acquired a total of six saloons in Sacramento, including one at the corner of Eighteenth and M Streets, which had a back room for boxing.[4] The saloon business was a source of great profit for him.

During Prohibition, however, the government shut down his saloons and bought out his immense stock of alcohol—but not before Hoffman buried his best scotch.[5] In 1919, he used the government's large payout, believed to be $1 million, to buy a forty-acre orange orchard in nearby Fair Oaks, a town established in 1890. With his saloons closed, he went into the next best business—promoting boxing.

Hoffman became a matchmaker for the Sacramento Athletic Club on Ninth, between I and J Streets. He refereed eleven fights in Sacramento at the L Street Arena from 1919 to 1924. He started the career of "Fighting Billy" Murray, from Petaluma, California. In 1921, he took George Washington Lee, bantam, to New York, hoping for a title. In 1922, Hoffman took Lee to Manila to fight Pancho Villa. Under Hoffman's flair for promotion, Lee was billed as the "Yellow Peril" and the "Chinese Champion Bantamweight of the World." (Lee's father was Chinese, his mother Mexican.) Hoffman dressed Georgie in a flashy Oriental robe and hat to impress reporters. He would do something similar ten years later for Max Baer.

Ancil Hoffman, Baer's second and lifelong manager and friend, as a Sacramento lightweight boxer.

With boxing in full legal status in California in 1925, Hoffman relocated from Sacramento to San Francisco to manage and promote bigger fights, all the while keeping his real estate in the Sacramento area. In the fight racket, he was known to be a "square shooter," shrewd in deal-making, a genius at promoting, and fair to his fighters, always paying them even when his promotions failed. One of his great skills was that he could hold his own with promoters (and racketeers) in Chicago and New York, dealers who could eat others alive. Ancil had a quiet resolve of steel.[6] Max Baer was now solidly under Hoffman's wings, in a relationship that would turn out to be one of the closest between boxer and manager in ring history.

With cash in hand from Hoffman's $5000 payment, Baer was eager to escape the crowds and questioning in California. By September 1, only days after the Campbell tragedy, Baer left his worries behind and set out for a week of distractions in Reno, the pleasure-dome of Nevada, where the nightlife was endless, liquor was accessible, gambling was almost legal (it would be by 1931), and divorce laws were liberal. There, he attended the Labor Day fight, which matched San Francisco junior welterweight Joe Bernal with

Oakland's Jack Kirk. When Baer was spotted at the event, he was asked by the promoter if he might be introduced in the ring. Baer refused, saying that "it was too soon after his fight with Campbell."[7]

Before the week was out, Baer's cash was gone, and he was back in California; but not before meeting the sizzling New York screen actress Dorothy Dunbar.

Both Dunbar and Baer were in Reno to ease their sorrows. Baer was a destroyed man emotionally and Dunbar had just ended another marriage. The starlet had taken up temporary residence in Reno for legal reasons only, to obtain a quick (four-month) divorce from South American millionaire Jaime de Garcon, owner of a Spanish tours bureau in London.[8] Dunbar had married de Garcon on March 19, 1930, only six months earlier. Prior to that marriage, she was married to Thomas Bucklin Wells II. Tommy Wells was a man of inherited wealth from Minneapolis, and a part-time movie actor who shared the screen with her in *Ain't Love Funny*. He died in Dunbar's arms in London in 1927, while she was divorcing him. His death left the widow with a nice monthly annuity from the Wells family, after she took them to court.[9]

Max Baer and his sexy consort were seen together around town, but Dorothy Dunbar Maurice Wells de Garcon denied any romantic connection, engagement, or marriage possibility with the young Californian, saying they were "merely friends."[10] However, everyone in Reno assumed Dunbar was in town to obtain a divorce to move on to her next conquest: Max Baer. While she denied all rumors, Baer was smitten. He so loved the lights and attention and the complete distraction (lovemaking) with Dunbar, that he made several trips from California back to Reno over the next few months while she was in residence.

Baer admitted to the press, "I never had a girl friend of any kind until after I was nineteen. My first girl was Olive Beck, a high school girl, later a waitress, the first girl I ever really courted. [Dorothy Dunbar] was the second girl of my life-time."[11] (Unfortunately, many of these girlfriends ended up suing him.)

Manager Ancil Hoffman was none too happy about the relationship, especially since he had just invested in Baer for the next six months and had already begun his ballyhoo campaign in New York, sending newsmen and managers telegrams and "ring shots" of Baer. Max had enough entanglements in California. Facing a manslaughter charge in a state that wanted to "clean up boxing," he didn't need another noose around his neck in Nevada. Add to all of that, any future Hoffman envisioned for Baer was in boxing; yet Baer was telling him that he didn't want to box anymore. Now, Hoffman had to extricate his charge from a love interest with a siren in Reno before her divorce became final in January 1931, when the newspaper headline would read: "Reputed Movie Actress Freed."[12]

Baer's Reno experience was a fairy-tale saga with the characters reversed. It seemed the fabled damsel was about to save the knight in distress. Few knew at the time that Dunbar was encouraging Max to return to the ring. She was a star attraction, and she liked him for the same reason—he had a powerful allure as a champion boxer. Harry Grayson wrote with tongue in cheek in 1934 that it was Dorothy Dunbar who saved Max for boxing. His comment referred to their rocky personal relationship, explaining that when Baer tired of arguments, etiquette books, and her lessons in "proper" behavior, he turned back to his friends in the masculine sport.[13] Max told the boys that the only etiquette he remembered from Dorothy was that "one should not shake hands across a dinner table and that one should take off one's socks before retiring."[14]

No doubt Dunbar's interest in having a star boxer on her arm—a strong, virile man to accompany her—was the impetus for encouraging him to return to the business. He was really nothing to her without boxing. He certainly needed the money to entertain his new flame in the manner to which she had been previously provided for. On November 3, Max Baer announced his engagement to Dorothy Dunbar. It was a time-sensitive tug-of-war between manager and girlfriend.

Before the year was out, Hoffman had removed Baer from the complications in the West and had taken him to New York to show off the new young face and to capitalize on the Californian's "killer" reputation. With his confidence and ambition restored, the brave knight realized that if he wanted to be a leading contender for the heavyweight throne, he had to take New York, because that throne was firmly rooted in boxing's castle, Madison Square Garden. A lot was at stake. Ancil Hoffman's publicity bell had been answered. Through manager Joe Gould and promoter Jimmy Johnston, Hoffman arranged a fight with James J. Braddock. However, the New York Boxing Commission refused to let Baer meet Braddock because they thought that Baer was "too inexperienced."[15] It is interesting to wonder how history might have been altered if Baer and Braddock had been allowed to meet in 1930. A fight with Paulino Uzcudun was also turned down because Paulino had fought Carnera in Barcelona while Carnera was "a suspended" fighter. Such was the nature of boxing's politics.

A match was eventually made for the famous Garden: Baer would fight Ernie Schaaf (the Oakland paper originally spelled his name "Shaff") on December 19, 1930, in New York (the *LA Times* said the fight would take place in Boston). Baer was definitely going to New York, and everyone in California believed that he would return as world champion. The news was sensational.

The knight would *not* be off on his steed to the East alone. His original departure, planned for November 27, had to be postponed—twice. When the New York fight was announced, managers began coming out of the woodwork. Whenever Max needed money, he offered a piece of his contract. Now all those "pieces" wanted a spot on the train for New York. J. Ham Lorimer showed up as manager of legal record, reminding everyone that Ancil Hoffman was only acting as manager, matchmaker for six months. Frankie Burns had a five percent spot on the trip as trainer, and father Jacob was supposed to get ten percent off the top. The Jacklich brothers were on hand, as were others, such as Alden Humphries, "who either owns a piece of Max or who represents somebody who does."[16] It seemed that anyone who had ever met Max had been offered a piece of his pugilistic pie. Added to the entourage was Baer's attempt to invite a secretary and chauffeur.

Bob Shand of the *Oakland Tribune* noted that in the last decade the East had never provided a fighter quite like the one the West was about to give them. It was at Baer's grand send-off that one sportswriter renamed his boxing column to "With the Knights of the Gloves." Meanwhile, the train that waits for no one had to wait for Max Baer. He eagerly boarded the Overland Limited on Saturday, November 29, at Oakland's Sixteenth Street depot before the photographers arrived. The train waited an additional five minutes while Baer de-boarded and posed for the cameras. Ray Carlen (one of Max's seconds, later to become manager for Lou Nova) predicted that Baer would return heavyweight champion of the world. It was quite a send-off.

In addition to his killer record, Baer looked incredible. Taking in his dark features, the lightning in his right fist, and his boatload of charisma, New Yorkers sized him up as the second coming of Dempsey. The experts there hoped that Baer might be the answer to what boxing needed to invigorate the sport. In short, New York needed Baer, and Baer needed New York. It was a match made in boxing heaven.

Baer would start at the top. Unfortunately, it was not quite enough at the top for his expectations. In his first big interview with a United Press associate, the twenty-one-year-old didn't wait to be asked any questions, he was ready to talk: "A fellow really has to come to New York to get anywhere, and when I leave this town to go back West, I hope I have the title in my trunk to tote back with me. In fact, my only regret is that my first go in the East isn't a championship fight." Baer added, "If I ever get into the ring with [German Heavyweight Champion] Max Schmeling, I guarantee to bring the title back to the United States."[17] The reporter was entirely taken with Baer's charm and noted that while he was a confident boy who "talks a good fight," his talk didn't sound like "bragging." Baer continued, like "John L. Sullivan ... I'm ready to take on anyone, and what's more I have a good punch in each hand to back up what I say." The reporter was awed, as were most others: "The youthful Californian is a colorful lad with an instinct for the dramatic and bids fair to become one of the most interesting figures in the ring since Dempsey."[18]

Grantland Rice, sportswriter for the *New York Tribune* whose columns were printed around the country and visualized in Paramount newsreels, hoped that Baer might stir up public interest in the heavyweight division. His judgment was not restrained: "The heavyweight division is now deader than a brace of mackerel."[19]

Rice complained that there were no heavyweights like Dempsey. Unlike the diatribe against sluggers in the *San Francisco Examiner* after the Campbell affair, Grantland Rice wanted to see a puncher who wasn't afraid to mix it up in the ring "without the defensive restraint shown by most of the others." "Schmeling," he went on to say, "has been almost forgotten. Sharkey and Stribling get only so far and then stick at that spot. They gain ground on one fight and lose it to another. It may be they have been around too long to have the needed keenness left for any extended campaign. At any rate Baer has a great chance. He is also in a great spot. No young heavyweight ever had such an opportunity to hurry to the front and make a clean-up."[20]

"Take my coming bout with Schaaf...." Baer had attracted another group of glossy-eyed reporters whose pens raced across their notepads to capture his every word. "I understand that he is supposed to be a good boxer. Maybe he is, but he is going to know that he is in a fight. On the Coast I would be a 3 to 1 favorite in a match like this. But here I'm the underdog. I'll take Schaaf in five rounds, but I wouldn't be surprised if I get him in the first. Most of these world beaters fold up with the first good punch."[21]

Like Lochinvar, "dauntless in war," Max Baer was determined, confident, fearless, and eager to show his skill. But to some he sounded brash: "Another heavyweight 'loud-speaker' has invaded New York ... a cocky, talkative youngster vaguely reminiscent of Jack Sharkey in the earlier days. Baer is supremely confident that he can stop Schaaf in a few rounds and then he'd like to get a shot at Sharkey. After that Schmeling or Stribling, or anybody for that matter, will suit the youngster."[22]

Baer always seemed in a hurry to clean up. Except in this case, Ernie Schaaf would be no dust-rag. Schaaf was a formidable challenger. He was experienced, with a record that already included decisions over the Who's Who of Boxing, like Tommy Loughran and Johnny Risko (men Max was expected to battle after Schaaf). In over 100 fights, Schaaf had never been knocked off his feet. Champion Jack Sharkey had just bought into Schaaf's contract with Johnny Buckley, convinced that the former Navy man would be the next champion. Schaaf was to the East Coast what Baer was to the West, a young man who packed a wallop and could prove he was ready to be a contender. Most importantly, the match between the two would show New Yorkers where the newcomer belonged in the big pool.

For his debut, Max felt he needed a natty set of boxing trunks. While in New York, Max was introduced to Mr. and Mrs. Harry Fine. Harry was the proprietor of Fine's Gymnasium and his wife was a seamstress. Max went to her and requested something unusual, satin trunks in pastel colors, even royal purple (anticipating the championship). He was going to be the best-dressed boxer in New York. She made the special trunks (and others throughout his career), and after Baer wore them, additional boxers wanted her custom-made trunks. Max started a trend, and Mrs. Fine was grateful for the new business that kept her busy for the rest of her life with orders from all over the world. She would eventually make trunks for Joe Louis, Henry Armstrong (who wore them in every fight beginning with his title win), Manuel Ortiz, Tommy Loughran, Fred Apostoli, and many others. During World War II, the Navy ordered 180 pairs, an order too large for her to fulfill.[23]

In addition to his fancy boxing attire, Max bought a new car, his third one, while waiting for the Schaaf fight. The promoters at Madison Square Garden were not happy when they heard the news. They sent manager Ancil Hoffman a polite demand. The letter, written December 8, 1930, from Garden President William F. Carey, was addressed to Hoffman at Wilson's Training Camp, Orangeburg, New York. It read, "We are considerably disturbed because of rumors to the effect that Mr. Max Baer is having delivered to him today, a high-powered automobile. And that he is inclined to fast driving. I dislike to put a damper on his fun, but nevertheless, I am forced to ask you to prohibit him from driving this machine until after his bout at Madison Square Garden on the 19th of this month."[24] Baer just smiled. He wouldn't be driving the high-powered machine because he had brought a chauffeur from California, formally attired for the purpose of shuttling him around.

By the time of the fight, Baer had convinced almost everyone that he could beat anyone, from Schaaf to Max Schmeling. Grantland Rice, however, was one of the few who didn't believe Baer could beat Schaaf.

At the official weigh-in, Schaaf weighed 203 pounds, and Baer, "the fistic chatterbox" from Livermore, weighed 209. Jack Sharkey was chief second to Schaaf, and Gus Wilson to Baer.

Ernie Schaaf, December 19, 1930, Madison Square Garden

Grantland Rice had been correct. Although Baer had an impressive record of knockouts in California, he could not cope with the better ring generalship of Ernie Schaaf. Max lost the judges' decision after ten rounds. All agreed that it was a hard-fought match. Like many of Baer's fights to come, it was close. Some thought that Baer should have won. Regardless, it was a match that failed to justify his killer reputation.

Schaaf, the boxer, was clever and more experienced, with short sharp punches. Baer, the slugger, did his best, most aggressive work in the first half. He plowed steadily into Schaaf's punches and dominated the first four rounds. He definitely had the stronger punches, but whenever Baer smashed his right hand into Ernie's chin and Schaaf would waver, Baer hesitated too long to put him out.

In the opening round, both were cautious. Baer followed Schaaf around the ring, sending out awkward, long left leads before making contact with two short taps to the chest. They exchanged body punches and were each connecting to the head with fierce punches when the bell rang.

Baer also won the second round. He leaped at the bell to connect his long left to the head and then buried a right into Schaaf's ribs. Ernie missed and Baer followed up with a volley of lefts and rights to the body. Schaaf backed into the ropes, and Baer sent a left hook to the chin that made him hold. Then Schaaf hit Max in the nose with lefts that brought blood before the bell. It was Baer's best round, but he failed to put Schaaf away when he had him on the ropes.

The third round saw Baer leap out and connect two left hooks to the body. He then tried to box. Schaaf was the better boxer, landing a half-dozen lefts. Baer landed two hard lefts to Schaaf's face that drew blood. Battling close and furiously in the center of the ring, both landed to the head and to the body as the crowd cheered wildly. Both were bleeding heavily when the bell interrupted the exchange.

In the fourth, Baer relaxed and tried to box. His punches were only light taps to Schaaf's head and body. Schaaf hit Baer with a hard right to the chin, and Baer came back with an even harder right to Schaaf's chin. Baer attacked again with a blow to the body and another to the chin but couldn't put him down. Schaaf took everything that Baer had to give; he buckled a couple of times, but came back.

Schaaf was ready for Baer's opening leaping lunge in the fifth and hit him on the chin. The pace was slow as they wrestled and fought at close quarters, each exchanging body punches. Both left the round tired.

In the sixth, Baer's opening hook sent Schaaf to the ropes. Schaaf came back pummeling, sending sharp lefts to the body and a right to the head. They slugged at the ropes, and Baer hit Schaaf on the chin and made him wobble. Schaaf came back and they both slugged away, avoiding any defense. The crowd came to their feet and cheered wildly. Baer went back to his stool exhausted.

In the second half of the fight, Baer wilted. He reeled from punches, and his legs appeared to weaken. There were no knockdowns, but powerful blows to the head and body; and in almost every round one or the other wavered and clutched.

Both fighters were tired in the seventh and fell into a clinch early. The crowd wanted more action. Schaaf worked in close, jabbing Baer's ribs, and guarding himself from Max's powerful right hand. Schaaf landed both hands at will on Baer's chin and had him dazed. Baer danced away from the action, but Schaaf came after him until the bell sounded.

Again in the eighth, Baer drove in a blow to the head and fell into a clinch. Schaaf landed volleys to the bloodied face. Baer was game but wild. Schaaf landed accurate short punches with both hands. Schaaf backed him into the ropes. Baer pulled his right as though about to let go a hard one, but Schaaf prevented it from landing with steady left jabs. Baer staggered to his corner.

Baer came out for the ninth dancing, and when he took a fighting pose, he switched to a southpaw stance. He missed and switched back to an orthodox stance. Schaaf punched with his left. Baer connected with a wild right hook, but Schaaf came back with a hard right to the chest. Baer was tired. A right to Schaaf's chin seemed to lack power. Schaaf continued punching to the face, and at the bell, Baer had a large lump over his right eye.

In the final round, Baer tried to land hard shots to Schaaf's head, but the punches bounced off. Whenever Schaaf hit Baer's right eye, Baer flinched. Schaaf never let up with rights and lefts to the head that eventually closed Baer's eye, eliminating his sight from that side. Baer tried valiantly to hit with both hands, but Schaaf battled back. Baer was bloodied and exhausted at the end of the round.

The crowd booed the final decision. The critics were divided, some scoring as high as eight rounds for Schaaf and two for Baer, while others thought Baer had an edge in five, with four for Schaaf, and one even. The score card by the Associated Press gave Schaaf five rounds—the fifth, seventh, eighth, ninth and tenth—with four for Baer—the first, third, fourth, and sixth—and the second round even.

Spectators got a good look at Baer's skill set. The fight showed New York sportswriters that he had punching power, speed, ring mobility, a granite chin, and gameness. He was eager to be the first out, in fact, leaping at the bell with his "opening" left hook lunge, either to the head or to the body. His attempt to switch to southpaw at one desperate point at the end was uncoordinated and awkward. And he seemed to lack the stamina necessary for a full ten rounds of hard fighting. (He had only gone ten rounds twice before, winning one and losing one.) Schaaf was a battle in the learning curve, but Californians may have wondered if Baer held back at any point, remembering how he had finished Campbell.

But Baer proved game, and the crowds loved him for that. Edward J. Neil wrote for the Associated Press, "A husky, colorful young puncher ... [a] welcome addition to the rising crop of youthful heavyweights, came out of the West for his first big league battle tonight and though he failed to conquer he left his mark, both on 10,000 of New York's faithful, and on the person of Ernie Schaaf.... Schaaf, as blonde [sic] and big as Baer is dark and big, won the unanimous decision of the referee and two judges after ten thrilling rounds, but the plaudits of the crowd as well as the votes of several of the ringside critics went to the loose-muscled grinning curly head from the Pacific Coast."[25]

Max appeared bigger in defeat than Ernie in victory. Baer was colorful and wild, "Homeric," one writer noted. Schaaf showed more polish, but it was said that he could not improve. Everyone agreed that Baer had room for growth. They said he had to improve his boxing and defensive skills. Baer had earned admirers in the East, and they believed his real glory was still ahead. Tom McArdle, matchmaker for the Garden, advised Hoffman to stick around. McArdle knew that even if tickets only sold for five dollars (the highest in the Baer-Schaaf bout), spectators got a bigger bang for their money than for a fifty-dollar ticket to see a Sharkey-Schmeling or Stribling bout or other big-name dancer.

Baer's purse amounted to $4800. After the various managers and ten-percent owners had taken their cuts, expenses had been paid, and $800 had been sent home, Max was left with $100. Baer was humiliated and said this about the fight: "The day after, the experts agreed on one thing—that I could take a pounding.... After that the opinions differed, but most of them were different only as to what sort of adjective they should place before the word 'bum.'"[26]

Baer came to New York with his reputation as the "killer," the Butcher Boy. But as Dan Parker assessed years later, "The trouble with him as a fighter, however, was that he had too much heart. I use the word in the sense denoting compassion rather than courage, without meaning to stamp this broad-shouldered giant as cowardly. There are fighters who don't know their own strength. Maxie wasn't one of them." His previous experience "proved the lethal quality of his punches and if they made him afraid, it was of himself."[27]

Schaaf would go on to have twenty-five wins and two losses before meeting Max again the next year. Only a few weeks after the close fight with Max Baer, Ernie Schaaf met and beat Jim Braddock (former light-heavyweight contender) at Madison Square Garden. Schaaf was an eight-to-five favorite over Braddock. Playing the "What If?" game, we can wonder what would have happened if Baer had beaten Schaaf and gone on to meet Braddock back in 1931.

Although Baer had lost his debut fight at the Garden and failed to live up to his KO reputation, he was not finished. His one fight in New York before the year was out had given him the publicity he needed to make it into the year-end rankings. Even if he had made the list by only one vote, he was now a bona-fide contender.

Rankings of the World-Class Boxers

At the end of 1930, the *New York Evening Sun* ranked the best of all fighters, regardless of weight class, according to the votes of sixty-four sportswriters. Mickey Walker, who fought both light-heavyweights and heavyweights, had twenty-four votes for "best all-round performer in the ring." Jimmy McLarnin, welterweight, was second with eleven votes; Jackie Kid Berg, British lightweight, third, with nine votes. Fidel Labarba, featherweight, received six votes, and Tony Canzoneri, lightweight champion, three.[28]

The heavyweights were at the bottom of the list, reinforcing the judgment of Rice and other sportswriters about the field. Young Stribling was given two votes; Max Schmeling and Max Baer tied with one vote each.

Mickey Walker had won the top honor the year before, but his manager Jack Kearns was having a difficult time getting the favorite a match. The *Syracuse Herald* lampooned, "Mr. Kearns has numerous inducements being ready to offer a guarantee of a couple of banks in North Dakota he doesn't remember the names of, an 80-acre squirrel farm atop Pike's Peak, a couple of shares in the Chicago River, several slightly used umbrellas and an old pair of dice."[29]

Ratings for the leading heavyweights by the *New York Sun*, using 70 sportswriters, put W.L. (Young) Stribling as number one. The others in his class were Jack Sharkey and Max Schmeling; Carnera was below them in a class by himself; Griffith, George Godfrey, Vittorio Campolo, and Tommy Loughran were in a class below Carnera; and Max Baer, Tommy Loughran, and Risko were at the bottom.[30]

The National Boxing Association (NBA) had its own rankings. In the heavyweight division, Young Stribling was number one, followed in order by Jack Sharkey, Jimmy Maloney, Primo Carnera, Tuffy Griffith, George Godfrey, Johnny Risko, Paulino Uzcudun, Ernie Schaaf and Max Baer.[31]

By December of 1930, the New York Athletic Commission pressed Schmeling for a title fight with Sharkey within 15 days. When manager Joe Jacobs and Schmeling refused, the commission canceled both of their licenses. Chicagoans jumped on the situation and offered Schmeling $500,000 to fight the winner of a Stribling-Carnera bout. Madison Square Garden proposed its own set of elimination bouts.

Grantland Rice assessed the situation, saying that it would be a feat to work out who would be fighting Max Schmeling in 1931. "Max Baer is still at least a year away [actually he was two and a half years away] and Carnera is still 4,000 miles away. Would Sharkey meet the winner of Stribling-Carnera or Stribling-Campolo?"[32] There was even a call for the great Jack Dempsey to return to the ring and take on Schmeling. And there was also Tuffy Griffith, who turned heavyweight in 1929, and wanted to take part in any elimination tournament. California promoter Ancil Hoffman was quick to offer Joe Jacobs a tune-up bout for Schmeling with Baer—a "Maxie-Maxie bout." The idea sounded good and Jacobs would file it away for the future.

Grantland Rice was so frustrated with the heavyweight championship situation that he said, "Why not declare a moratorium for at least a year and let nature take its course?" Let Jack Dempsey "shadow box and at least bring back a reminder of the days when one wallop was worth more than 10 dancing maneuvers."[33] He seemed displeased by the fact that the losers were getting more notoriety than the winners. As one pundit quipped, the breakfast greeting nowadays for managers and their valiant boys is: "If we can only lose this one, we'll own Broadway."[34]

The latest figure in the "lose and become famous" game was Max Baer. Promoters wasted no time matching Baer, still rated as one of the finest heavyweight prospects in the country, for his second appearance at the Garden with Tom Heeney of New Zealand, in the fight of the week.

Much has been said over the years about Baer's failure to reach the pinnacle and hold onto it due to a disdain for training. However, during the time of his early Madison Square Garden fights, nothing seemed unusual about his training regime. After the Schaaf fight, Max was mentally defeated, homesick, and in love. Hoffman gave him some time off. Max explained what happened: "I came here. There were hotels, restaurants, night clubs, theaters, blondes, brunettes and redheads. I was twenty-one years old and I had $10,000 in my pocket. If you had been in my place, what would you have done?" he asked Frank Graham, a journalist in New York.[35]

Dorothy Dunbar had followed his entourage to New York while keeping some distance away. Max wrote in an article, "I didn't play 'hookey' training for that fight. Ancil allowed me a few days for skylarking after the Schaaf battle."[36] Hoffman knew Max was lovesick.

Hoffman questioned him, "Why don't you marry her and settle down?"

"Because she won't have me," he answered. "I guess it's because I don't have enough class."

"Well," said Hoffman, "If she doesn't want you, why annoy her by hanging around?"

"I'm not annoying her, I'm entertaining her," Baer shot back.

"That may not be her story," the mentor replied. "You're so lovesick I get sick of looking at you. You're thinking more about a girl than you are about your career, and if that keeps going you'll end up with your nose in the water bucket."

"You're right," Baer told him, "I'll call it quits with Dorothy." He left the hotel and went straight to see Dorothy Dunbar. Instead of calling it quits, "[Max] took his little verbal banjo around to Dorothy's and sang songs." He said, "She kidded me and asked if the great big bad man from California was going to knock out Heeney like he had knocked out Schaaf."

Max replied, "This is one bird I'll wing, sure."

But Dorothy replied mockingly, "Sounds familiar."

Whether it was humiliation or inspiration, Max had a different showing in his next bout with Tom Heeney.

He trained hard at Gus Wilson's gym. Two days before the bout, "Baer worked five rounds, three with Albert Nokin, the Belgian, and two against Billy Schwartz, Alexandria,

Virginia, light heavyweight." In the afternoon, he was "scheduled to box four rounds, do about five miles on the frozen roads and three sessions of calisthenics."[37] (No current trainer would have his charge out running on frozen roads, risking a possible slip and fall.)

Gus Wilson charged $15 per day for room and board for each trainer and fighter. Sparring mates cost $15 per day. The manager usually stayed at a hotel nearby. (By comparison, the Yosemite gym in Oakland charged $2 per month for dues, and sparring partners were available for $5 per day.) After paying Max's expenses, Ancil Hoffman had probably given serious consideration to his six-month contract with Lorimer, set to expire in March.

Tom Heeney, January 16, 1931, Madison Square Garden

Baer entered the fight with New Zealand's Tom Heeney, called the "Hard Rock from Down Under," as the betting favorite three to one. "Old Tom" had been in Gene Tunney's last career fight.

Henry McLemore with the United Press predicted that the ten-round bout would not go the full rounds. "Even if Heeney has that 'one real scrap' left that he claims, the young Californian should put a stop to things in the sixth round or thereabouts. Baer

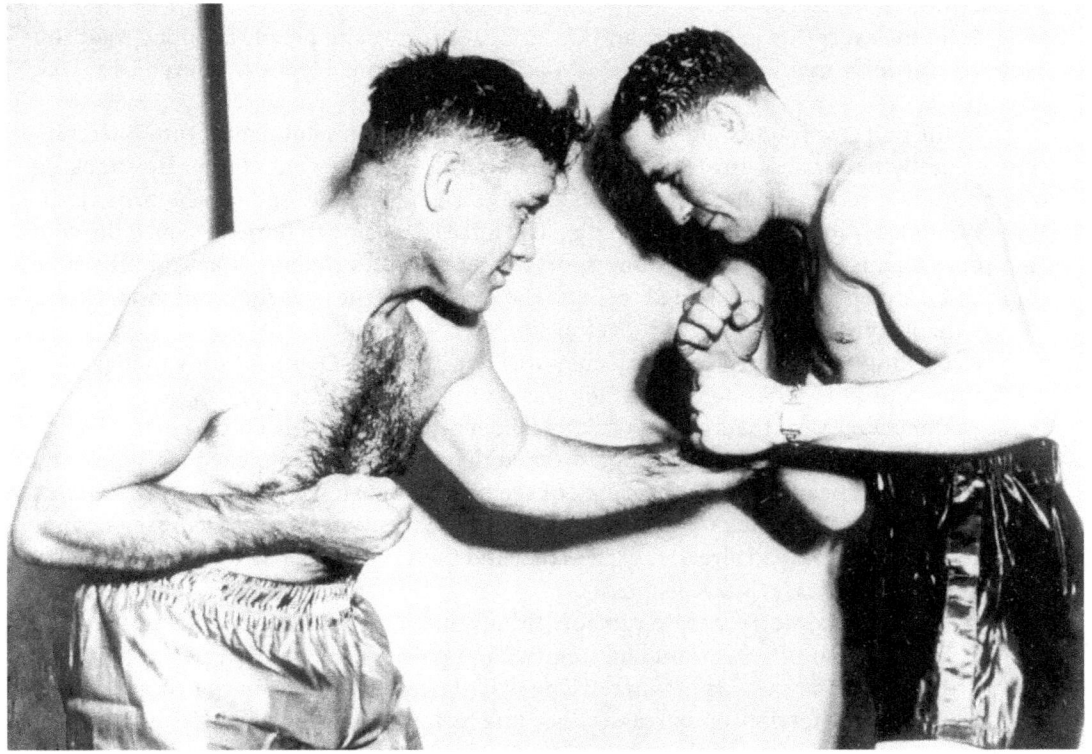

Tom Heeney (left) squares up with Max Baer (right), January 16, 1931, Madison Square Garden. Max wears a nice watch for the photograph.

has everything but experience—a crackling punch in either hand, speed, and a willingness to wade in there and shoot the works. Heeney, never a great fighter in his prime, now has little more than a stout heart that keeps him moving forward as long as he can lift an arm."[38]

Baer was criticized in the Schaaf fight for leading with his chin, and if Heeney connected, he might have a chance to win. But if Baer could put away Heeney, he was expected to be given a bout with Johnny Risko, early in February. (He did get that fight, but not until May.) Most felt that if Baer failed to beat Heeney, he might just as well pack up and go home.[39]

When the doors of the Garden opened for the fight, officials from the New York State Boxing Commission were positioned inside the foyer, standing guard. As soon as Primo Carnera of Italy and Paulino Uzcudun of Spain tried to enter (they had purchased their tickets in advance and had no idea that anyone was waiting for them), they were stopped by the guards and refused entrance. Unbeknownst to them, a provision existed in the boxing laws of New York that prevented a "suspended" boxer from entering a licensed fight club. The commissioners had been tipped off that the two foreign heavyweights were going to try to attend the Baer-Heeney fight. Carnera had been suspended in New York for having been involved in an alleged "fixed fight" in California. Paulino was suspended because he met Carnera in Barcelona on November 30, 1930, and was now guilty by participation. The Carnera-Uzcudun episode was the first imbroglio of the evening. The visiting heavyweights would miss the second one—another fight for the history books.

With the exception of Carnera and Uzcudun, ten thousand people attended Madison Square Garden's main event between Max Baer and Tom Heeney, refereed by Jack Dempsey.

In the first two rounds, the men went at each other, landing punches, with Baer having a slightly better showing. But in the third round, Heeney went at Baer by attacking the body. Baer returned with a two-fisted attack to Heeney's body and face before smashing his famous right hand to Heeney's chin. The force of the punch hurled Heeney through the ropes against the shoulder of one sportswriter and into the lap of another. Heeney quickly cleared his head, struggled through the ropes back into the ring, and took a knee. It was the Dempsey-Firpo fight all over again.

According to the timekeeper, Heeney was out. But Jack Dempsey only managed to get to the count of "nine" before Heeney was on his feet, ready to fight.

Arthur Donovan, the knockdown timekeeper, had begun his count when Heeney was initially knocked off his feet. But it seemed that Jack Dempsey picked up Donovan's count, missing a beat or two in the shock of seeing Heeney blown from the ring. Heeney waited for Dempsey to pick up the count, and he rose from his knee at Dempsey's count of nine. But Donovan had already reached ten, and then yelled "You're out" when Heeney was attempting to rise. Chaos erupted.

The officials conferred, trying to sort things out. The crowd yelled for the fight to go on. And the two boxers stood chatting like old pals, all the while ready and willing to continue from the same spot where Heeney had been ejected from the ring.

Dempsey was terribly embarrassed, became furious, and argued with everyone that he had not ruined the count, that there was a discrepancy between Donovan's pounding and the man watching the seconds on the clock. No one could argue with Dempsey, so they simply declared the fight over after one minute and three seconds of the third round.

Max Baer (left) knocks Tom Heeney out of the ring while Referee Jack Dempsey tells Max to go to a neutral corner, January 16, 1931 (courtesy IBRO).

Max Baer was credited with another of his famous technical knockouts with his powerful right.[40]

The Baer-Heeney fight resulted in an important ring change for boxers everywhere. The New York Athletic Commission ordered that there be a "resting place" for those boxers knocked or pushed out of the ring or otherwise fallen out. Before the fight, outside "ring aprons" of canvas and decking had only extended 1½ feet from the ropes. The new regulation required the canvas to extended 3½ feet from the ropes.

The bout drew $24,000, from which Baer's take at twenty-percent amounted to $4800. After expenses and fees paid to managers, there was little left over for the boxer. Ancil told Max he had to fire the secretary and chauffeur. Ancil was seriously toying with the idea of giving Max back to Lorimer at the end of the New York jaunt. But first, Hoffman needed to get Baer out of his red ink. He put him on a strict $5 per day allowance. Then he signed him to fight Tommy Loughran.

Tommy Loughran, February 6, 1931, Madison Square Garden

After the bout with Tom Heeney, the Garden offered Hoffman and Baer another fight. Ancil chose the formidable opponent: Tommy Loughran of Philadelphia.[41]

Max asked, "Why Loughran?"

Hoffman replied, "I'm choosing Loughran because you can learn something by being beaten by him."

"Well, who says he'll whip me?"

"I do," answered Ancil. "Loughran is a very strange man. You could almost call him a freak. He has 575 left hands and the more remarkable thing about him is that he pumps all of them at the same time into other people's faces."

"When I clip him…."

"When you clip him, I'll guarantee to have Woolworth's sell you their nice big building for a dime. A couple of years from now, you'll wish you were only half as good then as you think you are now."

After the tongue-lashing, Max said he "read up a lot on Tommy Loughran, and asked plenty of people before I fought him just how good he was. They told me that if I hit him six times in ten rounds I ought to get a Congressional medal. The fight—let's see, now," Baer reminisced. "Was it a fight or just a bag punching exhibition by Tommy?"[42]

Baer was set to meet a difficult opponent who had now entered the heavyweight ranks. Tommy Loughran, the dancing master of Philadelphia, had been the king of the light-heavies as a result of his deadly left. And when the doors of Madison Square Garden opened for the fight with Baer, the crowd (at 12,000) was even larger than the attendance at the Baer-Heeney fight.

Tommy Loughran of Philadelphia, a fast light-heavyweight, used his left to defeat Max, winning all 10 rounds, February 6, 1931. Afterward, Max asked Tommy for a boxing lesson. Loughran said that when Max hit him with a right, "I thought the roof fell in."

In the dressing rooms, ring savvy Tommy beat Baer to an early punch. He knew that Baer was a nice guy who liked everyone and had a habit of trying to pick an argument with his competitor in order to get mad enough to fight him in the ring. With that knowledge, Tommy rushed into Baer's dressing room and grabbed his hand and told him how glad he was to meet him and hoped he had a swell time in the East. Baer could not possibly be mad at such a nice guy!

In the ring, Loughran jabbed his way to a "ridiculously easy ten-round decision over Max Baer, willing but clumsy. Stepping around with all his old-time speed, Loughran stabbed Baer off balance with a stinging left jab all evening, evaded almost all of his wild rushes, whipped right uppercuts when opportunity presented itself and won the unanimous decision of the two judges and Referee Jack Dempsey."[43]

Baer said, "Along about the seventh I just quit trying to hit Tommy. It was a waste of effort. He made me look and act so much like an amateur that I just had to stop and laugh. It was my salute to a better man. I think I drove a few into Tommy's body, but I guess that was because Tommy was charitable and didn't want me to go ten rounds without landing at least a couple of times."[44]

Loughran commented on Baer's sledgehammer right. "He hit me in the ribs with that right in the second round, and I thought the roof fell in. I was hurt badly, but I didn't want him to know it and kept on the move. Max sensed something wrong, but when he saw me come back at him with a punch after hitting me there, he didn't know what to think."[45] He said Baer kept trying to knock his block off with his right, but he would move his head to one side, and Baer would miss; he would move to the other side, and he would miss, he caught one in the air, and he would duck under another one. When they were in a clinch, Loughran whispered in his ear, "Keep trying, Maxie, I've got at least 12 more ways of making you miss with that punch."[46]

When a belligerent spectator yelled to Max, "Why don't you hit him with your right hand?" Max yelled back, "Why don't you come up here and hit him with your right hand?"[47]

Baer lost every round of the fight. Ancil Hoffman was as disappointed as anyone. He called partner Lorimer and told him the situation, and Lorimer said to bring Max home, that he believed he could get the California commission to grant him a license.

Hoffman also answered a phone call from reporter Bob Shand of Oakland, who asked what had happened to Max? Hoffman could only reply that "the lad had lost all his old fighting instinct." Otherwise, he couldn't really explain why "Max stood still and let Loughran jab him at will. He showed the same lack of ambition in his fights with Schaaf and Heeney."[48] Baer's best asset was his fearless fighting spirit, especially when he had his man hurt. But Hoffman explained that the killer instinct was gone. "In the fourth round he clipped Loughran right on the chin and had him helpless on the ropes." The California Baer would have finished it up, "but Max stood back and allowed Tommy to recuperate. Again in the ninth he had Loughran on the verge of a knock-out, but he failed to follow up."[49] The same had happened in the Schaaf fight. Max simply couldn't finish him off. It was as though he remembered looking at Frankie Campbell, and when he finished him off, Campbell was dead. Baer's killer instinct was gone.

Hoffman even said, "We tried to stir him out of his lethargic attitude. We insulted him between rounds and Gus Wilson, one of his seconds, even slapped his face. The old Max Baer would have become fighting mad at this kind of treatment but the Baer of today is meek as a lamb."[50]

Max earned $8000 from the fight, and after managers' cuts he would have $2400 from which to pay training expenses. Bob Shand said those training expenses cost $100 per day.

But Max had learned some valuable lessons about ring psychology and put his resolve to good use. Baer went to Loughran's dressing room and asked him to show him how he connected with his left. "I'd like to hit some other fellows' noses the same way. How about showing me?" Tommy laughed and told him to meet him for lunch the next day. In that meeting, Loughran drilled Baer on his technique. Tommy said to keep practicing and it would come. "Just shorten your punches."[51]

Later, Max walked into Jack Dempsey's hotel room. Dempsey saw so much of himself in Max. Grantland Rice was visiting Dempsey and said that Baer was cut in "the Dempsey mold." Dempsey reminisced about his early fight when he came east to meet Lester Johnson. Dempsey said that when he was jabbing Johnson with his left, Johnson grabbed his arm and broke two of his ribs. Dempsey had Max throw a left jab to demonstrate. Dempsey showed Max how to catch that left with a left hand, lift it up, and with a right hand, smash the body. Jack said that Johnson won the fight because he couldn't straighten up after the broken ribs.

Dempsey showed Baer another trick. Again, he had Max throw out a left jab. With his right fist, Jack hammered the muscles of Baer's upper arm. Baer recoiled, saying his entire arm was either numb or broken. "Two or three wallops like that won't help any arm," Dempsey grinned.[52] Dempsey told Baer that he had to punch faster—keep throwing punches with both fists, even if you miss with one. He also told him to punch with his whole body, not just his arms. Dempsey stiffened his right shoulder and brought up his fist with a quick turn of the right hip. "Loosen it up and let the hip follow. Keep your body weight back of the punch. You can knock down an elephant with what you have." Dempsey let the punch whistle past Baer's chin. Grantland said Dempsey was in full force now, "and there has never been anything halfway about the Dempsey model." Dempsey told Max that the approach to infighting was important. Never walk in facing your opponent; walk in "half-sideways" with one or the other hip out. And "rip in hard," no tapping, and keep both hands busy.

Another interesting tip Dempsey gave Baer was to practice missing with the right, so his opponent focused on that. Then he could barrel in with a swift left, so his opponent didn't know what hit him. Speed counted. The goal was to keep your opponent off-guard. One of the most important ideas Jack told him was not to think about knocking your opponent out. With that idea in your head, "You'll tighten up and press or hit too soon." Hit naturally and hard without crowding the effort, he advised. "Don't try to knock somebody's head off every time you swing."

What was Baer's reaction? Grantland Rice said he was attentive to every word. He reported that Baer said, "I have learned more today than I ever dreamed was in the game." Rice said that he was "far from being the arrogant, headstrong fighter that so many believe him to be."[53]

Max Baer's time in New York was full of momentous occasions. He went to see a stage show starring former Heavyweight Champion "Gentleman" Jim Corbett. Before the show, Max and Ancil went backstage to greet the champ. Max recalled, "When I walked into his dressing room and saw this man dressed in a robe, jet black hair, putting powder on his face with a powder puff. 'This is the man who licked John L.?' I asked myself."[54] Max would never forget the connection between the heavyweight champion and his access to the world of show business. It is possible that this meeting was as important a stimulus as any for Max to return to boxing to try to become champion so as to attain similar star status.

The fighter and manager were ready to leave for home when they were called before the New York Athletic Commission. It had been brought to the attention of the members that both Baer and manager had a background marred in California and that Hoffman had been acting as manager in New York when he was really a San Francisco promoter. Because he was without a manager's license, Baer's matches had been called into question. Hoffman explained that both men had been denied licenses in California for the Campbell death. Hoffman assured the commissioners that when they returned to California the situation would be corrected—an optimistic wish on Hoffman's part.

Three • New York Meets Lochinvar, 1930, 1931

The loss to Loughran again forced Baer to eat humble pie. It is interesting to hear Grantland Rice's insight on Baer and Baer's own words regarding the fight:

> The general public's opinion of Max Baer as a chesty, arrogant, swellheaded kid is all out of line. I saw him the day after the Loughran fight. He had no alibis, but he had this to say: "I was so ashamed of myself I could hardly hold my head up. I did my best, but I knew it ought to have been a lot better. I knew what that crowd must be thinking about me, and whatever it was I couldn't blame 'em. I deserved to have my nose punched off, and I almost did. But I'm still not discouraged. I know now how much I have to learn and I'm going to learn it if I can. I may be a lot of things, but I'm not a quitter. I only hope I never look so foolish again in the ring."[55]

In his defense, Baer had come up through the ranks very quickly. His early competition and quick knockouts may not have given him the experience he needed as a contender.

Jack Dempsey had taken up his cause. Dempsey had a true affection for Baer; so too had Grantland Rice, and just about anyone who was around Max for any length of time. Dempsey told Rice, "Baer can still be a great fighter if he will put his entire attention on ring work, and not upon outside matters."[56] When he spoke to Baer, Dempsey minced no words: "I have at least one thing to my credit. From the time I started, up through the Firpo fight, I went into training with just one thought in my mind—how to get ready to beat the other fellow. That took in just 100 percent of my ability to concentrate. If you do the same thing, you can go a long way. They need your kind now. If you don't, you might as well quit. You can't play two games at the same time." Max said afterward, "I only wish I could get good enough to go one round with that fellow. What a great fighter and what a grand guy!"[57]

It remained to be seen if Max had the tenacity and focus to go back to work.

If Max Baer wanted to fight, he had to leave New York. There were no more fights for him there. His coveted fight with Johnny Risko of Cleveland was canceled. It was a great disappointment as well for the "Rubber Man." But Madison Square Garden had canceled Baer's contract. He was no longer an attraction. And he was starting to be less of an attraction for Ancil Hoffman.

Ancil had decided to go back to California by ship rather than by train, sailing through the Panama Canal. He needed a rest. Max had done well during his stay in New York financially. His gross earnings were: Schaaf, $4,879.72; Heeney, $5,062.33, and Loughran, $8,130.18, for a total of $18,072.23. Baer's personal take on his earnings at thirty percent was a little more than $5400. Because Baer had already spent his portion and more (on a car and other extravagances) before the Loughran bout, Baer was in debt to his manager, who held all the money. After Hoffman put Max on the $5 allowance, the spendthrift seemed to be doing better, or so Hoffman thought.

On the morning the boat was to leave for California, Baer entered Ancil's hotel room and said in a panic, "I've got to have $1200."

"You what?" Ancil asked.

Baer demanded, "By 10:00."

The problem was that Baer couldn't live on, and hadn't lived on $5 a day for quite some time. The boxer had borrowed $800, and he needed to pay it back before he left the city.

Ancil swallowed hard and then asked, "And what about the other $400?"

"Those are charges on my room." Max had bought flowers, theater tickets, food, etc., with much of it going to court Dorothy Dunbar, who had been consoler-in-chief during his stay in New York.

Ancil, the 5'4" business manager, who could not have scaled more than 140 pounds, stared his 210-pound, desperate heavyweight directly in the eye and said, "No! You're already overdrawn $2500."

Max walked over to the window, pried it open, and looked somberly down at the street, 34 floors below. "Twelve hundred bucks or I go sailing out of here," he threatened. "And then how are you going to get back that $2500 overdraft, and where will you get another champion like me?"

Ancil drew in a deep breath and thought about it for a minute. Then he replied, "Jump, Dearie, jump! And then my champion headache will be gone."

"If that's the way you feel about it, I won't oblige you," Max said, his bluff called.[58]

Hoffman paid the debt so the pair could leave New York.

With Max's excessive spending, Hoffman had made no money on the trip. In fact, he lost money. Little did he know that things would get worse.

With the New York battles now behind them, Baer's trainer Frankie Burns returned to California via train. Dorothy Dunbar took a plane to Reno, where she would sign her final divorce papers and pick up her monthly alimony check of $1500. Max and Ancil boarded the liner that passed through the Panama Canal, with Max's new 16-cylinder "steed" stowed away in the hold compartment. It was Valentine's Day, 1931.

Hoffman was ready to return to California and turn Max back over to Ham Lorimer.

But in the two weeks the boat was in passage, the pair had time to think. Hoffman had his lawyer request a California manager's license. Contract documents with Lorimer showed that Hoffman was to have one-fourth of Baer's contract after six months. It was also noted that he had never taken any money from Baer's earnings while in New York.

Baer would prove to the world that he was no "quitter." He had tasted the big fights and bathed in the bright lights of New York. He had expected a quick and glorious ride to the championship. And although his opportunities resulted in disappointing setbacks, they were not career-ending ones. He was still young and full of promise; and more importantly, he had ambition, a desire to learn, and the determination to avenge his losses. Nothing was going to keep him from the national spotlight. Even though the Garden didn't want him, and the New York commissioners were soured, Max still had offers coming in from Chicago, Denver, Detroit, Reno, and Tijuana, Mexico, including an offer from Mike Jacobs and his Twentieth Century Athletic Club in New York. And Hoffman had plans for Baer to work out with faster sparring partners. He felt that Baer was too slow. His punches were good with Schaaf and Heeney, but his attempt to keep up with Loughran was "laughable."

Baer hoped that the three new members that made up the California Athletic Commission would change their minds and give him a license. One new commissioner was sportswriter Bob Edgren. His attitude toward Ancil Hoffman and Max Baer was downright hostile. As a manager of fighters, he said "Ancil is a good country hotel keeper." In speaking of the Baer-Loughran bout, he said it was "a very idiotic thing to do," adding, "They say Baer is a year away. He's more than that from the eyebrows up."[59] Hoffman and Baer would not be granted licenses, but Ham Lorimer was granted a manager's license on February 15, 1931, while Ancil and Max were still on the boat.

Edgren was right about the Loughran-Baer pairing. On March 13, Tommy would make mincemeat of Ernie Schaaf. Edgren's feelings about Baer were bitter. When the commissioners planned a dinner party in Northern California, Edgren told the group that Baer was not invited to his mansion, and that he didn't want to see him in Monterey County, Alameda County, or any other county. The license request for Hoffman was tabled.

Max and Ancil came into port at San Pedro, California, on February 28, telling the press that if they were denied licenses in California, they would fight in Mexico. They continued on the boat to San Francisco. Max went back to the Yosemite Gym in Oakland to work with Puggy Buckley, trainer when Max was under Bob McAllister. Word was that if Max tried to apply for a license it would be denied.

At the end of March, Max Baer went to lunch with Chaplain Kelly, one of the new state commissioners. He also attended Kelly's church sermon on March 22, to show that his heart was in the right place. Kelly's sermon was titled, "The Prodigal Son."[60]

Ernie Owens, April 7, 1931, Portland, Oregon

Max would start his comeback away from the controversy of California. Max and Ernie Owens, two California battlers, had to fight in Portland, Oregon. Baer was back with Ham Lorimer and without his trusted trainer Frankie Burns. Word was that these were not good omens, but in fact, Baer probably saw his fight with Ernie Owens as the knockover that it was.

The magnificent body of Max Baer in his prime: lean, agile, and powerful (courtesy Mike Silver).

The bout was over by the second round. Baer weighed 197 and Owens 185. Baer lunged from the start, landing two fisted punches to Owens's midsection. He kept up the attack until he struck him with an overhand right that sent Owens to the canvas. He was saved by the bell.

In the second round, Owens came out bravely, but was floored by Max with a hard right cross to the jaw. Ernie came up at the count of nine, when Baer was waiting to drop him again. Referee Tom Louttit stopped the fight.

After the bout, Max returned to Hoffman's ranch at Fair Oaks to prepare for the Risko match, which had been canceled previously in New York. The new fight would be in Risko's hometown.

Johnny Risko, May 5, 1931, Cleveland, Ohio

On April 23, the day Max left for Cleveland, he filed an application for a California license. It was turned down on April 25, without comment. Baer's train arrived in Cleveland on Sunday, April 26. He began training at the Argonne Athletic Club for the May 5 ten-round bout at the Cleveland Public Hall. Even before the fight, Max had an idea that he would be in the running for a big fight scheduled in Reno for Jack Dempsey's July Fourth celebration. But first he had to get past Johnny Risko.

Risko had cratered many battlers' hopes in the ring. He was known as the "Rubber Man" because punches and boxers simply bounced off the man. He almost destroyed Gene Tunney before Tunney met Dempsey. Risko put away Jack Sharkey in 1928. Risko had boxed professionally for six years before Max Baer ever entered the ring. In addition to his experience, he was at his peak, in the middle of his fighting career. His last two wins were over King Levinsky and Tom Heeney. He had beaten Ernie Schaaf, Vittorio Campolo, and Paulino Uzcudun.

In front of a crowd of 7,000, Johnny Risko proved to be another spoiler of a near contender. In a barrage of left and right combinations to the body and head of Baer, Risko won the judges' decision. Baer did manage to stun Risko with several hard rights to the head that caused him to fall into clinches. But whenever he came out of the clinch, Risko managed to land a hard punch that would even things up. In the final two rounds, Risko managed to take the advantage.

It was another humiliating loss for Baer, in a series of significant losses, in his attempt to become a contender. The loss was witnessed by none other than Max Schmeling, who watched from a special box. Any good coming from the event (something Baer could not have appreciated at the time) might have been that this loss, along with the previous losses to Ernie Schaaf and Tommy Loughran in New York, had given Max Schmeling a false sense of confidence over the young up-and-comer, now down-and-outer Max Baer.

"And so poor little Max Baer took another licking from washed up Johnny Risko in the east last night. Too bad, too bad," said reporter Russ Allen of the local *Hayward Review*, tired of Baer's big dreams, big money, and big automobiles. "That finishes Max on an eastern attraction. And if he is smart he will come back to the coast and gather up some of the smaller but more certain money. Max's performances in the East have been little less than disastrous. Declared a pending champion and possessed of everything except, perhaps, gray matter, the Livermore butcher boy has proved a flop. But he will still be a drawing card in Oakland. Mark our words, the next fight Max stages in or near Oakland will result in an overflow house. He may be a piece of cheese to the Easterners, but to the Eastbayers he still is our little boy Max, with a wallop and a personality and a good chance to redeem himself and again hit his way to the top. But little Maxie should forget about 16 cylinder automobiles."[61]

While Little Maxie was still endeared to many Eastbayers, the California Commissioners remained intractable about granting him a license. Bob Edgren was entrenched. Chaplain Kelly said he might be swayed to give him a license if Max would "use cheaper transportation," and wear "less gaudy raiment."[62]

Everyone knew that was not going to happen.

Four

Pied Piper's Road Back to Contender, 1931

By May 1931, Jack Dempsey was at work on his Dempsey Bowl in Reno, Nevada.

Dempsey was tired of the stranglehold that New York had on major fights. He was comfortable in Reno. The city was the playboy capital of the West, where the wealthy came to be entertained through gambling, drink (illegally) and horseracing. He would place his bet on boxing and try his hand at promoting. After all, he was trained by the best promoter in the business—Tex Rickard—in how to place the biggest bets using other people's money.

After Rickard's unexpected death in Miami in 1929, Dempsey accompanied Rickard's casket on a train from Florida back to New York, where the great showman would lie in state in Madison Square Garden. Thus, the promoter's torch was passed to Jack Dempsey. And just as Rickard had championed the boxer Dempsey, now manager Dempsey would champion Max Baer.

Backed by Reno's mob money, Dempsey was granted permission to build a $100,000 race track, with 600 stables, a clubhouse, and a boxing pavilion. There he planned to stage twenty- and twenty-five-round "finish" fights, like those of yesteryear when boxing was a more "manly" sport, in his estimation. Dempsey did not like fights limited to fifteen rounds, and since the laws were lax in Nevada, he could do as he pleased. Dempsey explained the "finish fight: "If there was no knockout, [the match] will continue for 20 rounds to a decision."[1]

Dempsey planned to stage the first bout in his new arena on July 4, an event he hoped would equal that of Rickard's promotion of Jack Johnson and Jim Jeffries in Reno, twenty-one years earlier, in 1910. Like Rickard, Dempsey dreamed big, especially since by 1931, the nation was two years into a dreadful financial depression. But he knew that even in any lean time, the very wealthy had money to spend, and they spent it on entertainment. It helped that Dempsey had a blueprint from Rickard's earlier event to ensure a successful Independence Day celebration in Nevada.

It also helped that the entire production was funded by two prominent men of the Reno mob: William Graham and James McKay, "Dempsey's associates," as they were called in print.[2] McKay and Graham owned their own casinos or gambling clubs but also were given cuts in Wingfield's Riverside Hotel, the fancy six-story building built in 1927, to house large suites for divorcees in residence. When called upon, Graham and McKay hid their questionable associates in Reno, and gladly accepted their wealth of deposits in their bank.

In short, Dempsey was only the front man for the occasion. The mob figures, described by some as "business leaders," loved sports as much as they loved gambling, and they were willing to spend a lot of money to indulge their friends on these occasions. J. Edgar Hoover of the FBI had box seats for any racetrack in the country.

Mob money was not the only money in town. With its beautiful alpine lake nearby, the area was home to the very wealthy who built exotic escapes from the congestion and exposure of the cities. Reno's other calling was to the celebrity divorce crowd. Dempsey was there for the same reason. He was divorcing his wife Estelle Taylor.

Dempsey had tried his luck promoting fights in Chicago, but had to fight politicians and competition. Here Dempsey was in control. When asked about prospects, he threw out names like Campolo, Griffith, Loughran, Risko, Maloney or Schaaf, to test the water. Tex Rickard had always liked Uzcudun, so maybe he would invite him. He also mentioned that Ancil Hoffman, agent for Baer, had made an interesting proposition. Hoffman had offered a percentage of Baer's fight. (For Baer's later fights, Dempsey would be in for seven percent, either as trainer or promoter.) It did not appear to matter that Dempsey was promoter and referee.

Paulino Uzcudun, July 4, 1931, Dempsey Bowl, Reno, Nevada

One month before the fight, the ballyhoo for the "Gold Rush to Reno" was going strong. The stage was set for a revival of the "sport of kings" in Nevada. In a publicity number taken out of Tex Rickard's promoter playbook, women were admitted free to the day's events to ensure greater numbers. The opening day horse race for a mile and 70 yards was billed as the Dempsey Handicap. Miss Elsie Dempsey, his sister, would crown the winner. There was no formal mention of Dempsey's father and his new wife. They had made the news earlier. The couple lived one state over, in Salt Lake City, Utah. In March, Hiram Dempsey, 73, had married his neighbor Hanna Chapman, 37.[3]

Everyone eagerly awaited the holiday celebration.

The week before, advance ticket sales indicated that the fighters would share a purse of $50,000 or more. The guarantee for each was $10,000 plus a percentage of the gate. After taxes, Uzcudun was to receive 30 percent of the gross and Baer 22 percent. The open-air racetrack arena could seat a maximum of 22,000. Parking was available for 5,000 vehicles. Admission tickets covered both the horse races and boxing—six preliminaries and the main bout. Ringside seats sold for $20, reserved seats $15 to $5, and general admission went for $3.[4]

To accommodate the 18,000-plus visitors that swelled the city, every hotel and residence room was made available. People came by train, automobile and airplane. They slept in special train berths and rented Pullman cars lined up one after the other, 120 in all. Over a hundred film personalities arrived on a special motion picture train. Among them were Eddie Cantor, the four Marx brothers, Buster Keaton, W.C. Fields, and many studio executives.

It was estimated that 6,000 or more Basques from the Western United States, California, Oregon, Utah, and Nevada attended to see their hero.

On July 1, Dempsey was given an offer to meet the winner of the Schmeling-Stribling bout in Cleveland. He turned it down. But just to see what skills he still possessed,

Four • Pied Piper's Road Back to Contender, 1931

Jack Dempsey's big promotion in Reno, Nevada, July 4, 1931. *Left to right:* Max Baer, Jack Dempsey, Leo C. Owen (sportswriter hired to publicize the event), Paulino Uzcudun, and Leonard Sacks (Uzcudun's business manager) (courtesy David Bergin).

Dempsey met Pat McCarty, Chicago heavyweight, "for nothing" in the ring at Paulino Uzcudun's training quarters in Steamboat Springs. Dempsey floored the 240-pounder five times. McCarty had to be carried out of the ring. After watching that, Lou Briz, Uzcudun's manager, said, "I wouldn't concede Paulino a chance with Dempsey if they were matched and the old champion were in condition."[5]

Max Baer worked hard at his training camp at Lawton Springs, a resort about 12 miles from Reno. Dempsey had given Max a lecture on the need to train hard for this fight. He told him to forget the bright lights, colorful clothes, and fancy car until after the fight and concentrate on the work of training. No horseback riding and absolutely no trips to Reno. Ancil Hoffman had already impounded his car, released the chauffeur for the time being, sealed the gear shifts, and ordered the garage attendant not to let "anybody, not even Baer himself" drive the car until noon of July 4, when the chauffeur could bring the car to his training camp to pick him up for the match.[6]

"Whoever has been telling [Dempsey] I was not training seriously," Baer exclaimed, "is an outright liar. I was never more serious in my life."[7] Hans Birkie worked hard with him. Sometimes Baer went through as many as seventeen rounds with partners. He ran six to ten miles per day. He shadow-boxed, punched the bags and skipped rope, all vigorously, under trainer Dolph Thomas. Two weeks before the battle, Max flattened two sparring partners, Sylvester Nolan and Henry Spilletti. But when Pat Doyle of San Jose sparred, he split Baer's lip and Max had to have three stitches to close the wound. Dempsey came to check on him and thought nothing of it. When he fought Jess Willard, he had five stitches in his lip. Baer was lighthearted, but nothing suggested he was slacking off.

But Alan Ward, journalist for the *Oakland Tribune*, came clean eighteen years later about a rendezvous he shared with Baer. Ward stayed on the same premises while covering the fight camp for his newspaper. One night, when everyone was supposed to be in bed, after the lights were out, Max, Buddy Baer, and Alan Ward got into a car and headed for Reno. They toured all the "joints," with Max even leading the orchestra at one of the clubs while Ward was gambling. Before daylight, the pack tiptoed back to camp and crawled into their beds. The camp trainer was never the wiser. "Wotta Night!" Ward exclaimed.[8]

By all accounts, Baer seemed noticeably different, and supporters said they liked what they saw. Baer had never looked in better condition. Everyone was anxious to see him face the gold-toothed Basque, a great fighter who had already been tested by Schmeling, Carnera, Risko, Heeney, Griffith and others.

At the end of their training, both combatants felt confident. Max couldn't imagine losing the match. Paulino was quietly confident.

Everything seemed to be going smoothly, when, at 11:00 p.m. sharp on July 3, the evening before the fight, forty federal agents from California and Nevada began to execute prohibition raids in Reno and Sparks. They made forty-one arrests of proprietors for selling illegal alcohol. All the major roadhouses, hotels, and speakeasies were searched. Even Baer's training quarters were raided. Luckily, he was asleep and missed all the excitement. Government duty had its rewards. The agents were permitted to stay to see the fight. The next day's event was unaffected, but a damper was put on the evening's revelry since the agents were still in town enjoying the festivities.[9]

On the day of the match, it was quite noticeable that almost half the seats of the stadium were filled with women in colorful attire. By noon, it was hot under the cloudless summer sky. Vendors effortlessly sold their wares of hats, seat cushions, and nonalcoholic beverages.

When Dempsey came into the ring, the crowd shouted a lusty ovation—many were there just to see him back in the ring. The boxers entered at half-past noon. There had been rumors that the fight had been "fixed." So when Referee Dempsey called the boxers together for instructions, he made it plain, especially to the newspapermen working at ringside, that if he sensed anything fishy, or if either man was about to lay down, he would stop the fight and their purses would be canceled. He expected an honest fight, and he expected the men to continue to fight, *no dancing*. People came to see an old-fashioned fight.

Max, 22, and four inches taller than his rival, wore gold trunks trimmed in purple. Paulino, 30, wore black trunks trimmed in red. Max had a lot riding on the fight. If he won, Dempsey would promote him in a match with Jack Sharkey. If he lost, he would be out of the heavyweight picture.

Fifteen thousand ticket-holders entered the arena. After three preliminaries, Dempsey opened the doors to another 3,000. He figured that since the holders of the cheaper seats had moved down to the more expensive seats, he could let the people still standing in line to enter for the price of the cheapest seat.

The main event was viciously fought, with both men throwing punches furiously, trying to knock the other down. There was butting, clubbing, cuffing, heeling, wrestling, gouges, grunts, and groans. Both men threw kidney and rabbit punches.

Paulino waded in, head down, and started punching. Baer got in some hard punches to Paulino's chin in the second. But by the third round, Baer's nose was bleeding from lefts to his face. Baer was at his best landing uppercuts to the head and jabs to the body.

Whitey Bimstein, Paulino's second, had brought a bathtub filled with water and ice to his fighter's corner. Bimstein said it was 110 degrees in the shade. He had a stack of towels that he soaked in the ice water during the rounds, and during each rest break, he draped them around Uzcudun so that he was totally refreshed for his upcoming stanza. Bimstein said, "I had eight one-gallon bottles of mineral water, and another bottle that was filled with brandy and un-chilled water for drinking. I also covered the soles of his feet with adhesive tape and kept pouring ice water into his shoes, so the burning-hot ring canvas wouldn't bother him."[10]

Paulino came out refreshed from his corner for the fifth round and hit Baer with a heavy blow to the jaw. But by the eighth round, Baer was leading and pushing his rival around the ring. Uzcudun never seemed to lose his head or his cool, quite literally. In the middle rounds, both let go of some wild sweeping swings that missed their marks, or were ducked under. Most of the action occurred at the ropes or in clinches when they exchanged body or kidney shots. They wrestled and pulled each other around the ring, and Dempsey just smiled. It was everything he wanted in a fight.

Trainer Bimstein complained that Baer was fouling his man, and Dempsey called back for all to hear, "Whitey, tell your boy to foul him back."[11]

The last real lightning bolt Baer threw from his right hand landed on Paulino's jaw in the sixteenth round. The Basque staggered, but he was able to come back in the seventeenth. The fight seemed even. Some said the pace was fast for a heavyweight bout, and it even increased during the last five rounds nearing the decision. Reporters from the West Coast said, as if they were watching a different fight, that the pace was slow, but most of them had never seen a fight go beyond ten rounds. This twenty-rounder occurred under such grueling heat that the colored dye from the men's trunks started to trickle down their legs, resembling blood.

In the break before the final round, Dempsey told the newspapermen that the twentieth round would determine the winner. As the sole referee and judge, he had called the fight even at the end of the nineteenth round.

Baer was suffering in the heat. He lost his speed and punch. He seemed to lack the power or the stamina that Uzcudun had in the final round. Paulino rushed Baer into the ropes and landed hard punches to his midsection. Baer rallied, but only weakly. His resilience was gone in that last round. When he went to his corner, he was battered and bloody. Those who had seen both his California and East Coast bouts said Baer looked better and performed better than they would have imagined for twenty rounds over the course of an hour and a half. They were impressed. Some said that the old Spaniard, eight years Baer's senior, just outclassed the boy.

After the brawl, when Bimstein talked to Dempsey about all the fouls, Dempsey said he "thought Uzcudun out-fouled Baer." Anyway, "We got the decision," said a relieved Bimstein. Dempsey commented later that he thought Baer was the better fighter, but he was a mess at the end of the twenty rounds, and Paulino looked like he could go another twenty.

Ringside scores varied. The *San Francisco Examiner* gave Uzcudun eight rounds, Baer four, with eight rounds even; the *San Francisco Chronicle* gave the Basque eleven, and Baer five, with four even; the Associated Press called the fight even until last round;

the *Reno Gazette* called it a draw at six-six, and eight even. Dempsey, the only scorer who mattered, gave Paulino six rounds (5, 6, 10, 18, 19, and 20) and Baer four (8, 9, 13, and 15), the rest even.

Uzcudun left the ring with his forehead bruised and his eyes discolored. He admitted, "Baer was a little tougher than I expected but I was confident of winning the fight." At his camp back at Steamboat Springs, he told reporters: "And he is a dirty fighter.... He butted continually in the clinches. It was very hot out there in the ring and whenever I drew a deep breath it was like sucking in hot flame. My feet felt like balls of fire."[12]

Both boxers lost weight under the scorching sun: Max lost ten pounds and Paulino, nine. Dempsey credited Paulino's win of the "bathtub battle" to Bimstein, but others said that Baer could not focus on anything but Dorothy Dunbar, who sat at ringside.

When Dempsey was asked if it was a good financial venture, he just smiled and said he was looking forward to next Labor Day. Outsiders said he "cleaned up."

That night, the city came alive with gambling houses packed. Fireworks showered down, and firecrackers popped all around. Bankers talked to celebrities, and cowboys partied with miners and lumberjacks. It was the biggest night the city had seen. And everyone remained orderly, except for the two women who got into a scuffle in a back alley. Playing at the Roxie Theater was *The Big Fight*, based on David Belasco's stage play in which Dempsey was the star.

To mitigate the sting of his ring loss, Max turned again to Dorothy Dunbar. Four days after the bout on July 8, 1931, Max wed Dunbar at a private ceremony in Reno. Baer's mother had objected to the marriage, saying, "[She's] old enough to be Max's mother. She's 38 years of age and Maxie is only 22. She's taking a mere boy to raise for a husband. Jacob and I will not be there."[13] His father didn't have anything positive to say about the marriage either. "Matrimony has no place in the life and career of a prizefighter just beginning in the game," said Jacob Baer. "Such a marriage can have but one ending—unhappiness and divorce."[14]

The private evening nuptial took place at banker Harry Sheeline's home with thirty attending, including Dempsey. Afterward, Baer told the newspaper, "I have been deeply in love with Dorothy ever since I met her. She has taught me what is best to read and pointed out the proper things to do. In fact, she's the only person who has been interested enough in me to try to make me like real folks."[15] That Max thought Dunbar represented "real folks" was an irony Baer could not see at the time. Rather, he was the one who had come from humble beginnings, and would find in his ring friends the value of "real folks." Little did he expect to seek divorce in less than a year, but not before seven separations and six reconciliations.[16]

In pursuing a title during his adventure east, the Larruping Lochinvar had lost four big fights: Ernie Schaaf, Tommy Loughran, Johnny Risko, and now Paulino Uzcudun. The only thing Max had captured was a bride with a history of failed marriages.

Added to the situation was Ham Lorimer's decision not to sell the balance of Baer's contract to Ancil Hoffman. "He'll have to fight for me as often as I see fit," demanded Lorimer, even though Baer was without a license in California.[17]

On July 25, 1931, the California State Athletic Commission took up the matter of Baer's license with regard to promoter Louis Parente. "Hard Hat Louie," as everyone called him because he always wore a black derby as stiff as steel, said that Baer still owed him fights from a previous contract. Reluctantly, the commission issued a license to Baer, but only because of his obligations to the promoter.

The next stage of Baer's fighting life, from September to December of 1931, proved that Max had the heart to come back. But his career would be at the mercy of a war among managers and promoters, the outcome of which would determine his fate.

Parente originally proposed Jack Van Noy as Baer's first opponent in the contract obligation, but the match was turned down because the commission figured it was a set-up. Van Noy served as a sparring partner for Baer when he was training for his previous match with Uzcudun in Reno.

Max worked out at the Yosemite Gym in Oakland, anxious to get back into the ring. He fought three exhibition bouts on August 9, at a health club picnic at Neptune Beach. By the end of August, Ancil Hoffman was in Reno trying to convince Jack Dempsey to a match with Baer.

Louis Parente proposed a bout for Jack Van Noy with Tom Corbett for a six-round main event to prove that Van Noy could be matched with Baer. In the bout, Van Noy floored Corbett in the first round for a nine count and another in the second, after which he failed to rise. With Van Noy's four consecutive sensational knockouts in local rings, the commission could not refuse him a match with Baer. Bob Edgren had originally objected to matches with both fighters Jack Van Noy of Los Angeles and Les Kennedy of Long Beach; but on September 12, the commissioners relented and approved both bouts.

Jack Van Noy, September 23, 1931, Oakland

Baer trained with his former trainer Bob McAllister at Yosemite Gym, and Van Noy worked at Duffy's. Reporters noted that for his "Start-Over Come-Back," Max was more subdued, without his usual bombast. "He says he will do his best and thinks that best will be good enough to win," reported Bob Shand of the *Oakland Tribune*.[18] Bob McAllister said, "Max may not look very good in the gym after his long absence from the ring," but "he only has to land once with his right to end the battle and I don't believe Van Noy is fast enough to get out of the path of the punch. I believe Baer is on his way to the top again."[19]

Van Noy's manager Henry Stummie had this to say about his boxer: "Van Noy is no master boxer, but he hits harder than Baer and nobody ever pinned any medals on Max for his boxing ability."[20] Actually, Van Noy had beaten his early opponents as decisively as Baer had done when climbing to the top.

Baer, with a two-to-one betting advantage, won the decision on an eighth-round technical in front of a crowd of 8,000, with fans yelling for Baer to finish Van Noy off in the seventh. Shand summarized the results: "Max Baer of a year ago was a fightin' fool. The Max Baer of today is a lamb in comparison. Instead of being a free-swinging, swashbuckling gladiator, Baer tried to be a methodical boxer last night and he looked bad."[21] It was an easy win for Baer in his comeback from the 20-round loss to Uzcudun two months earlier, but his heyday was over. Critics said that "Max was a complete washout and you can write him off the books as a total loss."[22]

After the Van Noy fight, Mrs. Dorothy Baer decided to become her husband's manager. She offered Lorimer $2000 for his share of Baer's contract. Lorimer said he would accept nothing less than $25,000. She responded, "Mr. Lorimer paid nothing for his part of the contract and has been getting his cut right along. We want to change that and feel that $2000 is a fair price. Both Max and I feel that we would be better off if we possessed

Lorimer's share of his contract."[23] Lorimer refused the offer, saying that he had fifty percent of Baer and Hoffman had twenty-five percent of that. Hoffman probably thought of his minimal percentage as more of a liability than an asset, saying publicly that he was not willing to pay any more for Baer's contract: "Right now Maxie is no gold mine."[24] Max's pugilistic affairs were always complicated.

Ancil Hoffman was never granted a California promoter's license, but since he was chairman of the executive committee of his friend George Putnam's new fight club, the Seals Stadium Athletic Club in Oakland, he was free to arrange a card featuring Max Baer. Opponents he considered were Victor Campolo, Paolino Uzcudun, or Johnny Risko. Baer needed to prove that he could beat Risko, but Risko was currently tied up in negotiations for a fight with Tommy Loughran.

The wrinkle in the Putnam schedule was that Max still owed Parente another bout, but not before he was called to answer questions before the Athletic Commission. Max was asked about his poor showing in the Van Noy fight. He explained that he was distracted by all the legal complications with Lorimer. Lorimer told Baer that he was dropping McAllister as his trainer and hiring someone else. He also expected Baer to use other sparring partners. Lorimer had signed Baer to fight the giant Portuguese, Jose Santa. When Parente announced the bout at a local Oakland fight, there was no response from the crowd, only dead silence. The bloom was off the rose.

Jose Santa, October 21, 1931, Oakland

Lou Parente promoted the Baer-Santa bout at the Oakland Auditorium. The day before the fight, the newspapers tried to hype the main event, but there was some confusion about who would fight on the undercard. The *Bakersfield Californian* ended its coverage with, "The Mexican fighter Tony Fuente was to box Flinker but he landed in jail or something."[25]

Jose Santa, whose surname was Santa Camarao, stood 6 foot 7½ inches and had fought six other bouts in Parente-sponsored events at the Oakland Auditorium before meeting Max. Actually Santa was more experienced than Max, having fought for four more years in Portugal, Brazil, France, Germany, and the U.S. His previous two fights had been with Tom Heeney.

In spite of Ham Lorimer, Max trained for the fight with Bob McAllister. Baer refused to see Parente until the night of the fight. Even Santa's management team was upset with the promoter. Parente wanted to stage the fight in the indoor Oakland venue that he controlled. But the venue was limited in space. Santa's team felt they were losing valuable gate by not holding the fight at the larger outdoor ballpark.

At two o'clock in the afternoon, all the one-dollar seats had been sold, with 2,000 people left outside hollering. Four rows of five-dollar seats were still unsold, so before the main event, the crowd was admitted for one dollar per person. The rafters bulged.

The day after the fight, the Oakland paper read, "The Baer growled again like the grizzly of old," in a fight "as hectic a heavyweight fight as was ever witnessed in any ring."[26] Baer had closed Santa's eyes with knots the size of eggs in the sixth round. Since it was almost impossible for Santa to see through his slits, Baer danced around until the ninth when he put Santa down for a five count. Baer knocked him down twice in the last round: for a six count, the result of a hard body shot with the left and a right cross to the cheek; and then with a right to the head, leaving him cold on the canvas. Doctors and seconds worked on the man, leaving Baer clearly worried in his corner. The three state commissioners who sat ringside were equally concerned. Baer kept asking, "Is there anything I can do?" But there wasn't.

When Santa regained consciousness fifteen minutes later, Baer visited him in his dressing room. Both of Santa's eyes were closed and his face was a mangled mess. Baer apologized profusely, saying that he would give him another bout, or "anything else you want," reporters heard him say.[27] Then Baer threw his arms around him in a big hug, telling him what a big heart he had. The three commissioners left without commenting.

Baer told the crowd outside how game his opponent was. Baer then drove his own car home, with his wife, father and sister inside. Max was a noticeably changed man, but no one was willing to give any credit to wife Dorothy.

The event drew $19,000. Surprisingly, the public was told afterward that it resulted in a loss of $500. Parente paid Max $7500. Ten years later it was reported that Lou Parente and his partner Oscar Klatt exploited both Max Baer and Jose Santa in this fight, knowing that it would possibly be Parente's last fight promoting Baer from a Lorimer contract. It was said that Santa paid good dividends to the Parente team over time.

Johnny Risko, November 9, 1931, San Francisco

George Putnam inaugurated his new San Francisco Seals Stadium with a match between Johnny Risko and Max Baer, with the help of unlicensed promoter Ancil Hoffman. Hoffman promised each man $5000 and an additional twenty-five percent of the gate. Actually, Hoffman had Risko under contract as soon as Putnam received his promoter's license back in July, but he had to wait until after the second fight promoted by Parente to clear Baer for any new activity. Hoffman believed that since Risko was the victor in their May 5 bout in Cleveland, the rematch would make for an exciting fight and productive gate. Ticket prices ranged from fifty cents to three dollars.

A win over Johnny Risko was even more important to Baer now because Risko had just been beaten by Tommy Loughran in a ten-round battle on October 20. It was Loughran's eleventh straight win and placed him in line to battle Jack Sharkey for the right to meet Champion Max Schmeling. Because Loughran had beaten Risko three times, it was important for Baer to best the Cleveland spoiler.

Risko was an experienced boxer. He was seven years older than Baer and had started his career in 1922. He was born in Austria, but after coming to America, he adopted Cleveland as his hometown. Standing only 5-feet 10½ inches, he was known as the "Giant Killer," or the "Spoiler." In 1925, he had beaten Jack Sharkey and gone the twelve-round distance with Gene Tunney. He had lost to Ernie Schaaf in 1928, but had come back the next year to beat him. (He would come back in 1932 to beat King Levinsky, and in 1934 to beat Tommy Loughran. By 1939, he would be totally broke, back in Oakland at age 37, begging promoter Tommy Simpson for a fight with anyone. Before his career ended—his last fight was in 1940—he had fought them all: George Godfrey, Max Schmeling, Paulino Uzcudun, Tom Heeney, Mickey Walker, and Paul Berlenbach.)

Fifteen thousand fans poured into the new Seals stadium. Chief second for Baer, Bob McAllister, had an awkward time getting in since Hoffman left strict instructions not to let anyone enter without a paid ticket. McAllister pleaded with a police officer standing guard, telling him he was part of Baer's staff, but he was told that only the chauffeur had a ticket waiting for him at the window. So Bob went to the ticket window and said he was Max's driver. When Ham Lorimer and his associates went to the window expecting tickets, they too had to pay the $3 cost per person.

Ring action was slow because of a heavy rain that made the canvas slick. Risko opened aggressively and landed a hard right to Max's jaw. Although the fighting was steady, the second through fifth rounds went to Baer. Baer simply landed harder and cleaner shots during those rounds. They traded blows such that the sixth round may have been even. In the eighth, Baer slipped on the wet

In a must-win battle to remain a contender, Baer redeems his previous loss to Johnny Risko in San Francisco, November 9, 1931 (courtesy IBRO).

canvas, and later Risko slipped and fell down. Baer helped him up. They were in a clinch at the end of the round, and in breaking from it, Baer blasted Risko out of the ring. He then helped him back in. The next round was wet as the rain increased and both slipped about the ring in the sloppy conditions. In the tenth, Risko rallied and Baer pounded at his midsection. They were battling away when the final bell rang. All three commissioners sat at ringside and agreed with the decision that went to Baer.

The next day a second fight broke out when Baer tried to claim his $5000 purse. (In California at this time all fight purses were paid through the commission's offices. The rule also stated that the fighter must be paid two-thirds of the purse and the manager one-third.) Ham Lorimer was officially the manager of record in California for Baer and he was first in line to claim his due. The commissioners told Baer that unless he filed legal documents against Lorimer, there was nothing they could do but to issue Lorimer the money.

On November 14, Baer went to an attorney and had a document drafted serving notice to Ham Lorimer that explicitly stated he was no longer connected to Baer for any future fights. Lorimer had been given one-third of Baer's last three fights, even though he had nothing to do with them. In addition, Lorimer stated that since he had a signed contract with Baer for five years (which had started two years earlier), he had the legal authority to sign Max to fight anyone he selected, and he told Baer his next bout would be with Les Kennedy. Now Max seemed to have his fists tied to California. In addition, trainer Frankie Burns, who had traveled east with Max, also had a five-percent interest in Baer's fights, even though he was not training him either. Burns graciously reduced the amount to three percent since he really wasn't doing anything. He received $120 for the Van Noy fight, $225 for Santa, and $150 for the Risko battle.

There was good news outside of California. Baer was getting national attention by the boxing writers. The bad news was that when he tried to avoid fighting Kennedy under Lorimer, the commissioners told him that if he bowed out, he would face indefinite suspension again.

Les Kennedy, November 23, 1931, Oakland

Max Baer went back to the Yosemite Gym. Les Kennedy worked out at Duffy's. If Max had to fight Les Kennedy again, he might as well use the occasion to even the score. About his last fight, Max said that Kennedy was as puffed up as ever: "I shellacked him in Los Angeles with a left hand and rocked him with my right. He has been licked plenty since that night, so I cannot see where he has improved." Les planned to box, but vowed to slug it out if Max wanted that.[28]

Max's lawyer tried to have the fight canceled because Max was under stress from all the legal issues. The attempt failed, and Ham Lorimer introduced Arthur De Kuh in the ring before the main event as being the next opponent for the winner. Lorimer was signing them up as fast as he still could.

Max proved that he was mentally capable of smacking Kennedy to the canvas in the third. At the beginning of that round, Max came out crouched, ready for the kill. He frightened Kennedy into the corner. Max had been practicing a combination weapon: a left hook to the stomach, a right cross to the chin, and a right-hand uppercut that no one saw coming. Pow! The short right uppercut was a well-kept secret. Max never practiced his three-punch combination in the gym. Sans sparring partners, he could only practice the combination on the golf links with trainer McAllister. Max walked to his corner without turning around. The bout was over.

Lorimer had no intent to relinquish Max's contract now that sportswriters were saying it was worth $500,000. Max filed an injunction to prevent Lorimer from making any further matches. On December 19, Lorimer was hospitalized for unknown causes, assumed to be stress related.

Arthur De Kuh, December 30, 1931, Oakland

For his last fight of the year, Baer took on Italian Arthur De Kuh of Boston, taller and heavier than Baer and believed to be a better fighter than Johnny Risko. De Kuh had defeated Dynamite Jackson, a black heavyweight from Los Angeles who was also on the radar as a possible contender. De Kuh was known to throw punches from all directions. He lost close decisions to Jack Sharkey and Young Stribling. (He would be Baer's sparring partner in his camp for the Carnera fight.)

When ticket sales lagged, Baer had his wife call and order twenty-two tickets to be sent to the Oak Knoll Country Club the morning of the fight. Max and Dorothy had rented a house on the golf course.[29] When asked why so many tickets, Baer said he heard De Kuh had his own cheering section, and he needed one too. He donated the tickets to all the caddies at the golf course.

Bob McAllister told the press that sparring partners for Max were difficult to find. They offered $10 a day and thought that was a reasonable offer, considering it was the Depression. Nevertheless, none showed up. Again, there were no sparring sessions for Baer other than shadow boxing along the fairways of the golf course.

De Kuh outweighed Max by 16 pounds. In the battle, De Kuh won the first round, but Baer worked with the precision of a machine and won the middle rounds, two through seven, with damaging body shots. De Kuh won the eighth and ninth rounds, and they split the tenth. Baer's face at the end was marked and bloody. The middle rounds, when Baer carried the fight, gained Baer the decision. Many thought that Baer should have been called out for fouls—low blows, kidney punches, hits on the breaks and behind the neck.

After the fight. Baer learned of Lorimer's hospitalization. He called off his lawyer and said that he wanted Lorimer to get the pay. Baer explained his change of heart: "Ham did a lot of things for me and I feel sorry for him."[30] It was a new year, and he wanted a fresh start without fighting with anyone. It seemed Max could never be mad with anyone or hold a grudge. His heart was really too soft for his own good.

Five

Elimination Battles of 1932

Max Baer was not the only boxer looking for a new beginning in the heavyweight division in 1932. When Jack Dempsey left the ring in 1927, after losing to Gene Tunney, he was a wealthy man. But like so many others who lost their fortunes in the crash of 1929, he needed new income. After multiple offers and a layoff of four years, Dempsey was ready to return to the ring. He said he had been training in Reno and had signed for a nine-bout tour, each fight for four rounds. He considered meeting King Levinsky, Johnny Risko, Tommy Loughran, KO Christner, Paulino Uzcudun, Dynamite Jackson, and Max Baer, all top heavyweights.

Soon after announcing his tour, Dempsey's manager Leonard Sacks clarified: the tour was actually a series of tune-up matches for a Dempsey title fight. Dempsey planned to meet the winner of the Schmeling-Sharkey bout in June.

Like Grantland Rice, Dempsey was sick to death of the heavyweight situation and wanted to settle the issue of heavyweight champion once and for all, even if it meant he had to take matters into his own hands.

Dempsey knew through manager Joe Jacobs that Max Schmeling was contractually tied up with the Garden for a Sharkey fight. But after that, Schmeling was free to negotiate. Dempsey wasted no time in jumping on the possibility of a fight with the champion. Dempsey used his own celebrity for the ballyhoo: "I think it is the only possible bout with a chance to draw a million dollars."[1] No fight had produced a million-dollar gate since the death of Tex Rickard. Promotions for big heavyweight contests were up for grabs. (It would take Mike Jacobs a few years to gain a foothold in a new monopoly.)

Executives at Madison Square Garden who held the trump cards on the big fights were not about to let Jack Dempsey move into their territory as a fighter, manager, or promoter.

Dempsey's announcement set in motion a series of elimination battles that would last for the next two years. Jimmy Johnston, matchmaker for Madison Square Garden, announced that New York and the Garden would hold quarter elimination bouts to determine who would face the winner of the Schmeling-Sharkey battle scheduled for June. Johnston had no plans for Dempsey spoiling the waters. Johnston announced his matches: King Levinsky of Chicago vs. Max Baer of San Francisco for ten rounds January 29; February 5, Ernie Schaaf of Boston vs. Paolino Uzcudun of Spain for ten rounds. Then February 26 or March 4, the winners of the first two bouts would meet for fifteen rounds in New York.

After paying his dues and running through eight challengers since losing to Tommy Loughran, Baer's star was back in the heavens, and the Garden was ready to have him take on Kingfish Levinsky in an elimination battle. With Ham Lorimer still in Merritt hospital after six weeks, Ancil Hoffman accompanied Baer to New York.

King Levinsky, January 29, 1932, Madison Square Garden (Quarter-Elimination Battle)

Levinsky, whose birth name was Harris Krakow, was the son of a fish-seller in the Jewish section of Chicago. A year younger than Max, but having fought a year longer, Levinsky was considered a contender in the heavyweight division for his back-to-back wins over Paolino Uzcudun and Tommy Loughran. (The "King" would wage a great comeback in 1932 and 1933 fighting Primo Carnera, Tommy Loughran, KO Christner, Johnny Risko, Tuffy Griffith, and Jack Sharkey. He would fight Joe Louis in 1935.)

Levinsky was a wild swinger. Nothing got in his way, including the referee. When B. Bennison of England met the "King" of Chicago, he said he found "nothing unpleasant in his cocksuredness. He has, at some time or other, been hit with everything short of a trip hammer, but in a magical way he still finds it possible to dream of the coming of a day when he will beat the world. He has vast punching power ... by way of being a specialist in haymakers."[2]

Levinsky was managed by his sister, "Leaping Lena" Levy. She was smart and aggressive. In addition to preparing his food, Lena knew the business and made his matches. Like Ma Stribling, who managed her son Young Stribling, Lena was not allowed by the boxing commissions of the day to apply for a license as a manager or a second, although Lena frequently appeared in her brother's corner.

Levinsky was just coming off his KO win over Tommy Loughran when he met Baer for the ten-round elimination battle in the Garden. Unfortunately, everyone in the East remembered Baer's earlier failure when he lost to Schaaf, Loughran and Risko. This time around, Max was no playboy. He was married and his wife was in charge of his training at Gus Wilson's camp in Orangeburg, New Jersey. Dorothy Dunbar Baer had learned to punch the bag and skip rope, and she could do the same roadwork as her husband. This fight would be a first—with two women significantly in charge of their male heavyweights. At least one sportswriter said that it would be a more interesting fight if the two ladies got into a tussle at ringside. They certainly had the sharp wit to get things going.

Over 11,000 spectators watched Baer outpoint Levinsky with persistent attacks to the body. Fans had come to expect a knockout with Baer's big right fist. Instead he used his right to methodically hammer his opponent's left side. The crowd was a bit disappointed.

As soon as the bell rang, Baer attacked Levinsky's left side, for which the Chicagoan seemed unable to muster a defense. Body punches turned into barrages. At one point Levinsky grabbed Baer and pulled him into a clinch on the ropes, where Baer overheard the radio announcer speeding through the punches: "Baer hits him with a right—a left—a right to the head—a left to the body—a right." Still clutched tightly by Levinsky, Baer looked down at the announcer at ringside and said, "Take it easy, pal, you're away ahead of me."[3]

Referee Gunboat Smith and Judges George P. Kelly and William P. Dunn gave Baer seven of the ten rounds. Levinsky spent most of the rounds trying to tie up Baer's hands. In the ninth and tenth, Levinsky tried for a knockout with his roundhouse punches, but

After their wedding, wife Dorothy Dunbar took on the management and training responsibilities for husband Max Baer, 1932.

Baer evaded the blows. Even though Baer clearly won the fight, the crowd felt that the Baer-Levinsky match did not live up to its hype as a championship elimination bout, with many saying the fight was boring.

Boring? Baer was unusually affected. Never again, he vowed, would he appear "uninteresting." It wasn't his nature to be uninteresting, and he would try to bring that quality to his fighting life. From this point on, he would give his audience its entertainment dollar's worth.

Baer returned to California to await the winner of the other elimination battle, Uzcudun and Schaaf, the following week to see who would become alternate for the Jack Sharkey and Max Schmeling fight.

On February 18, Jack Dempsey would take on Levinsky in his experimental comeback tour, to see how he stood among the current heavyweights in the division and to make some money. Levinsky earned $11,000 and Dempsey $35,000. After four rounds, the newspaper decision went to Levinsky.

In only a matter of weeks, Baer had beaten Levinsky, and Levinsky had beaten Jack Dempsey. And while Dempsey was making a pile of money, he was not considered a contender in the elimination battles after his loss.

While Baer waited to see where he stood in the elimination process, a storm was brewing back in California over who owned his contract and who had the right to schedule his bouts, especially now that he appeared to be back on the big-money track.

Tom Heeney, February 22, 1932, San Francisco, Seals Stadium

Ancil Hoffman scheduled a ten-round rematch with Baer and the veteran from New Zealand, at the new Seals Stadium in San Francisco. The match attracted a large crowd, estimated to be somewhere between 7,000 and 10,000, because folks remembered the Dempsey-Firpo–like previous bout one year earlier when Baer knocked Heeney out of the ring in the third round.

Baer was considered a three-to-one favorite in the bets because of his recent good showings. Betting odds were even that Baer would score a kayo. Heeney had six pounds on Baer, but Baer was nine years younger and had the advantage in reach by four inches and height by three inches. And although the *Bakersfield Californian* headlines the next day read, "Max Baer Defeats Heeney by Decision in Last Round Spurt," the subhead read, "Butcher Boy Fails to Give Impressive Account of Himself."

In the first three rounds, Heeney was able to absorb Baer's punches. Then Baer found Heeney's jaw and took the lead in the fourth round. Heeney seemed to rally in the ninth and have the edge on Baer. But by the last round, Baer was soundly in charge and had Heeney covering up to protect himself. Many spectators thought Baer should have put him away with a knockout, having had all the advantages. Referee Toby Irwin awarded the decision to Baer. Someone even suggested that Baer "carried" his opponent for five rounds in order to have him standing for the tenth. But Harry B. Smith, journalist from the *San Francisco Chronicle*, who had been observing fights on the West Coast since the days of Joe Gans, said, "Baer doesn't know enough of the tricks of the game to 'carry' an opponent without it being obvious!"[4] The take for each man was $2500.

Paul Swiderski, April 26, 1932, Los Angeles, Olympic Auditorium

Before the rent was due the first of April, Max gave up his palatial home on the golf course in Oakland and returned to live with his parents, an indication that his marriage was on the rocks. Dorothy had rented a home in Beverley Hills, near Los Angeles.

Baer's match with Swiderski of Syracuse was under the promotion of Jack Doyle at the Olympic in Los Angeles with the help of Hoffman. Swiderski had never boxed in California, but his reputation preceded him. He had beaten King Levinsky, Babe Hunt, and Frankie Simms, and had been substituted to fight noted champions. He said, "I honestly believe I'm a man of destiny."[5]

Swiderski's last bout with Mickey Walker in Louisville, Kentucky, turned out to be a free-for-all. A last-minute substitute, as he had been with other champions, Swiderski came out for the first round and knocked Walker down with the first punch. In those first two minutes, he knocked Walker down four times. At that point Jack Kearns, Walker's manager, and Teddy Hayes climbed into the ring and started fighting everyone within reach. It took eight minutes to revive Walker and clear the ring for the start of the second round, yet no one was counted out or disqualified.

Walker was knocked down twice more in the second, and again Kearns jumped into the ring and started smashing anyone and anything, including the light fixtures. After the lights were repaired, the battle resumed. Walker came back to floor Swiderski in the fourth and fifth rounds, winning the battle.

In his bouts with other champions, Swiderski hit Max Rosenbloom so hard his eye was split open and he couldn't continue, but Swiderski was disqualified for hitting with an open glove (something Rosenbloom was known for doing). In his battle with Pete Latzo, Swiderski brought Latzo to his knees with a hard punch in the solar plexus, but Latzo's management claimed foul and Swiderski lost again.

Swiderski didn't worry about being unmatched in the Garden's elimination bouts of 1932. He said, "I'll be the last-minute substitute for Jack Sharkey in June against Max Schmeling."[6]

Baer went into the fight having a 10-to-8 advantage over Swiderski. Max had a slight weight advantage, 205 to 194.

The first four rounds of the main event were slow, but fairly even. Max took some punishment in the clinches. Then, Max nearly ended the battle in the fifth when Swiderski went down two different times for a count of nine, but managed to come to his feet and stagger through the rest of the round. Swiderski was cheered in the sixth when he managed to protect himself from Baer's attempt to put him out with a hard right. Referee Abe Roth stopped the bout 1 minute and 20 seconds in the seventh, after Max sent Swiderski down again for another nine-count. Swiderski came up but was too wobbly on his feet to continue. He complained of "California justice" when the fight was stopped.

The 7000 spectators were pleased that Max had regained his desire to knock out his opponent instead of merely winning on points. Baer was paid $4500 and an additional $500 for training expenses. Swiderski was paid twenty-five percent of the gate after preliminary expenses of $500. The gate was reported to be only $7000, a suspiciously low total considering the number of attendees.[7]

Reporters commented on how changed a man Baer was now. He looked 100 percent better than when he previously fought Ernie Owens and Les Kennedy at the Olympic.

Ham Lorimer, now out of the hospital and again considered Baer's official manager of record by the California Commission, signed Max to a bout with Walter Cobb two weeks later. It was not a bout that Max wanted, but he was told by the commission he must fight, and that if he refused it, he would be suspended.

Walter Cobb, May 11, 1932, Oakland Auditorium

The ten-round fight with the 221-pound Walter Cobb (born in Hutchinson, Kansas, but working out of Baltimore) was scheduled for the benefit of the American Legion. Referee Toby Irwin stopped the fight in the fourth round on a technical knockout after Baer gave the man a hard beating with a combination: long looping left to the jaw, right to the jaw, and another left to the jaw. Cobb went down for the count of nine and came up for more. Max hit him again with a right to the chin and a left to the chin. Referee Irwin felt Cobb could not go on and raised Baer's hand in victory. At that point Cobb's manager, Eddie Eichner, said a few unpleasant remarks to the ref, and Irwin called in Inspector Louie Broderick and ordered him to take away Eichner's license.

The fight had been rough, more of a street fight than a heavyweight boxing match. Spectators said that Cobb started the rough stuff, and then Baer head-butted him in the second. Blood covered both men and Cobb cried foul, but the referee told them to continue. Coming out of clinch, Baer hit Cobb with an uppercut, and again Cobb cried foul. Cobb came after Baer in the third with a barrage of body shots. As Baer was fighting back, just as the referee was telling them to fight by the rules, Referee Irwin was accidentally hit in the chin by Baer's wild swing. Such was the free-for-all. The referee recovered and the fight continued—all for charity.

After the match, Cobb told reporters that he was given a bum lead about Max—that Max would go down if hit hard enough in the stomach. But Max never went down.[8]

On May 19, after his fight with Cobb, Baer was signed for two more fights by Lorimer. The management contract was still in limbo, and both managers, Lorimer and Hoffman, continued to do business on "behalf" of Max Baer. Something had to come to a head.

Lorimer signed a contract for Baer to fight on June 8 against Italian Arthur de Kuh, an opponent Baer had met six months earlier in December. But Hoffman had also signed Baer for a Fourth of July fight at Dempsey's bowl in Reno with King Levinsky, an opponent Baer had also faced previously in January, and a bout that was much more important now to Baer's national standing and pocketbook.

In Reno, Dempsey's manager Sacks tried to avoid any conflict with Lorimer by stating in Baer's July contract that Baer could not fight between May and July for anyone else. Baer had to make a decision. Baer (along with his trainer, Bob McAllister, who left Lorimer to come over to Baer's side on May 26, 1932) went with Dempsey's promotional offer. It would be a decision that would cement the Dempsey-Baer bond, even though it put Baer in another legal entanglement.

The California Athletic Commission was livid with Baer's decision to fight in Nevada and would try to force him to fight in California through the power of sanction. When the commission met on May 24, Baer was ordered to keep the fight that Lorimer scheduled with de Kuh in June or risk permanently losing his license. With the backing of the California Commission, Oakland promoter Louis Parente was going ahead with Lorimer's fight plans.

Baer said he was not going to fight in California, and he didn't. He kept his word with Dempsey and fought July 4 on Dempsey's card in Reno. With the exception of a charity bout for the Campbell family and special permission for one exhibition, Baer would never again be allowed to fight in California as a native son. He could have made more money in California during the leaner years of his later life after he lost the championship, but he was forced by necessity, instead, to places like the Ada County

Fairgrounds in Boise, Idaho; Tyler, Texas; Ada, Oklahoma; Ogden, Utah; and Twin Falls, Idaho.

In addition to losing his boxing license for the second time, his marriage was falling apart. In making the decision to go with the Levinsky fight, he had also made up his mind to seek a divorce from Dunbar. He told the press he would establish residency in Reno while he was in training so as to qualify for a divorce there. Five weeks before the Levinsky fight, when he was in training in Reno, Baer told the press, "Dorothy's a swell girl, but I've decided that she'll be better off without me. Perhaps she can find someone else who'll make a better husband than I have been and with whom she'll be happier."[9]

Dorothy Dunbar Baer "beat Max to the punch" when she filed for divorce in Los Angeles on June 4, 1932. Her legal complaint stated that Max "called her objectionable names, criticized her care of the household, associated with other women, and struck her on several occasions."[10] They had been separated since May. She also asked for either $20,000, which she said she loaned Max, or an appropriate sum of money for her financial support.

But by June 18, 1932, they had apparently patched things up, and she was eager to be seen at his Lawton Springs training camp, posing with the boxer for the cameras, saying "everything was sweet again."[11]

King Levinsky, July 4, 1932, Reno (20 rounds)

The Fourth of July bout in Reno was a wise choice. It kept Baer at the top of the list of contenders. Max Baer "stood firm among the front-rank heavyweights today as a result of an impressive 20-round decision over King Levinsky, Chicago's ex-fish peddler."[12] Fans numbered 9,000 in Dempsey's open-air arena in the late afternoon, much cooler than the fight the year before. Some waited in line for two hours to get last-minute seats for the 20-round "finish" fight.

Dempsey started to get nervous when Levinsky and his handlers failed to show up for the preliminaries. Photos of celebrities were taken in the ring while waiting for the main bout. On the ring's stage appeared actors and notables: Tom Mix (in a white cowboy suit), Wallace Beery, Jim Tully, George Wingfield, Mayor Roberts, Jack Dempsey, Young Corbett, Morley Griswold, and others.

After a short delay, Levinsky showed and the battle began. Baer waged a determined, "ceaseless" body attack throughout the entire twenty rounds. Levinsky came back gamely to take the punishing body blows that turned his sides raw. Levinsky did throw some haymakers to Baer's jaw, but they failed to floor him. After the tenth, the fight was all Baer's. There was no question about referee George Blake's decision. The spectators were satisfied. There were no knockdowns. Levinsky led the slugging attacks in the first, second, ninth and tenth rounds. All the others went to Baer. Levinsky's handlers explained that he appeared to have broken bones in his right hand from Baer's elbow in the third round, essentially disabling him for the duration. Still he managed to stay on his feet for the entire 20 rounds.

Max Winter, owner of the Minneapolis Lakers pro basketball team, recalled the fight in 1949: "I'll say that Max Baer the day he fought King Levinsky in Reno was the greatest heavyweight of all time. On that afternoon Baer could have torn Joe Louis apart, were Joe in his prime. Into little pieces.... Baer had the stuff of greatness, of immortality, in his body. Max just didn't turn on the steam [for Louis]. But what a fighter that handsome mug from Livermore was the day he took everything Levinsky had to offer and laughed in the King's face!"[13]

After the fight, and during his many stays in Reno, Baer partied at a casino called the Ship and Bottle. It was the grandest of the many casinos at the time. One hundred thousand dollars had been spent remodeling the former Sign of the Ship at 242 North Center Street. It was outfitted with crystal chandeliers hanging above hardwood floors covered in Persian rugs.[14] When Max was in town he was the life of the party and a good source of the Ship's income. Baer always held what looked like a mixed drink in his hand, but he never drank more than one, and sometimes he didn't even drink what he was carrying. He was more comfortable being the main attraction, cajoling the crowd with his comedic wit.

Kingfish Levinsky spent most of the rounds trying to tie up Baer's hands, July 4, 1932.

Reno was an exacting town where dollars were exchanged for every angle of business, including slot use, casino charge, and protection. Many of Chicago's criminals retreated there when they needed anonymity, although everyone knew almost everyone in town. Thus, the protection business grew. Reno visitors "of note" expected to pay this "security" tax. Ancil Hoffman had to pay a hefty fee from the fight purse for his charge's protection by the mob during the stay. Protection meant that Max's group had been silently followed so as to prevent anyone from harming them. The mandatory payment greatly annoyed Hoffman, but he paid it nevertheless.[15]

Ernie Schaaf, August 31, 1932, Chicago

The elimination tournament continued in the attempt to find a suitable opponent for Champion Jack Sharkey, who had beaten Schmeling in June. Although Baer had beaten Levinsky, the Kingfish was still a contender. In August, Levinsky was scheduled for twelve rounds with Johnny Risko in Cleveland. Primo Carnera faced Art Lasky of Minneapolis for ten rounds at St. Paul; and Schmeling and Mickey Walker were expected to meet in September. If Baer won his match with Ernie Schaaf, he would get one step closer to the title by getting a chance to meet the winner of the Schmeling-Walker bout.

Although Baer had ten consecutive victories, he was not predicted to win the Schaaf

Many blamed Max Baer (left) for Ernie Schaaf's death months after their fight, August 31, 1932 (courtesy David Bergin).

battle. It was the first time a newspaper headline predicted that Baer, now called "ex-butcher boy," would lose.

Reporter Charles Vackner admitted that the first time these warriors met "was the hardest heavyweight duel I ever witnessed. After ten rounds of savage slugging, Schaaf was returned the winner."[16]

In preparation for the Schaaf fight in Chicago, Baer established a pre-training camp at Arrowhead Springs in Cold Water Canyon in the mountains, ten miles north of San Bernardino. By August 13, his wife was at camp. Before setting out for his more extensive training camp in Chicago, he went back to Beverly Hills with Dorothy.

Baer knew how important a win over Schaaf would be for his career. More importantly, his wife knew it. The newspapermen had a field day covering Baer's "very unusual training camp," in Chicago seeing his starlet wife working out alongside her husband.

August 23, nine days before the fight, a sportswriter commented: "No heavyweight champion or challenger ever went to as much trouble for a title fight as Max Baer has gone to as he prepares for his ten-round encounter a week from Wednesday with Ernie Schaaf at the Chicago stadium."[17]

Baer's trainers placed a ring in front of the Aurora race track. He had the use of the track for roadwork with jockey showers and locker room. He was staying at the Exposition Hotel near the track with access to a swimming pool. His wife worked side by side, and was responsible for keeping him to his rigorous schedule: Up at 6:15 for a short plunge in the pool and 4 miles of roadwork on the track. Mrs. Baer ran with him for the last two miles dressed in "lounging pajamas and running shoes." Rubdown, breakfast, and a walk or a game of billiards afterwards. She was a sharp pool player and declared she would beat him before training camp was broken. Then back to the track for ring work: several rounds of boxing, pulley, bag work and calisthenics; then a rubdown, short rest followed by an evening meal prepared by Mrs. Baer.

Ernie Schaaf had only lost two decisions in the past two years. Schaaf was a 7–5 favorite in the betting odds over Baer.

Baer, at 23, and Schaaf, at 24, were the youngest of the heavyweight contenders. Both Schaaf and Baer were considered powerful body punchers, with Baer being more of an old-fashioned, long-distance fighter. The crowd of 6500 at the Chicago stadium declared the fight to be one of the most astonishing finishes ever seen in a ring. It was a ten-round decision that should have gone into the record books as a KO.

Papers noted, "Baer spent most of his time in the early rounds posing, laughing, making faces and generally disporting himself in strange contrast to the vicious fighter he was."[18] More than likely, Baer was either determined to entertain his audience and thereby gain notoriety for his antics in the ring that would make the news, or he was psychologically befuddling his serious opponent to mask the effects of Schaaf's hard hits.

In those early rounds, Schaaf was the aggressor, landing the cleaner and harder punches. But in the last three rounds, Baer unleashed his two-fisted attacks. Strangely enough, in the ninth and tenth rounds, the referee warned the two fighters to pick up the pace. Baer began to hit Schaaf on the chin aggressively, "knocking him groggy." Baer kept up the attack until, in the last round, he fired short shots from both hands to the chin until Schaaf's legs buckled, and only the ropes held him up. Schaaf staggered off the ropes, and with two more rights to the chin he fell face-first to the canvas.

Schaaf's seconds jumped into the ring, poured water on his head, rubbed under his heart, and lifted his legs above his head. He remained out for a full five minutes before he was pulled to his corner and sat upright, finally regaining consciousness.

The bout was not considered a win by kayo because the final bell rang at the count of nine, and it was not a unanimous decision. Referee Tommy Thomas and Judge Ed Klein voted for Baer. Judge Livingston Osborne voted for Schaaf, or felt he deserved at least a draw. On the East Coast before the Baer fight, Ernie Schaaf had been proclaimed the next heavyweight champion. But afterwards, papers reported that this fight was the most decisive defeat of his last 29 bouts, of which he had won 27. Gate receipts were estimated to be $75,000.

When Ernie Schaaf fought Max Baer, Schaaf was ranked third in the heavyweight division. After Max, Schaaf went on to battle and lose to Hartford's "Unknown" Winston, who was really Eddie Winston. He also lost to Stanley Poreda. The *Fitchburg Sentinel* called Schaaf a "once-promising youngster" who had taken a long rest after a disastrous summer when he was beaten by Stanley Poreda and Max Baer.[19] Schaaf planned to even up the score with both Stanley Poreda and Max Baer.

Tuffy Griffith, September 26, 1932, Chicago

Despite what the newspapers reported, Ham Lorimer wanted to make it clear that he and Max were still friends. In fact, Ham was pulling for him in the Griffith bout, a match made by Chicago promoter Nate Lewis.

Tuffy Griffith was floored by Baer at the end of round six, but saved by the bell. Referee Phil Collins stopped the fight in the seventh and declared Baer the winner (courtesy IBRO).

Griffith had come to Chicago in 1927, from Sioux City, Iowa, to see the Dempsey-Tunney fight, and he stayed to become one of Chicago's favorites. While Griffith had a large local following, Max Baer's reputation and popularity had swelled to the top.

The *Chicago Tribune* touted Max's record in its headline as the "Best in Modern Times." According to Nate Lewis, who had been in the fight business for three decades, Max had evened up his losses with the exception of only two battlers, Loughran and Uzcudun. He had never been stopped. Nate went on to say, "I have seen other brilliant records, such as Schaaf's string of knockouts that numbered nine or ten, and Jack Dempsey's stretch of quick victories, but when you take the whole record into consideration, the mark set by Baer stands alone."[20] Lewis pointed out that Tuffy Griffith was a fast heavyweight, and that you would have to go back to Tommy Loughran to find any faster heavy.

Chicagoans were proud that they had captured such a good show. Both heavyweights were ranked in the top ten. The bout allowed Griffith to "reestablish himself" and Baer to move another step closer to Jack Sharkey. "Baer has the color that all champions must have and his finish of Schaaf indicates that he carries a punch that deserves comparison with the famous 'Iron Mike' that Jack Dempsey toted around in his prime. If he gets by Griffith there will be only the winner of the Walker-Schmeling fight ahead of him. Chicagoans saw him against a slow-moving but dangerous puncher in Schaaf. He faces an exact opposite in Griffith, who has the speed of a lightweight and a flickering left hand that is continually in the other fellow's face."[21]

Because the Walker-Schmeling fight was on the same night, those results would be announced ringside.

Griffith went into the battle lacking size, power and reach. Griffith weighed only 188 pounds, but he was expected to box in close to avoid Baer's long reach. If he remained on his feet after ten rounds, he was expected to take the decision. Baer admitted that he had fought a slow pace when he fought Schaaf, and he expected to speed it up against Griffith.

The bout attracted a crowd of 9,500. From the first to the third rounds, Tuffy seemed to hold his own, but gradually he lost strength from Baer's strong body punches. The bout was almost over at the end of the fourth, when Baer shot a right into Griffith's head. He wobbled into the ropes, which held him up until the bell rang. He walked very unsteadily to his corner. At the end of the sixth, Baer had him on the floor when again Griffith was saved by the bell. One minute into the seventh, Baer hit with a straight right hand and Referee Phil Collins stepped between them to declare Baer the winner. Tears streamed down Griffith's face as he was led to his corner.

The gross receipts of the fight totaled $21,829.20. Griffith received $3,900 and Baer $5000.

Many said Baer could have won as early as the fourth, and others said the fight was essentially over in the first round.

On September 27, 1932, the sports pages were filled with boxing news. In addition to the results of the Baer-Griffith battle, the *Chicago Tribune* announced, "50,000 See Schmeling Knock Out Walker" in the Garden's Long Island Bowl. Mickey Walker, the Bulldog from Rumson, New Jersey, was knocked down for a count of seven in the first round. Again, he took another bad hit in the second but remained on his feet. Walker came back in the next few rounds to continue his mauling attack. Westbrook Pegler said, "There was a minute in the fifth when Walker stood Schmeling in a corner and worked on him as though he were a body bag in a gym."[22] And by the seventh, Walker was the clear aggressor. But in the eighth, he failed to duck Schmeling's right-hand chop and he went down for two nine counts, which Pegler said "dressed up the fight with that gorgeous gruesomeness which marks the really artistic fight."[23] Manager Jack Kearns jumped into the ring after the bell and called for Referee Jack Denning to halt the bout. Walker's mouth had been "ripped," and his face was a "hospital case," said Pegler. Now Schmeling waited for Sharkey.

Max hoped for Schmeling or Carnera next. But on October 18, Ancil Hoffman denied the rumor that Madison Square Garden had signed Baer to meet Carnera in December. Jimmy Johnston did call Hoffman with the proposal, but Hoffman refused the bout, saying, "There is nothing to gain by meeting Carnera, as we are after Schmeling or Sharkey."[24] Johnston took offense to Hoffman's rejection. Johnston would be snubbed again by Joe Jacobs. And all hell would break loose.

Schmeling's manager Joe Jacobs had a mandatory contract with the Garden for a title fight between Max Schmeling and Jack Sharkey. But when Jimmy Johnston handed Jacobs the details of the contract on October 20, 1932, Jacobs erupted in rage. Schmeling would only get ten percent of the gate. Jacobs thought that Schmeling deserved more than ten percent, so plans for the 1933 title bout between Jack Sharkey and Max Schmeling went bust. Jacobs's personal contract with Schmeling guaranteed the Black Uhlan $100,000 per year or Jacobs had to make up the difference. The ten percent offered by the Garden wouldn't begin to cover his contract obligations. "Just a lot of wise guys! A bunch of double-crossers and cheap, shyster promoters," Jacobs said, not mincing words about the dealers at the Garden. "But they can't get away with that. I've arranged for Schmeling to fight Max Baer in June."[25]

Ancil Hoffman had offered Joe Jacobs an astounding $100,000 cash guarantee for Max Schmeling to fight Max Baer. Jacobs was quick to sign the deal, sans promoter or matchmaker. Neither the German boxer nor his manager would have to work another fight the entire year to satisfy Jacobs's $100,000 a year contract to Schmeling. Hoffman was sure that a Baer-Schmeling fight would be the biggest fight of 1933 and would repay his guarantee. Ancil Hoffman had just shoved Madison Square Garden out of the picture.

Jimmy Johnston would retaliate. As soon as he heard about the deal, he sent Max Baer a telegram with an unbelievable offer. Johnston would guarantee Max Baer the title in a fight with Jack Sharkey if Baer would dump his manager and sign with Johnston's brother Charles. He promised that Charlie would also "attend legally to your other managers."[26] (It was well-known that Johnston used his brother Charlie as a mere "figurehead.") Reporter Ed Hughes explained the "sordid pug squabble." Hughes called it "an amazing proposition" in the "larcenous texture of the stuff" of fisticuffs, but no surprise to those who followed boxing. He stated that the telegram said that if Baer would sign with Charles Johnston, "Mr. [Jimmy] Johnston guaranteed that brother Charles WOULD MAKE BAER THE HEAVYWEIGHT CHAMPION OF THE WORLD" [Hughes's caps].[27] After the press exposed the offer, there was no reason why Sharkey would accept a title fight with Baer if it had been guaranteed that Baer would win.

Baer declined the lucrative offer, his first opportunity for the title, albeit unsavory. Some may think today that Johnston was merely offering Baer a chance at the title by offering a fight with Jack Sharkey, since the Garden owned Sharkey's first fight defense. Johnston may have believed that Baer could beat Sharkey. But no reporter at the time believed that Johnston did anything other than to promise to "rig" the fight in Baer's favor, which he had the wherewithal to do. At this juncture in history, heavyweight boxing took a turn in a different direction. But Jimmy Johnston and the Garden were not out of the picture yet.

From Joe Jacobs's point of view, if Schmeling could put away Max Baer, there would be no significant contender to stand in the way of a Schmeling-Sharkey match and a chance for Schmeling to regain the title.

The shockwaves of the set-up were still being felt in December, when Jack Dempsey brokered a deal that sent aftershocks through the boxing establishment. The story in the news ran:

> The monopoly Madison Square Garden has enjoyed on prime heavyweight attractions since the days of Tex Rickard was threatened today from a new and formidable quarter. William Harrison Dempsey announced yesterday he had signed Max Schmeling and Max Baer for a fifteen-round bout sometime in June. Dempsey also believed the fight would draw a gate that would pay Schmeling's $100,000 guarantee. The site was not specified, either New York or Chicago. Other promoters have sought to "buck" the Garden in the past, but most had two strikes on them before they went to the plate, either because the Garden had the best locations or the best fighters or both tied up with air-tight contracts. Now the Garden has the champion Sharkey, but no one to fight him.
>
> Not so with Dempsey. Jack has his fighters safely signed and through his association with Tim Mara he will have his choice either of the Polo Grounds or the Yankee Stadium should he decide to stage the fight in New York. Mara has the two big ball parks under lease for boxing and through his Aram Athletic Club is duly licensed in this state as a promoter. Chicago, it was understood, is

Left to right: Max Baer, Ancil Hoffman, and Jack Dempsey. The three were set to take over the heavyweight situation in New York.

genuinely anxious to stage the fight as a world's fair attraction and probably will have some persuasive arguments for Dempsey's ear. Under the terms of the contract, the Garden is obligated to find someone for Sharkey to fight by June 20. With Schmeling and Baer both unavailable, the Garden will be forced to look elsewhere, possibly in the general direction of Primo Carnera.[28]

Dempsey had just put Baer on the top of the boxing world, landing Yankee Stadium and Max Schmeling. It would free Primo Carnera to fight Jack Sharkey for the heavyweight crown, and settle the question of which Max would eventually fight the winner for the crown.

As a result of this turn of events, the 1932 end-of-the-year poll by the *New York Sun* gave first place in the heavyweight ranks to Max Schmeling of Germany for the third straight year, despite the fact that he had lost his world championship to Jack Sharkey. Of 60 writers polled, Schmeling was voted the best of the heavyweights by 38, while only 18 thought that Sharkey's disputed fifteen-round decision entitled him to top ranking. The list was: 1. Max Schmeling; 2. Jack Sharkey; 3. Max Baer; 4. Stanley Poreda; 5. Primo Carnera; 6. Johnny Risko; 7. King Levinsky; 8. Mickey Walker; 9. Young Stribling; 10. Ernie Schaaf.[29]

Probably the most radical change in the year's ranking was the elevation of Max Baer, the Livermore Walloper, to third place from a position in the "honorable mention"

Five • Elimination Battles of 1932

list in 1931. "Baer knocked out Walter Cobb ... King Levinsky, Ernie Schaaf, Tom Heeney, P. Swiderski and Arthur de Ku and now stands in the finest position of all the young contenders, matched with Schmeling by Promoter Jack Dempsey."[30]

Dempsey came in and clinched the big fight before the year-end rankings appeared in the news, which moved Baer to third place in votes and Max Schmeling to first, solving the heavyweight elimination problem, but creating a big headache for Madison Square Garden.

Moneyman Hoffman would be left to transfer the actual $100,000 guarantee to Max Schmeling some time before the big fight.

Six

Battle of the Two Maxes, 1933

> To think that in college I gambled four years
> On Plato and Horace to win....
> Oh, why did I bother with Pliny or Pope
> Or follow the calculus chart
> When I might have been crowding some cove to the rope
> And socking him over the heart?
> No wonder I murmur like someone bereft,
> "Why didn't they teach me to lead with my left?"
> —Grantland Rice
> (Homage to the Baer-Schmeling fight)[1]

Baer would not fight again for nine months as he waited for his semifinal elimination bout on June 8, 1933, with Max Schmeling at Yankee Stadium to determine the challenger for the winner of the Sharkey and Carnera bout. Max had wanted to fight Schmeling before Carnera because he thought Schmeling the tougher of the two opponents.

In late October 1932, Baer went to Oakland to work out with Bob McAllister. In a postal mix-up, his boxing trunks were shipped to Sacramento, and there were none to fit him in Oakland. At this time Ancil Hoffman asked trainer Bob McAllister to talk with Max about the idea of having him insured for $100,000 during the period before the bout. Hoffman was about to hand Max Schmeling $100,000, and even the rich promoter needed some kind of guarantee if something should happen to Max before the fight.

Max would stay home for the winter holidays to help his wife. In turn, she would see to it that he followed strict orders from Hoffman and McAllister. The Baers lived with Ancil Hoffman and his wife Maudie on their ranch at Fair Oaks in California. With her big picture days over, Mrs. Max Baer offered her services to a local theater. Max helped her to learn her lines in the play *The Mask and the Face*, debuting with the Sacramento Community Players for two nights in December.

January 1933 began a new year of boxing hostilities. Writer Jimmy Donahue summarized the scene in New York: Jack Dempsey "took advantage of a situation, of course, but that's why promoters were born."[2] To begin with, there was the feud between Joe Jacobs, manager of Schmeling, and Jimmy Johnston, matchmaker of the Garden. Then there was the antagonism between Johnston and Ancil Hoffman when Johnston tried to steal Ancil's fighter and tie him to the Garden. Then Dempsey rode in from the West and stole the only show in town that could bring in the money (Schmeling and Baer). Sharkey added to the uproar by calling Dempsey a *bum* and Schmeling a *yellow rat*.

Meanwhile, back in California, Baer was back in the news again, not for boxing, but for a previous romantic liaison. In Oakland, on January 14, Miss Olive Beck, Baer's first girlfriend, filed suit against him for $250,000 for breach of promise. She claimed that Baer jilted her to marry Dorothy Dunbar. As proof of their engagement, she produced several love letters Baer had written. Not until the month after Max's big fight with Max Schmeling would he learn that the California court had ruled in his favor because Miss Beck failed to prove sufficient facts.

Nationally, it was announced in January that five states had entered bills in legislatures to extend boxing matches from ten rounds to fifteen: Colorado, Illinois, Ohio, Pennsylvania and Wisconsin.

Since a rematch with Max Baer did not make, Ernie Schaaf was rematched with Stanley Poreda, from Jersey City, on January 7, 1933. Poreda was considered the favorite for his showings in 1932, over Risko, Schaaf, Carnera and Loughran. Some said this bout was considered one of the ongoing elimination battles. Poreda had been ranked recently as high as fourth among heavyweights.

Schaaf came into the fight ready for a brawl with Poreda. And after Schaaf landed a crushing blow on his opponent's jaw in the second, Poreda was never able to come back. He was down two times in the fifth and was saved by the bell as trainer Joe Jeanette dragged him back to his stool. He was knocked down again in the sixth and Referee Arthur Donovan called a halt to the bout.

Two weeks later, for four days, January 20 through 23, Schaaf was hospitalized with the flu. His doctor said he would be over his illness in a few days. Instead of a rematch with Max Baer, Schaaf was matched with Primo Carnera.

On February 10, 1933, in a Madison Square Garden elimination match between Primo Carnera and Ernie Schaaf, it soon became apparent that Schaaf was making a mediocre showing and was in no condition to be in the ring, although he continued through twelve rounds. However, in the thirteenth round, Primo half-hit or punched Schaaf and he collapsed. The punch was so slight that fans yelled, "Fake." But Ernie Schaaf, the Blond Viking from Boston, fell to the canvas unconscious and died only days later. The coroner ruled the death resulted from natural causes, but the surgeon who operated on him said the death resulted from a blood clot from the boxing match. His body was escorted home by his mother from New York to Boston on February 14, for burial three days later.

Many said that Baer's beating of Schaaf was the true cause of his death. Much like in the Campbell fight, Ernie had taken a bad beating from Baer and was left unconscious at the final bell. But Schaaf's match with Baer was over five months before he died. Schaaf had been in four additional battles after Baer. It was later discovered that Ernie had not completely recovered from either flu or meningitis, a condition which may have caused swelling in his brain when he went into the ring with Carnera.

Baer was not responsible for Ernie Schaaf's death, but the rumor persisted, and it greatly bothered Max. With fans claiming Max was responsible for two deaths in the ring and a two-year winning streak, many believed that the Californian had a good chance of beating the German.

Meeting with Adolf Hitler

Early in 1933, Ancil Hoffman and his wife Maudie traveled to Germany to cement the details for the Baer-Schmeling fight and deliver the guarantee money. Hoffman was an easy man to work with compared to the New Yorkers who had given the German the runaround in the past, and Schmeling wanted to thank him for coming to Germany personally to complete the fight arrangements.

Eager to entertain and thank Hoffman with the best of German hospitality, Schmeling arranged for him to attend a luncheon meeting with the new chancellor of Germany. Adolf Hitler had been recently appointed to this government position in January. (He did not declare himself Fuhrer until 1934.) Schmeling was a star in Germany and a particular favorite of Hitler's in his admiration for physical strength. Baer, too, was admired and compared to German body-builder Lionel Strongfort, considered the strongest man alive.[3] (America's equivalent was Charles Atlas.) Strongfort, whose physique was favored by artists and sculptors, was born in Berlin in 1878. (He lived to be 92, advocating for a vegetarian diet.)

Another top American leader of note, Henry Ford, was also on the invited guest list for the special luncheon. Ford Motor Company had a significant number of auto manufacturing plants in Germany—complexes that were later taken over and converted for purposes of the Nazi war effort.

Hoffman and his wife were staying at a Berlin hotel when Schmeling arrived to pick them up for the important date. Upon seeing Maudie waiting expectantly outside the doorway, hand in hand with her husband, Schmeling uttered a very guttural and emphatic, "No, no women!" Apparently, and unbeknownst to Ancil, this was an all-male luncheon and Ancil had failed to communicate any of these details to his wife. Surprised and insulted, Mrs. Hoffman darted back inside the hotel to avoid further embarrassment. Her husband would pay dearly for this affront. While he was attending the luncheon, Maudie mitigated the situation by buying, at the hotel's priciest boutique, a very expensive fur coat. Ancil reported to his American friends that the trip had been both unpleasant and costly.

Hoffman went into the luncheon feeling miserable, and things only got worse. According to details Ancil told his good friend Judge William Pettite, Hitler was a vegetarian; therefore, there was no meat served. In addition, Hitler didn't drink alcohol, and as a former saloonkeeper, Ancil had been used to the best of brews. No alcohol was served. Hoffman was left to drink a bitter mineral water that he despised. The luncheon conversation didn't improve matters. Baer and Hoffman were German surnames, so Hitler assumed Hoffman shared his Aryan pride. It was true that Hoffman did not consider himself Jewish. (Hitler would have ascertained his background in advance and would never have extended an invitation if he thought he was Jewish.[4]) During the meal, Hoffman was offended by Hitler's exhaustive talk about a "pure race" and white superiority. As a boxer, manager and promoter, Hoffman had spent his entire business life mixing with people of all races and religions. He never forgot Hitler's arrogant Aryan remarks. And Hoffman's personal encounter with Hitler would leave an indelible imprint on Baer's legacy when Max fought Schmeling.

As part of the contract with Joe Jacobs and Ancil Hoffman, Dempsey had to announce the location of the fight, either Chicago or New York, by March 10, so that training camps could be established. Chicago had hoped the bout would occur at the World's Fair there. But with the unexpected death of Chicago Mayor Anton Cermak, a good friend of Dempsey's, the Chicago plans were off. The mayor was shot March 6, in Miami, Florida, by an assassin's bullet assumed to be intended for President Franklin Roosevelt. After Cermak's death, Dempsey turned his attention to New York.

Six • Battle of the Two Maxes, 1933

Madison Square Garden executives were not happy about a summertime event for New York in direct competition with the Garden's planned Sharkey-Carnera title fight. After Schaaf's death from the Carnera fight, New York Commissioner William Muldoon said that he would not permit Carnera to meet Sharkey because the Italian was too dangerous. His comments were dismissed by the other members of the commission because the Garden needed a good fight.

Muldoon had been an early chairman of the New York Commission, and, in many minds, the only chairman. He was a stern, tough man, but well-respected. Muldoon had seen a lifetime of fights, but sadly he would not live to see the Baer-Schmeling bout. He died June 3. Gene Tunney, Jack Dempsey and Jack Sharkey were present at William Muldoon's funeral at Valhalla, New York. He would be honored with a military tribute at the battle of the two Maxes.[5]

The state's commission approved Dempsey's bout for June 8, in New York. And so began one of the greatest promotional wars since Rickard's tenure at the Garden. Now Jimmy Johnston needed a date for the Sharkey bout that would not conflict with Dempsey's. The Sharkey-Carnera fight would be June 29. It helped the publicity fodder that Dempsey planned to donate a part of his gate to the Calvary Cancer Hospital. But as the Dempsey team was to find out when ticket sales were less than expected, another publicity angle was necessary.

Beginning in April, there was something printed almost daily about the fight. Dempsey recommended that both Maxes start their individual promotional work two months prior to help stir up national interest. The promotions would help both parties regardless of who won. The public felt that the next champion would come from this New York fight, so they flocked to see the boxers. Max Baer planned exhibition stops on his way from California to New York, in Denver and Chicago. Baer stopped in Denver on April 5, where he kayoed Sam Greer in the second round and Wee Willi Medivitch, also in the second. Two days later he was in Chicago, where he knocked out Ed Willis in the first round.

Promoter Dempsey was as much the subject of the upcoming event as were the boxers. He was only 38, weighed 200 pounds, and looked every part the athlete he was in the 1920s. Grantland Rice said Dempsey reminded him of a leopard or tiger caged in a room with a nervous energy. He never relaxed. "He is courteous and sincere, always willing to sign an autograph, never showing resentment. When asked why Baer-Schmeling was his first big promotion [he had already staged two promotions in Reno] he said that Schmeling has proved his place over three years and he is the best in the game."[6]

Dempsey recalled:

In the meanwhile, I had watched Max Baer come along from a raw novice and a careless kid into a greatly-improved fighter, one who at last was taking his profession seriously. In my opinion, Baer today is one of the best heavyweights we have seen in a long time. He is big, strong and fast enough. He can punch and he can take a punch. He has everything a good heavyweight needs, and Schmeling will have to be an outstanding fighter to beat this big fellow in 15 rounds. There was another reason I picked this pair. I always like the aggressive side of the game and I know this is what the crowd likes. Schmeling likes to wade in and start punching, especially if the other fellow will meet him halfway. Baer feels the same way about a fight. Neither can be classed among the defensive types. Both like to punch—and both can do their share. I think Baer is one of the hardest hitters I ever saw. You see, Baer is only 23. I was 24 before I got my shot at Willard. I showed Baer what a great spot he was in—only two fights away from the heavyweight crown at 23. Few have ever been in this spot before.[7]

Manager Joe Jacobs, left, with German protégé Max Schmeling, April 8, 1933, *New York World Telegram* (courtesy Library of Congress. Prints and Photographs [LC-UsZ62-135653]).

    Maximilian Siegfried Adolph Otto Schmeling was four years older than Baer, born September 28, 1905, at Klein-Luckow, Germany. Like many boys at the time, he left school after the eighth grade to go to work. A short spell at an advertising agency left him yearning for something more physical. He left to work in the Rhineland coal mines. And it was during this time he became interested in pugilism. His first purse amounted to $5. Originally, he worked the corner for his trainer, Max Machon. With the help of Machon, Schmeling turned professional at the age of 24, and with his victories became the German heavyweight champion, a hero in his homeland. In 1925, he met Jack Dempsey in Europe, and Dempsey consented to box one round with him. After that experience, Schmeling became a lifelong admirer of the famous mauler. Schmeling came to the United States in 1928, and his first battle earned him $1000. He earned $15,000 when he defeated Johnny Risko. His defeat of Carnera earned him $74,000. American audiences were struck by his uncanny physical resemblance to Dempsey. Schmeling even said he learned the finer arts of the sport by studying the Dempsey-Carpentier fight film.[8]

Schmeling landed in New York on April 14, 1933, and was greeted by his manager Joe Jacobs and promoter Jack Dempsey, along with a host of reporters. They questioned him first about the condition of Germany. His response reflected what Hitler wanted people to think: "It is my personal impression that Germany was never so quiet as now.... I saw no physical molestation of any Jews. I'm so confident reports of mistreatment of Jews are exaggerated I would like to take my manager, Jacobs over there as a test."[9]

Like Baer, who was on an exhibition tour in the West, Schmeling planned an exhibition tour in the East, including parts of Canada. His stops included Pittsburgh, Boston, Montreal, Quebec, and Portland, Maine. The tour was expected to conclude at Reading, Pennsylvania.

Dempsey was stirring the publicity pot in New York. His two Maxes were introduced as guests of honor to one thousand diners at the annual Sports Dinner on April 27, sponsored by the New York Athletic Club. Dempsey announced that the training camps were to open May 1, and he would make periodic visits to ensure that the men were working as he expected.

Very few reporters believed that Baer could beat the German. But Grantland Rice predicted May 1:

> Of the four [in the semi-final tournament], just at this stage, I like Max Baer's chances above the lot. But I believe he will have a harder time of it against Schmeling than he will against the winner of the Sharkey-Carnera brawl. Easterners, especially New Yorkers, underrate Baer because they saw Tommy Loughran outpoint him when he was a raw kid, barely past 20. The big Westerner is a different fighter today, older, bigger, a better boxer, with a flock of tough battles under his belt against such competition as Paulino, Schaaf, Griffith and King Levinsky. Over 6 feet 2, weighing around 215 in top condition, he will be a rough customer for anyone to handle. Schmeling will have to be 50 percent better than he was against Sharkey to have an even chance.[10]

By the end of May, it was obvious to all concerned that there was a serious problem in ticket sales. Max Schmeling had been given his guarantee of $100,000, and to make that up, along with other monies needed to make a profit, something had to be done. The problem wasn't with the fight, because it was a good, competitive match. The problem was that the Jewish fans did not want to pay for a ticket that would help support Hitler's golden boy. To remedy the situation, the fans needed a boxer to support. It was a reach back two generations, but Max could tout his Jewish connection.

Was Max a Jewish Boxer?

The Baer-Schmeling fight cannot be fully discussed without addressing the fact that for the first time Max wore a Jewish symbol on his trunks into the ring, which identified him as Jewish for the rest of his life. Prior to this fight, no one really cared about his heritage. He was simply identified as the son of a butcher from Livermore, California. Because the name was spelled "Baer," German for "bear," he was assumed to be German. After

Jack Dempsey (left) and Max in an exhibition fight in preparation for Max Schmeling at Atlantic City, New Jersey, May 28, 1933. Dempsey went one round with each boxer and said Baer knocked the wind out of him, but Schmeling didn't hurt him (courtesy Mike Silver).

the Schmeling match, Max was enshrined in the imagination as being a Jewish boxer. To fully examine the subject, because writers have held various opinions, the following topics merit consideration: statements in the boxing literature; Max's own statements; the family's lineal history; his family's practicing faith; traditional circumcision; and the origin of the use of the Star of David as an emblem on his boxing trunks.

Boxing Literature

Up to 1988, literature on Jewish boxers excluded Max Baer. Max was not listed in the *Jewish Boxers Hall of Fame: A Who's Who of Jewish Boxers*. Between 1900 and 1940, there were 27 Jewish world champions, but Max Baer was not listed as one of them.[11] Highly respected boxing historian Hank Kaplan, former editor of *Boxing Digest*, did not include Max Baer in his introduction of the great Jewish boxers from Abe Attell through Barney Ross.[12] Max Baer was not listed in Lester Bromber's *Ten Greatest Jewish American Boxers*, "The Jewish Boxers' Hall of Fame," "Jews in Hall of Fame," or "Boxers in Jewish Sports Hall of Fame in Israel."[13] Baer was not mentioned during his day, or shortly after, with the other Jewish boxers of note like Lew Tendler, Mushy Callahan, Izzy Schwartz, Abe Goldstein, Benny Bass, Jackie Fields, Art Lasky, Abe Simon, Kingfish Levinsky, or Max Rosenbloom. Max Baer knew many of them, fought many of them, even entertained with some, but he was never listed among them, or identified with them, as being Jewish. In 1953, for example, a photo was printed of the boxers who starred in the 1933 movie *The Prizefighter and the Lady*. It showed Max Baer, Art Lasky, Primo Carnera, and Jack Dempsey. The caption for Art Lasky read, "former United States and Jewish heavyweight champ." The caption for Max Baer read, "Another former great world champ and called 'Clown Prince of the Ring.'" The photo illustrated that by 1953, Art Lasky was considered Jewish, but Max Baer was not.[14]

Max's Statements

Max addressed the topic on several occasions, but he never settled the issue in public before he died. Privately, it was a different matter. It was generally assumed by his friends that he did not consider himself Jewish (outside of the ring). When asked the question by reporters directly, he did not answer them. When he did comment, it was usually by way of a joke or casual remark. For example, after taking a severe beating to his nose, he looked into the mirror and remarked that if anyone didn't believe he was Jewish, they should take a look at that "snozzle."

Max rarely attended any church, but he could recite passages from the Bible. Sitting next to sparring partner Curley Owen at a table in Baltimore in 1951, photographer Ralph Dohme wrote that Max recited the genealogy of Jesus Christ, directly from the Gospel of Luke, quite a feat in that the list, from Jesus, son of Joseph, comprises 76 names back to Adam, son of God.[15]

Family History

That others considered him Jewish was fine with him. None of the core Baer family members actively practiced the Jewish faith or any faith until they married. Baer's father Jacob was not a practicing Jew, and hog farmer would have been an undesirable profession for a Jewish man. Family stories do indicate that Jacob's father, Max's paternal grandfather, was Jewish. He did not practice the faith, and a paternal lineage (instead of a maternal link) excluded Max from Orthodox consideration. Max's mother, Dora Bales, was Scotch-Irish, born in Iowa and raised Catholic. Neither Max nor his parents, Jacob and Dora, identified with or practiced any specific faith. Max's second wife, Mary Ellen Sullivan, the mother of his children, was Catholic, and she raised their children in the Catholic faith. But Max attended church only for weddings and funerals or other special services.

Before he died, Max declined to be baptized Catholic, but was buried in a Catholic cemetery.

Circumcision

In the early twentieth century, one proof of being Jewish was whether or not a man was circumcised. Circumcision was historically a sacred mark identifying a male with the Hebrew faith. If they were not Jewish, most men of Max's generation were not circumcised at birth. A generation after Max, when more babies were born in hospitals, the procedure became more commonplace for male babies from other faiths for health reasons. Stories told by Max's trainers and boxing friends (including this writer's father) indicated that Baer was never circumcised. Trainers, sparring partners, even newspapermen who hung around the very open gyms, dressing rooms, and showers in those days were not timid about seeing naked bodies. Baer's trainer Ray Arcel, who wrote the foreword for *The Jewish Boxers Hall of Fame*, told Ken Blady that while they were training he "used to take showers with Max" and he assured the author "that Max wasn't Jewish."[16] However, on this same subject, Nat Fleischer said that Max was circumcised as an adult just prior to and for the occasion of the Schmeling fight. That simply did not happen. Sparring partner Ike Aycock was in the gym with Max after the Schmeling fight.

Lineage

Many writers explain that Max Baer was one-quarter Jewish because his father was half Jewish. This language of ethnic or religious identity by percentage fell into common practice historically when it was used for economic or political purposes. Americans were aware of this type of language (so very offensive now, but common prior to the Civil Rights Movement) when black Americans were identified for census and other records as, for example, one-quarter black, or "quadroon." The same percentage of identification occurred with Native Americans for purposes of government identification and later for "benefit" purposes. It is awkward, however, to make a similar analogy with religions. For example, would a descendant of a Catholic be called half or quarter Christian or Catholic? The measure, however, became commonplace in Nazi-ruled Germany.

This percentage marker was an important measure in the 1930s for Hitler, who wanted to cast the widest net possible for his criminal labor camps and later extermination camps. Anyone who was one-quarter Jewish would have fallen victim. If the Baers had been in Nazi-occupied territory, the family most likely would have been incarcerated or exterminated if they identified their grandfather as Jewish.

Star of David

Where, when, and why did the Star of David appear on Baer's boxing trunks, a matter that has so identified Max with the Jewish faith? Why didn't he talk about it?

Certainly, Max had empathy for the Jewish people who were fighting for their very existence in Nazi-controlled parts of Europe during the time he was fighting in the ring to claim a title. But early in his rise, he was concerned, like most boxers, and Americans in general during the Depression, with a paycheck and the next meal. Non-Jewish Americans' attention to the Nazi situation in Germany was not front-and-center until the second half of the 1930s. Baer's great heart, however, did extend to those who were suffering in Germany, Austria, Finland and Poland, as proven much later in his career as a world-famous celebrity.

Five years after the Schmeling fight, the source of the star was revealed by Bill McCarney, the "Professor" and member of Schmeling's camp. McCarney was at Hymie Caplin's Sixth Avenue Pub with a group of friends, which included sportswriter Bill Henry, and they were talking about the Louis-Schmeling match. McCarney said that the reason Schmeling wanted to beat Louis was to avenge his loss to Baer. "Neither the official nor the German fans have forgiven him for losing to Baer," he said, "a fellow they believe is Jewish."[17] As he told this story, one of his listeners objected, saying that he thought Baer *was* Jewish, pointing out all the ballyhoo from the Baer-Schmeling fight. McCarney declared that it was just that, that he made it all up to sell tickets.

He explained that ticket sales were starting to pick up in the weeks before the fight, but not at the rate promoters expected. They had expected a $300,000 gate, which Dempsey said the fight would draw (and which they needed to pay guarantees and expenses), but at the end of May it seemed unlikely, with all the negative publicity about a German fighter, that the gate would reach $200,000. Writer Bill Henry commented that for only $200,000, "Jack Dempsey himself wouldn't have walked across the street for it."[18] The Germans were afraid to attend and the Jewish population didn't want to buy tickets because they didn't want to support a German. In addition, the Jewish War Veterans loudly advocated boycotting the fight.

So Bill McCarney, working for the Schmeling camp, devised a plan. The Jewish people might come to the fight if they had someone to support. It didn't matter to him who they supported as long as they bought tickets. "Of course Baer isn't Jewish at all," McCarney steadfastly declared five years later when he explained what he had invented. But: "Tickets weren't selling any too well when Baer got in town, so I suggested that we spruce it up a bit by concocting the German-Jewish angle. Too, it is New York's great Jewish population that provides the bulk of the fight crowd. It worked mighty fine."[19] And Max played the part wonderfully, he said.

Ancil Hoffman loved the idea of putting Max in the ring as a Jew, particularly after Hoffman's distasteful luncheon with Adolf Hitler. He saw it as a way to snub Hitler for his remarks a few months earlier. Hoffman, however, was initially wary of how to carry it all off since neither he nor Baer knew anything about Judaism, and if they asked any questions about the religion from the many Jewish fans in New York during the build-up, they would be exposed as impostors. But Ancil was never at a loss for how to solve a problem. Hoffman's friend William Pettite explained in a 2017 phone conversation to the author that Ancil hired a rabbi, paying him to field any questions about the Jewish faith. And Ancil and Max walked freely around New York, advertising the fight, meeting people, and being seen with their rabbi.

Journalist Dan Parker wrote in 1959, "Baer's adoption of the Star of David as fighting emblem and his claim that he was Jewish (later admitted by him as untrue) won him a tremendous following in New York, where Schmeling represented Hitlerism, although as discreetly as he could. Considering that he had to go back to Germany, he disclaimed any connection with the Nazi party."[20]

After the Baer-Braddock fight, Bill Corum wrote, "Indeed it is generally understood that the better box office he found it to be, the more Jewish Maxie became. With which nobody should find fault. The best and freest spending fight fans in New York are Jewish."[21]

In a question-answer column called "Things They Ask the [*Oakland*] *Tribune*," one reader asked, "Is Max Baer Jewish or Portuguese?" The columnist answered simply, "Max Baer is an American."[22] This question epitomized the confusion over Baer's race and ethnicity. But after the Schmeling bout, Max was roundly labeled as Jewish.

On May 6, at Lake Swannanoa, New Jersey, Max Schmeling began his training by boxing four rounds with two sparring partners: Jack Shaw and Gus Rodenberg. Rodenberg took the worst of the damage when Schmeling almost floored him with a right and left to the chin and body. Five hundred people were at ringside to watch. Schmeling had more experience than Baer, better boxing skills, and a good right hand from short range. He was smart, cool, game, fast and a good puncher. New York heavyweight Lou Barba had been in Schmeling's five previous training camps and knew how fast he was. "You seldom get a clean shot at his jaw. He's as quick as a cat and if you make one little mistake he'll bring over that right and you finish up on the canvas. Max Baer will have a tough time hitting him on the jaw with his left."[23] Schmeling was a 2-to-1 favorite over Baer. Schmeling could expect trouble in the early rounds, but was expected to win at the end.

And at Baer's training camp? Max wanted golf to be on his daily schedule, but Ancil Hoffman said that was *out*. He told Baer, golf was something you played to relax, not something you did to train for a heavyweight boxing match.[24]

In the build-up to the fight, newspapers compared Baer to other young champions. Max was now 24. Dempsey and Jim Jeffries were both 24 when they won the championship. Max's punches were certainly harder, but he was wilder. Max had trained harder for this bout than any other. He had worked with champion trainer Whitey Bimstein, and it was Bimstein who said Max was in the best shape of his career. Some called Whitey "a philosopher strategist, buffer and probably one of the best leveling forces any scrapper ever had with him to prepare for battle."[25] Bimstein was a trainer in full; he readied his charges psychologically and physically. Baer was a trim 210 pounds, and his arms, shoulders, and chest rippled with muscles. Even his forehead wrinkled when he posed with a seriously mean look for the camera. By comparison, Schmeling's muscles were loose, not as clearly defined, and his boyishly handsome face looked serious but never mean.

The combatants were both young. Max Schmeling was 27. They were the last two great heavyweights before Louis that could wallop. Schmeling was more deadly accurate, hit hard and blocked well. Both had deadly rights. Baer snorted and growled and heaved punches recklessly with both hands. There were several reasons for the 2-to-1 odds for Schmeling. He was a proven champion. And while Baer had never been put down (he had a granite chin), he was not the best at defense. The only experience Baer lacked was facing Sharkey, Carnera, and Schmeling. He had gone through the rest of the contenders and everyone agreed that Baer, in his present condition, would be Schmeling's greatest test. Both had long winning streaks.

Max Schmeling seemed to appear as a blaze from out of nowhere. He had only 8 fights in the United States, but he won all with the exception of Sharkey, and that was a disputed decision. The only way Baer could win, said the pundits, was if he could take away Schmeling's Sunday right-hand punch. If Schmeling won the title he would be the first to lose and regain the heavyweight crown.

One week before the fight, ticket sales were still lagging. Newspaper editors did what they could to promote sales. They predicted attendance to be 80,000. They promoted the battle with greater shemozzle than a title fight. They compared it to a Dempsey battle: "There's a suspicion among the experts ... that Max Schmeling's 15-round duel with Max Baer in the Yankee Stadium Thursday night may wind up the closest thing to a two-man riot the ring has seen since the night of the Dempsey-Firpo Brawl."[26] Dempsey cut off radio broadcasts locally to encourage fans to attend. Yet some worried that the weather would not hold.

Dempsey traveled back and forth to each training camp and even sparred with each warrior to hype the fight with his personality and energy. At one point Joe Jacobs thought that Dempsey gave Baer some pointers. But Dempsey boxed a one-round exhibition match with each boxer.

Two days before the fight, the gate was at $100,000 tickets sold with $50,000 in reservations, far less than the originally expected $300,000. Hope was that the last-minute rush would make up the difference, especially since the weather was expected to be clear. Dempsey had worked harder on this bout than for any of his previous fights, and there were still many details left to attend to. The New York Yankees had played a game with Boston only two days before the fight, and the stadium had yet to be turned into a boxing arena.

The day before the fight a constant stream of ticket buyers was seen at the window. Dempsey and his workmen were busy setting up the ring and arranging chairs.

On his train trip to the fight, Papa Jacob Baer stopped over at Denver to pick up his brother Ben, a Denver policeman, who accompanied him to the fight. Jacob bragged openly that "Max would knock the German loose from his shoe laces."[27] After their arrival in New York, their cab became caught in traffic. When Jacob told the traffic officer he had to get to the stadium to see his son fight, the two Baer brothers were given a police escort through the city that landed them an hour early to the stadium.

Max Schmeling, June 8, 1933, Yankee Stadium, New York

On the day of the fight, wagering odds moved Schmeling to a 5-to-2 favorite. The boxers rested in the morning.

The weigh-in was held at the New York Athletic Commission headquarters at 2:00 in the afternoon. Baer weighed 203, seven pounds under what he had expected. Schmeling was at 190. Baer had a five-inch longer reach. Baer was 6'2½" and Schmeling was 6'1". Each had a 33-inch waist and looked fit and trim.

Gates at Yankee Stadium opened at 3:00. Twenty thousand rush seats in the bleachers were sold for $1 starting at 4 p.m.

The gloves for the fight were a novelty for boxing: a mixture of badger and horsehair. Typically, gloves were stuffed solely with horsehair, but they became knotted and full of lumps toward the end of a championship fight. Dempsey was fanatical about his gloves, and he hoped that the new mixture would make for more evenly distributed padding. The special 6-oz. gloves were delivered to Dempsey for his inspection in ample time for the fight.

Nervous Papa Jake Baer entered Max's dressing room and was reassured by his son, "Don't worry a bit, Dad. I'm going to knock out Schmeling and I'm not going to get hurt myself. Everything is going to be all right. Now you run out and see the preliminaries and I'll be along when the main event starts."[28]

The first preliminary began at 7:00 p.m., with the main bout expected to occur between 8:30 and 9:00. It was a night of all heavyweights on the undercard.[29]

A lot was riding on the main event. If the fight was exciting and the men fought hard and put on a good show, big money was predicted to come to town. If not, Henry McLemore quipped, "The game will fall three notches below bowling as a money-maker."[30] Jimmy Johnston needed the fight to be a scorcher or his Sharkey and Carnera bout June 29 would lose serious money. McLemore said the unspeakable: that if this bout turned out to be a love feast, then Johnston can pack all his attendees for his next fight into a phone booth with room for calisthenics. McLemore predicted a win by Schmeling. He told his readers that if Baer won, they could send all their "I told you so" letters to his new address in Siberia.[31]

A crowd of 50,000 cheered Baer as he entered the ring with a smile on his face. Some mistook the look for cockiness when, in fact, his trainer Mike Cantwell had told him a joke to get him to relax. Baer was kept laughing all the way down the aisle and up through the ropes. At ringside Max recognized Mr. and Mrs. Al Jolson from Hollywood and blew them a kiss.

Dempsey, by contrast, looked haggard as he raced among the guests at ringside: "Hello, hello ... good to see you ... thanks for coming ... hello, hello." "At ringside," wrote Paul Harrison, "were the highest and lowest [of society]; officials of state, and men and molls of the underworld, celebrities of stage and screen ... those are elements that make ... a gloriously irrational experience of a prize fight."[32]

Venerable, and now frail, ring announcer Joe Humphreys bellowed his introductions to the audience, with forehead perspiring. The Californian was announced first and then Schmeling, "the most popular fighter from the Old World." When Baer disrobed and approached ring center he was wearing the Star of David on his trunks. It was as surprising to Schmeling as it was thrilling to the Jewish attendees. Schmeling knew about the publicity, but he never expected Baer or Hoffman to take it seriously, after the kindness he had extended to them. Schmeling never considered himself anti–Jewish or a Nazi, and he didn't consider Max to be Jewish like his manager Joe Jacobs.

Hitler, listening to the fight on the radio, must have thought that he had been duped if his luncheon guest had been sponsoring a Jew in the contest against Schmeling.

Max remembered what Dempsey had taught him: "Whenever you get tagged and see seven or eight guys in the ring, go for the one in the middle." That's exactly what happened early in the bout. Baer said, "He hit me with a right in the first round that straightened my broken nose. I looked up and saw 10 of him. So I rushed the guy in the middle and it was him."[33]

Schmeling didn't seem up to his ability. In the fourth round, Schmeling only pawed with his left. He seemed distracted. He spent a lot of time hitching up his shorts. At certain times it looked as if his trunks would fall to his knees, they were so loose. It seemed a curious wardrobe misfit.

Referee Arthur Donovan warned Baer about holding Schmeling's neck with his left hand while he punched with his right. (It was the same kind of cupping action that Louis would use later on Schmeling, and Donovan would not warn Louis.) Baer was also criticized for using a "backhand blow," the same bad habit that would cause the referee in the future Braddock fight to deduct points. In this fight Referee Donovan warned Baer of his frequent use of the blow, but he did not deduct any points. Baer offered an explanation: "When I missed a right I brought the glove back just hard enough against

Schmeling's jaw or head to keep him off balance. But I've got a right to hit with the glove."[34] Baer seemed impervious to punishment. Schmeling hit him at least six good times on the chin but nothing fazed him.

Ancil Hoffman's strategy for the fight was for Baer not to open up until after the fifth round. But when he saw an opening, Max launched his two-fisted attack in both the first and second rounds. After he saw that he could batter his opponent around the ring, he was content to bide his time. Max told Grantland Rice afterward, "It's a funny thing about fighting. No one can plan anything in advance. I had planned a body attack in the early rounds. But the fight never worked out that way. It worked just the opposite. So I swung in with the tide of the fight. No use to buck it."[35]

Baer had hammered Schmeling in the stomach in the first round, and when Baer was slow to get up for the second round, Schmeling came in and "caught me right between the eyes with a full right hand and it like to have took my head off. I remember that the tears jumped right out of my eyes and nearly blinded me, but I took it and went on to punch him silly."[36] Baer let up only for a moment. He had Schmeling against the ropes twice in the second.

In the third, Baer landed an uppercut at the belt-line and he was cautioned to keep the punches up. They fought at close quarters, Baer landing to the body and Schmeling landing on the head.

In the fourth, Baer landed hard punches, left and right to the jaw, and Schmeling backed up. They slung wild punches in the middle of the ring that brought the crowd to its feet, but no one hurt the other. Schmeling drove Baer to the corner as the bell rang. Some thought the round was even.

In the fifth, both men came out dripping with sweat. Schmeling took the offensive for the first time. Baer seemed to have let up. He explained later that it was the terrible heat that caused him to do so. His experience in those 20-round fights taught him everything he needed to know about pace. If he was going to make it to the end with strength, he was going to have to pace himself. When Baer let up in rounds 4, 6, and 7, Schmeling waded in with short, sharp attacks that won him his only rounds. Some reporters said he won round 5. Ringsiders were certain that Baer was finished and that the German was about to cut him to pieces. Some in the crowd booed the Californian.

Schmeling came out in the sixth and rushed Baer, but he was kept at bay with a long left. Three punches landed on Baer's chin, but he responded with a hard right that jolted the German's head back.

In the seventh, Schmeling ducked one of Baer's wild punches. He took a series of punches to the head without any power, and he came back with a series of lefts that popped Baer's head. Schmeling was able to guard against most of Baer's blows.

By the eighth, any listlessness was over, playful smiles were gone, and the fireworks began. Baer rushed into Schmeling wearing a frown with deadly seriousness. He landed a left uppercut to the body and left and right jabs to the head. They went to close quarters and exchanged body punches. Baer was warned for hitting with his backhand.

Jack Sharkey and Primo Carnera, both at ringside, must have realized then that Baer had been underrated, that he was impervious to damage. Both must have wondered what it would be like to face this young man with the "killer instinct."

In round nine, Baer put Schmeling on the ropes and nailed him twice on the jaw. And when Schmeling's guard went up, he attacked the body. They were slugging away when the bell rang and the referee had to separate them.

Max Baer's hand is raised by Joe Humphreys after Baer defeated Max Schmeling, June 8, 1933, at Yankee Stadium (courtesy David Bergin).

The fight ended in the tenth. When coming out of a clinch in the middle of the ring, Baer struck Schmeling squarely on the chin at short range with his hard right. Schmeling went down and the count began. He came up, Baer hit him, he covered up, and then he slid along the ropes as Baer kept up the attack. Baer screamed at the referee, "Do you want me to kill him?"[37]

Donovan stopped the fight one minute and 51 seconds in the tenth round. Baer shouted jubilantly, "I'm going to win that championship!"[38] Baer went to his ring corner and threw kisses to the crowd.

Schmeling was "shell-shocked" at the loss coming five rounds before the scheduled finish. He explained later that he must have gotten careless and opened up. "Wham. I thought a house had fallen on me," he said.[39]

The "young blade from out of the West with thunder in his brawny fists and all the 'killer instinct' he has any use for, stood today a threatening menace to Jack Sharkey's heavyweight crown," read the lead line from New York.[40]

Henry McLemore was awestruck: "[Baer] is magnificent to gaze upon. What a sweetheart of a punch. It starts from somewhere just south of Topeka and whistles towards its mark like a through freight whamming past a flag stop. Schmeling never knew what hit him.... When it landed it started a flood of headaches. Schmeling got one. Jacobs got one and the three score experts who picked the German got one."

When asked if he had gotten a big kick out of winning, Baer responded, "To tell the truth, my first thought was feeling sorry for Schmeling. I remembered how I felt after the first Schaaf fight—bruised, and battered—and beaten—no one around caring whether I lived or died. I was sorry for myself that night—so this time I felt sorry for Schmeling. It's the toughest game of them all when you lose. Talk to Schmeling? No, the only thing I said was just before the fight. 'No matter who wins, Max, I hope we'll still be good friends.'"[41]

Sportswriters pronounced Baer the new Dempsey, fistiana's man of destiny. Dempsey was thrilled. Headlines like these read, "Boxing's Comeback Rests on Shoulders of Young Star," "Baer, New Dempsey to Lead Boxing to Its Old Popularity." Jack Dempsey was ready to match Baer with the winner of the Sharkey-Carnera match, but Carnera was still under contract with Madison Square Garden for another fight, so Dempsey took Max on a quick barnstorming tour to eight cities. Dempsey told AP sportswriter Edward J. Neil, "Boxing has found in Max Baer the kind of fighter who can bring the game back to the old days—the days when big men fought to knock each other out, and you couldn't find places big enough to hold everyone who wanted to see it done."[42] He seemed to think Baer's potential was just beginning to be uncovered. Dempsey predicted that with more fights, Baer's boxing skills would only improve.

The fight had not been as financially successful as Dempsey had hoped. Over 3,000 of the tickets had been complimentary.[43] Newspaper reports of the gate varied: from $250,000, to $239,193, to as low as $201,092. Uncle Sam got 10 percent from the top, and the state 5 percent, in taxes. From Max's 15 percent of $30,000 or less, Ancil Hoffman gave Max $100. He knew Max's spending habits. The wise manager took the rest of the money and tucked it away in an annuity for Max's future. Schmeling received 40 percent. But at $80,000 it left a $20,000 shortfall from his already paid $100,000 guarantee.

The day after the fight, there was no mention of the Star of David on Baer's trunks. It was not a big news item at the time, not by AP reporters in New York, such as Damon Runyon, Hype Igoe, Henry McLemore, or Dempsey. The upset of Schmeling, former titleholder, and Baer's advance from the elimination battles to the heavyweight championship bout captured the news.

And while Baer's name was everywhere, and proposals for matches came in from 40 states, it was not all good news. Promoter Lou Parente in California claimed Baer still owed him two fights. And Baer's former manager said he owed him big-time for the current fight. J. Hamilton Lorimer wasted no time in attaching a lawsuit totaling $36,436.14 to his earnings. Ancil Hoffman scoffed when he heard about it the next day, saying that Lorimer was going after an empty pocketbook, that Baer had already spent those earnings before the fight.

Papa Jake was very proud. He told the *Oakland Tribune*, "He looked great, simply great. He has cut out a lot of his foolishness and is down to business."[44] The problem, Jake told the *Santa Ana Register*, is that "he's just a kid, always wanting to romp around with somebody, whether it's a little kid on the sidewalk or one of those Broadway dolls."[45] Both Papa and Uncle Ben planned to stay in town for the Sharkey-Carnera bout before returning to the West.

At a post-fight dinner given by Dempsey at Gallagher's Chop House the week after the bout, Baer shook hands with Schmeling and asked him for an autographed photo. Baer told him, "You are the best sportsman I ever met or hope to meet. I congratulate you on your coming marriage."[46] Schmeling left the next day for Germany to marry his sweetheart Anny Ondra, a musical comedy and film star. His trainer Max Machon would be his best man.

Baer felt a deep sorrow for Schmeling. "When he left for home," Baer told Grantland Rice several years later, "he was the loneliest-looking, most depressed fellow I ever saw."[47] Baer was the only person in the fight game to see him off at the boat when he left for Germany. Baer sent flowers to Schmeling's stateroom.

With Baer's astonishing win, Jack Sharkey's title was threatened.

Sharkey was eager to offer up his view of the fight. He told Henry McLemore, "Baer is just a chump, I'd like a crack at him."[48] McLemore titled his column, "The Boston Sailor is Same Old Blushing Violet as he Compares Self to Californian."

Sharkey elaborated:

> I don't know any words strong enough to describe the Dutchman's showing. He wouldn't do anything. He didn't hit but one good lick in the whole fight. That was a right to the stomach in the seventh round that drove in so deep it jerked Baer's left leg off the floor.... Baer [was] wide open as a farm gate. The Dutchman refused to let fly. He never was that way against me.... Both guys spent half their time apologizing for hitting with an elbow, butting and holding. It was the politest thing I ever laid my eyes on. I expected to see 'em sit down for a cup of tea at any moment. I counted 37 clean smacks and still [Schmeling] wouldn't go down. What kind of punching is that? Naw, I can't get excited about the guy. He's still just a big strong chump that's in for a licking by me. Boy, I hope I get a shot at him.[49]

Jack Sharkey wouldn't get that shot. Within the year, his "champ" to "chump" remarks would boomerang. He would lose to both Primo Carnera (on June 29, 1933) and to King Levinsky (on September 9, 1933). The man Sharkey called "chump" was about to become Max the champ.

Seven

The Heavyweight Championship, Carnera, 1934

The elimination battles were over. Max Baer had beaten Max Schmeling, and now he had to wait until June 29, 1933, to see who he would battle for the title, either Champion Jack Sharkey or Italian Primo Carnera.

Carnera started his U.S. career in 1930 at Madison Square Garden. Initially, the 6'6" Italian giant was considered "the last of the mastodons," more of a huge carnival attraction than a serious boxing threat. He weighed 260 pounds and, by boxing standards, was considered crude and inexperienced. New Yorkers had forgiven him any indiscretions in California, and by the time he met Champion Jack Sharkey for the title, he had paid his ring dues. He had posted wins over the same men other top contenders had faced coming up through the ranks: Ernie Schaaf, King Levinsky, Jose Santa, Les Kennedy, Art Lasky, Jim Maloney, George Godfrey, Paulino Uzcudun, Young Stribling and Tommy Loughran.

His contract was funded and manipulated by the mob. With very little understanding of financial matters (including a language barrier), he was easily duped regarding his earnings and investments and was left in financial ruin by unscrupulous management when his fighting days were over.[1]

Primo Carnera became the largest man of his era ever to win a world championship. Eighty years later, men at 6'6" weighing 260-plus pounds fighting for the title was not earthshaking news, but no one called Wladmir Klitschko or Anthony Joshua "mastodons." Molds from Carnera's fists preserved at the museum of the International Boxing Hall of Fame in Canastota, New York, prove just how enormous the Italian was.

During his lifetime, William Muldoon of the New York Boxing Commission argued against letting such big men fight against the average-sized heavyweight. With his size and reach of 85," the giant would usually outweigh his opponents by 60 pounds. Carnera, who had the muscular build of a modern-day Arnold Schwarzenegger, had survived 15 rounds with Jack Sharkey after being knocked down for a count of nine in the fourth round of their 1931 fight at Ebbets Field. Sharkey was the only opponent who had floored Carnera with a fair blow. Biographer Joseph Page noted that while Carnera "was down three times prior to the first Sharkey fight—all three were low blows that left him writhing on the mat."[2] Now, many believed that with 81 fights under his belt, the 25-year-old Carnera had improved, while Sharkey had only gotten older.

Sharkey had been battling at the top for years.[3] At 31, he was either going to show he was really good or that he was past his prime. (The comparison seemed lost at the time, that at 30, Sharkey was the same age as Gene Tunney when he took the laurels from Jack Dempsey.)

Unlike a battle of sluggers, the Sharkey-Carnera fight would be more complex in that both were good boxers. Carnera had a good defense, and Jack Sharkey was still considered the best ring craftsman of the big men.

About 40,000 spectators filled the Garden Bowl on Long Island on June 29, 1933, for the title fight. The odds were slightly in favor of Sharkey (by KO in 7), but by the time of the bout the odds had dropped to about even.

Publicity was fueled by Sharkey's revenge over the recent death of his protégé Ernie Schaaf, who died after the match with Carnera. Immediately after the Schaaf bout on February 10, Sharkey stood in Carnera's dressing room and roared at a surprised and frightened Carnera, "I'll get you for this."[4]

Four months later, Sharkey had the chance to avenge Schaaf's death. A win for the ex-sailor who learned to box in the Navy would continue his title legacy and also land him a bout with Max Baer and a chance to earn $100,000. If he lost, he said he would quit the ring. But no one expected him to lose to Carnera.

Spectators were stunned when Referee Arthur Donovan counted Jack Sharkey out as he sprawled face down on the canvas in the sixth round. One observer remarked that there was more action in that sixth round than in all of heavyweight boxing the past year.

The earlier rounds had favored the Sailor, but in the sixth when the two were near the ropes, Carnera smashed a short uppercut to Sharkey's jaw which almost lifted his head off. It was a punch everyone said Carnera didn't have—a right uppercut. "Every day I practice it for months," said Primo proudly back in his dressing room. "Nobody thought Primo had uppercut. I show 'em, huh?" Primo sat without a mark on his face. "I fight anybody now—Baer, Schmeling, anybody. I whip anybody they say. Primo's champion of the whole world."[5]

It had been a summer of spectacular upsets. In a few short weeks, the two dominant heavyweights, Schmeling and Sharkey, had been eliminated by Baer and Carnera. It was murmured that the next fight might bring back the million-dollar gate.

Max Baer would have to wait for a year while Jimmy Johnston at Madison Square Garden, owning the contractual rights to the future title match, put him on hold while Johnston got a game plan together to line his pockets. During the year, Baer was denied a big-money fight, and Carnera was forced to travel around the United States making money on dinners and exhibitions. (It would be the same for Baer the following year.) Customary income during 1933 for champion exhibition engagements was $2500 plus 50 percent of any receipts (approximately $50,000 in current dollars), quite a good sum for a country still in a financial depression, but not the earnings a big fight could make.

With Jimmy Johnston in no hurry to schedule a title bout, Primo went to Rome and successfully defended his European title against Paulino Uzcudun in front of 65,000 fans on October 22, 1933. Premier Benito Mussolini and his three sons attended. Italy was proud to own the world title.

While Max was waiting for his fight with the new champion, he and Dorothy Dunbar reconciled, but by the end of the summer they would be separated again. Jack Dempsey married New York's Hannah Williams, musical comedy star and former wife of Roger Kahn.

By September, the Associated Press announced that Dunbar planned to file for divorce. Dunbar's comments were: "Max had gone Hollywood and he may decide to be a film star rather than remain a good prize fighter."[6]

Seven • *The Heavyweight Championship, Carnera, 1934* 99

Left to right: John Reed Kilpatrick, President of Madison Square Garden, presents the Heavyweight Champion Belt to Primo Carnera, as Jimmy Johnston, matchmaker at the Garden, looks on, October 13, 1933. *New York World Telegram* (courtesy Library of Congress, Photographs and Prints [LC-USZ62-133794]).

While Jimmy Johnston and Madison Square Garden stalled, executives in the movie industry did not. They beat the ring promoter to the punch, creating their own movie version of the upcoming title match. On August 14, 1933, it was announced that Baer was signed as the lead in a movie about a prizefighter and a lady. Baer would play the contender, but the actor for the champion's role in the movie had yet to be selected. Baer offered his advice. Since Primo was the existing champion, why not get him to play the part? The idea was brilliant for both movie publicity and for the upcoming title match. The storyline had to be tweaked, and Primo had yet to accept the role. The deal was sealed after the boxers accepted $30,000 each for their roles (a half-million in current dollars), as much money as might be earned from a big fight, and safer.

It was said that there were two versions written for the final fight scene: one for Hollywood, that would end in a draw, and the other for Europe, in which Primo would knock out Baer. "Shhhh!!! Max Baer Agrees to Lose to Carnera; But It's only a Movie Bout," announced the *Syracuse Herald*.[7] The irony was not lost on sports followers.

When asked how he was selected for the role, Baer said the movie executives noticed his smooth and melodic voice from the radio broadcasts. He gave this interview at the studio sitting behind a desk smoking a cigarette. "Sure, I smoke," he said to the puzzled reporters. "I don't have to worry just now." And the fight game? "Dempsey's got me matched up to fight Carnera in June," he announced. "I'm not worrying about that, either."[8] Dempsey was in for 7½ percent of Max's contract for the title fight.

The Prizefighter and the Lady

"That's the way Tex Rickard would have done it," said Jack Dempsey as the cameras rolled.[9] Baer's character Steve Morgan and Champion Primo Carnera then signed articles of agreement in front of Dempsey, who played the promoter. The movie showcased Myrna Loy as the beautiful lady who leaves her rich mob boyfriend for a boxer who fights for the title. In an unusual twist, Max Baer and Primo Carnera were about to make a dramatic picture of a title bout seven months before their actual title fight.

The film was a huge success and would cement Baer's reputation as a lady's man. After Dunbar, he had been linked romantically to Myrna Loy, Jean Harlow, Carole Lombard, June Knight, and Mary Kirk Brown of New York. All the ladies denied the rumors

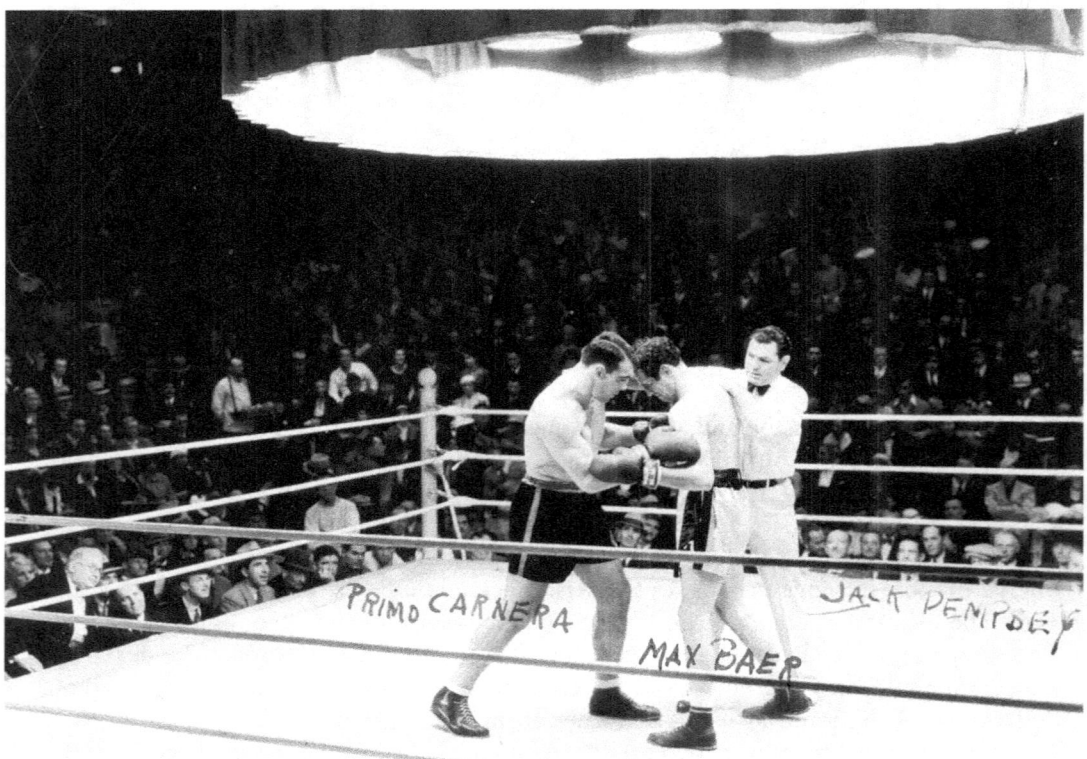

The movie *The Prizefighter and the Lady* predated the actual title fight, featuring Max Baer as Steve Morgan, Primo Carnera as himself, and Jack Dempsey as referee. The studio had to build a massive set when Madison Square Garden refused to let the fight scene be staged there (courtesy David Bergin).

publicly. In fact, Max didn't score too many points with the actresses while on set. It appeared that the film people didn't "take to his kidding." He chirped: "Hi'ya baby," the first time he met Joan Crawford. And when he tried to help the spicy actress Lupe Velez up from the floor one day, she responded that he shouldn't do that, her husband Johnny might not like it. "Who the heck is Johnny?" asked Baer, knowing full well that husband Johnny Weissmuller was the famous Olympic athlete who won five gold medals, set over 60 world records, and played Tarzan in the movies. Then he added, smiling, "Oh, he's just a swimmer."[10] It was his way of kidding, but his wisecracks were not well received by the Hollywood set.

Working with Carnera on set gave Baer insight about his future opponent's size and reactions, physically and emotionally. Baer learned what would get under his skin. And of his boxing technique, Baer realized that Carnera only used his right hand to block, and that his 270-plus pounds were likely to wrestle you to the ground in a clinch. Baer got the feel for his reach and balance. He also discovered that Carnera wasn't a natural fighter. He had only been taught certain moves, moves that Baer memorized in the film takes. Baer realized that for the title fight, he had to come up with new ring tricks that Carnera didn't expect and for which he had no defense. He also learned that the giant couldn't hurt him.

With a successful movie behind him and a boxing title ahead of him, Max (like many famous people in the news) was a magnet for lawsuits. At the end of March 1934, Bee Starr, a circus trapeze artist in New York, sued Baer for $150,000. Her damages were necessary to repair her broken heart. Baer shot back that he would sue her for damages to his reputation.

Another lawsuit was settled in court regarding payments for jewelry he bought for Dorothy. His bill totaled over $5000, but when she contemplated divorce, Baer quit making payments. He tried to return some of it, but he still owed $954. The judge ordered him to pay the bill along with court costs and attorney fees.

John Lardner for the *LA Times* said that Max's taste in girls, clothes, and cars had cost him a pretty penny in lawsuits. He estimated that Baer's legal bills totaled over $33,000 before the title fight. Also costly were Max's "Hollywood-styled" suits, set off with shirts of baby blue, and gray or brown suede shoes. One reporter said his only rivals in the sartorial business were Jimmy McLarnin and Kid Chocolate.

Shortly after the film, Baer was offered a two-year movie contract. Jack Dempsey gave Max an ultimatum: decide if you want to be a film star or a prizefighter. Jack told him that while he may be the leading challenger, he wasn't ready for Carnera. "He was last summer," Dempsey said, "but he hasn't been in a gymnasium in six months. He isn't even ready for Schmeling, the man he knocked out last June. He has become soft.... I've gone into all this with Max. I've told him that without his ring ability, he wouldn't and couldn't make a nickel on the stage, but it's like talking to a child. He's dazzled by all this glitter and excitement."[11]

Max turned down the film offer. "I love to fight, and after I whip Carnera I will go back to Hollywood."[12]

On January 26, Benny Franklin, who had promoted three other world championship bouts in Baltimore, offered a $100,000 purse for a Baer-Schmeling rematch (offering Baer $75,000 and Schmeling $25,000).[13] But Dempsey, acting as Baer's co-manager/trainer/promoter, would not risk letting anyone fight Baer before Carnera.

At the end of the fistic wars of 1933, Max Baer was hailed as the "Miracle Man,"

Max shakes hands with engineer T.M. Stine before boarding for his trip east for his chance at the world title.

designated by *The Ring*'s consensus of 104 boxing writers as the fighter who had done most in 1933 to stir the imagination of fans and help boost the game out of the doldrums. Now, the only match anyone wanted to see was a Baer-Carnera fight. Finally, Grantland Rice could announce that heavyweight boxing had turned a corner as a result of Max Baer. He said, "After all, a faint streak of light has begun to show through the deep shadow of the fight game.... Baer is still the one big card that would mean a big gate. He is now the top card in the game."[14]

In January of 1934, Chicago bid for the Carnera-Baer title fight. But by the end of the month, Jimmy Johnston, the Garden's matchmaker, shocked everyone by saying that all negotiations with Baer, Hoffman, and Dempsey were off. The reason? Johnston found it impossible to tie Max up in a Garden contract in case he won the championship. After two years of elimination battles, and after beating Schmeling for a chance at the title, Baer now heard Johnston telling the press that "the challenger won't be Max Baer."[15] It was Johnston's way of enforcing "his way or the highway." Johnston would let King Levinsky fight Carnera for the title instead. And to pump more fights into the Garden, he told Levinsky that he would have to fight Charley Massera and Walter Neusel before he would get a chance at Carnera.

Then, Johnston told Carnera he had to fight Tommy Loughran. Johnston's masterfully inept matchmaking, or spiteful avoidance of the Carnera-Baer title fight, cost the Garden dearly. The Carnera-Loughran bout for the championship on March 1, 1934—Carnera's first title defense—would go down in the record books as was one of the smallest gates in heavyweight title history: only 15,000 people attended, with a third "on the house." And the champion's surprising unanimous decision over Loughran, after landing only two clean punches in the entire fight, smelled. The gist of the battle was that Carnera simply used his weight to push his opponent around the ring and attempt to club him to death. Carnera was repeatedly warned of the foul technique that many of the heavyweights used: he held with one hand and clubbed with the other.

Only in rounds 14 and 15 did it appear that Carnera connected consistently enough, "with a display of longshoreman's tactics," to have Loughran in any real distress.[16]

After turning down a movie contract and with no immediate fights on the horizon, Max told reporters that if Dempsey couldn't find him a fight, he might go on a barnstorming tour with him. Eventually, both Johnston and Dempsey/Hoffman caved. Johnston could not risk his job at the Garden with another disastrous title fight. In a mutual agreement, Baer would meet Carnera for a chance at the title, but Baer would owe Johnston his first title defense if he won the championship.

On April 1, 1934, Max and his entourage left California for Camp Baer, his title-fight training location, at Asbury Park, New Jersey. On the way he boxed in exhibitions at Tulsa, Oklahoma; Kansas City; and Jefferson City, Missouri.

Primo Carnera, June 14, 1934, Madison Square Garden, New York

While in training, Baer ran seven to eight miles daily in the morning. He typically sparred eight rounds, two each with partners Ray Lazer, Ceil Harris, Al Truman and Dynamite Jackson. He also had his brother Buddy in camp who was now 18 years old, 6'5" and 246 pounds, and aspired to follow in his footsteps.

There were several brothers in the fight game: the Dundees, Zivics, Conns, Petrolles, Attells, Braddocks, and Gibbons. On August 15, 1938, the 6 Finazzo brothers of Baltimore made Ripley's famous "Believe It Or Not," by fighting on the same card. Every bout had a Finazzo in it. But no brothers had held the same gloved title. Back in the bare-knuckle days, Jem Ward, the "black diamond" of England, held the heavyweight crown for nine years before handing it off to his brother Nick, who held it from 1835 to 1841. The Baer brothers would make history if each could win the gloved heavyweight crown. This became their mission.

When Max Baer arrived at camp, he weighed 215 pounds. Dempsey made it known to reporters that he was going to stay on at camp to whip the playboy into shape. So the uncorroborated story goes.... Max commented that he could beat Dempsey. Dempsey wanted to show him otherwise. An unknown source told Biddy Bishop, one year after the event, that Dempsey got in the ring with Max to make his point that Max wasn't ready for Carnera. Max joked and said "he would go easy and not hurt an old man."[17] Max clowned. Dempsey was serious. Jack waited for an opening and socked Max on the jaw with a hard left hook, knocking him cold for 20 minutes. When asked why this story was never published when it happened, the teller of the tale said because it would have "ruined the title fight."[18]

During his training camp for the championship, Max performed in the radio drama *Taxi*.

Baer killed two birds with one stone at his training camp. He performed in a radio drama called *Taxi*, airing three times a week. Baer played a cab driver with pugilistic aspirations. Before the 14th episode actually aired, Max joked, speaking into the microphone: "This program comes to you courtesy of the Nudist Colony. Your announcer is Willie Stripp." When asked if he ever became nervous in front of a mike, he said, "The only mike that ever made me nervous was Jack Dempsey's left hook," indicating there may have been some truth to the story told about the training-camp knockout.[19] Max enjoyed doing the broadcast, and income from the show helped to pay camp expenses.

Studio officials were pleased with the results and said that should Max turn out to be a "palooka" in the fight business, "the boy has got the stuff ... he could easily make the grade as a radio actor."[20]

Back in Hollywood, a few starlets were asked about Max's chances in the New York title fight. Lupe Velez Weissmuller said, "I doan geeve a damn who whips." Miss Harlow said, "Really, I'm not interested."[21] Dorothy Dunbar said, "Maxie's ring career interests [me] no more than yesterday's firecracker which has fizzled out."[22]

Others did have an opinion about the outcome. Jack Hurley, manager of Billy Petrolle, said that Carnera will "lick Baer without a great deal of difficulty."[23] Dempsey predicted a win by kayo with his right hand to the chin within the 15 rounds, after Baer first weakened Carnera with body blows. Former Champion Tommy Burns compared Carnera's boxing skill to that of Jim Corbett. Even Madame Senora Conchita Escobar, Gypsy fortuneteller who set up shop at Epsom Downs, England, for the Derby, was contacted by cable for her psychic opinion: "Baer by a knockout."[24] All agreed that Carnera had tremendous strength, good fencing skills, and a strong left. Most importantly, he had a determination to win because he had a burning hatred for Baer. He thought Baer made fun of him on the Hollywood movie set. Dempsey had the last word: "I expect a great fight and rich receipts. With that, boxing will obtain a good start toward the return to the golden days it enjoyed under the guidance of the prince of promoters, Tex Rickard."[25]

Two days prior, knockout bets favored Baer, but (like the results from the Loughran bout) the odds were 2 to 1 for Carnera's getting the decision if the fight went the full 15 rounds.

Because both boxers had injured men in the ring who had later died, the New York Commission required extensive physical exams. Max and Primo were examined by three doctors: William Walker, Vincent Nardiello, and Morris Beyer. Commissioner Bill Brown insisted that Baer wasn't in shape and had not trained properly enough for the fight. (This statement infuriated Max.) Even though the doctors found both fighters in splendid physical condition (Carnera weighed 263 pounds and Baer, 210), Brown maintained, "I'm sticking to my original opinion, that Baer has no right in there Thursday night."[26] Max just smiled, knowing that his humor and playful banter annoyed both Brown and Carnera. While the two boxers were stripped to the waist, they posed for pictures. Max turned to Carnera and started plucking hairs from Primo's chest: "She loves me! She loves me not!" "The roar that came up out of Carnera's throat was like an earthquake under a mountain. He wasn't fooling."[27] The fight almost started in the commission's office.

The next day, a reporter who had witnessed the physical declared that Maxie was in better shape for the bout than his opponent, considering Carnera was suffering from a cold. Baer showed no signs of anything, he said, "including serious thought."[28] The odds shifted 7 to 5 for Baer.

The day of the fight, Carnera drove into New York from his training camp at Pompton Lakes and settled into the Hotel Victoria, his favorite spot. Baer was secluded in a home of a friend.

Ringside tickets the day of the fight sold for $25 with seats that had been extended to row 34. Scalpers were getting $60 to $70 for ringside tickets. Not since Dempsey-Tunney in Chicago were so many press passes requested—about 700. Half of these would be given in the ringside section. The new Eighth Avenue subway from Manhattan was expected to run every minute.

The main event was scheduled to begin at 10 p.m. with preliminaries starting at 8 p.m. The preliminaries were all heavyweights and included a name that Baer would meet in the future, James J. Braddock.[29] By 8 o'clock only a handful of people had filled the vast stadium. But by the time of the final preliminary, it looked like 60,000 people had taken their seats.

In the Griffin-Braddock preliminary, John Charles "Corn" Griffin was supposed to be a "coming sensation," while Braddock was seen as ring-worn. Both Griffin and Braddock were knocked to the canvas in the second round. Braddock floored Griffin twice in the third before the referee stepped in to stop the fight. While Braddock was paid only $250 for this preliminary battle, the showing would pave his way to the heavyweight title in only one year.

While Max was in his dressing room waiting for the main event, two unsavory characters came in to have a serious talk with him. Ancil Hoffman ran them off. Since Carnera was owned by the mob, Hoffman knew Baer would not get a fair shot by the judges. He told Max that he was going to have to knock Carnera out to win.

The main event was broadcast in three languages to an international audience and across the U.S. by the National Broadcasting Company (NBC) over 88 stations. Graham McNamee described the action on the radio. Max Baer's mother was in Denver listening to the fight on the radio with family.

Celebrities of all sorts—political, stage and screen, and boxing—were in attendance. The first champions to be introduced by Joe Humphreys were heavyweights Tommy Burns, Jack Johnson, Jack Dempsey, Gene Tunney, and Jack Sharkey. Additional notables were introduced in the ring: Jack Root, Benny Leonard, Willie Ritchie, Tommy Loughran, Jimmie McLarnin, Steve Hamas, and Ray Impelletiere.

Carnera was first to enter the ring, wearing a blue bathrobe and some said a "worried look." Carnera biographer Joseph Page reported a thwarted assassination attempt of Carnera when he reached ringside. A man stood waiting for the champion to climb into the ring and then brandished a gun. Carnera's seconds struggled with the man, and apparently snatched the gun away. Goodtime Walter Friedman, friend of Carnera's money-team of Owen Madden and Billy Duffy, sat guard at the ring for the entire bout.[30] Apparently, someone saw an opportunity to retaliate against the mob bosses while Duffy was in jail for tax evasion. Boxers were always in the cross hairs of those in control.

Baer came through the crowd about five minutes later wearing the orchid-colored bathrobe he wore for the film, *The Prizefighter and the Lady*. Across the back was embroidered in large black letters the name "Steve Morgan," hero of the make-believe title.

Jack Dempsey thought the Baer-Carnera fight mirrored his fight with the giant Willard in 1919. Both Dempsey and Baer fights would end in savage beatings of the respective champions. Dan Parker called it an "11-round classic of ring butchery ... a strange combination of buffoonery and savagery." Max just "toyed" with the man, said Parker, who "left to his own resources, wouldn't have harmed a flea."[31]

Max tended to fight in flurries, which made his hard punch and "survival of the fittest" style so unpredictable. But the simple story of this fight was that Carnera was knocked down so many times that reporters stopped counting. There was no question about Carnera's gameness. In none of the knockdowns did Carnera take advantage of the nine-second count. Carnera went to the canvas 11 times in 11 rounds (6 times the result of a blow, 3 from slips, and 2 when Carnera caught Baer's left hand and pulled him down in a fall). Several times Baer hit Carnera next to the ropes where he would have fallen to the canvas had he not caught and steadied himself on the ropes.

Baer came out for the first round with a serious look on his face. His strategy was to circle to the left to avoid Carnera's big right hand. The Italian giant came to the middle to box. He hit Baer in the mouth with three lefts and Baer lashed back furiously with a left and right to the body. Carnera feinted and Baer's right hand came back to smash him to the floor. Carnera hurt his ankle in the fall. He was up before the count. With Carnera unsteady on an injured ankle, Max knocked him into the ropes.

Baer came out for the second round ready to put the kill on his opponent. But as he was landing a right hand to Carnera's head, Carnera locked Max's left hand under his right arm and they both went down. Again Baer crashed a right to Carnera's head, and they both fell to the floor. Baer stalked and Carnera pushed Max into the ropes for the champion's first real show of aggression.

In the third round, Baer sent a smashing right uppercut into the body. Carnera clubbed back. Then Max sent him down with a long right to the temple. He was up at the count of one.

Fortunately no one landed on the canvas in rounds 4 through 7.

By the fourth round, Carnera had regained his faculties and kept attacking ceaselessly with his left. Baer came out in the fifth and surprised Carnera by shuffling his feet in Carnera's rosin. Baer's attacks in rounds 5 and 6 were to the body. Carnera could scarcely stand but was still lobbing punches.

If anyone questioned Carnera's boxing ability, those doubts were put to rest in the next three rounds. In the seventh, Carnera chased Baer to the ropes with straight lefts. At one point Referee Donovan cautioned Carnera about his backhanded punch. In the eighth round, Baer came snarling back with rights and lefts to the body and head. With a left hook to the face, Baer made a stream of blood trickle down Carnera's face. Baer went after him again, and as Carnera moved to avoid his lunge, he fell to the ground. He rose quickly and Donovan called a low blow on Baer, which cost him the round.

In the ninth, they fought toe-to-toe with Carnera having the slight advantage. Carnera was beginning to weaken, but was still fencing Baer off with his left. Baer noticed that an elderly gentleman in the press row, sitting next to Frank Graham, had slumped over in his seat. He seemed to have experienced a "slight heart attack." When Max returned to his corner for the one-minute break, he screamed at his seconds, "Quick, get a doctor for Harry down there." Max was concerned about his friend, reporter Harry Smith from the *San Francisco Chronicle*, who had come to New York to see the fight. Then the bell rang and Baer had to attend to business in the ring. Once the round was over, Max leaned over the ropes and asked repeatedly, "How's Harry? Take care of him.... Take care of him...."[32] Baer kept a watchful eye on Harry at every rest break. A doctor attended to Harry Smith, but once revived, the reporter refused to leave his post and scored the rest of the bout.

In the tenth round Baer came out with a scowl on his face and crouched as a Dempsey-like panther. Carnera reached for him with an open glove, and the referee warned Carnera to close his glove. They fought in close, with Baer hammering away at Carnera's body. Carnera grabbed Baer and hammered back at his head. As they came out of the clinch, Baer dropped him. The referee went over and stood for at least ten seconds in front of Carnera, blocking him from Baer. (It would be an unfair advantage that Baer would talk about for the rest of his life.) The crowd was enraged and yelled, "Get out of the way! What are you doing? Let him hit him."[33] Then Donovan moved and Baer went in and knocked Carnera to the floor. Donovan had counted to 4 when the bell rang. One newspaperman jumped into the ring to ask the referee if the fight was over. Donovan said, "Yes." Then he asked if Baer had won, and again Donovan said, "Yes." Donovan was corrected. Carnera was saved by the bell and the fight was on again.

Baer knocked Carnera down twice in the eleventh and he came up both times for a two-count. Carnera flung his hands aimlessly, but couldn't connect. Baer battered him so severely that the referee stepped in to stop the fight. This time the fight was over. Later, Donovan was questioned if Primo had asked him to stop the fight, and he said, "Yes." But most sportswriters at ringside believed that Primo was too dazed to request or answer anything. What was evident was that Primo wanted to fight to the end, proving just how game he was throughout.

After Baer's arm was raised in victory, Max bolted out of the ring and put his arms around Harry B. Smith to make sure he was fine. "Is there anything I can do? I'll be right back...."[34] Here was a 25-year-old boxer who had just won the world heavyweight title,

Primo Carnera went to the canvas 11 times in 11 rounds when Baer won the championship, June 14, 1934 (photograph by W. Wallace).

explained Oakland reporter Art Cohn, and all he could think about was the reporter in the first row.

Baer left the ring wearing the Steve Morgan robe. The next movie rendition of this fight, twenty years later, would give a more sinister reflection of the story.

Baer would never get over Referee Arthur Donovan's actions in the ring that night. It would be an ongoing feud for the rest of Baer's life. He said that Donovan "stepped in front of my right hand no less than five times in the first round. If he hadn't done that I might have flattened Primo then." He said he didn't question Donovan's honesty as referee; he just thought that "he lost his head in the excitement."[35] Later, he would question the referee's honesty.

Amazingly, on Referee Donovan's scorecard, he gave the last round to Carnera, even after he had been knocked down and counted out. On Donovan's scorecard, Carnera had won almost every round. Baer was incredulous. Donovan accounted for the discrepancy by saying that it was his belief that Baer had fouled Carnera in almost every round. But writers at ringside said that Baer fought a clean fight and had not resorted to "objectionable boxing." On only one occasion could *New York Times* writer James P. Dawson point to anything that might be charged against him "in the State Athletic Commission's book of fouls, and this was accidental. In the eighth round the Californian was erratic with a sweeping left for the body."[36] Donovan would not hear the last of the repercussions from this fight from Baer and Hoffman.

From ringside, Max sent his mother a wire saying she was his only sweetheart, the one woman who never sued him. Baer was escorted by a line of policemen who formed a flying wedge to get him through the crowd. Baer said the walk to his dressing room was the toughest part of the battle. Jack Dempsey was waiting for him in the dressing room. Baer grabbed Dempsey's head and kissed him on the cheek. They shared an inside joke going back to the Levinsky fight when Baer surprised and unnerved Jack with a kiss on his cheek after the win. Dempsey yelled, "Sweetheart! That was the greatest fight I've ever seen. Bar none!"[37]

Then Max spotted his father: "Dad, didn't I tell ya? Look, not even a scratch. Only this," he said, and pointed to a bruise over his right eye. They kissed. Max was kissing everyone, including one newspaperman. "Say," Max said ironically to the newspapermen, "I shouldn't have been in the ring tonight, I wasn't in shape!"[38] It was a reference to New York Commissioner Bill Brown, who wanted to have the fight postponed, believing that the challenger wasn't prepared for the fight. As it turned out, Baer had put on some donnybrooks of sparring sessions and other activities before the fight, meant as a ruse to build up Carnera's false confidence. He did the same when Bill Brown visited his training camp.

Baer had done this on other occasions, when in fact he had trained hard. Many believed that he went into fights ill-prepared, that he disdained training. But it was a role that he played well to confuse his opponents. But as in the case at Asbury Park, his training was part stunt meant to be misreported. In fact, one person, after seeing Baer's workout one day, wrote to the sports editor of a newspaper to ask if Baer really trained this poorly. It was all part of his plan of attack.

Baer's trainer Dolph Thomas told Ronald Wagoner after the bout, "[Baer's] a natural fighter. And what an actor. He's not a hard man to train because he possessed such a great physique. If he had trained for two weeks more he couldn't have been in better condition for Primo."[39] In fact, it was trainer Mike Cantwell who said that for his training against Carnera, it wasn't girls or the bright lights that distracted him; it was practice for his radio show. Even after Cantwell turned off the lights at 9 p.m., Baer would practice memorizing his lines and test out different emphasis and gestures. Cantwell confirmed that there was no playboy stuff at the camp.

Max and his manager Ancil Hoffman had protested the choice of Arthur Donovan as referee. Fearing a negative outcome for Max, Ancil Hoffman told his friend Judge William Pettite that before the fight, he had positioned a couple of men ready to swipe the judges' scorecards immediately after the fight was over. Later in the evening, Hoffman showed Max those scorecards. Sure enough, if the decision had gone to the scorecards, Baer would not have won the title. The Garden had stacked the cards against Baer if the champion had gone the limit.[40] Baer's ire over the situation would remain throughout his boxing career.

As he sat on his rubbing table back in his dressing room, Baer was hammered with questions. He interrupted, "Will you fellows let me talk?" Baer said, "Primo's a nice chap, and he's got lots of heart, a lot more than I thought he had. I pleaded with Donovan to stop the fight. Primo was such a dead cinch to wallop that I was afraid I might crack something back here."[41] He pointed to the base of his skull, a gesture to his unmentionable fear of killing another opponent.

After his rubdown on the table in his dressing room, Max raised himself up and said, "Somebody bring the new champion a bottle of beer."[42] When asked if any of Carnera's punches hurt him, he joked, "You can't hurt a Bear!" Then his demeanor changed and he said of Carnera, "Primo is a good strong fighter. He is as clean as they make them. I don't like to say I'm glad he lost but I'm sure tickled I brought the title back to this country.... I was kind of surprised when he got up the third time in the first round but after that I felt I could beat him any time."[43] The only harm Max admitted from the fight was a chipped tooth.

Carnera sat in his dressing room, the left side of his face swollen and his ankle iced and bandaged. He wept like a child. His seconds tried to console him, but he interrupted them saying, "I lose. Don't you see? I lose the championship, that's all." Then he fell back into racked sobs, pausing only to say as an afterthought, "But I didn't ask Donovan to stop it. I didn't quit. I'd have fought until I couldn't move, but I'd never give up."[44] It was true, he never gave up. He was in visible pain when he walked to the shower. His manager Louis Soresi said that his injured ankle had handicapped him for the fight's duration. Two days later, X-rays revealed a fractured right ankle. Seen in the pictures was a "clean cut chip off the ankle bone."[45] In addition, he had a torn ligament in his right leg. Primo said that the injury to his ankle occurred when he went down in the first round.

Out on his farm near Burbank, California, Jim Jeffries had this to say: "So Maxie was out of condition, was he, and a clown and a bum? I wanted him to win and I'm mighty glad he did. This ought to prove that Max Baer is a real fighter and a real champion."[46] When asked about the two fighters, California promoter Sunny Jim Coffroth called the two boxers "Cheese Chumps." "Both should be disposed of. One is a piece of gorgonzola and the other is a piece of limburger."[47] Back in Denver, Baer's mother responded that she knew Max could do it: "God bless you Mickey boy." She said that Max had told her he was going to go after Carnera's solar plexus. She said she cried once when Carnera had the best, but said, "[Max] can take it."[48]

With this fight, Max Baer was credited not only for saving the Garden, but for saving boxing and bringing the title back to the United States. A crowd of 55,000 paid $428,392.80 to see the fight. The Free Milk Fund for Babies received 10 percent off the top after taxes. Baer's 25 percent amounted to $81,305.44. Carnera's share at 40 percent was $129,088.60. After taxes and his mafia managers' take, Carnera was paid $47.07, a fact hallmarked in the movie *The Harder They Fall*.[49]

Immediately after he won, Max was reported to have been given a $100,000 thirteen-week contract (a number which seemed high) to do a radio broadcast in New York until late July. In addition, two Hollywood studios offered Baer a chance to play a leading role in a film, upon which one actor was quoted, "If that guy comes back to this lot, they'll have to enlarge the front gate to fit his head!"[50]

Only five years after his first recorded fight, Max Baer became the 13th heavyweight champion of the world, a tremendous feat but a very unlucky number.[51]

Dempsey's fight strategy worked: Baer hit him in the body until his guard dropped. Robert Edgren, no admirer of Baer back in California, summed up Baer's style: he has a wallop in his right hand, "when he's able to land it, but no defense, he blocks with his chin. He has plenty of punch resistance and that's what saves him.... If he lands his punch he wins, if he doesn't he loses. He feints by making faces. That worked with Carnera. It was really funny to see Baer suddenly squat, stamp both heels on the ground, make a ferocious face, like a Maori warrior, and scare Carnera into jumping back two yards. It even gave Baer a laugh."[52] Edgren went on to compare Baer to other champions. He would have had an even break with John L. Sullivan, but Jim Corbett would have danced away from him. Fitzsimmons wouldn't have been caught by his left. Jeffries was too fast and

Seven • The Heavyweight Championship, Carnera, 1934

hit too hard in his day, and Dempsey could use either hand with only a few inches to drive in a knockout.

His showmanship was part of his boxing style and public appeal. By now he had accumulated even more ring names: the "California Adonis," the "Iron-Fisted Destroyer" (the same as Dempsey's), the "Big Mouthpiece," "Nabob of the Night Clubs," the "Sun Dodger," and the "Big Lip from Livermore" (the Big Lip from Louisville, Muhammad Ali, was still three decades away). Max's comment: "Call me anything you like but come out and see me."[53] He was going to get them coming to see him whether they were for him or not.

Now Baer was not only the undeniable champion, he was a draw—one who could certainly put on a show. Edward Burns of the *Chicago Tribune* ran the first newspaper serial biography on the new heavyweight boxing champion of the world. The tribute ran seven days. Burns predicted, "Readers of sports pages are likely to read and hear much of the madcap champion within the next twelve months. It is freely predicted that Max Adelbert throughout the year will be the central figure in bigger and better jams, financial and romantic, than any sports character in the memory of man."[54]

His ring earnings at this point were estimated to be about $200,000, and all he had to show for it was experience, a home in San Leandro purchased for his parents after they left Oakland, two pending lawsuits (breach of promise and managerial), and the installment payments for two big automobiles.

Baer and Ancil Hoffman wanted to give Carnera a rematch, but Jimmy Johnston denied it. In late October, Johnston tried again to woo Baer away from Hoffman, but Hoffman was already in negotiations for another fight. Baer would never again fight Carnera, although later, after Primo had been dumped by his managers, Max would find him jobs as a wrestler and set up an exhibition match for the two of them.

By contract, Jimmy Johnston owned Baer's first title defense, and to get as much financial mileage from Baer's win as possible, he wanted to set up another series of elimination tournaments at Madison Square Garden to determine who would meet Baer. Promoters and contenders were tired of all the elimination battles. Baer's management wanted a fight quickly to free Baer up to fight again under a Dempsey promotion, something Johnston did not want. Carnera's management wanted a fight in October, arguing that he had been overtrained for the bout, went into the fight with a cold, and broke a bone in his ankle when he was knocked down in the early rounds. Neither of those battles would occur.

Nine days after the fight, Primo was still recovering in the Columbus Hospital in New York with a broken ankle. Both Buddy and Max visited. Max grinned and they shook hands. The two men's fists were almost equal in size. "I want you to meet my brother Buddy," said Max. Primo waved his hand for his own brother to step up. "Meet my brother," he said proudly.[55] Then Max whispered into Primo's ear that he had guaranteed payment for his hospital stay. Max returned to the foot of the bed, pulled back the sheet, and grabbed a toe on his good foot, "This little piggie went to market...." Primo bellowed, "Leave go them toes!" "OK, OK," Max said playfully. The Baer brothers stayed a few more minutes and left with, each saying, "Take care of yourself."[56]

Max Baer was not the only boxer tied up in a breach-of-promise lawsuit. Carnera faced a judgment of $15,000 for the same to a London waitress. He also owed the American government $33,290 in income tax. Prior to the fight, John Lardner reported that Primo had been sailing between Italy and the U.S. once a month to attend his hearings

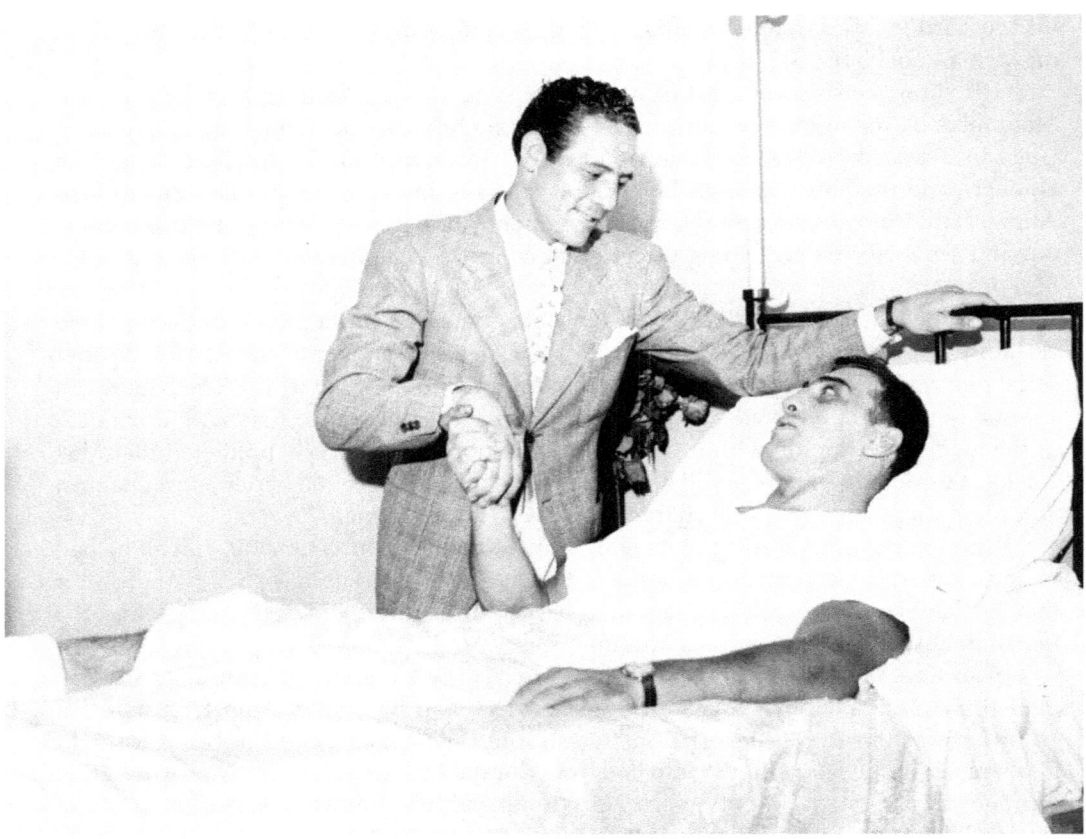

Max Baer visited Carnera at the hospital after winning the championship. Max told Primo that he would pay the hospital bill (courtesy David Bergin).

in bankruptcy court.[57] On top of that, Italy's Premier Mussolini was not happy with the outcome of the championship and called upon the Italian Boxing Federation to investigate the circumstances of the title loss. It was too little, too late to help the Italian fighter.

The night after the hospital visit with Carnera, Max performed on a radio show replacing Claudette Colbert on the 10:30 WEAF *Hall of Fame*. He played the lead in a dramatic sketch and sang in his melodic baritone voice. The next night he attended the Cort Theater to watch a prizefight comedy, *The Milky Way*. While there he was mobbed for autographs. He remained in New York for six weeks doing vaudeville and night club appearances, including one with Babe Ruth at the New York State Fair. Boxing had made him a true celebrity.

Despite Max Baer having received *The Ring* magazine's 1934 rating of "Outstanding Fighter of the Year," and being listed as the number-one heavyweight in his class alone, Max was prohibited by Jimmy Johnston from defending his title for one year. Max would spend his championship year fighting in exhibitions, on the road like a circus entertainer.

Eight

Championship Year, 1934 to 1935

Ancil Hoffman had promised Max that if he trained hard for his championship battle against Carnera, he could take a brief rest afterward to enjoy some female companionship. Now, as the world's champion, he appeared to start at the top to claim his reward. Mae West, with her sexy request, "Why don't you come up sometime and see me?" invited Max to dinner. After the rendezvous, reporters asked him what the pair discussed. Without a wink or smile, he replied, "European diplomatic events."[1] Max had been called the male Mae West, but it was reported that his true heart interest was with Jean Harlow (married and divorced three times at the age of 23). Harlow denied any interest in Max and the gossip quickly became yesterday's news.

Ancil Hoffman had planned for Max to make his first title defense with King Levinsky in Chicago on December 28, 1934, and afterward continue with title bouts throughout the next year with anyone who qualified. Hoffman wanted to capitalize on several big fights while public interest in the champion was hot. But Jimmy Johnston cooled the plan, telling Hoffman that as the Garden's matchmaker, he was the only one who had the contractual right to schedule a title defense—a right that was at his discretion. Johnston was not at all forgiving about Max's refusal to jump ship from his California management.

Johnston needed to control the fight market. His job at the Garden depended on it. For the time being, he would schedule elimination battles, which left Baer out of the picture for any big fights.

Ancil Hoffman, Max and Buddy (whom Hoffman now managed) took to the road in a "Championship" exhibition tour around the country. Max would fight four-round matches using 6-ounce gloves, and Buddy would begin building up his own ring reputation in the shadows of his older brother. It wouldn't be as financially lucrative as a title defense, but the trio would be out in the public making money. These exhibition battles would take a toll on Max's hands and influence his future in ways no one could have predicted.

Back in November when Max was under the impression that he needed to be ready to defend his title in December, he advertised nationally for sparring partners. Max always had difficulty attracting local sparring mates. Most were afraid to get in the ring with him. In the early 1930s the going rate for sparring partners was $15 per week, but the scarcity of prospects for many contenders upped the ante.

This author's father, Norman "Ike" Aycock, responded to Baer's solicitation, boarded a train from Donna, Texas, a small town in the Rio Grande Valley, and headed west. He had been fighting in South Texas and along the Mexican border, which had been the "Wildcat's" bread and butter. He would take the Baer offer and survey the possibilities in San Francisco, where he hoped the fight scene in Northern California would be better than what he had experienced in New Orleans. He had visited the Crescent City hoping to find matches there, but found only the mob. He was offered plenty of bouts, but had to agree to fight to orders (in fixed fights) and work as a bodyguard or enforcer in the mob's protection racket, offers he turned down. He hoped the situation in the Bay Area didn't carry the extra baggage.

In early December, Aycock became a sparring partner for Max for what was expected to be his first title defense, initially projected to be with King Levinsky. While only a welter-turned-middleweight, Ike was known for his fast hands and excellent footwork. Max liked to train with middleweights for their speed. My father said that he showed up in California with what must have seemed a rather pitiful-looking pair of gloves and trunks. Everything about him spelled Depression. Also, it must have surprised Max when he first saw Ike's hands.

Norman "Ike" Aycock, sparring partner for Max Baer in December 1934.

The Texan was rather unique in that he boxed with a missing left thumb. He had chopped it off with an ax, down to the nub on the palm, at the age of nine when he was squaring timbers into railroad ties for a penny apiece in Troy, Mississippi. Max probably felt sympathy for a man who, without the stabilizing force and guidance of a left thumb when throwing a punch, managed to get as far as he did in the sport.[2] Baer paid him $15 a session, top wages for sparring partners, which included two to three rounds per day with the champion. It was a nice paycheck, considering his previous club fights around South Texas averaged $25 with an occasional bonus—a percentage of the gate—which encouraged boxers to establish a following.

Most men were afraid to get in the ring with Max because of his killer reputation. But Max was kind and generous to his sparring partners, and always funny, as quick-witted as he was fast with his hands. Many boxers at that time, including Max, liked to display their hand

Eight • Championship Year, 1934 to 1935

speed by catching flies. When not sparring, the guys held fly-catching contests (with small bets) to see who was quicker or who could catch the most flies. Why all the fly-catching in the gym? It demonstrated and developed fast hands. The old boxers believed that a short jab had to be as quick, accurate, and powerful as the action of catching a fly.

Max never wanted to hurt a spar-mate. He could pull his punches. But my father told me that at any time when he was in the ring with the champion, he respected and always feared Max's unleashed power. Baer could have taken off any middleweight's head and killed him with an errant blow. On occasion, Max would look for an opening and send over a fast punch, intentionally missing his opponent's head or face by a fraction of an inch. My father recalled, almost fearfully, the sound that came from Baer's glove whizzing past his ear.

Recall of that sound came up again in our family. After World War II, when my mother's brother returned from Navy service in the Pacific, my father tried to teach him how to box. Neil Elder told me that the first time he heard that sound coming from my father's glove whizzing past his ear, he said he was finished with boxing. "No more. I'm done," he said, and walked away. He didn't want to hear that ominous sound ever again. Training with an experienced professional was far too dangerous for him. Here was a man who was no coward, who had sat in the back seat of a scout plane during every major battle in the Pacific Theater until the war's end, and who knew that if his plane had to make an emergency landing in the ocean, there would be no rescue—and he thought that the force of my father's boxing glove sounded threatening as it whizzed past his ear in a practice session! It gave me a true respect for that sound my father heard from the action of Max Baer's immense fist.[3]

Other sparring partners were equally respectful of the power of the champions while training. In 1933, Joe Louis visited his old gym in Detroit and selected five of his former teammates to be his sparring partners. Eddie Futch was one who politely declined the offer. When Futch was asked why he turned down a lucrative $10 a round, he said, "Yeah, but that's not going to be enough to pay your hospital bills."[4] Men like Joe Louis and Max Baer could inflict significant damage, even when they were just sparring. Max broke Buddy's ribs twice when they were just "playing around."

My father greatly respected Max Baer and enjoyed his time in the ring with him. Most importantly, my father couldn't say enough about Baer's big heart. "Max would give you the shirt off his back," he said. In fact, Max would give his boxing friends one of his suits when he thought it would fit. He never held a grudge, and he loved to entertain people. My father said he was always giving people something special to make their lives better. When his service with Baer ended, Max replaced Ike's old gloves with a new set of the best hand-crafted, kid-leather boxing gloves, made by Sol Levinson, ones my father cherished for the rest of his life. He signed the box to "Ike Aycock, Your old pal, Max Baer." He had begun to write the inscription to Norman, but changed it to read Ike instead. "Old pal" was a designation Max used only for close friends and sparring partners.

Even after my father became afflicted with dementia-pugilistica, he always remembered Max Baer with fondness as a gentleman, and he never spoke of him without great respect. Max truly loved everyone and everyone loved him.

Max had a tune-up exhibition with Les Kennedy in Kansas City, Missouri, on December 14, before he met Levinsky. On December 28, 1934, in Chicago, Baer met the "Kingfish" for what had been originally intended to be a title fight, but which now was

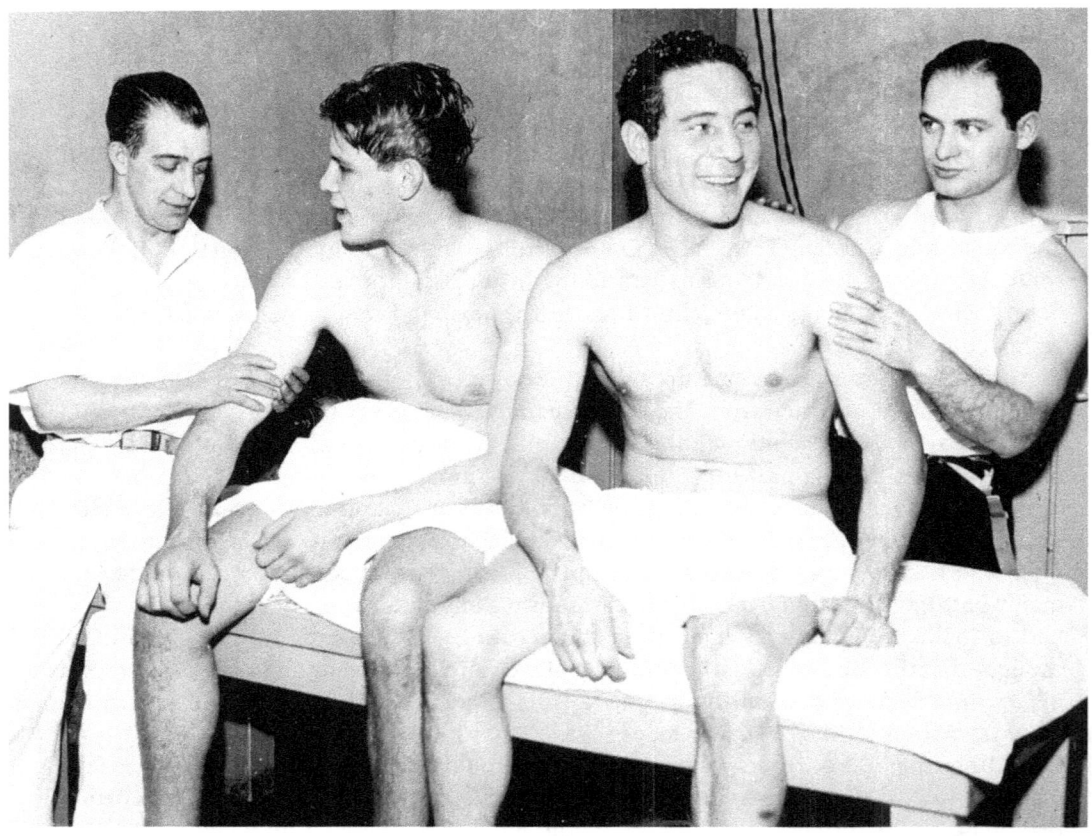

Buddy and Max on the rubbing table in preparation for their fights in Chicago. Max's fight with Levinsky was supposed to have been his first title defense, but those plans were canceled by Jimmy Johnston. Buddy fought Gene Stanton. Both Baers scored knockouts. *Left to right:* **Scotty Walton (C.Y.O. gym), Buddy Baer, Max Baer, Izzy Kline, trainer (photographs by Catholic Youth Athletics).**

stipulated to be *almost* a title fight. The Illinois State Athletic Commission insisted publicly that no title would be at stake—with one caveat: "The championship would be involved [only] in case of a knockout by Levinsky."[5] Because it was like a title fight if Levinsky could put Baer down, the battlers wore 6 oz. gloves instead of 8 oz. exhibition gloves, with only half the usual amount of tape and gauze for hand protection so that it would be official. Baer would follow a similar glove and knockdown protocol for other exhibition battles, an activity that would take a terrible toll on his hands.

For this fight, there would be no official score. In the event that the battlers were left on their feet at the end of the match, the decision would go to a poll of sportswriters. Baer had everything to lose and nothing to gain from the battle. It was with such an adverse decision that Levinsky had put an end to Dempsey's own title comeback plan, February 18, 1932. Levinsky was still a top contender, and in great condition.

The fight, the third in their trilogy, drew 14,000 people and a gate of $29,715. Baer received $9,508 for his effort and Levinsky received $3,565. Because the match could not be billed specifically as a title fight, seats were bought at bargain prices, which severely hampered a larger gate.

Eight • Championship Year, 1934 to 1935

Edward Burns wrote that Levinsky sat in his corner "like he might sit in Sister Lena's parlor smoking a perfecto."[6] Then he came out and refused to shake hands with Max, which rattled the champion. "He knocked my hand down when I offered it to him. Just a fresh mug," Baer said afterward. "And I had to take care of him."[7]

What irritated Levinsky, who was called the "Clouting Clown" before Max, was the fact that Max carried himself as a debonair who had the gall to wear a "slave bracelet."[8] (The bracelet had been given to Max by paramour June Knight four days after Max won the title.) Everything that drew attention to Baer's uniqueness was disliked by the "rough and ready" heavyweight.

In their previous matches, Baer had won the ten-round decision in New York and the 20-round decision in Reno. But through 30 rounds of fighting, Baer was never able to put Levinsky on the floor. In fact, Levinsky had only been knocked down once in his career and never had been knocked completely out.

Levinsky had the advantage in the first round, with a better left jab and four long lefts that rocked the champion. Baer came back in the first minute of the second with his "satanical leers." With a powerful punch to the stomach, Baer knocked Levinsky against the ropes and continued with rights and lefts to the body and then to the head—with four "fatal rights to the chin."[9] Levinsky was, for the first time in his career, completely knocked out. And, as one writer remarked, he was knocked out of his entire next year's estimated $100,000 earnings. Buddy Baer, now weighing 236 pounds, also knocked out his opponent, Gene Stanton, 216 pounds, from Cleveland, in the first round of the fight that preceded Max's.

Film of the fight was shown at various theaters throughout the year during Baer's championship. While the interstate transport of fight films was still illegal, the film was shown in cities wherever Baer appeared. It was billed as "the historic punch that knocked out Levinsky" and showed Baer's smashing right hand in action.[10] The popularity of the film helped to build up Baer's image as a powerful, indomitable foe.

On January 4, 1935, Buddy and Max shared the fight card at the Olympia Stadium in Detroit in front of almost 16,000 fans, the largest attendance at the stadium in two years.

In the afternoon before the card, Max sat in a chair reading fan mail. One letter caught his eye from a boy who had sent him a picture of himself in boxing pose and asked Max to give him advice. He also mentioned, "My gloves are worn out, and I need a new pair to keep up my practice cause I want to be a fighter like you some day."[11] There, on the spot, Max ordered a pair of gloves to be sent to the boy: "It would make the kid feel good," he grinned. That was Max, always trying to help someone. Said one reporter after the Hunt fight, "Max tried it in the ring Friday night but the public didn't understand."[12]

The audience had expected a real fight in the four-round exhibition with Alvin Earl "Babe" Hunt, of Ponca City, Oklahoma. Instead, Max entertained them with his antics. Babe Hunt had a good reputation. He had career wins over the likes of James Braddock, Ernie Schaaf, Johnny Risko, Les Kennedy, and Ray Pelkey. In the bout, Max let the Babe hit him occasionally, but the hits were not damaging. Baer pulled all of his punches. In this respect he was no Dempsey. When Dempsey stepped into a ring, he could never pull his punches—it was all fight. On one occasion, Max maneuvered Hunt into position for a knockout and then walked away, laughing. It was considered an acceptable act when working with a sparring partner, but not so in a real match. Max was jeered by the crowd.

Promoter Jim Mullen explained later to the press that Max had planned this. Baer told him prior to the match that he was going to carry the Babe for four rounds to let him make some money. Max said determinedly, "I'm not going to hurt him. He lost a lot of dough in poor investments and went broke. Now, the poor guy is trying to get some of it back. Why should I stand in his way? I'd rather help him. God knows Hunt needs all the dough he can get." Hunt was going around the country "picking up a little money here and there and a knockout would have spoiled his earning power," Max said.[13] Max knew so many men, like Ike Aycock, who were just trying to make a dollar in the only way they knew how.

Levinsky was another matter. Max explained the difference: "The King went around spouting off for weeks," telling everyone in Chicago he was going to "show me—the world champion—up before the big crowd."[14] Max was set on changing the "never-knocked-out" reputation of the King, which he did.

Brother Buddy was building a reputation and Detroit would give him his 13th professional fight. At 210 pounds, he scored a technical knockout in the second of six rounds over Detroit local Jack O'Dowd.

Both brothers got a firsthand look at the twenty-year-old Detroit Dynamo, Joe Louis, when he took on Patsy Perroni of Boston in ten rounds. Like Buddy, it was Joe's thirteenth professional fight; both had started their careers the year before. Louis was hit soundly by Perroni in the first round with a hard left to the head. It was the only punch Louis said he felt. Then he dropped his victim three times with a right hand that matched forces with the deadly right of Max Baer's. Louis's tactic was to bore in and unleash punches with both hands, and he had a noticeable short punch, a six-inch right. It would be another straight win for him. Both Buddy and Louis were on a streak of wins, but Buddy was still battling in six-rounders.

The most important event in Detroit, however, was not the interesting fight card, Max's generosity to a young fan, or seeing a young Louis in action—it was the powder keg waiting to explode. Reporter Charles Ward of the *Detroit Free Press* recorded it all.

Immediately before the fight, Jimmy Johnston and Joe Jacobs (Schmeling's manager) were in town to lure Joe Louis into their clutches. They came into the dressing room where Baer was talking to the preliminary fighters. Johnston's pretext was to thank Baer for drawing such a large crowd to the Detroit ring. Baer was in no mood to talk to Johnston, especially since he considered Johnston to be behind the attempt to derail him from winning Carnera's title, and now the promoter was denying him the opportunity to make big money through title defenses. When Johnston started into his speech, Baer interrupted, with the sharpest language reporters had ever heard from the typically jolly fellow.

"Yeah?" snarled Max. "And you say I am not doing anything to help the fight game. I gave the fight game the greatest boost it has received since Dempsey's time when I knocked out Levinsky at Chicago. You are the one who is ruining the fight game," he said, enraged. "You're the smart guy! Five years ago when I wanted to come back against Jimmy Braddock you turned thumbs down on the bout. You said Braddock was all washed up. Now you have Braddock matched with Art Lasky. Is it because you have a piece of Lasky?" This statement indicated that Max knew what was going on in the background of the heavyweight division. "When I boxed Carnera I entered the ring with everything against me. If I hadn't knocked the big Dago out, the decision would have gone against me."

"Whaddya mean?" frowned Johnston.

"Whatddya mean? What do I mean?" Baer shouted. "Why, Ancil has the judges' scorecards showing that one of your judges gave Carnera six rounds to my five. We are carrying that around for evidence." (This was reporter Ward's hearing of the story—according to Hoffman, all judges scored against Baer.) Baer continued, "You don't want to let me fight a double-header with Lasky and Hamas." (Both were turned down for Baer title defenses.) "Why? Because you are afraid I'll knock Lasky into your lap!" Baer was worked up and no one in the room was going to stop him. "Listen, Jimmy. You may have everything sewed up. You may have the fighters, the officials, and the politicians on your side, but you don't have these!" Baer held up his two very big fists. "I have these, you see." His fists were taped up and ready for battle. "And I'll use them to beat the living daylights out of every fighter you have tied up!"[15]

Johnston and Jacobs silently turned and left the room. Reporter Charles Ward summarized the event accurately: "The breach between Max Adelbert Baer and the Madison Square Garden Corp. became as wide as the Grand Canyon during Baer's stay in Detroit."[16] If Johnston didn't hate Baer before this meeting in front of a crowd of fighters, managers, and reporters, then he surely did afterwards. Unfortunately, Johnston would have the last word.

Ancil Hoffman continued to look for a fight for Max with a big draw. He considered Jack Sharkey, but that notion didn't seem to garner much attention from fight fans.

Shortly after Max's exhibition in Detroit, word circulated about a championship match between Max and Joe Louis. Jack Dempsey believed he could promote such a fight in Michigan and began looking for sponsors. In late January, he spoke with Floyd Fitzsimmons of Benton Harbor, Michigan, who staged his fight with Billy Miske. Dempsey was willing to go against the Garden and hoped to arrange a fifteen-round fight for the title in Michigan. In fact, he hoped to get the legislature to change the round limit from fifteen to twenty rounds for title fights, which he thought would make for more successful promotions. Dempsey was very politically active and would spend the entire decade arguing for twenty-round championship fights and other matters that he thought would help boxing.

Dempsey's plans for Baer sounded good to Ancil Hoffman. But Jimmy Johnston at Madison Square Garden didn't want anyone interfering with his fight plans. Johnston wanted a set of elimination tournaments to determine a challenger. Hoffman wanted the champion to meet the most profitable challengers. Baer's future remained undetermined, but many were starting to speculate that the new Detroit sensation, Joe Louis, would eventually figure in the calculation. One of the questions asked by the media was, if Louis became the outstanding challenger, would Baer draw the color line? Reporters worried that Louis might fall the way of other black greats, like George Godfrey, when good white boxers refused to fight them. But Max had never made color an issue.

Responding to the question of taking on Baer, Louis said, "I think I'll be ready for him in March. Yes, Baer is a pretty hard puncher. I've seen him in a couple of exhibitions and he showed me that he knows how to handle his mitts, but I think that after a few more fights I'll be ready for him."[17] While Louis had not yet engaged the crew of big names, he was still under consideration as a possible contender for Max.

But what would happen if Buddy Baer became a major contender? Would the two brothers fight? It was doubtful. Max and Ancil had brought Buddy along on the exhibition tour to give him some exposure and to train him up to take over if and when Max abdicated his crown.

Max appeared with Dick Madden in Boston, January 10, 1935 (courtesy David Bergin).

On January 10, 1935, Max appeared on a card in Boston. His four-round exhibition at the Boston Garden was with Dick Madden of the famous Madden mob family. Max quipped that he would let the mob decide if they wanted him to just toy with the man or knock him out. Madden owned a bar in Roxbury. The decision was clear: Max simply clowned his way through the four-round match before he won the decision. Attendance was only 1000. Buddy lost to Babe Hunt of Oklahoma in four rounds, the same opponent Max had taken on in the exhibition in Detroit the week before. It was Buddy's first loss, and he would make it up the next year in a rematch.

Max continued his battles in Florida, and from there he was expected to return to California for a benefit for Frankie Campbell's widow. After that he told the press that he wanted to go to England. Hoffman had been offered $15,000 for three weeks in London.

Campbell Benefit, Stanley Poreda, San Francisco, February 15, 1935

The Campbell benefit was the best part of his championship year. Max had always said that when he came into money, he would do something to help the Campbell family.

Eight • Championship Year, 1934 to 1935

The Baer brothers were home in San Leandro with their parents while waiting for the Campbell benefit. *Left to right:* Max, Jacob (former boxer), Dora, and Buddy in late January 1935 (International News photograph).

Max refused to take any money for his services, including expenses, and could not, since he was still officially sanctioned against fighting for any other purpose in California.

Ten thousand Oakland fans came out to the Dreamland Auditorium to see their hometown boy, who in five years went from an unpolished youth off a Livermore hog farm to a suave, sophisticated champion known the world over.

The event was billed as a fight and not an exhibition: four rounds using six-ounce gloves. Max was to meet Stanley Poreda of New Jersey. Only two years earlier, Poreda was considered a contender. He had faced Max's foes Tommy Loughran, Primo Carnera, and Ernie Schaaf. Poreda accepted $800 plus travel costs.

Max trained for five days at the Lakeside Gym, both clowning and conditioning, with two rounds of shadow boxing, two on the heavy bags, and two with the ropes. Then Ancil Hoffman decided to cut costs. He eliminated all sparring partners and put the two Baers in the ring together, a terrible mistake. Hoffman explained what happened.

It all started innocently enough. Max made the spectators laugh when he was shadow boxing and making fun of Buddy's wheezing and snorting. Then Max yelled, "Where's your crowd, Buddy?" Ancil Hoffman said, "You might not believe it, but these two fellows are desperately jealous of each other's ability, Max more so than Buddy. If Buddy gets into the headlines, Max is fit to be tied." Max feigned fright when his brother crossed his path. "They started off by tapping and laughing," then they went at it. Hoffman said, "Buddy came out with three of his right ribs broken and he was in a plaster cast for two months. He lost a couple of thousand dollars in bookings for fights."[18]

After the innocent sparring match, Frank Paccassi advertised for any heavyweight who wanted to work out with Max for $5 per round. A young college student, Frankie Riggi, from Brooks, Oregon, answered the call. While doing ring work with Riggi, Baer accidentally floored him. Immediately, Max was at his side apologizing. For the two remaining rounds, Bob Fraser, a heavyweight, engaged Baer. Al Trulmans, a middleweight from San Diego, who had helped train Max for Max Schmeling, also stepped in. Sparring partners faced challenging work, even if it was only for a charity match.

The night before the benefit, Max, Buddy, and Stanley Poreda attended a ten-round fight between Tommy Paul, former NBA featherweight champion, and Alton Black, a southpaw from Reno. Baer liked Paul and was at ringside to help Dolph Thomas, Paul's trainer. Just as Baer was stepping into the ring to be formally introduced, he was surprised by a court representative who served him with legal papers. It was a new lawsuit from former manager J. Hamilton Lorimer and promoter Louis Parente. They were suing him for $25,000, money they said they had lost on Baer for two fights they had planned.

After quickly thumbing through the papers, Baer said with dead seriousness that the former manager and promoter had made plenty of money when he was fighting in Oakland. Ancil Hoffman was present and said that no contract would have been valid at the time without his own signature on it since he had part interest in Baer. Max had already paid $50,000 in legal fees to date. And while he appeared to be a regular spendthrift, he wanted to spend his money the way he desired and not have it given away by a judge.

No one in the audience that night believed that Poreda had a chance to beat Baer. The public had gone to see one of the "greatest ring personalities of the century in action. Whether deadly serious or enjoying the role of clown, in which he is singularly adept, Max was a box office magnet."[19] Buddy Baer might have been on the card. Now he sat ringside in a body cast, courtesy of his brother.

Mrs. Campbell was introduced before Baer stepped into the ring with her. They had not met since Frankie's death. When one person heckled Max, he asked the audience for courtesy and then said to Mrs. Campbell, "If in the future there is anything that I can do for [you], I'll be glad to do it. Thank you all."[20]

For the sake of entertainment, "the champ was at his clowning best. He slapped. He hugged. He staggered under light jabs. He left himself wide open. He tied up Poreda artfully, then let him free without punching him. He crowded the Jersey boy into the ropes and wrapped them around his neck."[21] When Poreda connected with Baer's nose and drew blood, Max smacked him down. There were only two knockdowns: in the third, after the nose-bleed, and again in the fourth that ended the bout. The benefit netted $11,000 for Mrs. Campbell.[22]

Baer stayed in California as the Lorimer lawsuit prevented him from signing any other contracts or making any engagements, essentially preventing him from working during the most opportune time of his career until the suit was settled. Between breaks during the court hearing, Baer was asked repeatedly by the press if he planned to marry again. He was one of the most eligible bachelors in America.

Back on the East Coast, the New York Commission listed four possible contenders for Baer's crown: Art Lasky, Steve Hamas, Max Schmeling and Primo Carnera. All had

Eight • Championship Year, 1934 to 1935

to deposit $2500 as forfeit money. James J. Braddock was not on the list of plausible contenders, but he was scheduled to fight Art Lasky.

On March 1, Hoffman gave Madison Square Garden executives a 30-day notice that they must select a suitable title opponent and date according to their contract or Baer was going out on his own. If they failed to do so, Hoffman was going into deliberations with Walter Rothenberg of Hamburg, Germany, to have Baer meet the winner of the Steve Hamas–Max Schmeling fight as his first title defense. The bout would be staged in Austria in July or August. On March 10, 1935, Schmeling was victorious over Steve Hamas in Hamburg, and it looked like Baer was going to fight Schmeling again.

Jimmy Johnston was treading on thin ice at the Garden, in part because it appeared the big fights were leaving New York and going overseas. Johnston said he would go to court before he would let a fight occur in Berlin, London, or anywhere outside the Garden.

Primo Carnera was scheduled to fight 6-foot-7½-inch Ray Impellitier, "the Skyscraper," at Madison Square Garden on March 15. Johnston said that the winner of this bout would fight the winner of Art Lasky–Jimmy Braddock scheduled for March 22. The winner from those bouts was expected to fight Max Schmeling for the right to face Max Baer. So went the official elimination plans announced from Madison Square Garden. Those plans would not happen because after Carnera beat Impellitier, he went straight for Joe Louis in June. Hamas went off to Europe and was beaten by Schmeling. Schmeling ruled himself out of the contest by signing for a fight with Paulino Uzcudun in Berlin in July. In the strange set of complications, Jimmy Johnston at the Garden was left with Art Lasky and Jimmy Braddock, a boxer who was never considered a contender and had not been in the elimination matches.

Jimmy Johnston would turn his lemons into lemonade. He owned part of Lasky's contract. And to continue his legacy at the Garden, he arranged a match in which Lasky would fall to Jimmy Braddock. Lasky confessed the scheme to sportswriter Al Lamb the following year when Johnston failed to hold up his end. Lasky said he was "coming clean" because it was the right thing to do, but that was after Lasky was double-crossed. "It was agreed," said Lasky, "that if I lost to Braddock and he got the shot at Baer that Jimmy would consent to fight me in his first title defense." Lasky was not given Braddock's first title defense and Lasky left Johnston for Mike Jacobs. Reporter Lamb responded, "If that is true, it is bad. Scandals ... concerning the boxing game have been all too numerous in the past."[23]

On March 22, 1935, Lasky lost to Braddock. One week later, on March 27, the Garden and the New York Boxing Commission named James Braddock as the number-one contender for Baer's crown.

Baer had waited a year for his big fight:

> They call me a clown but I couldn't pull anything as funny as that if I sat up nights for a week. Why, five years ago the New York Commission wouldn't let me fight Braddock because they said he was a "set-up".... Now they gallop up with Braddock and label him the standout challenger for the title? Well, my answer is if these fellows like Braddock and Art Lasky and all the rest of that caliber want to fight me let them lick my nineteen-year-old brother Buddy first. Right now I think Buddy can beat either one of them without perspiring and he'd probably knock them right into Commissioner Brown's lap.... If I couldn't make better matches than what the New York Commission tries to cook up I'd go back to herding cows.[24]

Max and Ancil Hoffman should have taken the matter more seriously.

On April 4, 1935, Baer touted Louis's merits. He said that if Louis could beat Carnera, then a bout with him would draw a million-dollar gate at Chicago's Soldier Field.

Baer was on his way to New York to fulfill a radio contract with the Gillette Razor Blade Company. On April 6, Al Jolson premiered as the host of a new radio variety show in New York. His first show introduced guests Max and Buddy Baer. The two appeared in a comedy sketch and they also sang—both had beautiful voices.

Many other lucrative offers were on the table for Baer that Hoffman turned down: a fight in September under Mike Jacobs, promoter for the Twentieth Century Club, with either Joe Louis or Carnera; a fight in Europe with Schmeling under Walter Rothenberg, who was throwing out $300,000 for the champion; a fight in London sponsored by a Blackpool syndicate for $250,000. The decision not to take any of these offers cost Max some big bucks.

A year earlier no one would have bet that Braddock would rise to contender status. Madison Square Garden wasted no time in tying up Braddock's contract. No one knew at the time that the Baer-Braddock battle would be the last heavyweight championship entirely promoted under the umbrella of Madison Square Garden, the great house that Tex Rickard built for boxing. With his Twentieth Century Sporting Club, promoter Mike Jacobs would start a chain of events that would wrench power away from the Garden and create a trilogy of conflicts among his club, Madison Square Garden, and the New York State Athletic Commission, until World War II.

All agreed that Baer would knock Braddock over as chickenfeed and then go on to defend his title at Soldier Field in Chicago with Joe Louis if Primo Carnera didn't knock him off the list of contenders. But Baer had a few more exhibitions to fight before setting up training camp for Braddock, exhibitions that he now called tune-up bouts for his first title defense. Those exhibition tune-ups would cost him dearly.

The *Akron Beacon* announced, "Max Baer, king of the leather pushers, will trade honest-to-goodness blows with the hard-hitting Eddie Simms. Baer shocked boxing fans by insisting that the bout would not be an exhibition match but a no-decision battle and that regulation gloves were to be used."[25] On April 23, 1935, Max fought a fateful four-rounder against Simms in Cleveland. Newspapermen were amazed that the heavyweight champion was going around the country fighting exhibition bouts without using heavily padded exhibition gloves, especially now that he was scheduled for his first title defense.

Baer clowned his way through the four rounds. At the end of the fourth, when Simms landed a few good shots to Baer's head and jaw, Baer sent over a hard right to the head that rocked Simms. Afterwards, Baer complained about a sore hand. Three days later in St. Louis, Baer fought another four-rounder with Babe Hunt. Hoffman said, "His hands were so sore that we wanted to cancel the fight but the promoter objected so we went through with the bout."[26] After the Hunt fight, reporters were stunned when they saw that Baer went into the fight with a "beef steak" wrapped around his right fist and taped up. Since Baer couldn't hit with his sore hands, the bout was more of a wrestling match.

The next day, April 27, Max would fly out of Cleveland for his camp in New York to begin training for the most important fight of the year—maybe his career. When reporters saw Max and Buddy arrive in New York, they said the pair looked like they had been put through meat grinders. Both of Max's hands were badly bruised and Buddy's left hand was in a cast. Max told the press not to worry, that he had no broken bones and that his bruised hands would heal in a matter of days. He said the bout with Hunt only aggravated them. Shoveling sand at camp would help them heal.

It was at this point that Baer admitted that he may have underestimated Braddock. Baer said, "They say he hits like a pile driver and keeps pressing. Those kind of fellows are awkward to fight."[27]

NINE

Clown Prince Loses Crown to Braddock, 1935

It was said that Max Baer, "the eccentric pugilist, could clown and fight but was never able to do both at the same time."[1]

Many thought he merely clowned his way out of the title, although his clowning in the ring was part entertainment and part reaction to pain. But something about his first title defense never looked quite right, and reporters were left trying to figure out what had happened. Sportswriters had some part of the story and a theory that evolved over time. Dan Parker of the *New York Mirror* said: "The story of how his dethronement was brought about, just a year short of a day after he won the title, is incredible."[2]

Paul Zimmerman of the *Los Angeles Times* interviewed Max seven years after he lost the title: "It's hard to realize how Max ever lost his crown to Jim Braddock until you hear him speak of the matter." In Max's version of the story, he said he was "not feeling well," which was logical considering the condition of his injured hands. When it was suggested "that he tried to 'do too many good turns' for his friends on Broadway,"[3] his response was intriguingly sarcastic. Who were those "friends" that the slang term "Broadway" identified? And what "turns" did he do? Max was in the Broadway area for only a day before the fight, staying at an "unknown" penthouse where he had also stayed before the Carnera fight. Before that time, Max had been at his training camp at Asbury Park, New Jersey, the details of which were well documented.

Prior to moving to the training camp at Asbury Park, Baer was seen about town in early April with New York divorcee Mary Kirk Brown. She was the "girlfriend" for this fight.

By April 30, 1935, James J. Braddock was training at the Hotel Evans, a luxury camp at Loch Sheldrake in the Catskills. Less than a year earlier, he was getting $5 a day on the Jersey docks. On weekends he worked as a janitor for his apartment building. After a layoff of nine months in 1933, he won three fights under the spotlight: with opponent Corn Griffin for a $250 purse in the preliminary of the 1934 Baer-Carnera championship; with opponent John Henry Lewis in the preliminary of the Olin-Rosenbloom fight; and with opponent Art Lasky, who was considered a contender until he was beaten by Steve Hamas.

Braddock, never considered among the list of heavyweight contenders, would come into the title fight as a 12-to-1 underdog.

Baer told Grantland Rice about his own fighting strategy in general and for this fight specifically:

Nine • Clown Prince Loses Crown to Braddock, 1935

New York socialite and divorcee Mary Kirk Brown was Max's girlfriend prior to the Braddock fight. She was with him the night he lost the championship (International News photograph).

"You may recall that I told you a year ago at Asbury Park that I would never be a boxer. As I understand it, Jim Corbett had his choice. As a young fighter, he was a hard puncher. Jim was also a fine boxer from the start. He knew he couldn't be both—so he decided to take the scientific route. I had no such choice."[4] Max continued:

I'd never make a clever boxer, and I know it. But I could always punch and so far I've been able to take the other fellow's punches and still keep on my feet. As a boxer I may look terrible again in my training. I can't go there every day and knock out my sparring partners. As I've said before, all I want to concentrate on is the condition of my legs, hands and wind. I'm not taking any chances on these three important factors. When I throw a punch in a big fight, I mean it. I don't intend it for any caress. I hurt both thumbs early in the Schmeling fight and had to save my hands for a sure shot later on. I don't want to be caught again with bad hands in the middle of a scrap. I'll find plenty of work and exercise in the next five weeks. After all, I haven't been loafing the last six months. I've had a bunch of four-round exhibitions. I had to be on my guard in all of these against a sneak punch. In one of them I stopped Levinsky in two rounds. There wasn't any frolic about that one. I don't think anyone will have to worry about my condition by the date of the Braddock fight.... I've got five or six weeks in which to build up. I'm not sap enough to take any chances against a fellow who is game and can punch. I understand that Jim is coming right to me, crowding me from the start. I'm not bragging, but they can pick their own way of fighting and it's still all right with me—they can try to keep away or they can come tearing in. Every fight works out its own answer—after it begins.[5]

In 1929, Gillette was unsuccessful sponsoring radio ads. The company tried again in 1935 with Max Baer at the helm of a 13-week show. It was overwhelmingly successful. On July 20, after receiving over 200,000 prize entries, accompanied by proof of purchase, Gillette announced the winning name of the dog contest: the Livermore Gay Blade (ad from *Time* Magazine, July 15, 1935).

By his own testimony a month and a half before the fight, Baer was in good condition and not taking any chances on his hands, legs, or wind.

As he did during his training camp for the Carnera fight, Max broadcast a radio show from the seaside camp at Asbury Park. In early May, Baer starred as a detective in a series of live dramas every Monday night at 10:20 p.m. over WEAF-NBC sponsored by the Gillette Razor Company. The show was called *Max Baer's Lucky Smith*. The title was taken from Max's theme song "Lucky Fella," in the movie *The Prizefighter and the Lady*. However, at this training camp, Max Baer became the most Unlucky Fella.

During the late afternoon of May 10, the crew was rehearsing for the evening's skit. Jerry Casale, of Baer's boxing camp, heard the sound from the prop gun and decided it should be louder. He went to his quarters and brought back his .32-caliber Colt and loaded it with blanks. While he was showing the gun to Baer, it accidentally discharged, hitting the Champ squarely in the chest, causing a nasty wound. Baer was rushed to the hospital, seven miles away, where he was treated for a severe burn, given a tetanus shot, and released for several days of bed rest. "It scared me," Max admitted, "but I'll be back in a day or two getting in shape for that guy Braddock. I never did like guns. I'm afraid of them."[6]

In addition to the radio play, Gillette sponsored a dog-naming contest as part of its publicity. Prizes included 60 RCA Victor radio sets and tickets to the championship fight. A grand prize of $1000 would be awarded to the person submitting the best name for Baer's fox terrier on July 20 (six weeks after the fight, when Baer's radio contract ended).[7] Obviously, everyone at Gillette predicted a win for Max.

The week before the match, Jimmy Braddock announced his fight strategy: "I'm going to depend on my body punch. Baer is made to order for me and I'm in fine shape."[8] Braddock had a weapon in trainer Whitey Bimstein. Bimstein had trained Baer for his win against Schmeling, and Whitey knew everything Baer was made of. For that fight, he turned Baer into the best fighting machine of his career, and he would do the same for the underdog. "Whitey was one of the few who openly declared that his man Braddock had a chance against Baer.... When Whitey sends them into battle, they are ready physically and mentally." Writer Matt Jackson explained, "He putters over [his man] like a mechanic toys with an engine before a race. Everything has got to be just right."[9]

Braddock ran five to ten miles every day in the morning, sparred eight rounds with only a few seconds' rest between, rotating each two rounds with the roughest sparring partners available. Braddock focused on finding a defense against Max's long looping right-hand blow. He practiced moving forward into close quarters. Mike Cantwell, Baer's former trainer, watched Braddock's workout and summarized his chances: "I think he hits just as hard as Baer—and the important thing is this—that he hits straight, while Maxie doesn't. Those smashing left hooks to the body and crushing rights under the heart may be the punches that will bury Max in resin dust. Baer is in for the licking of his life."[10]

The difference in the two training camps was that Baer entertained his fifty-cent guests while Braddock worked seriously. One reporter said that Max's training camp was as close as you could get to an "insane asylum." "Baer stands around laughing, clowning, letting his sparring partners hit him at will, doing nothing of an offensive nature in rebuttal."[11] He even invited spectators to get in the ring with him to take a jab. The reporter stated that Baer looked in fine shape and admitted that all of this was just ballyhoo to make people believe that he was not taking his training seriously in order to get people to think that Braddock had a real chance. "I'm clowning here, sure, but I'll be the same vicious guy I was a year ago [against Carnera] when I get in there with Braddock. I'll flatten him as fast as I can. If I cut him, I'll never let up until I've got him torn apart."[12]

It was the same training regimen a year earlier that made Commissioner Bill Brown want to call off the bout because he thought Baer was not in proper shape. However, Grantland Rice said that Baer was in better form for Braddock than he was for Carnera. When Rice asked Dempsey what he thought about Baer's condition, Dempsey responded, "He has done enough road work to get his legs right. That's what I was worried about before the Carnera fight. I think he is now in better shape than he was for either Schmeling or Carnera. You know that championship means a lot, once you've won it. No one wants to lose it, especially within a year."[13]

But behind the entertainment curtain, Baer was not focused on his legs or wind. He was worried only about his hands that he had injured in the former exhibition bouts. So was Rice: "The one slight kink in the evening's entertainment is the condition of Baer's hands."[14]

As LA columnist Bob Ray said fatefully, "Maybe picking opponents with bum hands is the secret of Braddock's success."[15] Art Lasky's excuse for losing to Braddock was also a bad hand.

To everyone outside the camps, it was a foregone conclusion that Baer would win. Chicago promoter Nate Lewis visited Baer's training camp dangling $300,000 for Baer to meet Schmeling in September. Mike Jacobs was trying to match Baer with Louis in September in New York if Louis beat Carnera later in the month. Baer was prescient about Louis. He believed he could take the measure of Braddock, Schmeling, and Carnera as often as anyone liked. "Louis," he said, "[was] the most dangerous heavyweight on the fight horizon. I'd like to get him early, as Jack Dempsey got Luis Angel Firpo, before he was fully seasoned."[16] He suspected that next year might be too late.

In the two final days of workouts, June 8 and 9, both training camps were flooded with guests and onlookers: 500 fans in Braddock's camp and 600 in Baer's.

While people liked to think of Braddock as an old man, all "washed up," there was only three years' difference in their ages. Baer was 26, and Braddock was 29. The tale of the tape indicated that the two boxers were more alike than dissimilar. The size of their waists was 32 inches; their necks, forearms, wrists, fists, and ankles were essentially the same. Braddock at 6'3" was a half inch taller than Baer. While rumors circulated that Baer would weigh 220 pounds due to his lack of training, he weighed in at 209, one pound less than for his bout with Carnera. Braddock weighed 195½ pounds.

Dr. William Walker, physician for the New York Athletic Commission, examined Baer on June 8 to determine his readiness, and the news wasn't good. While his body was in fine condition, he was trim without an ounce of fat, and his heartbeat good, his hands were a mess. According to Dr. Walker, "The knuckles of the left hand were bruised badly and the bones in the back of the right hand were contused."[17] They had not healed properly. The doctor said that with four days of rest Max would be in shape to fight; however, he admitted that his hands may bother him. In fact, either Dr. Walker or manager Hoffman should have postponed the fight. Four more days would not heal his hands.

On June 10, 1935, the Associated Press obtained a copy of the letter written by Ancil Hoffman's wife to Dora and Jacob Baer explaining Max's condition. Maudie wrote: "Positively, Max is in the best physical condition of his career—aside from his hands which he complains about—but no one thinks they are as bad as he tries to make out. Ancil

Nine • Clown Prince Loses Crown to Braddock, 1935

has asked him to postpone the fight if they are bad—but he wants it to go on. The shape he is in he should go in there and tear Braddock's head off—and we are sure he will. Always fondly, Maude Hoffman."[18] It was stated in the press that Ancil disregarded Max's hands and refused to have him seen by a doctor. However, Max was also quoted as saying that he thought his hands would be better in time for the fight. Did Max and Ancil believe he could still beat Braddock with bad hands? Or was he "persuaded" to fight with bad hands?

All parties involved in the fight met with the New York Boxing Commission with Referee Arthur Donovan present. Hoffman objected to Donovan because of his handling of the previous Baer fights with Schmeling and Carnera. Hoffman said they would rather walk off than work under Donovan. The exchange was heated. Hoffman proposed a list of alternates: Gene Tunney, George Blake, Jess Kenworthy, Jack Kennedy, or Ed Dickerson.

Commission Chairman John J. Phelan replied to Hoffman's list: "None but New York referees will be considered. Any further remarks?"[19]

"Yes," said Hoffman, walking toward Phelan's desk. He turned and looked back at the other commissioners. "Gentlemen, I wish you would take a good look at my back. I'd like to know if you see a dandruff sign on it. I seem to be as popular around here as the measles." He continued, "If the Commission insists on being technical, then what about Lieutenants Kenworthy and Kennedy?" he asked. "They are officers of the United States Navy. I should think they would be qualified to officiate in any state of the Union." Hoffman simply said that Donovan was "incompetent." He told the commissioners that they had the proof if they would look back and see how he scored the Baer-Carnera fight.

Donovan admitted to the group that it was a "mistake" to give round 10 to Carnera when Baer knocked him out.

Max added that if he had not knocked out Carnera, that "mistake" might have cost him the fight. He didn't want that to happen with Braddock.

"Everyone was confused" in that fight, offered one of the commissioners. "Things were happening pretty fast."

"I'll say they were," Hoffman added. "Some of them were too fast for me." Hoffman stormed out of the office threatening to call the fight off. The commission replaced Referee Donovan with John McAvoy. Joe Gould was then asked about the forfeit fee for Braddock. The manager never posted nor did he have $2500, so he offered to put Braddock up as security. The Commissioners waived the guarantee. They knew Braddock would show up.

The day before the fight, something happened to Max that Hoffman said changed the course of the fight. He would later openly charge "interference and tampering with Max Baer." Hoffman told sports editor Davis Walsh that Baer was a "changed man" only the day before. That "change" was confirmed the day of the fight when Dr. Walker examined Baer and found his heartbeat extremely high, 150 beats per minute. Baer was nervous and highly agitated. Hoffman knew something was wrong. Someone had given him something or gotten to him.

Hoffman freely admitted he made a mistake on the hands issue, "thinking he had a cinch." Even the week before the bout, when Baer complained about his hands, trainer Dolph Thomas told Max not to "be a baby." But someone seemed "to have permanently borrowed Mr. Hoffman's prize fighter" on that day before the fight, said Walsh.[20]

Baer was confident leaving his training camp, but when he got to New York he

Madison Square Garden, New York.

became "low," "dispirited," and "nervous," unusual for the lively Baer. Hoffman was convinced and repeated, "Somebody came between manager and fighter right before the defense of a world's heavyweight championship, and bad hands or none at all, that's the real answer to Baer's showing."[21]

The night before the fight, Max had stayed with Leo Friede, a wealthy New York Stock Exchange broker, in his penthouse at 405 East Fifty-Fourth Street. On his own behalf, Leo Friede reported that all he did was give Baer "a place to sleep comfortably and quietly before and after the fight. Outside of that, I'm an innocent bystander. I wasn't there half the time, but I have reason to believe that he was visited only by his manager, his trainer, his valet and the millionaire sportsman, Jay O'Brien."[22] O'Brien was a good friend of Max. Reporter Walsh said that both Hoffman and Baer denied Friede's story.

So who were the Broadway friends that sportswriter Dan Parker alluded to that Baer said he had done a good turn for if not Friede? And what was happening on Broadway at the time? In short, at the time of the fight, the G-men were coming down hard, claiming tax evasion on the mob-owned Stork Club, a popular venue with the sporting crowd where deals were made; mob boss and former convict friend of Joe Gould, Owney Madden, was coming off parole; Jimmy Johnston was desperate and Gould was complicit in Johnston's plans for giving Braddock a shot at the title. With 12-to-1 odds, there was certainly big money to be made on an upset.

Sportswriter Dan Parker waited until after Baer's death to explain the fearful goings-on that he had heard happened to Max before the fight:

> The story told by the boxing men of that era who were in a position to know, is that Max was taken for a taxi ride by a tough guy [mob member] before the fight and told what would happen to him [or his family, as in death threat] if he dared to win. Anyway, Jim Braddock, a decent guy with a lion's heart, but not much equipment for a heavyweight champion at that stage of his career, knew nothing of what had gone on behind the scenes but obeyed orders to keep circling Maxie to the right and sticking lefts in his face. This he did with monotonous exactness for 15 rounds on June 13, 1935, and won the decision.[23]

Prior to the fight, after Hoffman had gone to observe the wrapping of Braddock's hands, he returned to Max's dressing room to find that Max's hand-wraps had been removed. Hoffman said that when he left Baer, everything seemed fine. Hoffman had requested and been approved by the commission to have extra hand-wrappings used on Baer's seriously hurt hands. But when Hoffman returned, Baer, or "someone," had unraveled the bandages. The tape was gone and the only wrappings on his hands were six feet of thin gauze. Baer's excuse was the tape hurt his hands and he wasn't going to wear any. Hoffman was told that Baer had made that statement to Braddock's representative. Hoffman was furious. Now Braddock was going into the fight knowing that Baer didn't have the full use of his hands and the protection of his hand-wraps. What handicap was exchanged or threat made? Who made Baer alter the hand-wrap at this crucial point in time? Were any other concessions promised? Dan Parker said that Baer "entered the ring looking as if he was walking his last mile."[24]

It was too late to do anything about the hands. The fight was on. Commissioner Bill Brown, who hated Baer, positioned himself at the radio broadcasters' table next to announcers Graham McNamee and Ford Bond. The radio table gave the trio the nearest view to the ring action apart from the judges.

Ringside Radio Broadcast, June 13, 1935

The fight was scheduled for broadcast at 9 p.m. Eastern Time over the NBC network chain. Rudy Vallee had the radio slot at 7:00, and Buddy Baer serenaded his brother as guest on Vallee's *Variety Hour*.[25]

Transcribed below is what the listeners heard that night from Graham McNamee in his breathless, staccato introduction and delivery of the fight, round by round. Ford Bond, sitting next to him, summarized each round and pitched the advertising for sponsor Gillette. Transcript of the introductory moments of the fight captures the essence of the quick-paced live broadcast, with McNamee's descriptive sentences slamming into each other (awkward to read in the written form) recording what he saw in real time.[26]

> This is Graham McNamee speaking, direct from the ringside of the Madison Square Garden Bowl in Long Island, New York, with a blow by blow description of the 15-round fight. This contest is the outstanding pugilistic contest of the year. For eight weeks the Gillette Safety Razor Company has been completing arrangements to broadcast from coast to coast over a nationwide hookup. Here to watch this heavyweight contest are scores of winners for their winning letters Gillette launched last April. For their winning entries, they receive free ringside seats and round-trip transportation between their home communities and New York.
>
> The last preliminary has just been completed, and we find that Mr. Hogan in the final preliminary, the bell of which you have probably heard, that Eddie Hogan has defeated Jack McCarthy. Of course

there have been other preliminaries preceding this, and in just a few moments the two contestants will be in the ring. Max Baer and Jimmy Braddock. Max Baer the champion who won from Carnera, you know, and in that great fight a year ago, and Jimmy Braddock who has come into a contending position from ups and downs. Jimmy has had lots of them [McNamee has difficulty explaining Braddock's situation], but was finally named by the Boxing Commission and the New York State Athletic Commission as the outstanding or number-one contender.

Mr. Bill Brown, member of the State Athletic Commission is sitting here with us and is at the ringside and is of course particularly interested in the radio broadcast of this event. [This is a curious disclaimer.] And we understand that Max has left the dressing room. I think he's coming down the aisle now. I see Ancil Hoffman has just stepped up to the side of the ring and is waiting for Max to come into the ring also.

And in the other corner we see a gentleman, elderly gentleman, with a pair of boxing gloves. [This is another strange detail in that McNamee fails to recognize someone tasked with such an important job as holding the gloves. In spite of McNamee's familiarity with the commissioners and those in the boxing world, he stumbles for a name here, leaving one to ask: who attended the gloves?]

And Max Baer is now stepping up the steps onto the edge of the ring, goes through the ropes which are held open by his manager Ancil Hoffman, and steps in clad again in that regular old silk robe with the name "Steve Morgan" on the back. You know he was Steve Morgan in his movie that he made a couple of years ago, and he has used that bathrobe or dressing gown, whatever you want to call it, ever since then. Max has now stripped off the gown, and it has been thrown around his shoulders by his trainer and we find that his hands are already taped and he is ready to slip on the gloves. And now I would like to turn you over to my friend next to me: Ward Bond, who has an interesting message for you.

Thank you, Graham. I know you listeners are plenty anxious to catch Al Frazen's [the announcer's] voice who is substituting for Joe Humphreys tonight. You of course heard the news about Joe. [He had suffered a stroke.] You're anxious to hear that gong, sending these two great heavyweights into action. While we are waiting for the boys to come into the ring, we want to tell you about the big new Gillette contest in which the Gillette Safety Razor Company is awarding thousands of dollars' worth of prizes just for naming Max Baer's dog, that wiry little fellow that Max recently adopted. Folks, you should see this dog of Max's; he's the most loveable little fox terrier you ever saw, white, wiry hair with spots of brown, and a snappy wide-awake look that says, "Boy, I'm ready for fun." And what a pal he's been to Max. Day after day, dominating Max's training camp, and he's been right up to the ringside and barks as the champ snagged a sparring partner. Right up to ringside when the champion uses that famous right. But let someone get one over on Max, the snappy little he-dog will bark and growl as if to say, "You can't do that while I'm around." You all would all love this little fella if you could see him, and we know you're going to get a lot of fun for suggesting a name for this dog. Be the first to submit winning names for this dog. Gillette is awarding over $17,000 dollars in prizes: a grand prize of $1000 in cash, 120 new 1935 RCA Victor "Magic Brain" radios.

All the dialogue above occurred in only one minute and ten seconds, which explains how the broadcasters could announce all the ring action in three minutes per round.

Ford Bond continued to explain the contest and how to enter[27]: "Graham McNamee will give you as usual one of his thrilling descriptions of the blow-by-blow account of each round. And between rounds we will come in to give you a résumé of the rounds." The ring action was described by one broadcaster and summarized by the other, giving little doubt about what happened in the ring.

Special guests were then introduced in the ring: Tony Canzoneri, Tommy Loughran, and Jimmy McLarnin. Bond continued, "And there's the introduction of Jimmy Braddock on the other side of the ring. We are in the neutral corner between the two boys. And as you know, Joe Humphreys, who has taken ill, Joe Humphreys has been announcing these boxing contests for I don't know how many years [since John L. Sullivan], for 43 years Joe has been around, and Joe has been taken ill suddenly, and we only hope that we can give you a good graphic description of what's going on."

Bond continued:

Al Frazen has taken Joe Humphreys' place in the center of the ring announcing. And now we find that Johnny McAvoy has just been announced as referee. Johnny McAvoy will referee this heavyweight contest for the championship of the world between Maxie Baer and Jimmy Braddock.

And now the boys are being called to the center of the ring, and Max throws off his robe and goes out to the center. Jimmy Braddock keeps his robe on. The boys go to the center of the ring, and are being talked to now by Jimmy McAvoy, the referee. And it won't be long now until we get into the first round of this contest. Both boys look to be in great shape, beautiful shape. The judges are Charles Lynch and Bob Cunningham.

Clearly Ford Bond announced the wrong judge from the radio desk, which suggests that the actual judge, George Kelley, was an extremely late substitute for Bob Cunningham, for reasons unexplained.

Referee McAvoy called the boxers to ring center. Their seconds followed. McAvoy announced the general instructions about moving to a neutral corner in case of a knockdown. When his instructions were over, one of Braddock's seconds put his arm around McAvoy's shoulders and reminded him of the "backhand." Audio from the film picks up McAvoy's statement that it would be a foul to backhand, but that it was okay to hold with one hand.

The following description comprises details from the film footage and the radio transcript. The broadcasters did not announce specifically who won each round, which may have been a condition of their broadcast.

"And there's the bell for the first round."

James Braddock, Madison Square Garden Bowl, June 13, 1935

(Judges' scores appear at the end of each round and at the end.)

Round One

In the fight film, Braddock circles Baer and shoots a left to his head, which is caught with Baer's right glove. Braddock misses with his right. He tries again. Baer catches him in a clutch and then jolts Braddock with a strong uppercut to the jaw. Max ties him up, and again breaks out of the clinch with an uppercut. Baer blocks Braddock's shots. Braddock swings wildly and misses. Baer ties him up and Braddock head-butts Baer viciously. They circle and as Baer ties him up, Braddock misses with a quick left, then tags Baer with a right on the face and another that lands only lightly on the left. They circle and Braddock misses two more times with a left.

Baer feints several times with his left but doesn't shoot. When Braddock lands, Baer looks surprised, as if Braddock is not following the game plan. Braddock throws more punches. They occasionally land, but when they do, they don't appear to do any damage. For the most part, Baer slips the punches thrown at his head, left and right.

Both are cautious in the first round, circling. Baer shuffles his feet. Most of Baer's actions are feints. When Braddock sends in a hard punch, it lands short. Baer rarely counters. Braddock is active, but Baer blocks or throws off the punches. Baer is passive as if biding his time and waiting for the round to be over.

The strongest punch of the round was Baer's early uppercut.
Braddock Braddock Braddock

Round Two

Baer doesn't jump out aggressively as he was known to do. Braddock hits first with his left to the face which is slightly off, and when he throws two more lefts, he misses and is blocked.

Baer takes a hit to the body. Baer sends in a left but is short. They come together and Baer lands a solid right to the body and a hard right to the head. Braddock tries a

Max Baer and Jim Braddock mix it up in their championship title fight June 13, 1935 (courtesy David Bergin).

haymaker with his right and misses. He tries two more times and Baer slips the punches and walks away from him clowning—strutting with his hands on his hips, elbows pointed out like chicken wings. When Braddock tries to punch, Baer ties him up. Braddock sends out four more lefts without a hit. Braddock tags Baer in the chest twice and Braddock falls away. When his back is turned, Baer follows him quickly from behind, shadowing him, so that when Braddock turns around, Baer surprises him with a "Boo!" It would have been a perfect time to land a punch, but Baer does not. Braddock is unfazed. They circle to the right. Baer holds Braddock off with his left. Braddock rushes into a clinch. His game plan is to fight in close. Baer punches out of the clinches with uppercuts.

Braddock Braddock Braddock

Round Three

Braddock again takes the lead, but Baer knocks off eight of Braddock's left leads as they circle. Braddock tries two overhand rights, and they fail. They fight in close. Braddock lands two punches, and Baer comes back with lefts and rights, four punches in all. Braddock's lefts are again knocked off or guarded with Baer's right elbow. He tags Baer lightly with a right. They circle and go into a clinch. Baer breaks out with an uppercut.

Braddock Braddock Braddock

Round Four

They come out slowly. Braddock shoots a left that slides off Max. They trade punches. Baer lands a short hard right to the body, and Braddock comes back with a punch to the face. In a clinch, they start to wrestle, and Baer throws Braddock out. He is booed by the crowd for this tactic. Braddock sends out a left, but it lands on Baer's shoulder. Baer flecks his left but lands high on Braddock's chin. They fall into several clinches with the referee breaking them up. Baer acts like he is going to land a big right. He lands a hard right cross, throwing Braddock into the ropes. They both feint. They exchange lefts. Baer catches Braddock's left in his mitt. Another left finds Max's jaw.

Braddock Braddock Braddock

Round Five

Baer holds Braddock off with his long left, sometimes touching Braddock's face. He backs Braddock around the ring. They circle. Braddock sends out lefts, and Baer blocks them. They fall into two clinches and Braddock lunges at Baer with a head butt. (There is no referee warning for the head-butting.) Baer backs up. Baer says something to Braddock, backs out of the engagement, and complains to the referee, but the referee does nothing. They come in and Baer lands a hard right to the body and two to the face. Braddock retaliates, and they exchange lefts. Braddock tries a left to the head, but it is deflected by Max's shoulder. Max tries for a haymaker and misses.

It was learned from the newspaper reports the next day that the round was taken from Baer by the referee because Max hit with a backhand right and the referee lifted a warning finger. However, neither Graham McNamee in his live description, nor Ford Bond in his round summary during the one-minute break, realize this warning or any deduction or they would have announced it to the radio audience. This round that went to Braddock on a foul may have been a determining round, with McAvoy determining the outcome.

Graham McNamee said very little about Braddock and appeared from his description to give the round to Baer. After saying initially that Braddock tried to tag Baer three times, but his lefts "slid off," McNamee commented that Max was backing Braddock around the ring. McNamee's verbs indicate the action: "Braddock misses..., Baer lands..., Baer drives a hard right..., Baer hits Braddock hard..., two more to the face..., Braddock retaliates...."[28] Braddock tags Baer on the side of the head, but does little more before the round ends.

Braddock Braddock Braddock

At this point, Baer had lost all five of the initial rounds. As Dan Cuoco, of the International Boxing Research Organization, noted, if Baer had actually used his left to jab instead of merely paw, or used it as a guard, he would have easily won some of these and other rounds.[29] The consistent loss of the early rounds supports the notion that Baer gave these rounds away. He certainly had the skill to do otherwise, even with bum hands, as the later rounds indicate. If he had not lost this round, the bout could have been even.

Baer gave different excuses later for his showing and many conflicted. He told Grantland Rice that his legs started to wobble after the fifth round, which hardly explains why his showing improved after the fifth.[30]

Round Six

Baer starts to fight. He lands a hard shot to Braddock's body. Braddock tags him with a right hook, a left, another left, and a right. Braddock connects as Baer walks into him. Braddock dives head-first into a clinch and appears to head-butt Baer twice. Braddock lands a left and right to Baer's face and then another left and right. Baer retaliates with a right to the head. They trade lefts. Max sends a left and right to the face, and Braddock is forced to hold. They trade lefts. Baer lands a hard right to the body, and Braddock lands on the face. While Braddock is scoring easily, the broadcasters announce that Baer's punches appear harder.

Even Braddock Baer

Round Seven

Baer is the aggressive one. Braddock bores in head-first to tie Baer up three times. Max sends in uppercuts to escape. The referee appears to call Braddock for head-butts. (This is what may have forced all scorers to give the round to Baer.) Braddock leads with his left and misses. Max swings wildly and misses, but later connects twice to the head with hard blows. Graham McNamee called it the hardest blow yet of the fight. Jim backs up. Max walks him down as if he could end the fight. Braddock is trying to regain his senses. Braddock lands a looping right-cross to the side of the face. Baer lands a hard body shot, and Braddock is forced to back up against the ropes. Braddock bores in with a head-butt. Max lands two uppercuts to Braddock's jaw and a right to Braddock's nose. But Baer cannot put Braddock down.

Baer Baer Baer

Round Eight

Baer is leading more and fighting harder, trying to end the fight, but Braddock is hard to hit. Baer tries to land a hard right uppercut, loses his balance and almost falls. Baer clowns. They both laugh. Braddock throws two lefts at Max's face, but McNamee said from ringside that nothing hard was landed during the round, and most of Braddock's punches were knocked down. At the end, they were fighting head-to-head, and while Braddock landed two good punches on Baer, McNamee said Baer landed the more accurate short rights and uppercuts to Braddock's body. From McNamee's description, Baer fought a better round, and Judge Kelly agreed, but the round went to Braddock.

Braddock Braddock Baer

Round Nine

Again they circle. Baer tries for the body, perhaps to bring down Braddock's guard, but he lands low and immediately apologizes. Braddock sends lefts to the head, but they land on Baer's gloves. Braddock bores in with his head, working at Baer's head, trying to keep Baer tied up at close range. Baer's corner yells, "Come on, Max." Then Baer bores in with his head. McNamee comments on the amount of "head-fighting" and that Baer is doing the better job at infighting, although his punches don't seem to inflict any damage. They circle and come in close again. When the bell rings, Braddock has connected with three shots to the head.

Before round ten, McNamee comments that it is "mighty hard to determine a winner," which suggests that in his eyes, at least, the bout is close or even.

Braddock Braddock Braddock

Round Ten

They both exchange lefts and rights—some land, many miss, and nothing is really damaging. In a clinch, Braddock hits for the head, and Baer lands three hard shots on Braddock's head and body. Baer misses a haymaker, and Braddock misses a short left. They come in close and both land. McAvoy comes to the center and has words with them. Max lands two uppercuts on Braddock's chin, and Braddock misses. Bond tells the radio audience that Braddock is swinging more but leaving them short or missing them altogether.

Baer Braddock Baer

Round Eleven

Max lands a hard right to Braddock's body and three shots to his head. McAvoy cautions Baer not to push with his hand. It is possible that his hands have given out. Max seems to be measuring Braddock with his left, but Braddock pushes it down. Max pounds away at Braddock's body. He lands a hard right to Braddock's arm, and another right to his head. Again McAvoy parts them. Baer is frustrated, either about McAvoy's interference or with his own failure to put Braddock out. Braddock lands on Max's face, and Baer comes back with three uppercuts. They talk to each other and Baer rushes Braddock to the ropes. In a clinch, Braddock lands an ineffective rabbit punch to the back of Baer's neck. Baer plays the head-butt game and is soundly booed for his effort. Ford Bond summarizes that Baer was landing the harder punches during the round.

Even Baer Even

Round Twelve

An aggressive round. Braddock comes out and sticks a right and left to Baer's head. Baer misses a wild swing and goes to the body. Braddock lands a beautiful left hook, and Max lands a swinging right. They trade punches with Braddock landing on the face and Baer landing on the heart. The referee talks to them. They are still punching toe-to-toe with each landing when the bell rings, and Baer appears to have landed the last punch after the bell, causing him to lose the round. The crowd loved the stanza.

Braddock Braddock Braddock

Round Thirteen

Both miss with their haymakers, and both miss inside a clinch. Baer follows Braddock around the ring. Braddock lands on Baer's head. Baer merely paws at Braddock. Again they clinch and miss. Baer lands a good punch on Braddock's head, but Braddock comes back and lands a hard punch to Baer's eye. Again, the round was about Braddock's throwing many punches, and Baer fending them off. It is apparent that neither can knock out the other.

Braddock Braddock Baer

Round Fourteen

They both come at each other firing quickly. Baer is still pounding away at the body and jaw with uppercuts, and Braddock is going for the jaw. In the clinches Baer is still desperately shooting uppercuts to the jaw. He tries for a haymaker but comes up short. Braddock follows him. In close, McAvoy separates them. Braddock lands on the face; Baer lands on the body. All judges give this round to Baer, who landed more punches to the chin in close quarters.

Baer Baer Baer

Round Fifteen

The last round is all about two bulls in the ring fighting bent over, with their heads touching, and each trying to blast away at whatever body part is open at close range. Braddock lands on the jaw, and Baer comes back with six punches to the body. Baer pounds away at Braddock's body, swings wildly with his right, and tries to land uppercuts. All Braddock has to do now is defend himself at close range where Baer cannot land a big punch. Baer is able to break away near the end and try for the haymaker. He lands, but the punch does not have the strength to put Braddock away. Braddock is groggy, but he weathers the storm.

Baer Baer Baer

At the end, Graham McNamee knows the fight is close. He begins to tell to the radio audience, "If the decision goes to Braddock it will be…" but he is interrupted. (Commissioner Brown is sitting next to him.) After a pause, which is assumed to be because he is awaiting official word, McNamee announces that "Braddock has won unquestionably by nine rounds."[31]

Reporter Dan Parker said that Baer "didn't seem either surprised or disappointed at the decision."[32]

Braddock stood at ring center in his lavender trunks and robe as the crowd cheered. Buddy jumped into the ring to kiss his brother.

Referee Johnny McAvoy, scored the fight 9 to 4 with 2 even for Braddock (exactly how the score would play out among the 3 judges). Judge Charles Lynch (the same judge who, questionably, gave the Carnera-Baer title fight to Carnera) scored the fight 11 for Braddock and 4 for Baer (high for Braddock, but enough to sway the balance should a third judge give more rounds to Baer). Last-minute replacement George Kelly scored the fight even, 7 to 7, with 1 round a tie (a better reflection of the fight).

Kelly's scoring resembled Nat Fleischer's: "For seven rounds Baer had the upper hand. He rocked Braddock with several flaming rights to the head that staggered Jimmy, and had the better of the exchanges."[33] Braddock never hit Max with anything that staggered him. Fleischer didn't indicate which rounds Baer won. But based on what he said of Baer, the fight was closer than the lopsided decision of the judges.

Below are the scorecards of referee and 2 judges given to newspapers by the New York State Athletic Commission[34]:

Round	McAvoy	Lynch	Kelly
1	Braddock	Braddock	Braddock
2	Braddock	Braddock	Braddock
3	Braddock	Braddock	Braddock
4	Braddock	Braddock	Braddock
5	Braddock	Braddock	Braddock
6	Even	Braddock	Baer
7	Baer	Baer	Baer
8	Braddock	Braddock	Baer
9	Braddock	Braddock	Braddock
10	Baer	Braddock	Baer
11	Even	Baer	Even
12	Braddock	Braddock	Braddock
13	Braddock	Braddock	Baer
14	Baer	Baer	Baer
15	Baer	Baer	Baer

The Aftermath

Even after puzzling over all the questions surrounding the fight at the time, this title fight remains as curious today as it was in 1935.

Two days after the fight, sportswriter Al Lamb was critical of the judges, suggesting emphatically in bold print that something was not above board:

> It was the first time in you-don't-know-how-long that the three officials working a fight have so closely agreed upon the tide of the battle, round by round. In fact, the uniformity is little short of miraculous. Usually there is a wide divergence of opinion among three official scorers of a fight. That is not strange.... **But Thursday night, Referee McAvoy and Judge Lynch marked their cards almost exactly alike. They agreed on the winner in 12 of the 15 rounds. Mr. Kelly was a little ways away from them but agreed on the decision** [emphasis in the original].[35]

Just like the Carnera fight, in which the scoring was arranged for Carnera to win, a similar arrangement seemed made for this fight, although the last-minute replacement Judge Kelly may not have known about it.

Several columnists were mad, believing they had been duped. Ed Hughes called it a pitiful fight, with Braddock "the hopeless case risen from the ashes of shattered hopes over the years, to emerge from mediocrity and worse when an old man, as Cauliflower years go," overcoming "the Greek god." Hughes asked, "In the grimy, vulgar terms of pugilistics, what was the matter with Baer?" Hughes simply wouldn't accept "bad hands." Fitzsimmons, at age 40, broke every bone in both hands fighting the much younger Jeffries. "So terrific were his clouts that [Fitzsimmons] nursed them one way or another for years afterward." "The point I'm making here," Hughes went on to say, is that Baer "fought as if it made no difference whether he won or lost."[36] Which may have been the case if the outcome was fixed.

Hughes spoke to Baer afterward in his dressing room and asked him, "What, no cocaine?" He asked him why he didn't shoot his hands with cocaine before the fight. (Hughes may have meant "lidocaine" or "novocain"; however, every reference in his column read "cocaine.") "Why didn't you use cocaine?" he asked Max.

"Well, I put it up to the Commission and they refused to allow it," Max answered.

"Well, why didn't you do it anyway? Why should you care about the squeamish airs of a fight commission in a matter that should be so personally important to you? Fighters and managers, as a rule, play this grim game with loaded dice, if necessary, scorn such sissy rulings. You can bet Billy McCarney [who used it on Luther McCarty's hands in the Al Palzer battle] wouldn't have conferred with a commission over the matter of ethics, or such hazy stuff." He walked out of the dressing room, perplexed and mumbling, "Baer is an incurable clown, they say, and that was why he lost."[37] But Hughes didn't believe that for one minute.

Paul Gallico said he was embarrassed by the man he had championed as "the most terrific hitter the ring has ever known, an invincible, indestructible tiger of a man behaving like a third rate vaudevillian."[38]

Most experts attributed Baer's loss to a lack of training or that he "clowned" his way out of the title. But film of the fight (albeit existing footage is sometimes shortened) suggests that Baer only clowned in the first half of the fight and fought the second half seriously. This suggests that Baer let Braddock have a good showing in the initial rounds, because in those early rounds, Baer didn't lunge out first; he didn't swarm his opponent; he didn't pulverize him in the first two rounds and then knock him out, as he was prone to do. He was not particularly aggressive in those early rounds, and his footwork was terrible, as though he was not prepared to stand and fight.

Was the first half of the battle a condition for the fight, or a threat from the mob? Was Max told or paid to carry Braddock for the first five or six rounds to even up the overwhelming odds against the challenger? It is quite obvious from the film that Max didn't fight to win until after the fifth. Grantland Rice confirmed that Baer had given away the first five rounds and explained Baer's poor showing: "He waited until the fifth round to go on the offense in which he broke both hands."[39]

Nevertheless, if Baer gave away five rounds in the first half, he clearly won five rounds in the second half for his harder, more powerful upper cuts and body punches. But because he could not KO Braddock, the fight would go down to the scorecards. Only one judge, Kelly, the last-minute replacement, scored the fight even. The two other judges gave the fight to Braddock.

Max needed a knockout, but he clearly did not have a knockout punch in his sore hands. Close examination of many of his punches indicated that his power shots were more of a clubbing-type of action. He did more pounding than punching. Did something happen in the day before the fight to further damage his hands? Or in his dressing room when his hands were unwrapped? Ancil Hoffman surely believed there was some kind of physical interference. Some thought the championship was stolen.

The only way the fight made sense, at least to sportswriter Joe Williams, was to point to Jimmy Johnston. Dressed in his "worst Hollywood outfit," Jimmy Johnston was the one who made out the best. Not discounting Braddock's courage, Williams noted that the outcome was good for Jimmy Johnston in that it assured him of being renamed matchmaker of the Garden when the board met two weeks later to determine his fate. It was common knowledge that Johnston's job had been in question, but: "How can they possibly throw a guy out who picks a battered fighter off the ash heap, maneuvers him into a battle for the heavyweight championship, predicts he will win—and he does?... There wasn't one lethal blow landed in the 15 rounds. There wasn't one knockdown. As early as the seventh round the crowd began to shower the arena with luscious razzberries." Most importantly, wrote Joe Williams, "If Braddock won, it meant [Johnston] still had control of the heavyweight division."[40] Part of the maneuvering of Braddock that Joe Williams referred to was Art Lasky's agreement to step aside and let Braddock win in their fight. Lasky's confession came only two days after Braddock's title win over Baer and was certainly a significant element in the unbelievable story of the Cinderella Man's rise to the top, which has been previously omitted.

Damon Runyon said that Jimmy Johnston, the Garden director, was "almost beside himself with joy over Braddock's victory because he hates Max Baer with a deep hatred." But Runyon added that his real interest in Braddock was affected by the Garden's contract with him.[41]

Max had little to say and only reiterated his congratulations to his successor. While still in his dressing room, Max was given a cigarette and a bottle of beer. He held up his right, and everyone was horrified at how the metacarpal bones in his hand moved out of position when he made a fist.

After the bout, Baer attended a dinner. It was supposed to be his victory dinner at a hotel, sponsored by Gillette. The only attendees were Baer, his brother, and some random hotel attendants. Tables were piled high with food and drink. The small party stayed and ate and drank until they were full.

Art Cohn said that afterward, Max wept.[42]

Conflicting with what Leo Friede said about a "quiet place for Max before and after the fight," Walter Winchell, society columnist, reported in his Broadway gossip column that Friede gave a party for Max after the fight. Waiting for Max at the penthouse was Mary Kirk Brown, the New York socialite romantically linked with him at the time of the fight. At the after-party, Winchell said "the host caught one of the sorrowing guests by the ankle, as the would-be suicide tried jumping from a window!" The reference was vague regarding who may have attempted the suicide.[43]

The fight was not a big money-maker for anyone, perhaps with the exception of gamblers, which may point to one aspect of the seedy-looking bout. It made only $205,366 because Braddock was not considered a big calling card as challenger. Demands for ringside seats (at $20, rather than the normal $50 price) were modest.

"One year ago," Joe Williams wrote, "Braddock was a pugilistic cadaver, his obituary

In his Steve Morgan robe, Max Baer congratulates new world heavyweight champion, Jim Braddock. *Left to right:* Whitey Bimstein, Max Baer, Ancil Hoffman, and Dolph Thomas (courtesy David Bergin).

written," today he's a world champion.⁴⁴ One thing was certain. The Clown Prince had handed the Cinderella Man the glass slipper.

As James Dawson concluded for the *New York Times*, "Braddock wanted to fight and did to the best of his ability. Baer, ever the clown, didn't want to fight, or just simply couldn't. That is the answer to this battle that was poor from a competitive standpoint and so stunningly amazing in its results."⁴⁵

The press refused to believe that the fight was not fixed. Fans suspected what William Weer called "another one of those curious denouements of the prize-fight business." The sportswriter asked, "Did the racketeer Owney Madden have something to do with it? Wasn't there talk of Madden's gang and a peculiar interest it developed, during the prefight days, in the heavyweight championship of the world?"⁴⁶

The night of the fight, Commission Chairman John Phelan said there would be an investigation into the "sensational upset." But the next day he changed his mind, saying emphatically, "There will be no investigation because there's nothing to investigate."⁴⁷

Baer's hands had puffed up to twice their normal size, "both swollen like hams. The middle knuckle of the left was puffed up as if stung by a bumble bee, and the back of the right was ballooned and discolored." All he could say, while a "big tear slithered from [his] purplish, swollen left eye," was that "I lost the title in Cleveland when I hurt my hands in an exhibition bout with Eddie Simms. I thought they would be all right." He was "grilled mercilessly on the most important question connected with the loss": "Was it phoney?" "Was the fix in?" he was asked repeatedly. He responded, "Jeez—it's bad enough to lose the title—to shoot a million bucks just like that. But it's worse to have people accuse me of laying down—of dogging it." He simply held up his hands.⁴⁸

His hands were X-rayed by Dr. Leo L. Michel, and he concluded that both hands had been broken. There were two fractures in the right (one from an old injury) and his left hand was broken at the wrist. "At the end of the third round," Baer explained, "both my hands were gone. All I could do was slap him."⁴⁹ Baer didn't offer his broken hands as an excuse for losing his title. He took the loss like a man. He said, "I know I deserved to lose the decision and I don't want to take anything away from Braddock. I thought my hands were strong enough when I went into the ring, and it's my own fault that I didn't knock out Jim early. Frankly, I didn't expect the fight to go more than seven rounds."⁵⁰

There were many scenarios surrounding the fight, any one of which could have affected the outcome:

There is innuendo and direct comment that Baer was threatened by the mob to lose the fight, and he certainly didn't look like the same confident fighter who pounded Schmeling or Carnera. He could have been induced to carry Braddock for five rounds, because he so obviously gave those rounds away, which was another anomaly in Baer's fighting style. He liked to get the job done in the early rounds.

Jimmy Johnston desperately needed Braddock to win to preserve his job at the Garden. The Art Lasky set-up fits this theory. If Johnston brought a fighter considered a has-been to the big ring and lost, Johnston would have lost his job as Garden matchmaker. If Braddock won, Johnston stood to control the heavyweight division.

Considering the deal Braddock's manager Joe Gould made with Louis's management before he granted Louis a title fight with Braddock, Gould and his mob-backer Owen Madden could have been behind any fight conditions. Gould was certainly indebted to Jimmy Johnston for moving Braddock to the top and placing him in the match.

Another consideration regarding Max's intriguing comment about doing a "good turn" for his "Broadway friends" was Mary Kirk Brown, the New York socialite whom Baer was seeing at the time and who was at the after-party. Was she involved the night before the fight? Had they stayed together at Friede's penthouse or possibly gone to the Stork Club and/or met up with Madden in one of the many private rooms? Even if Max had been with a woman the night before, his previous all-night forays didn't seem to affect his fight outcomes.

If anything affected the fight, it was Baer's hands. He was pressured going into a fight when he knew his hands were bad. In fact his hands were worse than Hoffman had seen before. Bad hands gave Braddock the advantage, and any of the unsavory management or authorities could have influenced Baer to proceed with the fight as scheduled. He could have been threatened with forfeit if he failed to go through with the bout. No medical professional, however, who saw Baer's hands would have let him go into the ring that night, except the doctor for the New York Commission, an agency that wanted Baer out of the picture.

Hoffman had reason to question the scoring and interference with his fighter, and was expecting a hearing before the New York Commission (where the world might learn of the facts of the case). There was no official investigation. Even with a hearing, Baer may have been reluctant to testify.

There is little doubt that Max was not able to win the fight by a knockout due to the conditions of his hands. Given that he couldn't win with a knockout, there is also little doubt that he could win the decision on the judges' scorecards.

Baer expected to get a rematch with Braddock and regain the title. (Was that part of a deal that stood to give bettors on the long odds a windfall profit from this fight?)

Walter Rothenburg was shocked by Baer's loss. He had been ready to guarantee Baer $540,000 for a Schmeling fight on August 17. Now the German promoter would make Braddock an offer; and if that failed, he would consider Baer for a fight but with a "sharp downward revision in the terms he had previously offered the former champion."[51]

There it was: Max Baer the *former* champion. He had just dropped the most valuable prize in sport. His opportunity for even greater fame, along with big dollars, evaporated. Schmeling declined to meet Baer again in any bout. But Schmeling did say that he would immediately set sail for the United States to meet Braddock in a title match. Only the previous spring he had turned up his nose at the idea that he would meet Braddock in an elimination bout, saying that Braddock wasn't good enough to fight him. Now his promoters were offering Braddock a $200,000 guarantee to meet Schmeling.

Baer received a check for $88,805, 42½ percent of the gate. Braddock received a check for $31,244.13, 15 percent of the gate. It was a far cry from just six months ago when Jim was Case No. 2796 on public relief, getting $24 per month in North Bergen, New Jersey. Eddie Brietz reported after the win that Braddock stood to get offers totaling 150 grand.

Max told reporters that he was going to quit the fight business. But Ancil Hoffman said, "Right now Max is a little disappointed in himself. But after a few days he'll begin to miss the adulation of the crowd, and will want to fight his way back to another chance at the championship."[52]

Baer would stay at the Asbury Park camp to help train Buddy for his bout with Frank Wotanski on the undercard of Joe Louis and Primo Carnera, June 25 at Yankee Stadium.

Nine • Clown Prince Loses Crown to Braddock, 1935

Buddy won his fight. And two weeks after losing the heavyweight crown, Max wed Mary Ellen Sullivan in Washington, D.C., on June 29, 1935, at the home of Judge F. Dickinson Letts. Jay O'Brien was his best man. Mary Ellen, born in Ithaca, New York, on September 30, 1903, was 32 at the time of this, her first marriage, five years older than Max. She was a 1927 college graduate from the Rochester Mechanics Institute, and worked as a dietician, supervising the coffee room at the prestigious Willard Hotel in Washington, D.C., where the couple met.[53]

Although Max had known Mary Ellen for two years, the wedding was a rather quick affair. As Max explained, "She's a home-loving person." Max was tired of the society girls and was ready to settle down. "She doesn't drink and she doesn't smoke. She's never seen a prize fight and she doesn't like them." Mary Ellen was also a devout Catholic. Max told the press he "might embrace the Roman Catholic faith out of love for his bride."[54] The thought never crossed his mind, until he married, but he didn't know if he had ever been baptized. "Even my mother doesn't remember," he said, which reaffirmed Max's limited religious participation, although he did mention two particular denominations. When told that many people believed he was Jewish, he said, "My father had Jewish blood in him, but he married a Scottish-Irish girl, and my mother is the sweetest mother in the world. My sister Frances married a strict Roman Catholic. I myself have gone to Episcopalian churches and Christian Science services."[55] For this marriage, Max had his parents' blessing.

Soon after the wedding, a member of the United Press asked Vatican officials to comment on a match between a devout Catholic with a divorced non–Catholic, perceived to be Jewish. The response was: "Membership in our church is open to everyone, including prize fighters."[56]

Braddock said that he would gladly offer Max a rematch in August. But Jimmy Johnston had other plans. He announced that Braddock was signed with the Garden, and his next fight would not be until June of the next year, 1936. Commissioner Bill Brown told the press that Baer was barred from fighting anyone in New York. Brown was quoted, "We had enough of that quitter."[57]

Baer's iconic punches had taken their toll on his hands. The New York Commission declared that Baer could not fight again until he had an operation on his hands. Baer was re-examined by Dr. W.V. Healey, the bone specialist who had operated on the hands of Gene Tunney. The doctor confirmed that Max had a "floating bone in his right hand" that must be operated on before he could fight again.[58] Hoffman set the date for the operation, but Max decided to have yet another opinion from doctors at Johns Hopkins in Baltimore. There, Dr. William F. Rienhoff Jr. told him that "he should not have fought Braddock with his hands in that condition," but that he didn't need an operation. His knuckles had been badly bruised over his left hand and he just needed to let both hands rest and heal.[59] He could fight again by September.

Hoffman realized that the only hope for getting Baer a chance again at the title was to sign with New York promoter Mike Jacobs. The promotional wars heated up. Jimmy Johnston refused to give Joe Louis and Primo Carnera a shot at the championship because, he said, "These opponents of June 25 are allied with the rival Twentieth Century club."[60]

The acrimony between promoters Jimmy Johnston and Mike Jacobs had gone back to the time of Tex Rickard. Jacobs's association with Rickard began in 1916 and ended abruptly with Rickard's death in 1929, when Jimmy Johnston was selected promoter at the Garden over Jacobs. Jacobs worked his way back into the New York promotional

Max married Mary Ellen Sullivan in Washington, D.C., on June 29, 1935.

scene when he formed the Twentieth Century Sporting Club in partnership with, and with publicity help from, Hearst newspaper reporters Damon Runyon, Edward J. Frayne (*New York American* sports editor), and Bill Farnsworth (*New York Journal* sports editor).

Baer's switch to the Twentieth Century Club gave Mike Jacobs the following heavyweight cards: Baer, Carnera, Louis, and Lasky. The Garden had Braddock and Schmeling, and those relationships were slowly eroding. Johnston had a spat with Braddock and refused to present Braddock his gold championship belt for eleven months until it was clear that he was going to stand by his contract with Madison Square Garden, aka Jimmy Johnston.

Johnston had the new

Did you hear what Jacobs was expected to make on his match-up of Joe Louis and Max Baer? With both gate attractions, Baer and Louis, signed to Mike Jacobs, Jimmy Johnston's monopoly at MSG was soon to end. *Left to right:* Max Baer, Ancil Hoffman, Mike Jacobs.

titleholder, but Jacobs had Joe Louis. When Johnston refused to split the fight proceeds with Jacobs, negotiations for a Braddock-Louis match hit an impasse.

With Baer and Louis on the same team, Baer would fight Joe Louis (the victor in the Louis-Carnera bout), hoping to get a rematch with Braddock for another chance at the title.

Dempsey convinced Baer's training staff that his upright, open style of fighting couldn't defend against the offensive blows from Braddock. That same style couldn't possibly defend against a Louis. So a new strategy was set with Dempsey in charge of training. Baer would have to change to a Dempsey-like crouch with his chin protected by his big left shoulder and his glove held high to block his side.

So Max, blessed with tremendous punching power and cursed with brittle hands, went back to Duffy's Gym in Oakland to train for Louis.

TEN

Former Champion Meets Louis, 1935

The first opponent Max Baer would face on the road back to regain the title he lost three months earlier would be—wham!—the Detroit Destroyer, Joe Louis. There had not been a battle of this magnitude since Dempsey-Tunney.

Louis was a young gun on his way to the top with a lust for victory, and Baer was coming off the big loss with his pride on the line. Both were hungry for the win. This match was expected to be an epic showdown, not a battle won on points. The victor would likely take his opponent with a knockout punch.

Interest in this fight was so hot that first-day ticket sales produced $250,000 in orders and reservations, the biggest advance sale since the Dempsey-Tunney days. Attendance was predicted to be 95,000, weather permitting. And if the weather was good, the gate could approach $1,200,000, an awesome amount for a non-title fight in the middle of the Depression. With each boxer signed for 30 percent of the net proceeds, each stood to make $300,000.

Early on in Louis's career, when manager John Roxborough contacted Madison Square Garden about a Louis fight, he had been told they were not interested in a black boxer who could not be trusted to lose a few on demand. It was Nat Fleischer who connected the Louis camp to his friend Mike Jacobs of the Twentieth Century Sporting Club. As a result, Jacobs was able to corner what would become the biggest fight name of the decade. Jacobs signed a contract with Louis's managers that gave the promoter sole proprietorship of all Louis fights for three years with a renewal clause. Jacobs had just shut the door on Jimmy Johnston's office at Madison Square Garden. The newspapers noted that promoter Mike Jacobs was starting to look and act like another Tex Rickard.

The Detroit threat to heavyweight challengers was variously called the "Black Menace," the "Panther-Man," the "Black Widow," and the "Brown Bomber." He had traveled to the top faster than any other heavyweight, in only one year and two months of professional fighting. With a brutal knockout record and nineteen professional wins without a loss, he made his Eastern debut on June 25, 1935, at Yankee Stadium, twelve days after the Baer-Braddock fight, with a TKO in the sixth round over Primo Carnera. Max Baer was Louis's 22nd fight. Jim Jeffries won his title in fewer bouts, but that was after three years of work. Jeffries retired after 24 total bouts. Joe Louis was predicted to be that new heavyweight phenomenon of the century. Even the president of the United States saw him as a new celebrity. Louis said that one of his biggest thrills was shaking the hand of President Franklin Roosevelt in Washington, D.C., on August 27, 1935.

Trainer Jack Blackburn had always told Louis, "Joe, a colored fighter is born with two strikes on him. You gotta be a killer to make money."[1] And in his all-in-a-day's work attitude, Louis was knocking over heavyweights like bowling pins. He was so good at the start of his profession that he never had to perform in a preliminary—he was always the main event. In July of 1935, the great heavyweight Sam Langford told the *Chicago Defender* that he thought Louis compared to another great black champion, the "Old Master," who was considered a "Marvel of the Ring." Langford said, "The Detroit Bomber is another Joe Gans who I think was the greatest fighter of all time.... I consider [Louis] another Gans. He can hit, he is fast and is no slouch at employing ring craft. He is the marvel of the age."[2]

On August 7, in Chicago, Louis beat King Levinsky in the first round on a technical at Comiskey Park. Louis's share was $47,688—a nice sum for one round of work and more than Braddock made on his championship win. In September, Louis would try to move up the heavyweight ladder by taking on another big man with a big name, Max Baer.

Frank Graham of the *New York Journal American* said, "Baer never saw the night that he belonged in the ring with Louis."[3] Grantland Rice used to say to Max before a bout, "Be mean when you get in there! For once in your life, try to hate somebody!"[4]

Baer would train hard and he would have iron-hard supervisors for his training. Manager Ancil Hoffman preferred heavy roadwork of 5-mile jaunts, one hour of wood chopping, and regular hours at training camp. And new wife Mary Ellen said absolutely no cigarettes, liquor, tea, coffee, or soda. Max was particularly fond of sodas. Actually, Max had substituted pipes for cigarettes, which were considered safer at the time. Parties, pals, and fun were a thing of the past. Even Papa Baer commented that Baer would toe the line in his training or he would "lick him myself," a formidable threat coming from a former butcher and boxer near equal his size and strength.[5]

Jacobs would control 100 percent of the promotion of the Baer-Louis fight. However, along with Louis and Jacobs came referee Arthur Donovan, whom Baer and Hoffman detested. Donovan was a connection made by Louis's questionable management. By 1944 Donovan was on the Louis payroll, having refereed 22 of the Bomber's fights. He came to be known in the trade as "Joe Louis's private referee." Many of his dubious calls were attributed to his contractual agreement with the Louis camp and his conflict of interest.[6]

The Louis and Baer match, September 24, was promoted as another "Battle of the Century." In the classic sense of a Tex Rickard promotion, this match was considered the best "mixed-race fight" staged in 25 years. It had all the earmarks of a Johnson-Jeffries or Nelson-Gans affair, along with the hope of a Dempsey-like battle that could bring back the million-dollar gate. The economy needed it and boxing needed it. One headline blasted, "Fists of Black Bomber Usher in New 'White Hope' Epoch."[7]

Before Baer could face Louis, the New York Commission required his hands to be reexamined. Commission doctors, headed by Frederick E. Elliott, took a dozen X-rays and declared: "There was no apparent sign of anything not normal in a fighter's hands."[8]

Both Buddy and Max trained at Speculator, New York, in the Adirondacks, approximately eighty miles northeast of Utica and 250 miles away from any distractions in New York City. Gene Tunney had trained there for his battle with Jack Dempsey in 1927. Max strengthened his hands by chopping wood, digging holes, and punching the bag. He soaked them regularly in the same brine Dempsey used, and he placed felt over his knuckles in training.

Max Baer went through many sparring partners in his training for Joe Louis. Here is Willie McGee, September 16, 1935 (ACME).

On September 19, Dr. William Walker of the New York Athletic Commission made an impromptu visit to see if Baer was conditioning properly. Everything the commission did annoyed Baer. The doctor watched him work out in four heavy rounds with sparring partners George Turner and Abe Feldman. Only the day before, Baer nailed Feldman with a left hook and a right cross to the chin. With Turner, Baer practiced getting inside a Louis left hook and throwing short rights from his shoulder. He let Abe's jabs bounce off his headgear, until he let go a barrage of punches that put his sparring partner on the ropes. After watching Baer, Dr. Walker admitted that he looked in better shape for this fight than he did for the Braddock fight. His breathing was better and his blood pressure was normal.

Everything about this bout seemed to annoy Max. Even his brother aggravated him. Buddy had been training for his own fight on the undercard with Ford Smith. At one point, Ancil Hoffman said the "movie people yowled" to take film of Max and Buddy boxing each other. "In an unguarded moment," Hoffman said yes. But after only a few seconds, Max had a bloody nose and Buddy a cut lip. Max couldn't pull his punches with his brother. The last time they were in the ring together, Buddy came out in a body cast. The movie people loved the realism until Hoffman called the impending carnage to a halt. "That is all, gentlemen, for today and forever!" Ancil swore, "These two have had the gloves on for the last time while I have anything to do with them."[9]

Several members of the Louis camp were also on edge. When Joe arrived at his training camp at Pompton Lakes, New Jersey, his first move was to close the tavern operated in conjunction with the camp. Joe didn't drink alcohol, but he didn't mind others drinking. He just did not want his sleep interrupted by a bunch of yelping drunks. He needed his sleep. The edict kept both manager John Roxborough and trainer Jack Blackburn sober. Joe had bet both men in his recent Levinsky bout that he would KO the Kingfish in the first round. If he lost, manager and trainer were promised a new suit of clothes. If he won (which he did), they would "go on the wagon" for two months. Both were known to over-indulge. It had been only a month into their sentence.

Joe Louis staged public workouts for the fans who came to visit his training camp. Crowds soared up to 1,000 on occasion. At one event, he sparred two soft rounds with Larry Johnson. Then he stepped up the pace with Lew Flowers, staggering him for two rounds. After that, he dropped Bobby Dean, of Newark, once in the first round and twice in the second round. Trainer Blackburn called for Paul Cavalier, of Paterson, to step up next. Blackburn would increase the number of sparring partners to five.

At the same time in early September, Max was also boxing six rounds daily. Hoffman was working on Max's speed. He told Grantland Rice, "Two men might be equally good shots, but the faster draw usually gets by."[10] Baer's slashing right had to come quicker and from an unexpected place. Hoffman added, "Hitting Louis is like trying to slap a timber wolf in the face. His head seems to be somewhere else when the blow arrives."[11] Max never trained more faithfully. He severely battered all three of his partners, Tony Cancela, Lou Scozza and Cecil (Ceil) Harris. On one occasion Ceil jumped out of the ring after Baer landed a vicious right on his chin. Like Blackburn, Hoffman was calling around for additional sparring partners.

Baer left his training camp for New York the day before the fight. He drove to Schenectady, where he boarded the train for New York. Accompanied by a state trooper, he was greeted in Schenectady by a crowd in the hundreds and by a second mob of fans when the train pulled into Grand Central Station.

For two days the fight followers poured into New York, flooding the midtown section and filling major hotels. The Commodore, Biltmore, Roosevelt, Vanderbilt, Ritz Carlton, Ritz Towers, Paramount, Edison, and Victoria hotels were all booked to capacity. Airplanes were added to existing routes to accommodate travelers. Special trains ran from dozens of cities as far away as San Francisco, specifically for the fight. Revelers thronged the nightclubs, and New Yorkers complained about the traffic.

Louis was irritable after having trained vigorously at his camp for three weeks. Managers Roxborough and Julian Black feared he was over-trained. He enjoyed his workouts. Without anything to fill his time, he became bored. As an old-school trainer, Blackburn would not permit Louis an auto ride. Blackburn took no chances of having his charge involved in an accident.

A regular part of Louis's training routine had been watching fight films of Baer-Schmeling and Baer-Carnera. Publicly, Jack Blackburn advised Louis to go at Baer from the first punch. Privately, he wanted him to stalk Baer and wait for an opening; such was the strategy Blackburn learned directly from the Old Master. Joe Louis was often called "a heavyweight Joe Gans." Blackburn's admiration for Gans meant that Louis was trained with daily reminders of the Old Master's strategies and deportment.

Louis was escorted by New York state troopers to the offices of the State Athletic Commission for the weigh-in. The only thing that occupied Joe's mind was his upcoming marriage to Marva Trotter.

When he learned of Louis's pending wedding plans, sportswriter Paul Gallico said that it was a bad omen. "Max Baer lost to Braddock and immediately married Mary Ellen. Fred Petty lost to Wiler Allison and immediately married Helen Vinson. Joe Louis is going to marry Marva Trotter the night of the fight. That's asking for it. He will be the third loser in the string—you mark the words of Paul Gallico, the old Hex-doctor." While Gallico's friends picked Louis to win, he held firm with Baer: "I am convinced that [Baer] has a great punch left and that when he applies it in rage and malice, it will do the trick."[12] Even James Braddock predicted Baer would win: "Maxie is a killer and I believe he will upset Louis."[13]

Baer was still wildly popular, as ticket sales indicated. And people like Gallico believed he had a punch that could put the new star to sleep. Baer was strong and unpredictable. No one doubted that he could have flattened Jim Braddock if his hands had been good. And regardless of Carnera's fight with Schaaf, or Schaaf's illness before he went into the Carnera fight, people still thought that Baer was at least partially responsible for putting Schaaf at death's door. And Baer had never been knocked off his feet in the ring. Ed Hughes, writing for the *Brooklyn Daily*, said, "Baer fighting with the spirit of the Schmeling, Carnera and Levinsky frays would surely have an excellent chance of whipping Louis." But, he continued, "Unless Joe is the most overrated fighter in ring history, this writer expects him to win from Max Baer somewhere in the tenth round."[14]

At the time of the fight, ringside tickets (extending back 35 rows), which were normally $25, were being scalped in the range of $80 to $125 each. A pair of seats behind the reporters was offered at $250. A pair of seats normally selling for $16.50 was exchanged for $45. These were still not the highest prices that had been set for a heavyweight bout. Ringside seats for Jack Dempsey's title defense against Georges Carpentier at Jersey City in 1921 were $50. The highest price of a ringside seat in 1927 for Tunney's defense against Dempsey at Chicago was $40. But these were still lean years and Jacobs thought $25 reasonable. Had he charged more, he would have easily made well over the $1 million mark.

More than one thousand reporters requested press passes. There were so many media representatives attending that an auxiliary section of seating had to be arranged. Louis made a polite demand that would change history. Prior to this fight, reporters from African American newspapers were denied press passes under the guise of no passes for the "weekly press." Since most African American–owned newspapers were weeklies, black writers were denied access to media passes in the press rows, consequently segregating ringside attendees. Old fight films reveal just how white the game was at ringside.[15] Louis demanded that black reporters be allowed to attend this fight alongside other press members in the press rows, thus desegregating reporters at an important boxing match and putting a new crack in Jim Crow laws. Writers like Billy Rowe and Chester Washington of the *Pittsburgh Courier*, Al Monroe of the *Chicago Defender*, Rowen Dougherty of the *Amsterdam News*, and many other black reporters attended the big fight in the media section.

Reporters came from as far away as England, China, Japan, South America, Canada, and Germany to cover the fight, advertised as it was—a return of the Golden Era and the million-dollar gate. Over 1900 policemen and detectives patrolled the crowd. In terms of bets, Louis was the favorite, 3 to 1. A great deal of money exchanged hands. Louis's manager Roxborough said Joe would win in five. But Baer's hometown Livermoreans wagered a total of $12,000 on Baer, the equivalent of $3.50 for every member of the city's population.

Max Baer and Joe Louis weigh in for their match, which would be the first million-dollar gate since the Dempsey era. Dempsey would be in this one as chief second to Baer (courtesy David Bergin).

The weigh-in at the Athletic Commission office in the afternoon was only a formality because no limit existed for heavyweights. Dr. Walker performed his routine medical exam and both Baer and Louis were declared in fine shape. Baer was given his purple shorts and Louis his red and black pair.

The gloves were still an issue. Baer had special gloves made in San Francisco. They were like any other set furnished for a championship fight: 6 oz., stuffed with horsehair, and made of kid leather. The only difference was that Baer's glove maker padded the inside area of the forefinger such that when a fist was made, there existed less space than normal between the thumb and forefinger. Baer felt that this padding added protection for his thumbs, which were frequently broken.

Baer had petitioned to wear his own gloves from California for both the Carnera and Braddock fights. For both title matches, the New York Athletic Commission denied his request. Again he submitted the gloves for examination, weeks before the Louis bout. The Louis camp raised no objection. But the commissioners, perhaps driven by the ire of Bill Brown aimed at Baer, rejected his request. Since there was no law on record governing a request of special, 6-ounce gloves, Baer's manager thought the commissioners were acting unreasonably and he was ready to call off the fight. Hoffman and Baer walked out of the office. They were called back. A compromise was offered. Baer could wear his gloves, but Louis would be allowed to wear twice the amount of hand-wrap.

Specifically, under his gloves, Louis was allowed to wrap his hands with twelve feet of soft bandages, two inches in width (instead of the normal six feet at one and a half-inch width) and use six feet of bandage to hold the wrap instead of two. Louis went into battle wearing the extra hand-wraps.

The combatants posed for pictures. In crouched photo shots, both fighters looked equally muscular and deadly serious. Heavily wrinkled brows appeared on both faces. Five thousand people waited outside the State Office Building at the Worth Street entrance for a glimpse at the celebrities or a possible autograph as they exited from the weigh-in.

A crowd also gathered outside an apartment house at 381 Edgecombe Avenue, the home of Mr. and Mrs. Vernon Porter, friends of Louis's manager. Joe went directly from the weigh-in for a few hours of sleep in a third-floor apartment. Waiting on the first floor was his fiancé, beautiful nineteen-year-old Marva Trotter, a woman Louis's handlers had approved for his career. At 7:30 p.m. a city clerk, Julius J. Brosen, arrived with a marriage license. At 8:00, Joe Louis married Miss Trotter, witnessed by his manager Julian Black and his wife. Marva's brother, the Rev. Walter Trotter, read the marriage vows. Marva was one of eleven siblings from Chicago. She worked full-time as a secretary at the newspaper the *Chicago Defender* while she was enrolled at the University of Chicago. She was introduced to Joe at one of his public training sessions at Trafton's Gym in Chicago as the man who was going to be the next heavyweight champion of the world. They saw each other infrequently over the next two years, and now they were married. Outside, policemen helped clear a path for the married couple so they could reach the car waiting to take them to the fight. At Yankee Stadium, Joe went to his dressing room and Marva took her seat at ringside.

Joe's dressing room was crowded with boxers, managers, and friends. He requested that he be allowed to sleep on his rubbing table, away from the other fighters dressing for their preliminary bouts and reporters eager to get a few words. He needed a nap; he had already had a full day and was tired. Promoter Mike Jacobs corralled a construction crew to build a makeshift fence of chicken wire, closing off a small area to allow him to sleep in seclusion until his match.

One of Baer's sparring partners, George Turner, was on the undercard. When time came for Turner to enter the ring, he couldn't find his robe, so he donned the robe of his sparring partner, Abe Feldman. The program literally stopped when the announcer asked everyone near the ring who was wearing the robe with "Feldman" on the back.

While Louis was snoozing, a doctor was in Baer's dressing room frantically trying to decide what to do with his injured hand. Max had broken his right hand in training camp, but the injury was kept secret so as not to affect the outcome of a possible million-dollar gate. Doctors had been treating the break with Novocain to deaden the pain. Because of the threat of rain on the evening of the fight, the boxers had to go into the stadium early. The main event didn't start until 10 p.m. Baer's hands were securely bandaged when the Novocain was starting to wear off. Max panicked.

According to Bayard Bookman, accountant for Hoffman and Baer, "As the hour neared, Max and the doctor slipped into the men's room where the doctor inserted the needle beneath the bandages. Apparently the needle missed its intended target and went in up near the wrist. Instead of merely numbing the hand, it deadened the whole right forearm. Within ten minutes Max was a frantic wreck, not far short of collapse." Max was determined not to go forward with the bout. Hoffman couldn't budge him. "Jack Dempsey almost literally had to drag him out for the fight."[16]

Marva Trotter was introduced to Joe Louis as the future world champion. On September 25, 1934, only hours before the Louis-Baer bout, she became Mrs. Joe Louis. Wedding card announcement.

Buddy Baer was originally scheduled for the wind-up bout after the main event, but at the last minute his heavyweight match with Ford Smith of Montana was moved to precede the main event, no doubt to accommodate Max's panic attack. Although Buddy rallied in the final round, he lost the unanimous six-round decision.

Max did not wear his customary "Steve Morgan" robe. On this night he wore a plain white robe with "Max Baer" stitched on the back, instead of a nod to the fictional champion.

One of the great ring announcers, Joe Humphreys, had been extremely ill, but he wanted to announce the fight. He entered the ring feebly, but when he clutched the microphone, his voice boomed. Radio hookups broadcast the fight from coast to coast. Clem McCarthy described the fight and Edwin Hill broadcast between rounds.

Jack Dempsey served in Baer's corner as chief second. He missed the introductions.

Jimmy Braddock was at ringside, along with Gene Tunney, Jack Sharkey, Jack Johnson, Benny Leonard, Johnny Dundee, governors of six states and noted mayors, Theodore Roosevelt, Jr., prominent judges, promoters, theatrical and sports personalities like Babe Ruth, who never missed a big fight.

The battle was short: Baer was cut down in 11 minutes and 52 seconds. Louis kayoed the former champion in the fourth round. Baer took the count on his knees while Louis was poised to come at him again if necessary. Baer struggled to stand with the help of the referee. He was dazed. Baer had been knocked down three times, and it was the first time in his boxing career that he had been sent to the canvas. In some respects it replayed the Johnson-Jeffries fight, insofar as crowds came from all parts of the country to see an "epochal struggle" between a black fighter and a white fighter. And in the end, the best man won, decisively.

George Kirksey typed from ringside, "A new 'White Hope' epoch was ushered in today on the murderous fists of Brown Man Joe Louis. He pounded former champion Max Baer to a pulp ... just as he did former champion Primo Carnera and boxing experts and fight fans realized with a terrible shrill that no known man, black, yellow, white, or red, not even Champion James J. Braddock, would have a chance against the unthinking, unfeeling, fighting machine."[17] Now Louis would be known as the greatest "fighting machine" since Dempsey. And even Dempsey, in his intimate proximity at the ring, knew that Louis had *everything*.

Sponsored by Buick, the bout drew 88,150 attendees. The gate, the largest for the decade, reached almost $1,000,000 ($932,944). Adding radio and film revenues, the Baer-Louis fight was considered a million-dollar fight. This was the fifth million-dollar event in American boxing history, and Jack Dempsey had been in all of them, as boxer and now chief second for Baer.

Each boxer was to get 30 percent. Louis received $217,337.03, bringing his total earnings to a half-million dollars. Baer's percentage had been reduced to 25 percent. What he actually received was even less: $150,000. Mike Jacobs explained that Baer had agreed to this amount as a guarantee. Jacobs took the balance of Baer's 25 percent, keeping $31,000.[18]

Because there were so many writers reporting to regional papers, the round-by-round reports varied greatly: in color, description and punch counts. Below are two versions from different newspapers: one from the *New York Times*, and another from the *Poughkeepsie Eagle News* (quoted in parentheticals), both printed September 25, 1935. Poughkeepsie was and remains a small town in the Hudson Valley of New York, approximately halfway between New York City and Albany. Of the two accounts, the *New York Times* was the more sanitized and proper; the *Poughkeepsie* version, the more colorful with diction a reflection of the times. The two versions seemed considerably different in the retelling.

Louis-Baer, September 24, 1935, Yankee Stadium, New York

Round One

They came out of their corners slowly.
(Baer came slowly from his corner hunched in a half crouch,)

Louis hooked a light left to the body
(and Louis stabbed his face lightly a half dozen times with lefts).
and missed a left for the heart.
(Louis missed a left hook in the body)
Baer landed a right to the head but Louis came back with a left and right to the body.
(and Baer slapped him savagely with a right to the head.)
They sparred cautiously until Louis unleashed a hard left hook to the jaw.
(They locked in a clinch, both cold and deadly, and pawed carefully at each other. His face never changing,)
Louis battered Baer's chin with two hard lefts and a right.
(Louis flicked a stream of lefts into Baer's forehead)
Louis sent Baer's head back with a straight left.
([Louis] hooked a hard left to the head then smashed Baer's chin with both hands. A right to the head brought blood trickling from Baer's nose.)
Baer missed a wild right for the head.
(Baer lunged in desperately, missing a long wild right.)
Baer stood toe-to-toe to Louis and exchanged punches savagely,
(Baer opened up with a savage attack,)
but Louis made the Californian stop with a hard right to the head.
(but Louis survived the storm and drove Max into a corner where he hammered his head unmercifully.)
Louis made Baer stand in the corner and punched him almost at will with hard rights and lefts to the head until the bell rang.
(Baer replied in the corner, pinned there and Louis hammered him savagely up to the bell. Blood covering his face, Baer slapped disdainfully at the Negro as he walked to his seat. Louis' round.)

Round Two

Louis tapped a light left to the head.
(Again Baer came up slowly, pawing with his left and Louis snapped a left hook into his face.)
Baer pawed for an opening with his left and retreated steadily.
(Baer approached low as the calm Negro stalked him and blood was trickling again from Max's face.)
Louis staggered Baer with a right to the jaw. Louis landed a left to the jaw and shook Baer again.
(They boxed carefully in mid-ring and suddenly Louis smashed Baer into a corner with three tremendous rights to the chin. Baer grinned foolishly, utterly unable to solve Joe's attack)
Louis hooked a left to the body and Baer sent back a left to the head.
(as the Negro nailed him first with a left hook, and another right to the jaw at the ropes. Baer's face was crimson from a stream of Louis' left jabs.)
Louis shot a left hook to the jaw.
(Joe whipped a left hook into the body, a smooth moving chocolate machine,)
Louis missed a left for the body and Baer held. Louis hooked two lefts to the jaw. Baer missed a left for the head and clinched.

(then belted the big white man into the ropes with another right to the head. They cuffed at close quarters, blood from Baer's face covered the brown man's shoulders and just as the bell sounded,)

Baer landed a right at the bell and followed with a left and right to the jaw immediately after the clang.

(Baer whipped a terrific right in the Negro's head. The Negro faltered for a second on the ropes and Baer lashed him furiously with both hands, keeping it up after the bell until Referee Donovan pulled him away. Louis' round.)

Round Three

They pawed with long lefts until Baer landed a left and right to the head. Baer shot a right to the body and Louis held. Louis hooked a left to the body. Louis drove a sharp right to the jaw. Louis sent two fast lefts to the face.

(With fresh energy, Baer punched at the Negro's head with his left, but Joe stabbed steadily, flicking Baer's face with left jabs. Louis' leads thudded a left hook on Baer's chin,)

Baer went into a crouch but straightened up immediately after taking a right on the chin. Baer drove a long right to the body.

(but Max, gaining confidence, roughed Louis in a clinch, hitting his head with both hands.)

Louis hooked lefts and rights to the jaw.

(Louis shot a clean right hard to the jaw, and poured a volley of left hooks into the side of the former champion's head. Baer took his hits magnificently, stalking after the Negro as Louis moved around the ring, lashing his face with lefts. Grinning through a bloody mask, Baer ripped a left hand into Louis' head, but)

Louis backed Baer against the ropes and dropped him with a right to the jaw for a count of nine.

(the Negro pinned him on the ropes and knocked him down with a barrage of left hooks. Baer came up at nine.)

Baer arose shaky and went down again under a left hook to the jaw and the bell rang at the count of four.

(He went down again under another volley of left hooks but the bell saved him at the count of four. Dempsey ran out, dragged the bloodied white man to his corner and they sought desperately to restore him. Louis' round.)

Round Four

Louis poked two lefts to Baer's face. Louis drove two straight lefts to the face as Baer retreated.

(They came out haltingly and Louis stalked him like a panther after stricken game. He stabbed Baer's head with his long lefts, and hooked Baer's chin with his lefts. He was setting Max up for the kill.)

Louis hooked a left to the body.

(A left sank deep in Max's body and he stumbled back. Another left and right caught him at the middle.)

Louis closed in and landed a left and right to the jaw. Louis drove both hands to the body at long range. Louis hooked a left to the jaw.

(A left and right in the chin rocked him and)

Baer went into close quarters and held. Baer caught Louis's arms at long range and drew himself into a clinch. Baer hit Louis with a backhand on a break.

(as he leaned back against the ropes he threw his first punch of the round, a light right to the head. Max backed into another corner, blood dripping down his lips, and Referee Donovan warned him for backhanding.)

Louis hit Baer a left to the jaw. Louis sent Baer's head back with a straight left.

(Louis was wildly deliberate as he flung a left hook at Baer's head, then smashed his mouth up with a biting volley of left jabs.)

Louis grazed Baer's chin with a long right.

(Louis missed a long right and they fell into a clinch.)

Louis dropped Baer with a right to the head and Baer took the count of ten on one knee. The time of the round was 2:50.

(A long right floored Baer. He sank to his knees, dropped his hands to the canvas and stayed there helpless as Referee Donovan counted him out, a knockout victim in two minutes and fifty seconds after the start of the fourth.)

Of the many acts of desperation was the noticeable fact that Baer hit Louis after the bell. Was he so desperate to disable his foe that he failed to hear the bell? Or as Hemingway noted in his report of the fight, had Baer intended to foul out?

Joe Louis knocked down Max for the first time in his career. *New York World Telegram* (Library of Congress, Prints and Photographs [LC-USZ62-135654]).

Louis told reporters in his dressing room after the fight, "Baer is a better fighter than Carnera and harder to hurt. I hit him several times with rights and could not feel him give way under them. But I knew he would feel them some time. He certainly has a tough chin."[19] Louis would return to his training quarters with his bride at Pompton Lake. Afterward, they spent part of their honeymoon at the World Series baseball games in Detroit.

Louis said in his memoirs, "When I knocked out Max Baer, I knew in my head that this was the turning point. He was a popular ex-champion and a good puncher. All my fights had meant nothing until Baer. I said to myself, 'Maybe I can go all the way.'"[20]

After the fight, the first thing Baer requested in his dressing room was a cigarette and a bottle of beer, his usual post-fight treats. He had been allowed four bottles of beer a day during his training camp.

Reporters asked if he was going to request a rematch. "No, sir," he responded. "This time I retire, and retire for good. No more fighting for me." He told them that he was going back to Livermore and raise cattle. Manager Ancil Hoffman was quick to say, "Let Max do what he wants. If he wants to fight, I'll manage him, and if he doesn't, I won't try to convince him."[21]

Izzy Klein wipes the blood off Max Baer's face after the Louis fight. Jack Dempsey, his chief second, looks on. September 25, 1935.

Jack Blackburn said that if Max Baer got in shape he would be the best white heavyweight fighter of the world. Jack Dempsey had the last word on the condition of the fighters as seen from Baer's corner. He wrote in an editorial for the *New York Times*: No alibis, but Baer hurt his right hand in the first round, and when his right hand went bad on him, "he couldn't go out and gamble, as I begged him to do. I cannot speak too highly of Louis. He is a fine fighter.... After the third round, it was apparent that Baer would be beaten. He told me he couldn't hit hard with his right. I asked him if he was O.K. after those two knockdowns. 'I'll go down fighting,' he replied. And he did."[22] Dempsey was disappointed in the outcome of the fight, especially since he had trained Baer in his new "crouching" style. As trainer he was cut in for 7½ percent of Baer's earnings.

Writing about the fight later, Joe Williams had this to say about the second round: "We never saw another fighter absorb so many thunderous punches to the head and body and still hold his feet. One punch to the jaw turned Baer completely around. Another wallop to the middle sent him crashing to the ropes. There was one period (it must have lasted a full minute) where Louis took a fixed stance and fired shot after shot, and Baer just stood there with a crazy grin on his stricken face. It was as if he were taunting Louis.... 'Go ahead. See if you can knock me down.' Louis never hit another opponent with more, or harder, punches; yet he couldn't drop Baer. Not in that round."[23]

Dorothy Dunbar Wells Baer Wells, who took the name of her former husband, was quoted in San Francisco as saying, "Max Baer is really too kind-hearted to be a great fighter."[24] Mrs. Wells was headed to Shanghai, where she planned to live and write short stories.

The movie of the fight was advertised the day after by RKO as the "Battle of the Century." Film of Buddy Baer's fight with Ford Smith, on the undercard of Louis-Baer, was also a movie attraction.

On Baer's train trip back to California, the Baer team was shocked by the outpouring of love from the fans. At every stop along the route, hundreds of fans waited to see Max and called out for autographs. It was estimated that between New York and Oakland, Max signed over 3000 autographs. If the Max Baer fighting era was over, the loss to Louis had only enhanced his popularity.

James Braddock made his own trip to California, appearing at an exhibition in Oakland on November 20. Reporter Alan Ward didn't take kindly to Braddock's or his manager's insults, saying the next day, "James J. Braddock has no fear of Joe Louis, a withering scorn for Max Baer, [and] an undersized but efficient manager." Braddock boasted: "You can quote me as saying, I don't think Joe Louis is so much. He hasn't licked anyone: Levinsky, who quit; Carnera, who never could fight a lick on earth, and Max Baer, who had all the heart taken from him after the licking I delivered." This was quite a bold act to appear in Oakland. Braddock couldn't have sent greater shock waves if he had performed on Baer's ranch in Livermore. "Yeah, that goes double," piped up Manager Joe Gould. "Jimmy is going to pull another surprise by licking Louis to a frazzle. Remember, he wasn't conceded a chance against Baer. Braddock has something the rest of these mugs haven't, and that's a good jaw and all the courage in the world."[25]

Braddock told the *LA Times* that he was not afraid of Joe Louis, but everyone who has fought him has been "scared to death." He said that he had watched the Louis-Baer fight "exactly twenty-seven times, and I'll probably see it twenty-seven more times before Louis and I meet...." He said he counted and Louis hit Baer "exactly twenty-two times in the second round. And what happened? Baer did not go down." So that told him, "Louis is not the terrific hitter he has been painted."[26] Braddock missed his own point: Baer was not "yellow." Louis was a strong puncher, and Baer had one of the best chins of the decade.

Roger Treat said in the *New Yorker* magazine, "[Baer] had the punch, the courage, and the physique to stand punishment. No one who saw it could say that Baer quit to Louis.... He took a terrible thrashing that night. Perhaps worse than Dempsey gave Willard. Worse because he could absorb more, and there was more of it coming over."[27]

Baer was sensitive, and the notion that writers held that he had "quit" to Louis bothered him severely. O.O. McIntyre, of the *San Bernardino County Sun*, ended his story of the fight by accusing Baer of having a yellow streak: "Max Baer whose faint streak of saffron had turned canary yellow."[28]

No doubt Max feared for his life in the cross hairs of the mob in the Braddock fight, but for the Louis fight, his hands *and* legs were gone (his legs from the terrific body shots). For the next seven years Baer would comment in disbelief, "Joe hit me 18 times on the way down, yet they say I laid down."[29] Baer told Paul Zimmerman, "There's a thin line somewhere between being yellow and smart. None of them knew how badly my mouth was cut inside or of my other hurts. My one regret is that I was not in the shape that night that I was when I beat Max Schmeling."[30]

It didn't help Baer's ring reputation or legacy that the weightiest of American literary figures at the time, Ernest Hemingway (who considered himself a boxing expert), was at ringside and called Baer's behavior "disgusting." As a correspondent covering the fight for *Esquire* magazine, Hemingway titled his lengthy article, "Million-dollar Fright." The sporting man of letters accused Baer of quitting—of being scared senseless. "The Louis-Baer fight," he said, "was the most disgusting public spectacle, outside of a hanging, that your correspondent has ever witnessed. What made it disgusting," he said, "was fear. Maxie took it numbed with fear."[31]

Fear, and how one dealt with it in sport and war, was a subject integral to Hemingway's fiction. He hated fear in himself and others, so his summary of the fight (through his fictional lens) was not surprising. Hemingway played spitefully with Baer's name, turning Baer, the "Butcher Boy" into the "butchered," like the brainless hulking Spanish bull in his stories. He said that fear reduced Baer to a dumb ox: "When he could not foul out that way Baer knew he had to be knocked out, and he never fought another lick, just took it like a steer at the stockyards. He never took a chance. He never threw another right hand. Louis finished him at the end of the third, but the bell caught him on the floor. So he came out to be knocked out in the fourth ... and the whole thing was more like an execution than a fight. I do not know how Max bet on the fight, but I do know he was scared sick and fear is a very ugly thing."[32]

Hemingway implied that it was possible that Baer may have bet against himself. That possibility was not as distasteful for Hemingway as raw fear and man's inability to conquer the yellow streak. Boxing was a favorite sport for the writer, along with fishing and hunting. And how one fought against the most primal adversarial elements was a fundamental theme throughout his body of work. Sadly, and ironically, when the famed hunter ultimately had to face his own death, he ended his life with a gun, like a stockyard "execution," as "disgusting" a behavior as he had accused Baer of exhibiting. Rejecting his own moral theme, the famous literary boxer ended his life without a fight.

At the end of 1935, Joe Louis was not only named "Heavyweight of the Year," he was also named "Sports Hero of 1935." In only one year he had skyrocketed to fame. Max Baer was named "Greatest Sport Disappointment of 1935." One title read: "Editors who voted on Questions Use Harsh Terms in Their Opinions of Ex-champion Who Quit Cold."[33] But Baer was not a disappointment to Louis. In the Brown Bomber's unbroken string of 26 straight victories, he ranked Max Baer as his #1 opponent: "I rank Baer first because I hit him harder than any other opponent. Any of the two punches I hit Baer with would have knocked out any of the men I have fought."[34]

Ancil Hoffman told writer George Helmer, "Max took the worst beating from Louis that I ever saw a man take from anybody. He didn't keep his hands up. He was easy to hit, and Louis certainly hit him plenty. I don't want him to fight again unless he's in shape. I wouldn't want him to get punch drunk."[35]

Since the fight, Baer and his wife had been living on the Hoffman's ranch near Sacramento. Hoffman was looking for an acting job for Baer. He had an offer for Max to go over to Paris in January to open the Café de Paris and then on to England to make a picture. Max Baer's future seemed destined for the "picture" business.

In the meantime, Buddy Baer and Jack Sharkey were negotiating for a possible match for December 5, 1935. Word also circulated that Buddy planned to meet Primo Carnera in February at Madison Square Garden. Ancil Hoffman hoped Buddy might be ready for Louis after two more years of training and fights. (It would be five.) Hoffman planned to bring him up slowly and carefully. Instead, he was looking for a good trainer and sparring partner for Buddy. Max was out of the question.

By the end of 1935, both Jimmy Braddock and Joe Louis had catapulted to the top of the boxing world, in part, as a result of Max Baer's reputation. Jimmy Johnston would keep Braddock's title defense in limbo for two years, stringing everyone along, a year longer than his contract allowed. All the talk now was of Joe Louis.

After Frankie Campbell, Baer had been called a killer. After Max Schmeling, he was a hero to the Jews. After Braddock he was called a clown. And after Louis he was called a quitter. No one really knew the true Max Baer.

He planned to retire from the ring.

Eleven

Madcap Exhibition Tour, 1936

"I've lived 15 years in the past seven and paid for 25."—Max Baer

By the end of 1935, Max Baer had vowed to quit boxing. His wife wanted him to quit, his father thought he had had enough, and Max knew the risks involved in the fight business. Even after he won the crown he said, "You can lay odds that I have no ambitions to get the toy balloon concession in any insane asylum."[1] Yet in 1936, he had more bouts in one year—31—than in any other year, and more after he won the title than when he was working his way to the top. All of these engagements occurred in only four months, from June through October. Max called them tune-ups for a comeback. His manager Ancil Hoffman had lost a great deal of money betting on Max to beat the underrated Jimmy Braddock, and now he needed Max to stay in fighting condition for when the call came for the rematch that he knew Baer could win. Thus, Max and Buddy were put into a carnival-like roadshow of boxing exhibitions across half the United States and parts of Canada.

Why the change of resolve six months into 1936, after deciding to leave the ring? Like many men during the Depression, Max was flat broke and he needed to make money for the here and now. Ancil Hoffman had been placing Baer's earnings in a trust fund for his future, and the fund could not be touched until 1942. It forced Baer to keep working. He was too young to retire.

After the loss to Louis, Baer turned to the movie industry, but Hollywood didn't return his call because he was no longer the champion. He had plenty of requests for appearances, but even a tainted celebrity status didn't pay the bills. He tried to stay in the public eye. He played golf, went to a few fights, and signed autographs. These activities were great for the public and his ego, but he needed to close a few business deals.

At the same time, the legal cogs were grinding to a halt at his front door. Another losing decision, this time in court, was waiting to sink him further into a crater of debt. On January 24, California Superior Judge Malcolm C. Glenn ruled against Baer in the lawsuit brought by his former manager J. Hamilton Lorimer. The judge ruled that Baer had no right to terminate a contract made by his managers, Lorimer and Hoffman, and that he would have to pay Lorimer $20,000 for his ring interest up to 1932.[2]

In addition, Hoffman was ordered to pay Lorimer a share of his manager's profit from Baer. The judge asked for an accounting of all of Baer's earnings—theatrical, radio, movie, nightclub work, and boxing receipts—so as to reconcile what the parties owed. It was estimated that Baer had grossed through the years somewhere in the range of $1 million, out of which percentage payments were made to his many partner-owners. Baer's legal problems with women, promoters, managers, even spectators seemed an endless shackle. After all was accounted for, Baer made a payment to Lorimer of $53,750, money that undoubtedly became a debt to Ancil Hoffman.

For the next six years, after which he could receive annuity payments, it was up to Baer to earn his bread and butter. Several novel offers came in, but eventually, he would have to fall back on the only thing he knew—boxing.

Baer was offered a job in a San Francisco nightclub as a master of ceremonies, and a similar job was offered in Los Angeles. But a more significant contract, for $25,000 a year, was offered by Lou Daro, impresario of California's "wrestling trust." (Some newspapers erroneously reported that the contract was for $100,000.) Baer considered the offer and countered for $35,000, considering all the training and work involved to average three bouts per week performing or refereeing. Daro countered with an offer to make Baer-Daro-Hoffman a combination entity that would take 20 percent of the gross entertainment receipts. Hoffman responded with a thanks, but no-thanks, saying, "We have too many irons in the fire to jump at a thing like this without careful study."[3]

Actually, the person nixing the wrestling deal was Mrs. Mary Ellen Sullivan Baer. After seeing a wrestling match at one of Daro's events, Mrs. Baer stated emphatically, "No wrestling for my Maxie if I can help it." One of the reasons for her decision was that she thought wrestling by such giant men was too dangerous. She pointed to the "horrible example" of Joe Malcewicz, "man of a thousand wrestling bouts." Joe's cauliflower ear was as big as a truck. "I don't want Max to get an ear like that."[4] Daro was not discouraged. He sought to influence Max privately. But his instinct was wrong and Baer didn't take the contract.

On February 25, promoter Jimmy Johnston of Madison Square Garden offered either Max or Buddy a fight with the winner of the Isadore Gastanaga-Primo Carnera fight, but Hoffman turned him down, saying Buddy was too inexperienced and Max was not in proper shape. Max weighed 239 pounds from his months of inactivity.

When it was clear that Max planned to return to boxing, and Braddock heard the news about Max's attempt to make a comeback, Jimmy spoke disparagingly of him. Sportswriter Henry McLemore was sensitive to this: "Braddock, above all people, should be sympathetic with comeback efforts. For certainly James J. holds the world record for coming back from nowhere.... Braddock started his climb to the heights from the last house, on the last street, in a town 250 miles south of oblivion." In fact, said McLemore, Braddock claimed he, not Joe Louis, ended Max's fighting days.[5]

Los Angeles promoter Joe Waterman offered Max $25,000 to meet Phil Brubaker ($15,000 to Baer and $10,000 to Brubaker). Hoffman responded to the offer tersely: Baer "is too fat."[6] Waterman made a second offer, saying that Max could have $25,000 and a percentage of the gate. Again, Hoffman refused.

A reporter found Baer at Duffy's Gym in Oakland. About a thousand spectators watched Baer's first (official and open to the public) training workout since losing to Louis. Reporters watched him go four rounds with middleweights Hugh Wedge and Jackie London. While the boys were giving Baer a working over, it was clear that at any time, Baer could knock them out with a powerful punch. Baer clowned with his audience. Playfully, he illustrated the punch that dropped Carnera to win the championship, and London was knocked flat on his back. The crowd loved it, demonstrating again the entertaining recklessness that made Madcap Maxie such a popular attraction. During a break, he spoke to reporters. Baer said that he was definitely going back into the ring, and Waterman's offer to fight Brubaker sounded good to him. He could be ready to fight again in about three months.

Baer's trainer Frank Pacassi chimed in with team pride, saying that Maxie "expects to be again wearing the heavyweight crown. Baer is in marvelous condition considering he hasn't had a glove on since last September, and would be a chump not to go back to the ring. He can soon fight his way into top condition, and can earn several hundred thousand dollars in the next two years. How else except fighting could he do that?"[7]

Max had just celebrated his 27th birthday the day before. He said pensively, "I've lived 15 years in the past seven and paid for 25. I'm through being a chump. I realize no man can go on forever in the ring, but feel certain I've a couple of good years ahead of me."[8] He said he thought Joe Louis had been sidetracked and deserved to meet Jim Braddock for the crown. Baer wanted to begin his comeback tour in California.

What Max needed now was a license from the California Athletic Commission. But promoters who were consulted said that the prospect was virtually dead in the water. Baer was entangled in too many lawsuits for the commission to reinstate his boxing license. It was frustratingly clear how much power and control managers, promoters, and commissioners had over boxers. Max would never regain his boxing license in California.

Baer seemed serious about his training and knew specifically what he had to do. "I've quit the bright lights once and for all. I haven't touched a drink in two weeks. I've reduced cigarettes to two a day. I've done a lot of road work and walking. My big problem is the hands. That's what licked me in my fights with Braddock and Louis. That and the playboy stuff."[9]

There were only two questions to be asked: Was he serious about trying to reclaim the heavyweight crown? Or was he simply going after ready cash with which to live? Some speculated that the only fight with a chance to draw big money was one between Buddy and Max. But like the heavyweight Klitchko brothers of the modern era, that would not happen. Buddy had also been on leave from the ring since the September Louis fight when he lost to Ford Smith of Montana on the undercard. It was, however, predicted that one of the Baers would be fighting for the championship within 18 months. But that was a year and a half away.

By the first of April 1936, any chance Max had for a comeback was thwarted by his old nemesis William J. Brown, Chairman of the New York Athletic Commission. The commission listed Joe Louis as the number-one challenger to the heavyweight champion James Braddock. Brown made it clear: "As likely successor Max Baer is omitted, but Buddy Baer is placed ninth."[10] Brown had knocked out any hope Max had for a championship comeback, and he would not fight a rematch or any elimination bout for the heavyweight title during 1936. It must have been a devastating pronouncement to have seen his brother listed as a top-ten contender when he was off the list entirely.

Only a year earlier Max had considered offers in the five and six digits from such places as New York, London, and Berlin; but a year after his losses, his name was gone from the list of major marquee prospects. Even after the omission of Max's name by the New York Athletic Commission, Mike Jacobs at the Twentieth Century Club still felt that Baer could be a big draw, and he would go to Europe on his behalf to see if there were any possibilities for a comeback tour there.

While Louis and Schmeling prepared for their bout in the East, the Baer brothers toured the West. Max had purchased a large sedan, more like a roomy limousine because the tax rolls indicated that Max paid the highest recorded taxes for a car in Roseville, California.[11] Before the tour was over, the car would be wrecked.

The exhibition roadshows had two main features: separate bouts for Max and Buddy, with the rest of the card filled with 3- to 6-round bouts. Max frequently met two or three different men for the exhibition, and race or background was not an issue. At one point he did have an issue with a referee—when Referee Arthur Donovan appeared in Toronto. On occasion the brothers clowned in the ring. Like the challenges issued by John L. Sullivan in the days of old, Baer announced that he would meet any heavyweight in the world. The novelty of the cross-country tour was in the unexpected—neither the audience nor Baer could predict what might happen.

Utah

Max had his first bout on the comeback tour on June 15, 1936, in Salt Lake City. He weighed in at 226, more than 20 pounds over his championship weight. He easily outpointed Tony Souza, a 220-pound Portuguese from Fresno, in a six-round bout at McCullough's Arena. Baer was a bit rusty and clowned and slugged. He floored Souza twice in the second round and three times in the fifth. The press was underwhelmed with his claim of being ready to fight his way back to the top. They said he looked nothing of his former self and labeled him ignominiously as the "Chumpion."[12]

Idaho

Two days later in Boise, Baer beat Bob Fraser, a black fighter who had been around San Francisco for several years, where he frequently acted as Baer's sparring partner. Fraser lost on a technical knockout in the second round. Baer's next stop, June 19, in Pocatello, matched him with Harold "Millionaire" Murphy, a 205-pounder from Ventura, California. Baer decisioned Murphy after six rounds. One reporter said sarcastically that if Baer was truly using these matches as his conditioning program, the "Kimeback Kid" wouldn't be ready for a top-notcher for the next forty years.[13]

On June 19, 1936, at the same time other former champions were being introduced in the ring in New York for the famous Louis-Schmeling bout, Baer was out on the road milling around in an Armory building in Pocatello. After wrapping his hands in his dressing room, waiting for his fight to begin, he was told the breaking news of the outcome of the big fight: Max Schmeling had beaten Joe Louis.

It was shocking. Louis had never lost a professional match. Max was overjoyed: "The fight proves that Schmeling came back and I can come back because the times I fought Braddock and Louis I should not have been in the ring with either of them. I knocked out Schmeling before, and I'd like to prove to the world I can do it again and then battle Braddock."[14] He said it all while caressing Bertha, his name for his big right hand.

The Louis-Schmeling fight pictures set record attendance across the country. However, royalties would not go into the hands of the boxers. Bill Duffy, mob associate in Carnera's management, had bought up all the film rights.

With Joe Louis knocked down, every manager of a top heavyweight was in a frenzy to challenge Braddock for the title. While on the road to Texas, Ancil Hoffman was also quick to send Jimmy Johnston an offer guaranteeing an astounding $200,000 for a Baer-Braddock fight. Hoffman's comment? Notwithstanding the New York Commission, "Let's see what Braddock and his crowd will have to say."[15] Hoffman told reporters that a fight between Schmeling and Braddock wouldn't draw and that a fight between Baer and Braddock was the logical moneymaker.

Promoter Mike Jacobs wanted to ensure that he was still in the good graces of Schmeling. To keep the German champion from going over to the Garden for a title defense, Jacobs sent Max and his trainer, Max Machon, a nice congratulations package. Each received a pricey new automobile.

Hoffman did not get an offer from Jimmy Johnston, but he did hear from Mike Jacobs. The promoter offered Baer the chance to meet Schmeling. Hoffman responded, "I think we'll wait awhile." Hoffman had been a veteran of the fight business for thirty years and Baer trusted his judgment. "I know Schmeling's victory over Louis has put us back in a sweet spot," Hoffman explained. "Mike Jacobs has Schmeling under contract, and he wants us to meet the German in September, the winner to meet Braddock. But after all, we lost the title to Braddock and we want to meet him first, if possible."[16]

Hoffman had turned down a solid offer to meet Schmeling, holding back his cards in order to meet Braddock. Little did he know at the time that the Garden and Jimmy Johnston were not going to let Braddock fight in the near future, although the contract required that Braddock defend his title before July 29, or lose his claim to the crown. Why this didn't occur is still a mystery only known to Jimmy Johnston, the executives at the Garden, the New York Commission, and possibly the courts. Some fight managers assumed that Braddock had given up his right to the title after one year. Jimmy Johnston insisted that a title bout was forthcoming. On the Baer front, Hoffman's decision "to wait" on Schmeling probably cost Baer an opportunity for a big fight with a big gate, especially since Mike Jacobs had access to Yankee Stadium in New York.

While on the road, Baer may not have known that his popularity in the East had not waned.

In a letter to sports editor Ed Hughes, one reader wrote, "I still think that our old friend Maxie Baer can lick both Louis and Schmeling if he would only settle down to that serious business of boxing, and I, like a good many people, would go to see him."[17] Little did reader Irwin Fields, of 181 Clarkson Ave. in New York, know that his friend Maxie was out in the hinterlands, turning down offers from New York and trying to make a comeback boxing every other day to make ends meet.

By late June, Jack Sharkey sprang back into the heavyweight picture as a result of a ten-round victory over Phil Brubaker at Fenway Park. Sharkey was another former champion barnstorming around the country when he met Brubaker.

With a Sharkey win and a $200,000 offer by Ancil Hoffman, Jimmy Johnston wasted no time in notifying Hoffman that he wanted to arrange an indoor bout in the Garden sometime in September between Max Baer and Jack Sharkey. Hoffman was not interested. This would be another match that would not occur in either boxer's lifetime.

Reporters were aware of these offers and gave Baer the nod with the possibility of a true comeback. Henry McLemore predicted, "Max Baer, the California wand waver, will be the first heavyweight champion in history to regain the title.... As big a bum as he was against Louis, Max is no bum when he's in there with a fellow he knows can't hurt him. He has the same sort of courage as a bully. Let him think he can bounce a guy around, and he'll nearly always do it. It's true that didn't work with Braddock, but the

Pacific playboy was in miserable physical shape that night. I'd certainly take him to lick Schmeling."[18]

Texas

Meanwhile, back on the road, instead of getting a return bout with Braddock, Louis, Schmeling, or Sharkey, Max Baer was on his way to Tyler, Texas, to meet Houston heavyweight George Brown, who, in 16 fights, had won only three with one draw. Baer's entourage in the large sedan included Buddy, Ancil Hoffman, and trainer Frank Paccassi, with Maxie at the wheel. As they were driving through Oklahoma on their way to Texas, the group was involved in a car accident that sent Buddy to the hospital with four broken ribs. Buddy would not fight in Texas while he was recovering. Max replaced the car with an eight-cylinder convertible coupe that he said he bought as a gift for his wife. (He must have bought an additional car to accommodate the rest of his passengers.)

In Tyler, Baer scored a TKO over George Brown in the fourth. After clowning for three rounds, he smacked Brown with three rights and Brown hit the floor each time. Brown's manager threw in the towel after the third knockdown. Baer's weight had come down to 218 pounds. Brown weighed 198.

After the Tyler fight, the group left the next day, June 25, for San Antonio. That night, Baer knocked out Wilson Dunn, from Ponca City, Oklahoma, in the third round, but not before being bitten twice by his opponent. It was amazing what Baer had to tolerate on the road. Irritated in the first round at being head-butted by Dunn, Baer dodged a rush and pawed his opponent through the ropes into the audience. In the second round, after some serious infighting, Baer launched him, this time violently, through the ropes with a backhand swing to the chin. Dunn landed again off the deck and managed to come back into the ring for the next round. In the third and final round, Baer hit the man's midsection with a whaling right and sent him through the ropes for a final landing.

Baer was roundly booed by 3500 attendees for his rough tactics. Max apologized to the crowd but pointed in his defense to the teeth marks on his arm and shoulder where Dunn had bitten him during a clinch in the second. Baer had a bruise across his nose from the head-butt in the first, and said, "I've got a future to think about, and I can't risk it against a fighter like that. In fact, I never saw a fighter like that before."[19] Hoffman just shrugged it off, remarking that it was all good experience. The gate came to $2077, and no records were found to indicate what the Baer camp made from the "bite fight."

Back on June 20, Baer was offered a match with Jack Petersen, British heavyweight titleholder. This fight didn't make either, and by July 2, Baer had moved on to Dallas to challenge Buck Rogers, 217, from Philadelphia. Baer won the six-round bout in three. Baer could have knocked the man out in the first round, but he entertained the crowd for two and half rounds before the KO. On July 5, Buddy was sent home to recuperate from his cracked ribs. A Texas newspaper reported, "Baer Has Several Irons in the Fire but None Getting Hot."[20]

In the past two weeks, Max Baer had been offered and lost the chance for a big fight with Max Schmeling, Jack Sharkey, and Jack Petersen. Instead Baer fought five journeyman heavyweights eager to make a name for themselves at his risk. Was Hoffman so in doubt about Baer's physical condition that he turned down offers that would benefit

Baer? Or was his interest in only one more big fight, a title fight? The group had traveled through three states and plodded on.

Missouri

Max and crew left for Springfield, where Max refereed a wrestling match on July 7.

Oklahoma

Baer's three-bout tour of Oklahoma lasted only four days. On July 13, Baer went to Oklahoma City, where he stopped Jimmy Merriott, 214, of Tulsa, in the second of six rounds. Moving on to Tulsa, Baer knocked out Junior Munsell, 187, Native American of Oklahoma City, in the fifth of six rounds. At this point Baer had reached one of Hoffman's goals. He had trimmed down to 213 pounds when he received word that Joe Louis had requested Max for a bout to start Louis's comeback campaign. It was another opportunity for a big fight.

Louis's managers wanted a match with Baer for Soldier Field in Chicago. They wanted the same set up that had been arranged with Louis-Levinsky in Chicago, which drew 39,000 people. They were quoted as saying, "We want Baer. Louis feels the same way.... There is only one place for the fight, Chicago. Chicago fans have never seen Louis in a major match, and they have never seen Baer in a bad one."[21] Hoffman could not sit on this offer because Louis's management wanted a fight as soon as possible. But the problem now was that Hoffman wanted too much money as a guarantee for Baer. Some said he wanted a $100,000 guarantee. Others said he wanted as much as $150,000.

The next night, July 17, Baer went on to Ada, Oklahoma, to fight local policeman Cecil Smith. Baer clowned his way through the four-round match to take the decision, intentionally refusing to knock the policeman out. Baer drew a great many laughs for an enjoyable evening.

While Baer was making his way back to Utah, he learned that Jimmy Johnston and the Louis camp were also considering Jack Sharkey and Al Ettore as possible candidates to start Louis's comeback campaign. Baer was still Louis's number-one choice. Sharkey was possibly out of the question now that he was being wooed by the Garden. Ettore had nothing to lose and everything to gain, but Mike Jacobs realized that the match wouldn't draw like one with Louis and Baer. But Hoffman was still sticking to Baer's large guarantee to get in the ring with Louis. Jacobs's response: "Nerts. If Baer wants to fight Louis again he can have the chance, but he'll have to do it on a percentage basis."[22] No deal was reached.

Over on the Braddock scene, Max Schmeling had deposited a $5000 good-faith guarantee in the offices of the New York Athletic Commission to fight Jimmy Braddock under a Mike Jacobs promotion. Max Baer was left out of the New York–Chicago boxing picture entirely. Max Schmeling would fight Joe Louis in June of 1936. Joe Louis would meet Jack Sharkey in August in Yankee Stadium and then he would fight Al Ettore in September in Philadelphia. Braddock would not defend his title.

One paper summed up the boxing situation: "This boxfighting business is getting to be a merry-go-round—what with four ex-champions, one authentic champion and one brown championship threat all in the picture at one and the same time."[23] In the good old days an ex-champion hung up his gloves, opened a saloon, and told stories about the good old days. One writer noted that every champion since the retirement of Gene Tunney was still in the ring.

Baer continued plodding along, performing in his roadshows, non-events on the big boxing scene, but major ones for the cities he visited. He was bringing celebrity to the home fronts, building up goodwill and loyalty among fans, and paying the bills. Ancil Hoffman said, "Maxie doesn't mind the brush-beating ... the comeback campaign nets, in addition to considerable booking, something between $3000 and $4000 weekly."[24]

Utah

Baer stopped in Utah on July 24 to appear in the Ogden Pioneer Days parade that included a boxing match during the evening rodeo. The men in the group ribbed him with Western humor: "Even a horse makes Max Baer hold on."[25] That evening Max received word that his father was seriously ill and the group decided to return to California. Max wasted no time knocking out Bob Williams of Houston, Texas, in the first round of six. Buddy Baer was back in fighting shape, and in the semi bout, was equally in a hurry to knock out his opponent Fay Jerricki of Pasadena, California, also in the first round. The Baer troupe left for California soon after the program.

Father Jacob Baer was at the Oakland Coast League Park for a baseball game when his nose began to hemorrhage. The vessels were cauterized at the hospital, but the loss of blood continued for eight days. Max's wife had already donated blood three times before the boys arrived on July 29. Max donated as well, and the newspapers reported, "Max Saves 'Papa' Baer from Death."[26] With headlines such as that, it was difficult for the California Commission to deny a license to Max. While they did not allow Max to fight in the ring, they permitted him to stage one exhibition in California in August.

California

On August 15, Max had a fight scheduled in Eureka, California, with Tony Souza of San Jose. But the California Commission ruled that Souza was not adequate competition for Max. Instead, Max was matched with Trent Fair of San Jose for an exhibition. Max shook the man several times, but spent most of time entertaining the crowd of 1200. Buddy got no better than a draw with Jack Casper of Tracy in his four-round event.

Canada

Vancouver, British Columbia, was celebrating its Golden Jubilee and Max Baer was a special guest. On August 19, Max entertained the crowd clowning and boxing through eight scheduled rounds with three different men. Max kayoed James J. Walsh of Kitscoty, Alberta, Canada, in two minutes of the first round that was scheduled for four. They came out laughing, swapped a few blows, and immediately went into a clinch. The KO occurred when Baer knocked out Walsh with a right coming out of the clinch. The second two-round bout was with Sonny Buxton of Victoria, and Baer held him off with one hand through the second. In the third bout, Max and Buddy played around boxing and joking, with Max taking a few make-believe falls to the canvas.

The exhibition occurred in the Vancouver ice hockey arena at the Fenner and Hood shipyard. A fire early the next day consumed the 17,000-seat wooden arena and swept through adjacent buildings. Only hours earlier, about 3,500 people had watched the fight.

Oregon

August 24, 1936, in Marshfield, Oregon, Max Baer scored a technical knockout in the second round over Nails Gorman, a Marshfield policeman. Buddy, whom the sportswriter noted had "developed into something of a moose since visiting here two years ago," kayoed Charles Simpson of New York in the second of six scheduled rounds.[27]

The next day, August 25, Baer decisioned Cecil Myart, an African American from Los Angeles, in six rounds in the Multnomah stadium in Portland. Buddy and Max were drawing big crowds to their training quarters at the Labor temple and 5000 people went to the evening show. Buddy kayoed Bill Deverer in six seconds of the second round scheduled for six. Max told the press he wanted to show those people "who said I was afraid of Joe Louis, that I quit to him in the ring, and never was more than a bum and clown at best."[28] The "quitting" reference still bothered him.

Idaho

On August 29, the group was in Lewiston, Idaho. Baer knocked out Al Frankco, 212, of Tacoma in the second and Buddy knocked out Don Baxter, 210, of Lewiston in the first round. Buddy weighed 237.

In Coeur d'Alene on August 31, Max Baer knocked out Don Baxter in the first round. The crowd booed because they thought it was not a solid punch. Buddy won a first-round kayo over Jack Conroy. Both were six-round bouts.

In Twin Falls on September 2 at Lincoln Field, Max, 217 pounds, delivered a knockout punch 37 seconds into the bout with Al Gaynor, 202 pounds, from Arizona. Buddy, 237 pounds, also won with a first-round KO of Jack Conroy, 200 pounds, of Toronto. Max and Hoffman were disgusted when they read in the paper that Garrett L. Smalley, Missouri State Athletic Commissioner in Joplin, had barred Baer from appearing in exhibition bouts in that state because "We do not intend to let a has-been come into this state with a buildup racket simply to make money."[29]

Utah

On the September 3 program in Provo, Buddy refereed the preliminary boxing matches. In the main event, Max easily kayoed his opponent Soldier Eddie Franks in the third of six rounds. Franks had claimed 47 wins over Army, Navy and Marine boxers, and the heavyweight champion of Manila. In addition to his boxing matches, Max was stumping for President Roosevelt's re-election effort. Jack Dempsey had assigned him the duty as part of Dempsey's Sports Committee of the Democratic Party.

Wyoming

On September 4 in Rock Springs, Wyoming, Max, 210, knocked out Cyclone Bench, 215, from Pueblo, Colorado, in the third round of six. Buddy, 240, kayoed Baby Hunt, 230, of Oklahoma City in the first of six rounds. Three days later in Casper, Max knocked out Cowboy Sammy Evans of Cut Bank, Montana, in the fourth round, and Buddy scored a two-round KO over Fred Schultz of Midwest. Both were 6-rounders.

Manager Ancil Hoffman was still fielding fight card possibilities in September from Mike Jacobs. Jacobs wanted Max for a main event in September with an opponent (yet to be determined) at Yankee Stadium. Jacobs was also working with London promoters who wanted Baer to meet the winner of the November 9, 1936, bout between England's champion, Ben Foord, and Walter Neusel of Germany. The Londoners preferred "the daffy Californian" over Joe Louis because he "has a greater hold on the public imagination than the deadpanned Louis."[30]

Iowa

After a 600-mile drive, Max and crew drove into Des Moines on the night of September 9, with plans to stay a week or longer depending on the fight arrangements. September 14, Baer took on Bearcat Wright, the "Negro Giant" of Omaha, Nebraska. They wore 16-ounce gloves in the six-round match and Wright was outpointed. In an interview, Max said, "I'm a serious guy now." But as one reporter said, he might go out and clown one night and then decide and "try to knock his foe's block off from the first round."[31] Really there were two celebrities in the ring. The Bearcat was a veteran boxer who had been in the ring with Jack Dempsey, Primo Carnera, Mickey Walker, Chuck Higgins, and Harry Wills in his heyday. He was a smart fighter and stayed in a crouch so as to give Max little target. Max seemed to rely on his left, because when aiming for his opponent's head, he intentionally missed with his right. The misses were a sign that he was nursing his hand. Max was booed after four rounds, but at the end, Wright was cheered for his keen defensive skills.

Veteran boxer Ed "Bearcat" Wright tests Baer in Iowa, September 14, 1936 (courtesy IBRO).

Buddy outpointed Pret Ferrar, another veteran black boxer, but was also unable to put him out. He had Ferrar down at the end of the first and second rounds, but for the next four rounds, Ferrar was too fast and smart to be put down again. But 4,000 boxing fans saw the opponents stay the limits with the two famous brothers.

September 19, in Cedar Rapids, Max clowned through six rounds with Willie Davies, Joe Louis's sparring partner. At times, "Max was taxed to withstand Willie's left jab and swinging blows."[32] Buddy pounded Tiny Tiger Blyttner, 210, in the first round, and flattened him three times in the second, after picking him up twice.

September 22, in Sheldon, Iowa, Max entertained the crowd by toying six rounds with Andy "Kid" Miller, 180, Sioux City, who barely reached the height of Max's shoulder. Buddy had to go five rounds before he knocked out Verne Trickle of Graettinger, Iowa.

On September 30, in their final stop in Iowa, Max fought Babe Davis in Keokuk four rounds in a no-decision bout. The fight had originally been booked for Quincy, Illinois, but was moved to Keokuk when the Illinois Commission refused to sanction the affair until after Baer first appeared in Chicago. A crowd of 400 persons jeered Max as he clowned his way through four rounds with Babe Davis of St. Louis. It was said that "Davis proved the better clown."[33]

Indiana

On October 8, Baer went to Evansville, Indiana, and kayoed Tim Charles of St. Louis. He knocked him down eight times before he was declared finished in the fourth round. The bout was so inconsequential that the Daily Chronicle of De Kalb, Illinois, reported in the title, "Max Baer Floors Someone by the Name of Charles."[34] The next night, Baer again fought Willie Davies of Chicago, Joe Louis's sparring partner. Baer floored him in the third round, but Davies came back to "pile up a point margin" that gave him the win in Platteville, Wisconsin. It was the first loss to Baer on his comeback tour.[35]

Canada

Baer's exhibition tour ended in Toronto, October 19. Arthur Donovan refereed the four preliminary bouts, but Max would not let Donovan referee his bout. Max knocked out Dutch Weimer of Phoenix, Arizona, in the second round. In his bout, no one connected in the first round, and when Baer connected with his uppercuts in the second, his opponent was out. Baer's bout was labeled a "fake, fiasco and disgrace to the sport."[36] But as someone at the bout commented, the promoter asked for a $400 opponent for Baer, and that's what they got. Buddy put his opponent out in the second with a right to the head of Salvatore Ruggirello. He came up after the count of eight only to take a volley of short rights and lefts. He was counted out after one minute and five seconds of the second.

At the end of the exhibition tour, Grantland Rice asked Max how he was "fixed." "O.K.," Max said. "I've paid off all my debts. I won a home and I have an annuity ready two years from now.... I picked up $2000 last week boxing and refereeing."[37] It wasn't a cut of the six-figure deals he had picked up the past, but he was paying his bills. With all the former champs out on tour, including Dempsey, many managers were able to arrange events for $3500 up to $5000. After Louis won the title, his managers started asking a $30,000 per-bout minimum.

Max, his brother, and their manager left the tour on October 22, 1936, for home. It had been a grinding three months since they had seen their families. The newspapers reported that everyone was homesick. The tour had not been a "howling success," but it paid the bills. Baer was no longer in debt, and Hoffman's mission had been accomplished: Baer had fought his way down from 239 to 210 pounds—he was back in shape.

Before they were home, Hoffman received another offer for Baer that he turned down: a match with Maurice Strickland, heavyweight champion of New Zealand. Hoffman had considered offers from unknowns, past champions, up-and-comers, and the American Olympic Golden Gloves heavyweight titleholder of 1936, African American Art Oliver.

It was beginning to look like the former champion would never regain the heavyweight crown. By the end of 1936, the only title fight offer came to Buddy. The six-foot, six-inch gladiator got on a train with Ancil Hoffman to go to Chicago for a December 10 fight billed as the Heavyweight Championship of the Emerald Isle with Patrick Michael Barry of Ireland. The bout lasted 2 minutes and 45 seconds. Buddy's knockout punch was a powerful right to the stomach, and Chicagoans declared Buddy the Heavyweight Champion of Ireland even though the fight was in Chicago.

Max and Buddy took what money was left over after expenses from the road campaign and applied it to their annuities as Christmas presents for themselves. Max said that in seven years, he would earn $1000 a month from his investment. So after lavish living, a lost title, lawsuit payouts, and a comeback tour that came close to extinction, Max was still investing for his future, and hoping at some point to regain the title.

Twelve

Baer Storms England, Farr and Foord, 1937, 1938

On July 8, 1936, a reporter asked Jack Dempsey about Max Baer's future. "He's all through," said the mentor, trainer and former promoter. "He couldn't draw 30 cents against any opponent."

"That's where you're wrong," said Trevor Wignall, a well-known British sportswriter on a specific mission to New York. "I have a contract in my suitcase and am prepared on behalf of London promoters to offer Baer $40,000 to come over there for a fight. London is still goggy about the fellow." He smiled assuredly, "They want to see him fight."[1]

For much of the decade, good boxers from England, Spain, Portugal, Germany and Italy crossed the Pond to the United States in search of top paychecks. In the second half of the decade, beginning in 1936, interest and direction shifted. The successful reopening of the National Sporting Club of London issued a universal invitation for boxers, managers, and promoters to return to the British Mecca.

News broke quickly on American soil that Max Baer might be going to England for a big fight. The proposal was the result of the entertainment interests of English multi-millionaire Brigadier General A.C. Critchley, owner of Harringay Arena in London. Critchley offered the Baer brothers full transportation over and all accommodations in his hotels for their boxing engagements. It was a big money-making detour and a shot at the top of Max's comeback campaign. American boxers, including Joe Louis, were excited about the new market and the chance to escape New York tyranny.[2]

In the fall of 1936, Baer signed to meet the winner of the match between Walter Neusel and Ben Foord. Neusel, Der Blonde Tiger from Germany, was a huge attraction. In 1934 he met and lost to Max Schmeling in the largest fight in German history to date, drawing between 90,000 and 100,000 fans.

"I'm coming back," Baer rejoiced. "This fight in England is the starting point."[3] He was given an initial $22,500 and four round-trip tickets from New York to London. His entourage of six included Mr. and Mrs. Ancil Hoffman, Mr. and Mrs. Max Baer, Buddy Baer and trainer Frank Paccassi. They planned to leave in January of 1937. The press remained skeptical. If there was a fight scheduled in England, it would be Max's last chance for a comeback. Always the optimist, Max outlined his plans: "If I can win in England and then beat Louis and then fight again for the championship, well, then I could make a million dollars for myself, couldn't I?"[4]

Baer began training earnestly in December for his February 1, 1937, bout abroad. He was at Hoffman's Fair Oaks ranch near Roseville, California, running four and five miles daily and chopping oak trees on the property. One reporter commented that Hoffman's ranch must be devoid of trees with all of Baer's wood chopping. On weekends, Max and Buddy went to Oakland to work in the gym.

However, in January, a suspicious event prevented Max from going to England, and the German champion, who won the November match, was paired instead with Jack Peterson for the February event. Baer was told he could fight the winner of that match.

The Fire

On January 27, 1937, the Baers and the Hoffmans would face a devastating loss. While Ancil was entertaining a small party of guests on his ranch at Fair Oaks, his beautiful home and its expensive contents were consumed by a sudden, raging fire. No one was injured, but the firemen were unable to control the inferno due to a lack of water in the vicinity. The $40,000 home had been a showplace near Sacramento. Baer and Hoffman were only able to salvage the piano and a few pieces of furniture. From his extensive collection of expensive suits and tailored clothing, Baer was able to save only two polo shirts. Four trunks already packed and tucked away for the pending voyage were destroyed. Only what the group wore at the time and what little they managed to carry out was saved. Baer's expensive car, parked in a detached garage, was also destroyed. The origin of the fire was questioned. Because it had started simultaneously in several places and everything went up in flames so quickly while the individuals were inside and unaware, it was believed to be the result of arson. Whoever ordered the fire wanted to ensure that Max would miss his prestigious bout in London.

Because Max and Mary Ellen lived with the Hoffmans, the fire and the loss of valuable possessions and his precious car stunned Baer like nothing he could remember since losing the title. He was helpless to save a pair of shoes, boxing or other. All clothing had to be replaced. Because of his enormous size, his suits had to be remade. He wore a size 13 shoe, which wasn't even a standard size in the 1930s. Art Cohn of the *Oakland Tribune* said that no shoe store in Oakland carried a size 13 shoe.

When the fire broke out, Max hurried into the living room to try to save Hoffman's valuable Asian rug and baby grand piano. With a surge of energy, he was able to throw off the heavy furniture and carry the rug out. He went back to carry the piano to the doorway, where firemen helped to pull it outside. The event was sobering. He told Art Cohn, "I was so worked up in that fire that if there had been two dozen Joe Louises in there, I could have kayoed all 24 of 'em."[5]

Oakland and San Francisco newspapermen followed the Baers during their buying spree to replace the lost items. They quipped that a couple of wardrobe factories forced to close during difficult economic times had reopened "on the strength of the order." Baer made light of his situation, joking that the only place he could go during his present condition was "to a nudist colony."[6] Baer was seen wearing his brother's shirts, which were four inches too long.

Mrs. Baer admitted that she had no problem replacing any article of clothing for herself, but buying even a pair of socks for Max was difficult. The newspapermen commented on a bracelet she was wearing that was not lost in the flames. It was a bracelet from which hung a tiny gold stork. Max had seen a picture of Mrs. Wally Simpson wearing one, so he had one made for Mrs. Baer. Max responded, "We haven't ever had a stork hovering around this household, so maybe this will bring us luck."[7] Mrs. Baer denied that she was pregnant.

Baer's life had been a roller coaster of events fortunate and unfortunate. A title loss, a divorce, a marriage, numerous lawsuits and even a fire could not destroy his ambitious spirit.

Some newspapers reported that the bouts in London were fabricated publicity stunts to get Baer's name in front of the media. Reporters clamored to see the contract. Nevertheless, proof that Baer was gearing up for something was his advertisement for sparring mates at Duffy's Gym in Oakland on February 3, 1937.[8]

That same day, Joe Gould, Braddock's manager, was in Jimmy Johnston's face at Madison Square Garden squawking about Braddock's right to face Louis rather than being forced into a contract of Madison Square Garden's making with Schmeling. Five-hundred-thousand dollars was at stake. Jimmy Johnston threatened that if Gould didn't keep the Schmeling fight, he would seek to have "the heavyweight title declared vacant, and that the commission recognize a bout between Schmeling and Bob Pastor, the New York heavyweight, as a championship match."[9]

Johnston's job at the Garden depended on his securing profitable matches. "We know our legal rights and we'll stop any Louis-Braddock fight until Schmeling has had his chance June 3."[10] The Louis-Braddock fight was scheduled for Chicago, and the Illinois Commissioners named Joe Louis the #1 contender. So essentially, Braddock had his choice of states and contenders: Chicago and Louis, or New York and Schmeling.

Joe Gould had an excuse for the Garden in that the Anti-Nazi League had threatened to boycott any fight involving a German from the land of Hitler. Actually, the threatened boycott might have helped to promote a bout in what otherwise might have been a lackluster fight between Schmeling and Braddock. But Gould preferred the $500,000 offer from the Louis camp. No one knew at the time that the deal Gould made with Louis's handlers and Mike Jacobs would set Braddock up for the next ten years if Braddock lost.[11]

While Johnston was fighting for a Braddock-Schmeling bout, Baer also got a bid from Jimmy Johnston for a match with his fighter, Bob Pastor, for either March 12 or 19. Hoffman signed a guarantee that Baer would fight Pastor. He did so for two reasons: he did not have a new date for Baer in London, and he could use the Pastor fight as a tune-up. But Hoffman also knew the New York Athletic Commission disliked Baer, so he made the guarantee on two conditions: license approval and a deadline date. The New York Commissioners had to approve Baer for the match with Pastor by February 19. He didn't want Baer to be tied up by the commission or the Garden and unable to accept a match elsewhere.

Sure enough, the New York bout did not receive the blessing of the Athletic Commission. This time, the man obstructing the match was Arthur Donovan, the referee Baer despised. The feud between the two was ongoing. It started when Donovan refereed the Baer-Carnera fight. The feud resurfaced in Toronto when Baer refused to have Donovan referee his exhibition. Then Donovan was eliminated for the Braddock fight. There was also the Louis fight, in which Donovan called Max a quitter. Now Donovan appealed to the commission to have Baer boycotted. In the words of Art Cohn, "Donovan [was] merely the mouthpiece for the Madison Square Garden in the present controversy; that Baer is still 'out' with the political bosses who run the fight racket and until he is 'in' he will never be in the National picture again; that regardless of who he meets, Baer will be kayoed."[12] It was Cohn's belief that Baer would never fight Pastor. And he was correct.

The Baer-Pastor contract blew up. Executives at the Garden said that Baer's management had signed a contract knowing that Baer did not have an adequate license in New York. Hoffman argued that the commission had until February 19 to issue a license. Fights were being lined up for Max in England, and Hoffman needed to know by the 19th. By February 24, it was clear that Baer was not going to be issued a license. Col. John Reed Kilpatrick, president of the Garden Corporation, was so mad about losing the deal that he contacted the British promoter Sidney Hulls and threatened legal action if Baer was aided in getting a fight in Britain. Now, it appeared that the Garden had not only lost an opportunity for a Baer-Pastor bout, but it was also losing the Braddock-Louis fight to Chicago.

Max Baer appeared at the New York Commission meeting on February 24, to appeal again for a license. Gen. John J. Phelan, chairman, and Dr. Walker Wear were not opposed to the license. But the third commissioner, Bill Brown, said, "I want to go on record as being against the return of Baer to New York. The last two times he fought here he left a bad aroma, which resulted in criticism of this commission from the press." Baer responded, "I can't understand why a good American should come all the way from California and have a man of Mr. Brown's background come down to the ringside and call him a bum [referring to the Carnera-Baer fight]." To which Commissioner Brown replied immediately, "I want to apologize for that. I was mistaken. You were a pair of bums."[13]

The commission had so inflamed the public's wrath regarding Max Baer's license denial and Brown's comments "on record" that even reporters who usually panned Max took offense. Art Cohn listed every "unsatisfactory fight" Jimmy Braddock had been engaged in, stating that he "was granted a boxing license by the august New York Athletic Commission." Yet Max Baer had been kayoed just once in his life, "and only Joe Louis at his best could do it," and he was denied a license by the same "bonehead" Commission. Then Cohn cited all the unworthy boxers who had been granted licenses in New York. Cohn concluded, "I, for one, refuse to close the strange career of Max Baer with the Shakespearean epitaph, 'The evil that men do lives after them; the good is oft interred with their bones.'"[14]

Five days later on February 29, the three commissioners backed down and approved the license. Bill Brown, under pressure, reluctantly voted to allow Baer a license. But Brown had the last word, repeating, "All of his bouts in New York had left a bad aroma," and Baer was still "just a bum."[15] But the offer was too late. Baer and Hoffman were off to England.

When it appeared that Baer was not going to be given a license for a fight in New York, London promoter Sidney Hulls deposited a $10,000 guarantee for Baer to fight either Jack Peterson or Benny Foord in London for March.

The Brits were not intimidated by the New York Commissioners or anyone associated with Madison Square Garden. After receiving notice from Commissioner Kilpatrick that the British promoter would be held accountable for "aiding" Baer in breaking his contract with the Garden, Hulls replied that his contract with Baer was signed back on October 16, 1936, and consequently predated any contract made with the Garden. Furthermore, he cautioned, "If Kilpatrick continues to persecute me without cause, I shall seek legal advice whether he can be held responsible for my mental anguish."[16]

The controversy over contracts with the Garden overshadowed Max Schmeling's arrival in New York on March 2, aboard the incoming Cunard White Star Liner, the *Berengaria*. Max had arrived expecting to fight Braddock for the title June 3, "if Madison

Square Garden can convince everyone concerned that his contract is good," reporters qualified.[17] It was a rather chaotic time for heavyweight boxing in New York.

By March 1937, the heavyweight situation could be summarized: Schmeling was in New York expecting Braddock to run out on their contract with the Garden for a title fight June 3. Braddock, unconcerned that Schmeling was in town, was pitching camp for a Louis fight in Chicago. Some believed that Max Schmeling had a right to own the crown if Jimmy ran out. Schmeling was the logical contender in that he had already beaten Louis. To his credit, Schmeling said that he would not accept a title without a proper fight: "Titles are won and lost in the ring."[18] When asked about the "Anti-Nazi League" boycott that may have forced the fight out of New York, Schmeling said that the boycott was just an excuse, that there wouldn't be a boycott if anyone thought that Braddock could beat him. The public lamented the lack of sportsmanship involved when a titleholder refused to live up to his contract. A reporter asked Schmeling if he thought Braddock was avoiding him because there was more money in a Braddock-Louis fight. Schmeling responded, "What about when Max Baer had to fight Braddock for the title? There wasn't much money in it for Baer, but he went through with it."[19] It was believed that Braddock had only one fight left in him and Joe Gould was looking for the biggest payday.

Meanwhile, the Garden filed two $50,000 lawsuits, one naming Baer and Hoffman jointly, and the other naming Sid Hulls and Brig. Gen. Alfred C. Critchley, London, for interfering with a boxing contract. Eventually, the lawsuit against Baer made its way to court in the amount of $12,000 actual damages and $10,000 punitive damage. Facing legal summonses, neither Max Baer nor his manager Hoffman could be found for comment.

On March 3, the outgoing *Berengaria* pulled away from the New York harbor headed to London on its five-day voyage. The Garden's legal process servers had searched for days prior for Max Baer. When word came that he was about to ship out, the servers were dockside waiting like hawks at every boarding plank ready to leap with legal papers in hand when they spotted Max. They searched on board the decks and peered into lifeboats looking for the any member of the Baer group.

Finally, when reporters contacted Hulls in London to ask about Max's whereabouts, the promoter told them that he was sure Baer's party was not on the boat—that they had planned to leave the next week from Boston. Just as the gangplanks were being hoisted away, Max Baer's face appeared in a porthole window, smiling. Women, who had been waiting on shore to get a glimpse of the fighter, shrieked in delight when they spotted him. Later, Baer appeared on deck waving, to the photographers' delight.

The Garden's legal mission had been spoiled. When asked about the incident, Jimmy Johnston said sourly, "Baer boarded the ship through the freight entrance late last night, but we'll get him in England. We got attorneys everywhere. He can't run away from us." Headlines read: "Madcap Maxie Baer Dodges Law, Press, Women; Sails for Merry England."[20] Ancil Hoffman had hired an armed bodyguard for the trip, so unsure was he of the volatile situation. While he was safely on board for the ocean crossing, reporters told Max that the French hoped he would fight in Paris. Outside America, the entire world seemed to love Maxie. The only thing that was certain back in New York was that it was going to take the Supreme Court to decide the heavyweight championship.

The Baer entourage stayed overnight on the ship after it docked. A large crowd gathered to greet him. "Gee. I'm going to like this," he exclaimed when he was off the boat.[21] His first sporting activity was to play a round of golf at Coombe Hill, Surrey.

By March 10, the Louis-Braddock fight was going forward amidst Madison Square Garden's legal attempts to stop it. Max Baer had been promised to meet the winner of the Braddock-Louis bout if he won in England.

Baer was at ringside March 15, to see Tommy Farr, 203, beat Ben Foord, 206, in a 15-round battle at the Harringay Arena. Max was scheduled to meet the winner, although he would eventually fight both men.

The New York Commission filed a protest with the British Board of Boxing Control requesting Baer be disqualified to fight in England because the boxer was under contract with Madison Square Garden at the time. After examining a copy of the contract, the British Board pointed to the clause that read the contract would be null and void if Baer did not get a New York license by February 19. The British Board decided that Max Baer would be allowed to fight Tommy Farr in April. Meanwhile, English promoter Hulls had contacted Joe Louis's team for a match in London in July, suggesting he might meet Schmeling, Max Baer or Tommy Farr.

When asked about the heavyweight situation, Louis was unresponsive, but his trainer Jack Blackburn had plenty to say. "There aren't any good young heavyweights that I've seen. Pastor? Yes, if he could fight as well as he can run. Max Baer could beat all the white heavyweights if he got in shape. He's the best white heavyweight in the world."[22]

When Baer left for London, trainers Izzy Klein and Jerry Cosale replaced Frank Paccassi.[23] In England, Baer trained at the Ace of Spades Roadhouse near Kingston, Surrey. On March 27, 1937, Baer was assigned a sparring partner: Bill Wainwright of Swadincote, Heavyweight Champion of the Midlands. Izzy Klein had agreed to make the trip to train Max if he stopped clowning. Baer agreed, and Klein would remain his trainer for the remainder of his important boxing matches. Baer worked hard for Klein and got down to 208 pounds. Word had it that the winner of Baer-Farr would take on Walter Neusel and then Joe Louis, in London.

Tommy Farr, April 15, 1937, Harringay Arena, London

Although Tommy Farr's British Empire Heavyweight Title that he had won the month previous was not at stake, there was so much publicity in America about Max fighting the British Champion that it seemed Baer's invasion of Britain had catapulted him back into boxing's big picture. Baer's personality had already made him a favorite with the British fans and they had yet to see him fight. At every restaurant, pub, theater, or hotel lobby, crowds gathered around him. They wanted his autograph, they wanted to hear his voice, or they wanted him to tell a funny story. They loved his style.

Max promised he would go after Farr right from the bell and knock him out with one punch.

The bout was scheduled for twelve rounds and odds favored Baer, 3 to 1. Most bets predicted that Farr would be off his feet in the fifth. Farr, the blue-eyed blond Welshman, weighed 198 pounds, and Baer, 208.

Max was guaranteed $22,500. Ringside seats went for $50. The gate at the Harringay Arena was expected to draw $100,000. Trainer Klein said that Farr had a stance that looked like one of those old-time boxing poses. Such description was not far removed from his background.

Thomas "Tommy" Farr, one of eight children, was born in 1913 at his family's home

Max Baer and British Heavyweight Champion Tommy Farr fought in London on April 15, 1937, at Harringay Arena (courtesy David Bergin).

in Clydach Vale, Tonypandy, Wales, from which he acquired his fighting name, "The Tonypandy Terror." Farr grew up in abject poverty, even by the austere standards of industrial Wales. His mother died when he was young, and his father, a boxer, was seriously injured in an accident that left him paralyzed. Thus, when Tommy was still quite young, he became the family's sole breadwinner. To escape work in the mines, he went into boxing and won his first professional fight in 1926 in Wales. He won the Welsh Light-Heavyweight Title, and later, the British Heavyweight Title.[24]

The Baer fight at Harringay was aired in England by the British Broadcasting

Twelve • Baer Storms England, Farr and Foord, 1937, 1938

Corporation. A crew from the American CBS radio network attended the fight and sent the broadcast back to the United States to air in the afternoon of April 15.

In front of an audience of 14,000, Farr, 23, kept Max on the defensive with his long left, successfully preventing Max from delivering any devastating blows.

In the first round, Farr hit Baer with a hard right that opened up a nasty cut under Max's left eye. The blood poured at such a rate that it kept Baer blinking through the blood. He said that it definitely hindered him in the first four rounds. Farr never let up, confidently unleashing both hands throughout the battle.

Each round was much like the first. Baer tried to land his right on Farr's chin, but Farr stepped away. And whenever Max let go a long right, Farr reached inside to batter his face.

Baer had the noticeable habit of hitching up his pants, and it seemed to the American listeners of the radio broadcast that he spent most of the rounds pulling up his trunks, according to the many times the broadcaster called attention to it.

Baer had Farr on the ropes in the fourth with accurate hits to his head, but the round ended even. Baer battered Farr's body in the fifth, but Farr chased him around the ring with left jabs. Baer seemed slow, allowing Farr to land two hard left hooks to his mouth in the sixth. Baer followed up with body blows to even the seventh round.

In the eighth it looked as though the end had come for Baer. He never attacked. Farr put him against the ropes and pounded away, but hard as he tried, Farr could not put him down. By the ninth round, fans were on their feet. Farr launched three left jabs and a hard right to Baer's head that staggered him. Max snorted and fought back savagely and the two were so locked in combat that they didn't hear the bell. At the end of the fight, Max was left battered and bruised. Farr won four rounds, Baer three and five were even. Photos taken in the ring after the fight showed Baer hugging Farr. Baer smiled through the blood and Farr grimaced as though he had just lost the match. The outcome was so astonishing that within an hour of the fight, Farr had two offers from America.[25]

Back in his dressing room, Baer was disconsolate and asked for two things: a cigarette and a doctor to take care of his eye. He said that it was the first time in his career that he had taken a cut on his face. His eye was gashed and terribly swollen, and his mouth was cut inside and bleeding. He said that Farr was the toughest fighter he ever met. Then he said with disgust, "I'm all washed up. I'm going back to the ranch in California and retire."[26]

The next day, it was said that "every Welshman with good lungs still" was singing the national anthem of Wales, *Land of My Father* (*Wlad Fy Nhadau*), and "Englishmen were stopping perfect strangers in the streets to ask if they had heard the news."[27]

The brutality of this fight was painful to Baer's father. Jacob Baer worried that his son was over the hill. He wanted Max to return home, settle down, and go into some other endeavor while he still had his brains.

Baer planned to stay in London through May to see Buddy's fight. Max would occupy his time doing film and cabaret work. But before he could sign for a picture, he signed for another fight, a 12-round bout with Ben Foord to take place at Harringay on May 27.

Buddy Baer easily won his match with Jim Wilde, former Welsh heavyweight titleholder, on May 6. Wembley Stadium was half-filled with 8,000 fans who watched the taller, heavier (by 34 pounds) Baer floor his opponent five times, three times in the first round, once in the third, and finally in the fourth when the referee stopped the bout. Wilde protested the stoppage and the crowd booed the referee, but it was clear that the Welshman had taken too much punishment to continue.

Max Baer and Tommy Farr after their brutal fight, April 15, 1937, in London (courtesy David Bergin).

Buddy's next match was in Swansea, England, May 24. Weighing 244½ pounds, he won a ten-round decision over Jack London, 220 pounds. London was knocked off his feet in the first round but managed to stay the distance. Buddy was making such a good name for himself in England that by the time he left London, promoter Sidney Hulls offered a guarantee of $100,000 for a match with the youngest Baer and Joe Louis. Ancil Hoffman's plans for Buddy were to forge ahead with a series of preliminary fights so that he would be ready to fight Louis in about two years.

Good news was on the horizon for Max Baer. On May 7, the day after Buddy's big win, Ancil Hoffman announced to Londoners that Mary Ellen Baer and Max were expecting their first baby. Max was elated at the thought of becoming a father. He said the first thing he would do if it was a boy was to send a telegram to Jack Dempsey, who had two girls. Pictures of the happy couple taken in London made the news in America. Max's parents learned of the news from the papers. When Max was back in California, he told trainer Frank Paccassi, "Yep, it's happened."

Frank responded, "What, another lawsuit?"

"Naw, I'm gonna be a father."[28]

Farr's victory over Baer was a bonanza for British boxing and Farr in particular. Immediately, his name was added to the list of heavyweight contenders for the title. Offers began coming in from the United States: one from Pittsburg for Farr to fight light-heavyweight John Henry Lewis. But Tommy's goal was to fight Max Schmeling in England.

Farr would fight James Braddock back in New York on January 21, 1938, and lose a very close decision. Max would take on Farr again in the United States in March of 1938.

Tommy Farr would win his greatest acclaim fighting Joe Louis. Arthur Donovan (who refereed the Louis-Farr fight) said that Farr "was the gamest fighter Louis ever faced ... his most rugged opponent."[29]

On April 30 in London, Max Baer signed to battle Ben Foord of South Africa in a 12-round bout in May.

Ben Foord, May 27, 1937, Harringay Arena, London

Max Baer was back in the Harringay Arena attempting a second foray in a comeback battle with Ben Foord. Foord began boxing professionally at age 19 in 1932. He had become the South African Heavyweight Champion on June 25, 1934, and only a year earlier had lost the British Empire title to Tommy Farr. Before meeting Baer, he had beaten Jack Petersen, Jack London and Tommy Loughran.

Fans generally thought that Baer was going into the last fight of his career. As a result, Foord's loss to Baer was as unexpected as Baer's loss in his previous fight to Farr. Unlike the bout with Farr, in which Baer was badly beaten, Baer managed to show something of his former self during the one-sided battle.

A crowd of 8,000 witnessed the wild-swinging event. With his smashing right hand, Baer knocked Foord down twice in the second round for counts of three and eight, from which Foord could never clear his head. The fight was made eventful when Baer accidentally tagged Referee Jack Hart with one of his round-house lefts. The referee was not hurt, but the crowd was amused.

The one-sided bout continued until Baer knocked Foord down for two nine counts in the ninth. Foord tried to rise at the end, but slumped back to the floor. His seconds threw in the towel. The timekeeper had counted Foord out, but Referee Hart discounted it and gave Baer the victory by a technical knockout.[30] Foord was out on the floor, face down and bleeding. British sportswriter Trevor Wignall was touched by Baer's reaction to the man he knocked out. "The moment I shall always recall," he said, "was that when he dropped to his knees and tenderly pillowed Foord's head on his arm."[31]

While Baer was cheered for ten minutes after the battle, many wondered why, during the Farr battle, Baer never displayed the terrific punches he was known for and that destroyed Foord. The press concluded that had not Baer "Foorded" the River Styx, he would have been carried to fistic oblivion.

Milton Bronner said that there wasn't much boxing or footwork going on. In fact, "Foord had all the grace and agility of an ice-wagon. Baer ... like a beer truck." He played with the crowd, with his opponent, and "stopped dead to pull up his shorts."[32] So the crowd saw the best of both the clown and the puncher.

Baer was well received by the British, whether he won or lost. He could be found at a West End restaurant crooning over the microphone while his brother Buddy played the drums. They were both talented entertainers—singing and dancing. Max was popular in England for the same reason he had been popular in America: he was the Jack Benny or Bob Hope evolved from a boxing ring. He had what publicists today call the "it factor," or "crowd appeal," something every promoter tried desperately to create. It helped that Baer was good-looking and confident. When he walked into a room, he filled it up with

South African Heavyweight Champion Ben Foord took a beating in his battle with Baer, May 27, 1937, at Harringay Arena, London (courtesy IBRO).

his charisma. Dempsey had "it"; Tunney did not. Baer had "IT" big; Schmeling and Braddock did not. "It" was what kept Baer in the game. And, of course, Louis had "it" in his quiet way.

British biographer Arthur Helliwell interviewed Max at the Dorchester where he was staying in London, and had this to say: "When you really got to know him well, you soon discovered that he was far from being the scatterbrain that most people imagined. On the contrary, he is an extraordinarily shrewd and astute person."[33] Helliwell pointed out what no one in America had given Baer credit for. "There never has been such a showman, but the capers and grimaces that set the customers rolling in their seats with mirth had a deeper significance than mere clowning." His antics in the ring were meant to frazzle the mind of his opponent. Helliwell said that his "pantomiming" paved "the way to a kayo just as the more skillful boxer uses strategy and ringcraft."[34]

Helliwell said of Baer's battle with Foord:

> No one who was at Harringay is ever likely to forget that fight. Poor Foord took a terrible lacing, but Baer's clowning, his mock snarls of rage and the ferocious grimaces in which he indulged between spells of murderous punching upset the South African even more than the punishment he absorbed. Like Carnera [Foord] was almost on the verge of tears before the fight was over. Baer would slug him dizzy with a succession of terrible rights and lefts, and then step back and stop with his arms akimbo, shaking his head sorrowfully. Or he would bare his teeth and roar like a cannibal chief as he stalked Foord with one glove raised like a club, and then, as Ben backed apprehensively away, he would suddenly smile and ruffle his hair like an affectionate elder brother.

Baer tried, but could never adopt a scientific boxing strategy. Still, the one he discovered that worked for him was one that so befuddled his opponent into distraction

Twelve • Baer Storms England, Farr and Foord, 1937, 1938

Max (tallest, rear left) and Buddy (rear right) were popular guests with the British public, especially when serving drinks behind the bar in 1937 (courtesy David Bergin).

that he could lay his sledgehammer right on the chin for a knockout few men could overcome. "He put on a great act of toughness and ferocity," Helliwell concluded, "but actually he was one of the most generous, good-natured and chivalrous fighters the ring has known. A nice guy, Maxie."[35]

Months after the fight, Ben Foord commented: "Max Baer is the finest fighting machine I ever came up against."[36]

The Baer brothers had been such hits with the British public that General Critchley offered them management positions at two of his biggest hotels: a health resort in Brighton-by-the-Sea and the Star and Garter in London. Both men could continue their boxing careers as long as one stayed on the job while the other was away. The salary and living conditions were said to have been "outstanding," and they accepted the generous offer. Unfortunately, family circumstances ultimately prevented them from relocating to England.

Meanwhile, Braddock was in training for his first title defense against Joe Louis.

Reporter Harry Grayson did note the hypocrisy that Braddock was allowed to run out of a contractual battle with Max Schmeling while Baer was held to a Garden contract with Bob Pastor when he couldn't get a license in New York. Schmeling had so much more to lose.

Americans were not the only ones who felt Schmeling's slight. The Germans were terribly upset, not the least of whom was Adolf Hitler. He was said to have been furious about the runaround from Braddock and was determined that the Germans should have a crack at the title. And if they didn't get a crack at it, Hitler would declare Schmeling the champion.

After Braddock's title defeat to Joe Louis, June 22, 1937, manager Joe Gould said that first on his list of preferred Braddock opponents was Max Baer. But it was a rematch that would never materialize, possibly because Gould couldn't arrange a payoff deal with Baer's manager like he had managed with Mike Jacobs.

Jimmy Braddock explained to author Ed Brennan in 1965, for *The Ring* magazine, "Gould went to Mike Jacobs, who was fighting the Garden. Jacobs said he would give us ten percent of all his heavyweight title fights for 20 years if I fought Louis. We went for that." Braddock told Peter Heller, "We might have got one hundred fifty-thousand out of it over the ten years, which wasn't a bad annuity." It was a huge annuity.[37]

Buddy, Max and Mary Ellen left England suddenly on the S.S. *Berengaria* back to the States after hearing the news of their father's illness. Jacob, 61, was recovering at his home at 880 Alice Street, San Leandro, having suffered another heart attack. He had been bedridden for three weeks. Max arrived on July 7, and was interviewed, saying that he would move to England immediately if he could convince his father to leave California. But that seemed unlikely now that his father was ill.

July was a busy month for Max back in California. He refereed eight amateur bouts in Santa Monica at the Municipal Stadium. On July 14, Baer was in Reno refereeing fights there. He had an exhibition fight on July 30 with Al Rovay in San Francisco. Also at the end of the month, Baer was either at Dolph Thomas's Gym in San Francisco or at Duffy's in Oakland training, expecting to fight Braddock in September, Schmeling the following May, and Louis in June. At some point between all the bouts, he said he was wanted in Hollywood to make a movie.

On August 26, Max went to New Jersey to visit the training quarters of Joe Louis in his first title defense of his heavyweight championship with Tommy Farr, scheduled for August 30, 1937. Max cautioned everyone not to write off Farr. What they were seeing at his training camp in Long Branch, New Jersey, was not his ring form.

Baer was never out of the news, or out of court. While he was visiting the training camps, the newspapers were notified that Max Baer had been issued a bench warrant for August 30, the day of the big fight. The warrant was for failing to appear in court, where he was charged with indecent exposure: appearing in public without a shirt. He was caught "walking in the heart of the [Long Branch, New Jersey] business section clad only in bathing shorts and shoes."[38] When first served with the charge by patrolman Antonio De Santis, Max thought it was a joke. He said, "What the hell, I've worn less'n that in the ring with ten thousand women looking." But it was no joke. The date for Baer to appear fell on the date of the Louis-Farr fight. "I gotta see that fight," pleaded Max.[39] Buddy was on the undercard. But the small-town prosecutor apparently didn't weigh the two events on the same legal scale. Baer's contempt of court charge was brought before the judge and dismissed if Baer would appear in a publicity photo in his court—in shorts, shirtless.[40]

For the Louis-Farr fight at Yankee Stadium, seven heavyweight title holders were scheduled to be introduced before the bout: Jack Sharkey, Jack Dempsey, Gene Tunney, Jimmy Braddock, Max Baer, Max Schmeling and Jack Johnson.

Max was also in the corner for Buddy's preliminary fight at Yankee Stadium with Abe Simon. Buddy had brought home a rabbit's foot given to him as a lucky charm when he was in England, and apparently the luck held. He stopped Simon in what would be the beginning of his serious campaign for the title. Buddy felt as though he had the key to Louis: to carry the fight to him "with short punches and plenty of them. Don't give him a chance to get set or send over a long range punch or wide left hook."[41]

Even though Tommy Farr did not win the fight against Louis, he showed plenty of courage. The British came to Farr's behalf, talking about the "spunk" of the man of Wales. Consensus was that Louis earned nine rounds, Farr five, and one was even. The referee and two judges gave Louis 10 rounds. Louis collected $102,585. Farr earned $51,202 plus $10,000 expenses. Promoter Jacobs was said to have cleared $20,000. Now it seemed like every former champion wanted to challenge Louis.

After the fight, Schmeling was asked if he would fight Farr for a chance at a title shot. Schmeling replied that he already qualified for a title shot, from 1930 to 1932, when he was champion, an excuse that held little weight considering all the champions who were still vying for a chance at the title.

On September 3, 1937, Max signed for a fight with Braddock promoted by Mike Jacobs for October 29, in an elimination tournament for Louis. But the fight would never materialize. On October 21, Braddock canceled out, citing his arthritic hands. The fight was postponed indefinitely. Max was still sore at the New York authorities. When his hands were bad, he still had to fight Braddock. When Braddock argued that he couldn't fight (or defend his title earlier) because of his arthritic hands, he got a two-year layoff.

The remainder of the year was rather mundane for Max in California. He served as Master of Ceremonies at various events, fought a 4-round exhibition with Nash Garrison, and jumped from arena to arena in California earning $200 a week refereeing fights.

Whenever Max refereed a boxing or wrestling match, the public turned out to see him because they never knew what might happen. On December 14, Baer refereed a wrestling match between Junior Heavyweight World Champ Due Chick against Pete Belcastro in Watsonville. Baer had admonished Belcastro for using dirty tricks, when suddenly the Italian grabbed Max by the leg and knocked him to the mat. Max immediately took an open hand and knocked Belcastro to the mat. Opponent Chick took advantage of his prostrate opponent by picking him up and slamming him to the mat a few times more. Then he won the match with a body press. What was Belcastro thinking to mess with the former world heavyweight boxing champ, Max Baer?

On Saturday, December 4, Marry Ellen Baer gave birth to a baby boy. At age 28, Max Baer became father to Max Jr. Max had walked the hallways of the East Oakland Hospital saying, "If it's a boy he's going to be a champ, I know."[42] Max said the baby resembled him. And the doctor even commented that he had some of the biggest hands and shoulders for a newborn he had ever seen. This was the happiest moment of Baer's life, and now he had a reason to resume fighting for the title. He was going to win it back for his son.

Max had become solemn. McLemore said he was not the "gay caballero who took New York apart, hitherto reckless and heedless."[43] But Baer was older now, and neither of his parents were well. He seemed to have his fighting priorities all lined up: "I've got the men I want to fight all in my mind and I've got things in order. I'd like to fight Braddock, who licked me when my hands were so bad it hurt to lace on the gloves. Then I want to fight Farr, who beat me when I'd been out of the ring so long I didn't know what I was doing." He wanted to fight Louis "most of all, because they said I was yellow the night that he licked me. I know I wasn't yellow that night, but that kid over in the hospital with his mother doesn't know I wasn't yellow. But he's going to. I'm going to fight a few fights for him now."[44]

Only five days after his son was born, Max had to take his father Jacob Baer, 63, to the hospital after Jacob suffered a heart attack (the same hospital where his wife and son were still hospitalized). Extremely weak, Jacob walked in on Max's arm. Jacob's heart condition was critical. But he seemed to improve at the hospital.

Max paid all of his father's hospital and doctors' bills along with his wife's.

The day after the baby came, Buddy left for New York to fight Eddie Hogan of Waterbury, Connecticut. Buddy was the betting favorite 8 to 5 for the fight scheduled for December 17, at Madison Square Garden. Attendance was expected to be at 7,000, and Joe Louis would meet the winner. Louis was on hand when Buddy won the fight. One reporter said that Buddy caught most of Hogan's shots in his gloves or they bounced off his shoulders. Another reported that Buddy took quite a beating until the third round, but withstood all that Hogan sent his way. The shot that first dropped Hogan was a long, looping right that practically came from the floor when Buddy came out of a crouch, a punch he no doubt inherited from Max. There were two more knockdowns before the referee stopped the fight in the third. One reporter described Buddy's style: "He plods around the ring with the speed of a plow-horse."[45] Afterward, Baer told the press that he wanted to meet Braddock next to revenge the loss by his brother. But at this time manager Hoffman thought he needed to wait on Louis. Until this bout, Buddy was considered just one of the many heavyweights in the large field of heavyweights. Now, this bout put him in the spotlight.

The next day, December 18, Max was served legal papers by Madison Square Garden, suing him for $1000 to collect the fight guarantee for the bout that never materialized with Bob Pastor.

At year's end, *The Ring* magazine's poll for 1937, ranked the top heavyweights in the following order: Joe Louis, Max Schmeling, Tommy Farr, Nathan Mann, Alberto Lovell, Tony Galento, Jimmy Braddock, Jimmy Adamick, Maxie Rosenbloom, Roscoe Toles, Arturo Godov, Bob Pastor and Max Baer. Baer was dead last and Buddy didn't make the list.

Mike Jacobs said he would match Max with the winner of Farr-Braddock of January 21, in his elimination battle for contenders for Louis. Farr had been training at Summit, New Jersey, running eight miles per day, working twelve hard rounds with sparring partners, and looking great with only two thin white scars under each eye from the beating he took from Louis. Farr was nine years younger than Braddock, and the odds favorite. One paper noted, "He's hard as pig iron."[46] Farr made it known to the press that after Braddock he wanted to fight Baer.

Braddock won the decision over his younger counterpart, and he did it by scoring with a barrage of punches which gave him just enough points in each round, including the last two rounds, to finish with the decision. Braddock planned to take on Baer next.

Baer had been training to meet the winner of the Braddock-Farr fight, applying a strategy for each man: a bob-and-weave style to meet Farr's boxing style, and a more stand-up style using a straight left and long right to meet Braddock's.

It was during a break in one of his public workouts at Duffy's when Max learned he would fight Braddock at Madison Square Garden. Max picked up the guitar and began to entertain the spectators. He liked to make them smile and feel good about getting their 10 cents per person, value at the door. He sang various songs and then gave his own rendition of a selection from Leoncavallo's *Pagliacci* (*The Clowns*). "I have gone in for the finer things of life," he quipped.[47] Oakland sportswriter Art Cohn responded that Caruso must be turning over in his grave.

In the opera, the actors are led onto the stage by a clown. Before the overture, the clown reminds the audience that actors have feelings too, and that the show is about real people. The lyrics must have resonated with Max, so frequently called the Clown of Boxing.

Then someone in the audience showed Max a newspaper that had quoted Braddock's manager Joe Gould saying, "Why should we take Baer? A fight with that guy would be a step backward." So that's the kind of gratitude he got for taking the man off the relief rolls and giving him a million-dollar chance at the title. Max responded, "That's a laugh. He never was anything but a bum, not even the night he licked me.... I just happened to be a bigger bum that fight. They should be grateful."[48]

He looked to his admiring audience and asked if anyone wanted to bet him $1000 that he could flatten Braddock. No one took the bet. The session was over, and Max turned to Buddy. He needed to bum a dollar to pay for his rubdown at the gym.

With the Baer-Braddock contract signed, Baer's camp arranged training quarters in Lakewood, New Jersey, beginning February 5. But what did contracts mean in New York? On January 24, 1938, the sly Joe Gould, Braddock's manager, said that he intentionally left himself some "outs" in the contract with Baer. Those outs stated that the "dates and the terms" of the fight must prove to be acceptable. Gould stated blatantly, "no terms and no dates will be acceptable." The fight was dead in the water. And if anyone wanted to challenge him about it, they only had to look back to see how he had managed to get Braddock a fight with Joe Louis even after he broke three Madison Square Garden contracts to fight Max Schmeling.[49]

All fights with Braddock were off the table by February 1, when the Cinderella Man decided to retire. Jacobs then offered Baer either Tony Galento or Nathan Mann. Hoffman declined the offers.

Tommy Farr was also disappointed in Braddock's retirement because he wanted a rematch. Braddock said that he wanted to continue to fight, but his manager Joe Gould said, "I put my foot down on it. I'm not willing to let such a grand guy risk the chance of getting seriously and maybe permanently hurt. You never can tell what will happen when you're in there against these young fellows. Jim was pretty well banged up in that Louis fight."[50] Quickly, Mike Jacobs replaced Braddock with Baer for the Farr bout scheduled for March 11.

Hoffman accepted the match. Farr wasn't too happy about the deal. He said that his loss to Braddock didn't obligate him to fight Baer. He had already beaten Baer once. He wanted Max Schmeling instead. But he changed his mind when Jacobs promised that he was to be given a title shot in the event that he beat Baer.

Baer wasted no time and left for New York on February 7, 1938. He didn't even stop on Broadway before he left for camp in Lakewood, New Jersey. Baer would turn 29 and train harder for this fight than any before. He hadn't smoked a cigarette for three months, since the baby came. Hoffman said that Baer was now the easiest of fighters to handle. Hoffman told reporters that Baer refused to let anyone in the camp smoke.

But before he could begin training in earnest, Max had another lawsuit to settle in New York. In 1933, New York showgirl Shirley La Belle had an unpleasant encounter with Max. She was now suing him for $50,000 for "making love to her against her wishes in a room in a midtown hotel in the early hours of the morning of December 20, 1933."[51] She said she had been invited to his room at 2 a.m. for a job offer. She was 18 at the time, and according to her complaint, the episode made her unsuitable to marry. Now, she wanted "vindication." La Belle was given $2000 and the case was closed.

Buddy was also training with Max at Lakewood for his fight with Gunnar Barlund of Finland. Many wondered who would win the title first, Max or brother Buddy. Unfortunately, Buddy was cut in the eye during training and had to lay off for fifteen days before the fight. In their off time, the boys played chess and ate oranges, a delicacy in the 1930s. Ancil Hoffman had a crate of oranges flown in twice a week from his California ranch.

Gunnar Barlund's manager Paul Damski filed a complaint with the New York Athletic Commission on March 1, 1938, against Buddy Baer's tailor-made boxing trunks. He said they were customized to rise a full three inches above the normal waistline. "They rise almost to Buddy's armpits," he complained to the commission, "and are a serious mental hazard to any opponent."[52] He threatened to pull out of the match if Buddy didn't cut them off a full three inches. The commission was shocked to learn of the deceit. No one, it seemed, had actually done any body damage to Buddy before, so the possibility that his high-water trunks were the reason for his career wins seemed plausible. It was ruled that Buddy would not be allowed in the ring wearing anything but store-bought garments.

Buddy was stopped by a technical in the seventh, wearing his store-bought trunks. Baer started off bloodying Barlund's nose in the first and ripping open a nasty cut above his left eye. But Baer was eventually overpowered. After he was struck twenty times in the face without a return blow, referee Billy Cavanaugh stopped the fight. Baer was never floored, but it was the first time in 44 bouts that Buddy had been beaten. Even wearing the new trunks, Barlund hit Baer low twice and was penalized for low blows. Both fighters left the ring bleeding heavily. The crowd of over 8,000 jeered Buddy as he left the ring with comments like, "Just a bum like your brother."[53]

Big brother Max was terribly upset by Buddy's defeat, but he vowed he would beat Farr to avenge his brother's loss. After Farr, Max wanted Louis. His heart was set on Joe Louis.

Tommy Farr (rematch), March 11, 1938, Madison Square Garden, New York

On March 11, 1938, Baer met Tommy Farr, who was the betting favorite 7 to 5 in their 15-round grudge match. Both fighters were considered unpredictable. A near-capacity audience of 16,000 hoped the fight would go down in the books as one of the most savage of the year. After losing a 10-round decision to Braddock, Farr had something to prove. Of course, Baer wanted to avenge his previous loss to Farr so that he could move on to a title match. But then he hadn't fought anyone since Foord, the previous year. Baer only had a six-pound advantage, weighing 212 to Farr's 206, but he had a new attitude and a new determination since the birth of his son.

Twelve • Baer Storms England, Farr and Foord, 1937, 1938

The next day, the papers proclaimed Max the golden boy. He had fought his way back to the heights, even though he was booed by the audience when he entered the ring. For fifteen blazing rounds, Baer was his old self, the warrior who bashed Schmeling and the puncher who demolished Carnera. Baer came out ferociously, hoping for an early knockout. Farr went down for a one-count in the second and for a six-count in the third. Baer's left eye was closed completely by the end of the third round, and he could never see from it through the remain-

Farr (left) and Baer in their grudge match at Madison Square Garden, March 11, 1938 (courtesy IBRO).

der of the fight. Farr seemed to pick up the pace in the fourth, fifth, and sixth, hitting Baer repeatedly with left jabs, but the referee penalized him for low blows in the fourth. Baer threw some wild punches, but when they connected he was able to drop Farr three times—twice with smashing blows to the chin. Baer took some heavy shots to his body, but came back in the seventh, sneering and snorting and landing some heavy head shots. One time when they were infighting in the seventh, Baer landed a heavy blow to Farr's ribs. The same occurred in the eighth. Farr's face was slashed, and both were still fighting at the end, although it took everything Baer had to fight on.

Brooklyn sportswriter Ed Hughes said it was one of the best fights he had seen at the Garden in years. Spectators couldn't have asked for a better fight. They punched and smashed and endured. Hughes said that there was no question that Baer had inflicted heavier damage. He had the fight close, eight to seven in favor of Baer. On the Associated Press card, Baer won eleven rounds, Farr three, with one even. The gate came to $74,409.22.

Years later, after Farr had fought Joe Louis, he told a London reporter that Madcap Maxie was a harder puncher than World Heavyweight Champion Joe Louis. "Punch for punch," he said, "Baer's are heavier, but Louis' come faster. They can be bloody annoying, if you know what I mean."[54]

With the win over Farr, Max Baer returned to the front rank of contenders for 1938.

Jimmy Johnston had this to say from Madison Square Garden: "Don't let Baer's victory over Tommy Farr fool you. Farr isn't much and Baer is just the same guy who played the el foldo for Louis."[55]

It wasn't until after the Farr fight that Referee Arthur Donovan, who had claimed that Max quit against Joe Louis, finally came clean and admitted that Baer had never quit. He said that Baer had not said anything when he got up after Louis knocked him down. "There was no request. I was convinced Baer had taken enough punishment for one night, and for one man."[56] It had taken Donovan three years to admit Baer had never asked him to stop the fight. Baer had never said "I quit," or "I've had enough," yet the repercussions from the conclusion of that fight would last long after Baer's death.

After Tommy Farr, Max wanted to meet Max Schmeling. But Hoffman was not so sure. He thought Buddy was a better fit for Herr Max. Gene Tunney agreed. But on the subject of Max, or Tommy Farr, for that matter, Tunney didn't think either would ever reach the top ranks again. But Max didn't count himself out. The decade was not over.

Max spent the next nine months without a big fight. He went back to refereeing wrestling matches in California, adding only one new job as a result of his interest in music: directing an orchestra. A dance was advertised where Max Baer would lead his own orchestra at Riverside Memorial Auditorium, Saturday, April 30, at 8 p.m. Admission was 75 cents plus tax.

Meanwhile, the most anticipated fight for the immediate future was between Joe Louis and Max Schmeling, scheduled for June of 1938. Max Schmeling had waited six long years for a chance to regain the world title he lost to Jack Sharkey. The Louis-Schmeling fight had the potential to make more money than the Baer-Louis fight of 1935. Including proceeds from radio and film, the Baer-Louis bout had been the richest, the only $1 million fight of the 1930s to date.

THIRTEEN

No Clowning for Nova, 1939

On May 1, 1938, Max Baer was at the Western Union Telegraph office in Los Angeles composing a message to send to Benito Mussolini. He had been asked by a group of prominent Italian-Americans to help with their mission to aid the Jewish people overseas. Since the Italian dictator was a lover of sports, it was hoped that Baer could use his celebrity to appeal for help. Baer sent a cable to Mussolini requesting the dictator speak personally to Adolf Hitler on behalf of the Jewish population in Germany and Austria.

After sending the telegram, Max left for San Diego with promoter Morrie Cohan. Baer was to meet Hank Hankinson and Odell Polee for two rounds each on a boxing card. Driving in a heavy rain, the pair spotted a young sailor near Oceanside whose car had taken a slide off the road and overturned. They stopped to lend a hand. Max single-handedly righted the auto, and Cohan was beside himself at seeing Max's incredible strength.

Sometime between helping the stranded sailor and arriving in San Diego, Baer was notified that his father, who had been bedridden after suffering another heart attack, had slipped into a coma. Baer canceled his engagement and headed north for San Leandro.

Max drove all night to reach his father. When he stepped onto the front porch of the house in the early hours of the next morning, Buddy met him in tears and told him that their father had died. Buddy, Mary Ellen, Dora Baer, and two daughters, Bernice and Fanny, and foster son August Silva were at his bedside. Jacob, 63 when he died, was remembered as a quiet, endearing man, who enjoyed stopping by Duffy's Gym whenever his sons worked out. Like Max, he was generous. He always had a cigar in his mouth and one in his pocket to give away. His funeral was Friday, May 6, 1938, at the Mountain View Cemetery, San Leandro, California.

Max had no sooner laid his father to rest than his infant son became ill. Five-and-a-half-month-old Max Jr. was hospitalized for pneumonia at the same Oakland hospital where he was born. He was placed under an oxygen tent for a week's stay. During this time, Dora Baer took ill. Max waited for Max Jr. to leave the hospital before he took off for New York.

In June, Max Baer and Ancil Hoffman were on the train to New York to attend the Louis-Schmeling fight. Mike Jacobs had promised Baer that he would fight the winner of the title bout in September. Max was the only man who had fought both, and he definitely thought Louis would win. In fact, he hoped Louis would beat Schmeling because he did not want Schmeling to become the first ex-heavyweight champ to regain the crown. Max wanted that honor for himself.

Pressure was on Joe Louis to win this fight: personally to avenge his previous loss to Max Schmeling, and publicly to prevent a German from winning the title. The stake in the world championship was now for more than athletic supremacy. If Schmeling won, Americans felt like it would be a win for Nazi Germany. Everyone feared that if Schmeling won, he would "duck out" and take the title to Germany, and America would never see it again.

All Americans, black and white, rooted for the black man to win. If Louis won, he would elevate his race to a position of athletic supremacy that had not been seen on a world stage since Jack Johnson. This fight was bigger than boxing, bigger than race, and the outcome was in the hands of one man, possibly two—Joe Louis and the referee, Arthur Donovan. It is fair to say that more political pressure was placed on the two boxers (and the referee) than at any other time in modern history.

Louis had already desegregated the press section, but a sign was posted ringside: "Ladies Not Admitted." Pressmen vied for ringside seats, and Max Baer took his seat in a working press chair near the ring. It was important for him to see the action up close in order to determine exactly how the outcome would be accomplished. Before the main event, the announcer introduced Max Baer as contender for the winner.

Baer watched carefully. It took Joe Louis only two minutes and four seconds in the first round on June 22, 1938, to slay the beast with his dynamite fists, so focused was he on his mission. And while Louis scored three knockdowns in that first round, it was the action before the first knockdown that determined the final outcome.

Louis had entered the ring mad, and Schmeling looked scared. The action was so fast and chaotic in that first round that many of the radio broadcasters tripped over their tongues, and radio listeners had trouble deciphering what was going on in the ring. They complained afterwards that the two-minute broadcast was a jumble.

The boxers came to ring center at the bell, circled, and sized each other up for about seven seconds. Then they engaged. They attacked toe-to-toe four separate times before Louis pushed Schmeling near the ropes and beat him so severely that he was forced to cling to the ropes. The action in that segment ended with Schmeling taking his first count.

Before that first knockdown, there were four distinct toe-to-toe engagements, with only seconds of disengagement between them. Louis started the first engagement with his left, testing the water. In the second engagement, Louis became more aggressive and unleashed a barrage of lefts and rights followed by an uppercut. After disengaging, Schmeling sent over a right cross to Louis's chin, but it lacked impact because the timing and distance were off. There would be two more aggressive entanglements. At the end of these encounters, Louis pushed Schmeling toward the ropes, where he was then set to demolish his prey.

At the ropes, Louis bore in and slammed Schmeling with a right uppercut and missed with a right. A left connected to the chin, and then Louis landed a vicious right to the head that knocked Schmeling senseless. Schmeling staggered backwards into the ropes and grabbed the top rope with his right hand, holding on desperately to steady himself. He maintained his grip on the rope for the rest of the punishment. Then Louis cupped his left glove to Schmeling's head and with his right, hit him directly on the side of his body, a punch that looked like a kidney shot; another left to the body; then a miss with the left. Louis was so angry at his miss while he had Schmeling vulnerable on the ropes (with his body turned at an angle) that he landed a powerful right into the middle of Schmeling's back. Schmeling screamed in such a high pitch that some said it sounded like a woman's voice. Louis must have realized that he had hit Schmeling squarely in the back because both of his hands moved up, and the next seven vicious blows were all directed to Schmeling's head. Like an automatic pistol: right, left, left, right, left, right, right and Schmeling sank with his right arm still hung over the top rope.

All of the blows of that final segment occurred with Schmeling essentially hung onto or over the ropes. Referee Donovan was jumping around the ring on the other side before he realized what had happened. By the time he reached Schmeling to wave off Louis, the German was semiconscious. Schmeling's corner yelled "foul," but the fight continued. Left in a haze of pain and disorientation that only his reflexive boxing training could overcome, Schmeling walked directly into the next refrain after taking a count of only one.

Upon viewing the film today, one might question the referee's decision. By today's stand-

Seated ringside, Max Baer watched Joe Louis (left) hit Max Schmeling as Referee Arthur Donovan looks on, January 22, 1938. Baer was scheduled to fight the winner. Baer declared Louis's punch to Schmeling's back a foul (Library of Congress, Photographs and Prints [DSO-8008-3]).

ards it is considered foul to strike the kidneys or the back spine. Holding an opponent's head with one hand while hitting with the other is also considered a foul. Rubbing a glove in the face or hitting an opponent who is partially out of the ring is forbidden.

The dark film footage showed Schmeling's right arm hooked over the ropes. It seemed as if Louis pressured Schmeling's head with his left hand to straighten him up for the kill. Louis had a habit of using a steady left hand either for balance or as a measuring stick, as seen several times in this short fight. In this instance it is difficult to tell if Louis was using his left glove for balance, for pressuring or pushing his opponent upright on the ropes, or for rubbing his glove in his face. Footage showed Louis landed what looked like one or two foul shots. A newspaper photo in the *Oakland Tribune* showed the moment Louis hit Schmeling in the side, and it is difficult to tell exactly where the blow landed. No newspaper photo was found of the punch that landed deep into Schmeling's back. Undoubtedly, these hits were the debilitating blows that fractured Schmeling's hip and spine.

In that fateful encounter, Schmeling sank to his knees still holding onto the ropes. The glazed look in his eyes showed only the urgent recognition that he was taking a count. Schmeling untangled himself during the count of one and walked feebly toward Louis for more punishment. After another barrage of blows, Schmeling's hands dropped, and Louis put him on the canvas for a count of two. Louis sent Schmeling to the canvas one more time.

At the final knockdown, Max Machon's towel flew into the ring from Schmeling's corner. Annoyed by the act, Referee Arthur Donovan wadded it up and threw it back. Throwing in the towel was a signal in Europe to end the bout, but was no longer used by Americans. Only Donovan could end the bout. Schmeling lay face down on the canvas, bleeding and semiconscious. From his corner Max Machon jumped into the ring to help his man. Donovan penalized Machon for entering the ring during the match, thus ruling the bout-ending loss a technical, rather than a KO. Manager Joe Jacobs screamed "foul," but this match would not repeat the fate of June 14, 1930, when Jacobs jumped up on the apron and screamed "foul" to cause the referee to disqualify Jack Sharkey for a low blow to Max Schmeling. A title-making foul was not going to be repeated here. America needed this opponent out of the picture.

Fans saw this action as a herculean display of heavyweight talent, and Joe Louis left the ring as a god. Even Grantland Rice admitted that Jack Dempsey's forty-seven-second blast of Jess Willard at Toledo (Willard had been able to stay at least two rounds longer) could not compare to Louis's fast and furious attack of Schmeling at Yankee Stadium on that historic night.

In his dressing room, Louis admitted that he "had to throw only three good punches to get him. I shook him up a bit with a left that was right hard. But the body punch that came right afterwards was the one that started him down the hill."[1]

Unfortunately, that "body punch" to the back was seen as a foul by Schmeling's cornermen, some newsmen, and at least one other American champion—Max Baer. Jacobs and Machon said the blow was a foul. Back in his dressing room, Schmeling gasped in broken English when asked about the blow. "Yah, yah, it was a foul. He hit me here in the kidney. I couldn't think. I couldn't move. Such a terrible blow."[2] He spoke to a German reporter in his native language and pointed to his back where Louis hit him. Afterward, Schmeling was taken to the hospital.

As Louis's next contender, Baer may have joked about his ten-cent mind, but when it came to assessing what Louis had done to Schmeling, Baer was no fool. He was the sole American boxer unafraid to give his honest appraisal that "Schmeling was a victim of unintentional foul blows in the recent debacle."[3] Baer had clearly gauged the fight a "debacle," not with just one foul but multiple fouls, though he qualified them as unintentional. Max fully believed that in the heat of the moment, fighting with rage, Louis had not meant to land such devastating fouls. But if Louis could mete out such damage to Schmeling, without Referee Donovan calling it, Louis could do it again. The image was seared in Baer's mind. Baer insisted that there wouldn't be a rematch for this fight because "[Schmeling] couldn't raise his hands after taking a couple of wallops on the kidneys."[4] It would have been difficult for anyone to raise an arm after such blows to the back.

When Referee Donovan was asked about the blow, he responded defensively, "It was a fair punch. That's what I was in there for, to see that everything was fair." He explained that a kidney punch was only a foul if it occurred in a clinch, "but this blow was struck while the fighters were two feet apart," he stated unconvincingly.[5]

X-ray examination of Schmeling's back showed initially a "small hip bone broken below the belt line." Schmeling said that Louis's left spun him around and his next right "caught me over the kidney. Everything went black and I couldn't see."[6] Max insisted that it was the kidney punch that debilitated him. Even if they didn't see the punch, everyone at ringside heard the cry. His seconds must have seen it because they threw in the towel.

The loss came as a shock to Germans who listened over their short-wave radio sets for the 3 a.m. broadcast. Adolf Hitler, known to be a night owl, was reported to have listened from his retreat in the Bavarian mountains. Although Schmeling and his camp cried foul, no one could question the power and effect of Joe's punching ability and his overall dominance. And no American referee was going to stop the most important world fight of its time on a questionable foul, certainly not Arthur Donovan.

The fight was Louis's fourth title defense since winning the crown from Braddock only one year earlier. With that fight he had now beaten all of the champions of the decade going back to Gene Tunney's retirement—a phenomenal, historic feat, five champions (Jack Sharkey, Primo Carnera, Max Baer, James Braddock, and now Max Schmeling). It was a grand slam of world title wins for Louis. The elimination battles among the contender champions of the 1930s were now over.

Louis would go on to make 25 total title defenses in a period of over 11 years. He would not only set a boxing record, he would set an example for other sports as well. He became the first black man to play in a Professional Golf Association tournament.

The fight in 1938 was the second biggest gate of the decade (a little over $900,000). The Louis-Baer gate in the same park three years earlier reached nearly $1 million with attendance at 83,000. Attendance at this event was 80,000. With radio and motion picture rights of $75,000, Mike Jacobs expected to approach his million-dollar goal. According to the *New York Times*, Louis's share at 40 percent (after federal and state taxes of 10 percent and 5 percent off the top) was $306,000; Schmeling's share at 20 percent was $153,000; Mike Jacobs's share was $306,000. (Ten percent of Jacobs's take on this fight was paid to Jim Braddock.)

The injury to Max Schmeling's back confined him to the Polyclinic Hospital in New York. After three days of additional tests and X-rays, Dr. Robert Emery Brennan, chief surgeon at the hospital, stated for the record, with X-ray plates in hand, that in addition to a "slightly swelled left kidney," Max was suffering from a "fracture of the left lateral transverse of the third lumbar vertebra."[7] (The lumbar spine is essentially the lower back. The transverse is a component of the bony part of the spinal vertebrae.) The injury would not be permanently crippling, but certainly painful, even by today's medical care. In laymen's terms, Louis had essentially broken Max Schmeling's back.

One of the reasons to re-examine this fight would be to ask the question, "What would have happened if Louis had lost the fight on a foul?" How might history have been altered? Would Baer have continued his quest to regain the crown? Perhaps not, in that Schmeling would have been the first heavyweight to regain the crown. But Baer had beaten Schmeling before and might have thought he could beat him again. In addition, Schmeling might have taken the crown back to Germany and never fought again. And what might Hitler have done to exploit the propaganda value of a German champion? Schmeling would never have been sent to the front line of battle as a Wehrmacht paratrooper in Nazi service. The thought of the world's heavyweight crown in the hands of the Nazis would have been an unfathomable consequence for Americans and their allies.

After the Louis-Schmeling fight, boxing in New York went into the doldrums. Max Baer was the only other fight promotion that Mike Jacobs had in the pipeline that could possibly draw a big gate as an opponent for Joe Louis.

Louis and his manager Julian Black agreed. Louis said, "I consider Baer always a dangerous fighter. You never can tell when a punch may fly at you when you're in the ring with Max."[8] Hoffman believed it was in Max's best interest to seal the deal with Mike Jacobs by signing Baer to a three-year contract giving Mike Jacobs exclusive right to control Baer's fights. The decision as to who and when Baer would fight was now directly in the hands of Mike Jacobs for the next three years.

Baer continued to get offers from Joe Jacobs, Tony Galento's manager, and Gus Greenlee, John Henry Lewis's manager. They were all passed on to Mike Jacobs. Jacobs told the press on July 14, 1938, that Baer would fight Joe Louis in a title fight. He said the contract was signed, and he was feeling good about it. Only "a miracle will be required to avert a Louis-Baer fight sometime, somewhere."[9]

Suddenly, Louis's management had a change of plans. Mike Jacobs was told that the Bomber couldn't fight for the rest of the year because income from another fight would put him in a different tax bracket for the year and would not be profitable. Louis's other manager Roxborough had been lukewarm on Baer anyway. Roxborough told reporter Harry Grayson, "All [Baer] has done since he quit to Joe on one knee is beat Tommy Farr, and who hasn't beaten Tommy Farr? I don't believe that Baer would draw more than a handful of people."[10] Mike Jacobs still considered Baer a drawing card by virtue of his win over Farr.

Matters became worse for Baer's mother. She had been ill since her husband's death, but on August 6, she took a sudden turn and Max was called to her bedside to give blood for a transfusion. The next day she seemed better. But as Art Cohn noted, "Baer's entire career has followed that tragic pattern.... By nature, Max is a simple homey fellow.... His sophistication is a pose. The Baer home, once the happiest of households, is now one of the saddest."[11]

That same day that Cohn noted Baer wearing a sad, hollow look, August 7, 1938, his mother died. Reporter Alan Ward said the cause of her death was a broken heart from losing her husband. Ward called it "a majestic beauty, rather than a heartbreaking tragedy." He recalled how in the past whenever he had written anything critical about Max, his parents would come back with good common sense and good nature saying, "Max is all right. He's just having some fun. After all, he didn't have much fun as a child. He'll settle down." Buddy, Ward recalled, was like "an adoring puppy trailing its mistress." He doted on his mother, loved her cooking, and would deeply miss her. Ward said, "No one will mourn her more sincerely than Max and Buddy Baer ... prizefighters who, by profession and nature, are supposed to have little truck with sentiment and tears."[12]

Dora Bales Baer, born in June of 1877, would lie in state in the private home of Judge A.W. Bruner in San Leandro, until her burial, August 10, 1938, next to her husband at Mountain View Cemetery. In her will, she bequeathed the family home back to Max, the one who purchased it for them originally. The remainder of the Baer estate (approximately $30,000) was divided among the other three siblings.

Rather than the expected fight with Louis in September, Max Baer went back to work doing exhibitions around San Diego and picking up a few hundred dollars refereeing boxing and wrestling matches.

In October, Hoffman thought it was time for a "working man's vacation." He scheduled several bouts for Max and Buddy in Hawaii. Max was to box one fight before an Elks Club benefit and one after. The exhibitions were expected to cover all expenses of the Baers and Hoffmans for three weeks, ending November 10. The Baer entourage sailed on the *Lurline*. It was not exactly a restful trip over because aboard the luxury liner was a troop of 250 club members who had brought with them a steam-whistle calliope, the size of a car, and the celebrations were nonstop.

In Hawaii the night before the Elks fight night, Baer fought Andre Adoree in Honolulu for a four-round no-decision bout. The next night, also in Honolulu, he knocked out Hank Hankinson in 48 seconds with his hard right in front of 2,000 spectators. Hank had only landed one blow when he was dropped on the Fraternal Order of Elks canvas. Max then proceeded to have a go with boxer/wrestler Al Baffert on the same card. Al went the limit with Baer. Two nights later, he met Adoree again, this time in Lihue.

On December 15, Mike Jacobs, who now controlled most of the heavyweights, issued a decree saying that before Max could fight Louis, he must fight another battle. He thought a preliminary battle would work up an audience. It was a blow to Max, who had been promised the next Louis battle. But as a contender under contract to Jacobs, he had no control of the matchmaking.

Baer was told he would have to fight the winner of the Nova-Farr battle. Louis would attend the fight to get a good look at Nova, a possible future contender for him. When interviewed for the fight, Tommy Farr said that he wanted nothing better "than to dispose of Nova and get another shot at Baer. Baer couldn't lick me again in a month of Sundays. He'd never fool me again with a left the way he did. I was paying too much attention to his right and he crossed me by nailing me with a left that caught me cold in the first round." Farr didn't expect to be beaten by Nova because he said, "He hasn't got a wallop like Baer that can shake you up for a round or two."[13]

Lou Nova beat Tommy Farr in December 1938, in 15 rounds to pocket $6540.76 for his win. So now there were three fighters on Baer's horizon: Nova, Galento, and Louis. With Baer in an elimination battle for the chance to fight Louis, Louis signed up to fight John Henry Lewis in January 1939.

A year earlier, Lou Nova had become California's No. 1 heavyweight. He had played football for Sacramento Junior College, but he discovered that he enjoyed boxing and left the gridiron to pursue a sport with greater financial potential. He went to train at Duffy's Gym in Oakland, where Max had been an idol to the young blond Californian.

It wasn't long before one of the trainers noticed Nova. Harold Algernon Broom saw that the boy had a good punch. Broom was obligated to Ham Lorimer, Baer's former manager, and Lorimer signed a contract with Nova. Nova entered the amateurs and won honors in Nationals and a Paris international competition. When he returned from Paris, he landed in New York, went into a Broadway restaurant, and found his former trainer. Broom was training Frankie Klick, junior lightweight champion, for Ray Carlen. (Carlen had been a second to Max's early fights in California.) Broom introduced Nova to Carlen and Carlen paid Lorimer $1000 for Nova's contract, a bargain compared to what Baer and Hoffman eventually had to pay Lorimer.

Nova was considered the best looking of the lot of young fighters, but the worst dressed. His new manager Ray Carlen told the Alameda Assassin to model his look on Baer. New Yorkers were infatuated with the new pug. They even considered him to be the new Baer. He was invited to nightclubs, parties, yachting trips, and weekends in the country.

Now it seemed Max Baer was the testing ground for Lou Nova. Many were starting to talk about a Nova-Louis fight, usurping Max Baer's first rights. Nova was even being talked about as the logical successor to the Brown Bomber. Jack Cuddy called Nova the new "white hope." Give him a year and Nova could beat Louis. Nova has a "splendid body, ring intelligence, plenty of dynamite in both hands, a genuine fighter's heart, the will to win and the necessary ruggedness."[14] Cuddy couldn't have built up any boxer any better.

Joe Gould, Farr's manager, was incensed that Farr wasn't getting a rematch with Nova. But publicity was set in motion for a Baer-Nova fight. After John Henry Lewis, Max Baer was the only one in the picture for Louis at the beginning of 1939. But the list would grow.

Max and manager Ancil Hoffman left California for Rome, New York, to appear as defendants in a $50,000 lawsuit on January 9. They had been sued by Frank R. McKeeby of Rome for negligence when a grandstand collapsed where the man was watching Max train for the Louis fight in 1935. Baer and Hoffman were asked to produce records regarding the grandstand, and when they could not produce them, they were charged with contempt of court. Their defense was that there were no records at all specifically regarding the grandstand. Seventy-five gratis tickets were given out for people to view the training camp. Lawyer Charles R. Hardles for Baer and Hoffman said that neither defendant was paid anything by the spectators.

When Max and Ancil hit New York, Baer appeared before sportswriters wearing a cowboy hat and red bandana, and talking with a heavy drawl about his new movie prospects. He had signed for a five-year contract to appear in a series of eight Westerns produced by First National Pictures. The movies were planned to be shot in color. He joked with the sportswriters, "Jest elect me sheriff of this yere county and I'll run every fight manager right out of town. I'll also do the same for some of the fighters."[15] The cowboy hat may have caught on because later in April, Joe Louis was seen wearing a 10-gallon cowboy hat at a baseball game. Max had always been a trend-setter in the sartorial division.

Max Baer had dressed up to play sheriff to bring attention to the corrupt boxing situation being decried by the sportswriters. Managers, promoters, and crooked judges seemed to be ruining the sport in their broken contracts and big-money schemes. At the end of 1938, the nation's sportswriters were polled to see what they thought could be done to clean up the sport. The result by a voting majority was to establish a national position, a ring czar or "strong man" to rule over the sport, much like Judge Kenesaw Landis over baseball. Those voting overwhelmingly selected Gene Tunney for the position. Jack Dempsey came in second. Such a position has never been established.

The headlines in the East were fairly typical when Baer came to town: "Max Baer in Town," "Tells Fight Plans," "Wants Louis Bout," "Certain of Victory." As for the rest of the ballyhoo, Max told reporters, "I want Lou Nova or Tony Galento, or both, outdoors, this year, and then you can put me back in there with Joe Louis. I think I can knock out both those other fellows and that'll build up a million dollar gate for me and Joe."[16]

Bill Corum thanked Max for coming down from Rome, New York, just to give the boys something to write about in "these dull days." He posted, "He has more color and makes more news in one week than all the other current heavies make in a month of Sundays. But underneath, Max still is the same boy who ran home from school in his youth because he did not like to fight." Corum called Baer the best "pretender" in the lot of heavies.[17] He didn't think anyone, much less Baer, really wanted to fight Joe Louis.

Baer showed up at Tony Galento's bar in Newark, New Jersey, hoping to obtain a fight with the man. It almost took place on January 12, 1939. Max was trying to be funny when he told his friends, "I never saw Galento fight but I've seen pictures of him back of a bar. That's a detriment to the best interest of boxing." Everyone laughed but Galento, who came back, "I don't think the public considers me a detriment to boxing but they do that bum Baer who is a quitter. He quit Joe Louis on one knee and he will never live that down.... Max talks a good fight and that's all—I openly accuse him of being afraid to fight me."[18] There it was: the challenge. And Baer left with an invitation to fight Tony Galento.

Then Ancil and Baer went to Mike Jacobs's office to sign for Nova. But in the meeting with Jacobs, Baer was told that he must now be obligated for *two* fights before meeting Louis. Ancil put his foot down: "We'll sign for the Nova match and that's all." Jacobs said, using the authoritative "we": "We're not guaranteeing Baer or any other fighter a title shot at this early date" (even though he had already promised the match the previous year). "Such a guarantee would destroy the incentive for other promising boxers to keep on winning." Mike Jacobs intended to line his pockets with elimination-match money. If Baer wanted a shot he would have to do like any other fighter, Jacobs said: "Keep winning."[19]

It was just another horse race. Three days later, Mike Jacobs told the newsmen that Baer was signed to fight Lou Nova in a 15-round bout at Yankee Stadium, the winner to get a shot at Joe Louis's crown in September. And five days later, Henry McLemore wisecracked, "Maxie Baer and Lou Nova of Alameda, California, should be brought together shortly in a sort of screen test for the supporting role in the next 'Gone With the Wind' thriller starring Joe Louis."[20]

Although Red Burman's name was mentioned, there were only three serious candidates for a future Louis bout: Max Baer, Tony Galento, and Lou Nova. The three would fill 1939's big fight schedule. Reporter Dan Parker weighed in on the trio for Louis, saying, "Joe Louis' next opponent will be either a novice whom he should be able to lick with one hand or a washed-up veteran he once made quit. Lou Nova isn't ready for Louis and Max Baer never has been. Why Promoter Mike Jacobs should pick Baer as the man to fight it out with Nova for the challenger's role passes understanding.... If he is the best man in the field of contenders, then the heavyweight situation is even worse than had been suspected.... Galento has courage and would give Louis a more interesting fight than either of the hand-picked contenders being warmed up for the slaughter."[21]

A Baer-Nova match was delayed until Nova's manager Ray Carlen felt that his charge had tune-ups adequate for him to meet Baer. Jacobs announced Tony Galento as one of those tune-ups. Galento had just knocked out Jorge Brescia in the first round. Brescia said he was hit a low blow, and the reporters were in his dressing room after the bout trying to get the story. Galento spent half an hour telling everyone how great he was in the fight when promoter Mike Jacobs interrupted, "You don't have to explain, Tony. You knocked the guy out!" But Galento wasn't through with his prattle. When asked about his next fight (Jacobs had just told him that he would battle Nova), he said, "Just bums. De both of dem. Dey're all bums—Louis, Baer, Nova. All but Galento. I'll be de next heavyweight champ."[22]

But the news scribes were moving on to the next big fight, which was Nova and Baer.

New Yorkers were skeptical that even if Nova beat Baer, the California youngster would not be ready to meet Louis by September. Regardless, the boxing scribes punched out the new story (as old as the last big fight, but with different names): "The fight has been one of the most talked-of battles in boxing circles here since Nova, clean-cut 23-year-old from Alameda, California, punched himself into the fistic limelight with victories over Gunnar Barlund, the big Finn, and Tommy Farr of Wales."[23] Madison Square Garden was left to match Tony Galento with Tommy Farr.

Even the fans back in California had given up on Max's ever winning a major fight again. Everyone thought that if he would train seriously, he could certainly win. Comparing the two Californians, Baer was said to have more experience, a harder punch, and a better ability to take punishment. All agreed that Nova could not be rated #1 contender until he had beaten Baer. And if Baer happened to want to fight and kill Nova in the ring, he could. But that was doubtful.

"Young men make reputations against old men. That's boxing history," said manager Ray Carlen, when asked about the Nova-Baer match.[24] Nova was coming up and Baer was coming down. That's all there was to it. The equation seemed obvious, yet the fight was expected to draw somewhere between $200,000 and $400,000 from the day it was announced. One man in Miami was said to have ordered 100 ringside seats as soon as he heard about the fight.

With contracts signed and lawsuits extended, Max and Ancil traveled by the "rattler," from New York back to Los Angeles. When the Santa Fe Chief made its layover stop in Albuquerque, New Mexico, at the Alvarado Hotel, the pair was met by a reporter. When asked about the upcoming fight, Baer said, "Yes, I expect a bit of a fight out of Lou Nova, but all I'm waiting for is another crack at the title." That was all the easy-going, mild-mannered man said to the Albuquerque reporter. The reporter even wrote that Baer's manner seemed "unconcerned." But when other reporters across the nation got the Albuquerque story, they changed it to read: "'All I want is one more chance at the title—and it'll be mine again,' he said, clinching his fist and scowling."[25] But that fist and scowl never happened as reported. Baer had to tolerate insults and inaccuracies, more after he lost the title than before.

The next week Bill Corum wrote that on January 16, 1939, he and Ernest Hemingway had gone to the Stork Club after the Friday night fights at the Garden. The Broadway bar was infamous and exclusive. The tables were assigned by number, and J. Edgar Hoover and his intimate friend occupied Table #1. Corum and Hemingway met up with Max Baer. After having been excoriated in Hemingway's *Esquire* article, Baer said to the famous writer, "Ah yes, I remember you, Mr. Hemingway. You sent me an autographed copy of a book once. Something you wrote, no doubt. Let's see now, what was the name of it?" To which Corum said Hemingway replied, "It was a little thing I wrote that I thought might help you…. *All Quiet on the Western Front*."[26]

On January 31, 1939, Jacob H. "Buddy" Baer, 23, was also making news when he married Miss Ralpha Pearl, 22, of Sacramento in Reno, Nevada.

Newspapers were filled with celebrity comments on the Baer-Nova fight. Tony Canzoneri picked Baer to win, saying, "He's bound to connect a few times with that devastating right hand."[27]

When Art Cohn told Baer that Galento had called him a "bum," Baer said, "The worst that can be said of me is that I'm washed up. But at least I WAS heavyweight champion of the world. At least I'm a has-been and that's a helluva lot more than a never-was."[28] In reality, what drove Max to keep fighting was his goal to be the first man to regain the heavyweight crown.

Joe Louis predicted Max would beat Nova, and "then I'll fight him in September."[29]

"Max is the best of 'em when he's right. He's best 'cause he can hit hardest. He's best of all but me."[30]

Nova said, "I like Max personally.... He's a good puncher but he's getting old. His legs are 'shot.' I think I'll pick him off about the seventh round."[31] Nova also thought Max was faster than Joe Louis.

Braven Dyer interviewed Nova for the *Los Angeles Times*. Did the fact that Nova grew up in Baer's shadows handicap him for the fight? "Yes," said Nova. He had idolized Baer, which he thought natural. But when Baer saw him working out in the same Oakland gym, he saw an awkward, inexperienced kid who didn't know how to punch very hard. He thought Max might go into the ring with that memory and false confidence. But he added, "You can believe me that when Max Baer is confident of winning he's an awfully tough man to meet."[32]

The New York State Athletic Commission gave its blessing for the Nova-Baer fight. No reason was given for the change of heart regarding Max Baer. Reporter Eddie Brietz said that it appeared that Commissioner Bill Brown, who had previously called Baer a bum, "now admits he had changed for the better."[33] Even a year later, the Commission refused to talk about the matter. During 1939, the New York Athletic Commission had closed its door to reporters. When they opened again in January 1940, Jimmy Johnston, Bob Pastor's manager, argued that the Commission had refused Baer a license three years earlier when he proposed a Pastor-Baer fight, but now they were allowing Baer a license to fight Nova, "and it's all right. Why?" Johnston demanded.[34] It certainly appeared inconsistent dealing when Billy Duffy, Louis's manager, never seemed to have a problem getting a license, and he had a known criminal record—he had even named at one time as a Public Enemy. No explanations were forthcoming.

Max left April 3, 1939, for the East. When asked if he had a chance to win, he explained, "I was born under a lucky star," and how could he be where he was today if he weren't? He felt confident that his "lucky star" would lead him back to the championship. The former champion said his hands were "hard as rocks." And while he weighed 220 pounds, ten pounds over his normal, he would get back to a fighting weight after a few sparring sessions. When asked what he would do if he lost, he said, "Retire for positively the last time" and take up a movie contract.[35]

Nova planned to spend two weeks training at the exclusive "members only" Clarkstown Country Club near Nyack, New York. The club, primarily used as a center for yoga teachings, was run by Dr. Pierre Bernard, "Oom the Omnipotent." The Club also advertised a menagerie of exotic animals: ten elephants, a gorilla, white peacocks, and any number of other creatures roaming the premises for the entertainment of the press and spectators. It seemed Nova had trained on the publicity stunts of his idol.

After his daily exercises, Nova posed riding elephants and llamas and "chinning up" with the monkeys. At one show, a trained elephant was dressed with a massive sparring glove. Lou played around with the elephant until he slipped and the elephant came back with a swing that missed Lou's chin by only inches. The press ate it up. Promoter Mike Jacobs just gritted his "store-bought" teeth.[36]

Nova would stay at a home among the 500 acres, with a wide lawn for a ring, and spectators could sit in elegant opera chairs while watching him train. Nothing was considered over the top for the heavyweight boxers. After his tour of the facilities, Jacobs responded, "What a joint!"[37]

Nova went into the fight rated #2 heavyweight, and manager Carlen wasted no expense in amassing a huge war chest for his charge. He hired both Jimmy Braddock and Doc Robb, Jim Braddock's old trainer, to work on Lou's left hand. Braddock showed him how he had used his left to beat Baer. McLemore, the cynical reporter, said that Braddock should have plenty of notes to show Nova. He said that Baer's fight with Braddock was so slow that Braddock "had plenty of time to lean over the ropes and dictate them to a stenographer."[38]

From a previous fight, Nova had turned a handicap into an advantage. Nova had torn a ligament in his right shoulder when he fought Tommy Farr. Nova had to wear a strap on his right arm that forced him to do everything left-handed. Maybe he would be lucky with his left jab, like Jim Braddock had been. After Braddock had worked with Nova for four hours a day for a few days, he said that Nova was as "stout as a bull after five or six rounds," and his short rights carried a lot of power. Furthermore, he didn't think Max had the endurance to go toe-to-toe with Nova for any length of time.[39]

The last day of April, Baer was in active training at Grossinger's Country Club Lake, midway between Ferndale and Liberty, New York, in the Catskills. Baer had turned 30 in February, but no one saw that as a disadvantage. If anything, Baer seemed to be in his best condition, near perfect. Trainer Izzy Kline felt that Max was "so serious" that he might be training too hard. Kline was afraid that he would reach his peak too early, so he thought about cutting back some of his training activities.

But he didn't. On May 18, during a sparring session, Georgie Youssef opened a gash across Max's nose. On May 20, Baer took on six different spar mates in six rounds. He was not letting up in his training. Added to the cut, on May 17, Baer learned that the judge had merged two lawsuits against him in Rome and Utica. The total lawsuit amounted to $70,000.

Reporters pondered the obvious: Nova had six fights the previous year; Baer none. Baer was 30 and hadn't fought in fourteen months. Nova was 24 and had won thirteen of his 26 professional fights by knockout. Nevertheless, Baer was in the best condition of his life.

On May 27, over 700 people came to see Max train.

Lou Nova, June 1, 1939, Yankee Stadium, New York

At the weigh-in at noon on the day of the fight, Baer scaled 210 and Nova 202. Betting odds were even. Dr. William Walker of the New York Athletic Commission said the blood pressure measurements of both men were high, but their pulses were equal. Baer stood 6 ft. 2½ inches; Nova, 6 ft. 2 inches. Baer's reach was 3 inches longer than Nova's. General John J. Phelan, head of the Commission, instructed both that any foul blows (low blow, head butt, backhand) would be the loss of the round. Everyone believed that Nova was a better boxer and Baer a better puncher.

The event would be the first nationally televised boxing match in America. (The Baer-Farr fight had been televised in Britain in 1937.) In language used to describe the television, a machine unfamiliar to most households, the boxing match was to be reproduced on the air "pictorially" in America. There were many more people listening to their radios than owned television sets. There were 150 dealers of television sets in the United States, and all dealers, according to ads in the newspapers and magazines, planned to carry the fight live. Neither Mrs. Baer nor Mrs. Hoffman planned to attend the fight or watch on television. They would listen to the radio broadcast.

Thirteen • No Clowning for Nova, 1939

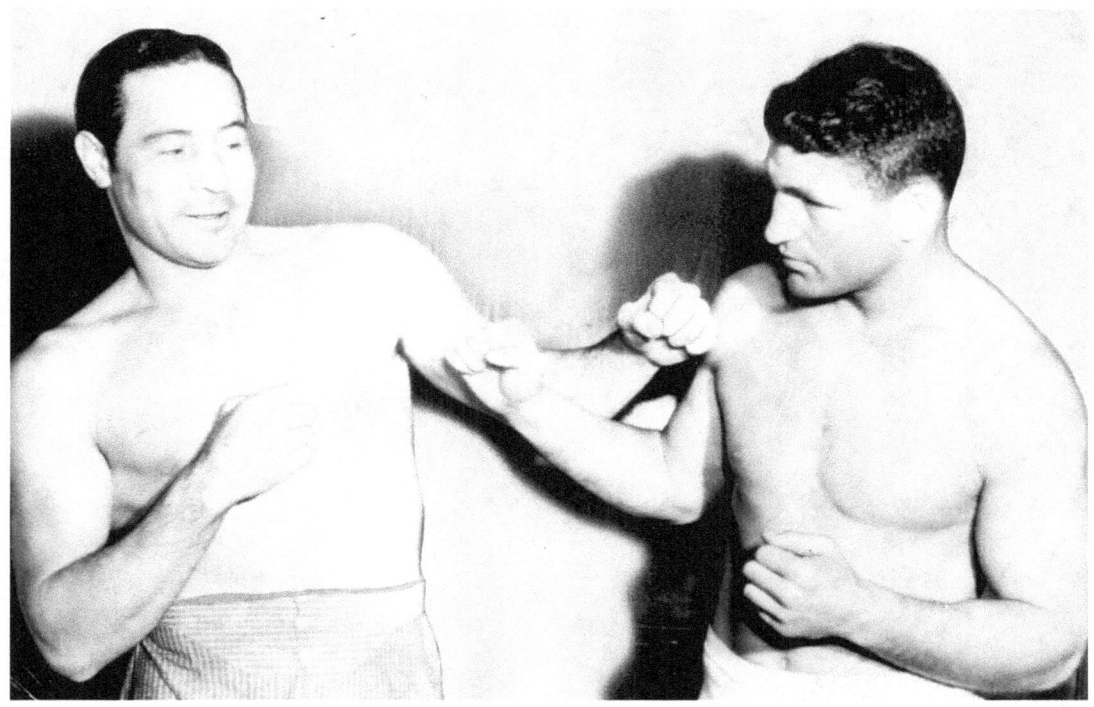

Max Baer (left) and Lou Nova pose for their rematch, June 1, 1939.

In the ring that night, Nova pounded the former champion with straight, slashing lefts. By the eleventh round, Baer was battered and beaten to a pulp. He was drowning in his own blood from a cut to his mouth from a punch in the second round, but not before Baer had staggered Nova with three right hands to the head. The punch from Nova forced the hard edge of Baer's mouthpiece through his lip. By the end of the fourth round, the bleeding had reached "hemorrhage proportions" and Max was choking on his own blood.[40]

Both fought at a torrid pace through six rounds. They simply stood in the middle of the ring and slugged it out furiously, with Nova doing a slightly better job in the first, Baer in the second, and Nova in the third, forcing Max to hang on. In the fourth, Baer cut Nova's right eye with a long left; and Nova, starting to show signs of wear and tear, hit Baer low, which cost him the round.

Although Nova was staggered by a barrage of Baer's best blows in the early rounds, he never went down. He was so disoriented in the second round that he walked to the wrong corner. One reporter noted that Nova's left ear looked like an eggplant, swollen from Baer's right.

Baer's face looked worse. By the end of the fight he only had slits for two eyes. Nova had stayed close to avoid Baer's long and dangerous right, and battered Max with short blows to the head and to the body to drain his stamina. The sixth was Baer's best round, when he hammered Nova with his right hand. In the seventh, after swallowing so much blood, Baer became sick to his stomach. He was penalized for striking after the bell in the seventh, which again left Nova trying to figure out which corner to seek. After the eighth, it was Baer's fight to lose. But after the ninth, his left eye was completely closed and he could barely see from the right.

In a torrid fight, some thought Max (right) won the early rounds. But after the fourth round, he was choking on his own blood from the beating he took from Nova. The referee stopped the June 1939 fight in the eleventh round, calling the fight for Nova (courtesy IBRO).

Max did not clown and he did not quit. The referee stopped the bout as a result of all the damage he was taking. Referee Frank Fullam halted the fight after one minute, 21 seconds in the eleventh. He had wanted to stop the bout sooner, but Baer wouldn't let him. When the referee saw Baer choking, he made the call. The bout ended, and Baer leaned over the ropes and told the press through a mouthful of gauze: "Don't say I quit. I couldn't breathe."[41]

Most agreed that the fight was close. Nova said it was his hardest fight ever.

Judges were Bill Healey and Joe Lynch. The Associated Press scoresheet gave Nova six rounds and Max four. Many said that Baer had won four of the first six rounds, and that if the cut to his mouth had not caused such blood loss after the sixth, he would have won the fight because Baer had left Nova disoriented at the end of the sixth. Others disagreed and said that Nova was slightly leading throughout. Mike Jacobs even accused Nova of moving the stuffing around in his glove so as to be able to slash Baer's face to ribbons with his bare knuckles. And then there was the question of Baer's faulty mouthpiece. Without doubt, the fight had been notoriously brutal. Nova lost two rounds on fouls and Baer one. The question of Nova's gloves came up again when he fought Galento—Jacobs insisted that they be put under lock and key until fight time.

After the match, Baer said he didn't know if he would ever fight again. Nova said he could have put Baer away had he not injured his right hand in the third round. Actually, no one knew until months after the fight that Lou Nova said that he had taken a brutal beating from Max. "That beating was far more serious than most people suspected. In fact, if it had been any more serious, it might have been fatal. I spent six days in hell after that fight. I never left the hotel room all that time. The doctor said I had a concussion of the brain."[42]

The fight was a disappointment to Mike Jacobs. Only 17,000 attended and the gate came to $82,364, not the $100,000 he expected. The fighters each received $22,517 for their efforts. But it was not a disappointment to the spectators. Even the habitual Baer detractor Art Cohn said that Baer made the most intelligent and courageous fight of his life, even though some said "he quit."[43]

With a technical win, Lou Nova knocked out Baer's chance to regain the crown. A new generation of fighters was coming of age, and Baer's comeback trail had come to an end.

Mary Ellen Baer listened to the radio broadcast of the fight, and when Max returned to their hotel room she was shocked to see her husband's face. She told reporters she was glad that he had lost because she didn't want him to face Joe Louis. Mrs. Baer told the media the real reason that he had gone back to try to regain the title: "He couldn't bear to read in the papers and hear people say that he was yellow, that he quit to keep from meeting Louis. It was on his mind all the time, and he felt he just had to vindicate himself.... If he had won, he would have kept on fighting, and now he won't be like other fighters who fought too long and couldn't remember their friends' faces." Max, she said, "never liked to be alone," and "he liked to be liked."[44]

Max Baer needed more than the adoration and approval of his fans. More than any external gratification was Baer's internal need or drive to be the first heavyweight to regain the crown. And in pursuit of that important goal, he needed to vindicate the loss he so painfully suffered to Braddock, the real cause for which only he knew. Baer didn't need the money another title offered, even though he joked that it would give him a million dollars. His motivation that such an all-passionate drive fueled was to resolve a deeply felt wrong, either from self-recrimination or anger over what may have been done to him. He never got over losing the Braddock fight, and he personally needed to regain the title. Even when he told the newspaper he was on the comeback for his son Max Jr., he qualified: "It would be swell if my kid grew up having as father a fellow who regained the heavyweight title less than three years after he lost it."[45]

Baer may have lost the Nova fight, but he won the respect of the people. As Alan Ward said, "The fire of that attack burned away virtually all the odium attached to his name and ring reputation."[46] He said that Baer would experience a personal popularity he never before enjoyed. Like Dempsey, it wasn't until he was defeated that he was respected.

Many writers commented that Baer went down fighting, that he showed no yellow streak and was courage personified. Even after defeat, Baer was still ranked fourth in the heavyweight division by the NBA.

Movie theaters across the nation carried the fight three days later. Newspaper ads called attention to eleven torrid rounds shown in graphic detail. Max left for California after his lip was stitched in New York.

In August, in Los Angeles, Lou Nova and Max Baer, rivals in the ring and friends

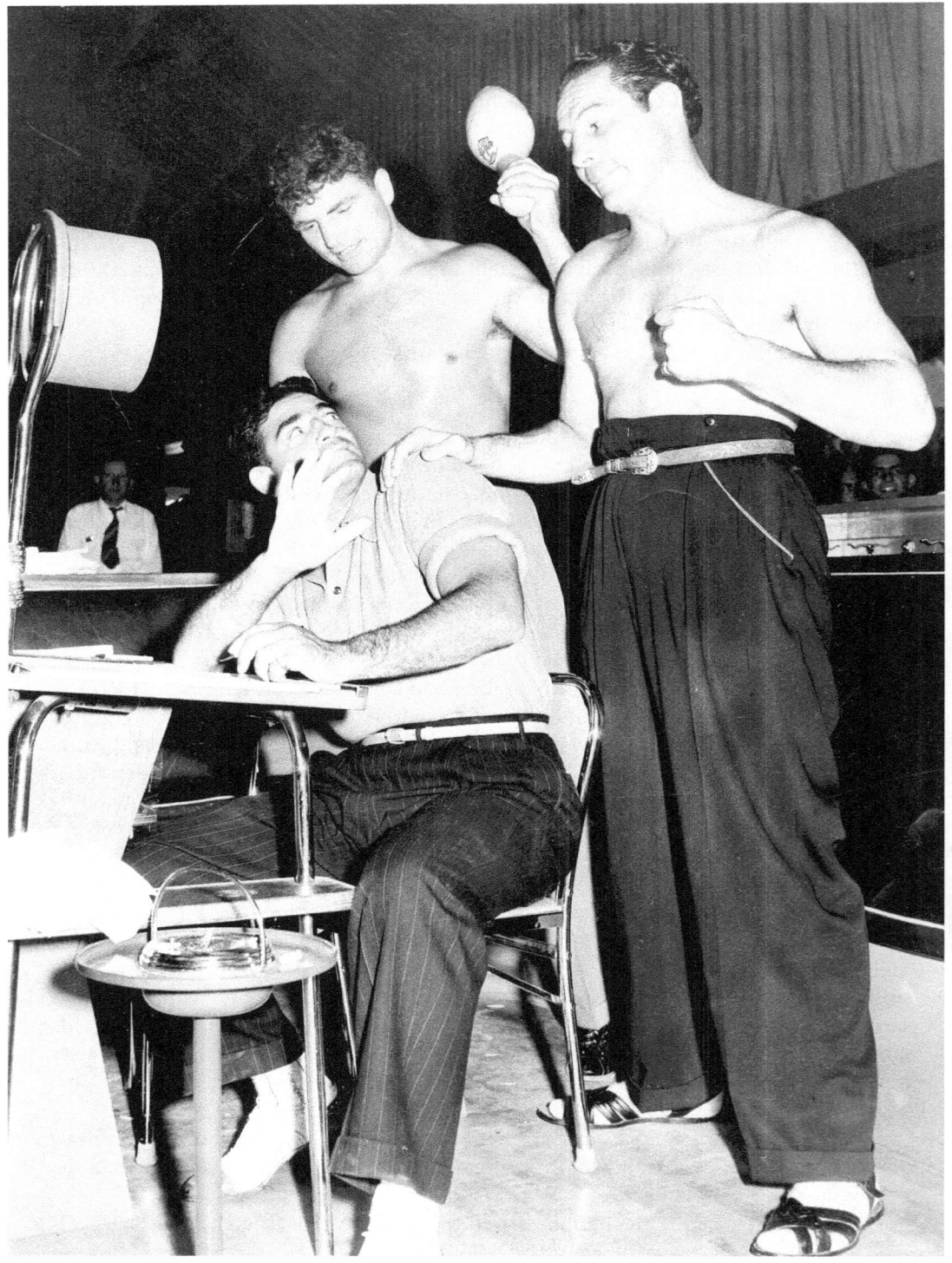

"Championship of the Pins." Scorekeeper (sitting) was wrestler Sammy Stein. Lou Nova (center) lost to Max Baer, August 1939 (courtesy David Bergin).

outside, got together for a bowling contest for what they called the Heavyweight Championship of the Pins. Three games were at stake. Out came the bankrolls, and the challengers put up a side bet of $10 for each game. Immediately, Nova cried "foul" on the basis that Baer was a "ringer," having bowled before.

In the first game Max turned in a score of 95 to Nova's 110. It looked like Nova was going to take the championship. However, Baer came back in the second game to score 193 to Nova's sad 96. In the third game, Baer again outscored his competitor, ringing up 161 points to 107. No one could ever predict when, after losing, Baer would come back to win.

FOURTEEN

The Screwball Championship, Galento, 1940

As early as November 1938, Philadelphia promoter Herman Taylor offered Max Baer a guarantee of $50,000 to meet Tony Galento. But Ancil Hoffman feared Max was in no shape to fight someone like Galento, thought to be next in line to meet Joe Louis.

So Lou Nova took the fight with Galento in Philadelphia scheduled for September 15, 1939. When Arthur Donovan was selected to referee the fight, Nova's manager Ray Carlen was suspect and argued against the selection. Carlen was afraid that through Donovan, "Galento might be herded into an unearned victory over Nova," and throw out his chance with Louis.[1]

The American public was tired of all the elimination battles for a Joe Louis fight, as promoter Mike Jacobs tried to line his pocketbook. On September 15, the National Boxing Association tried to correct the matter by ruling that only the top three ranking boxers in each weight class would be recognized as title contenders. It was a decision meant to restrict the numbers vying for Joe Louis's crown—and to prevent him from fighting what had become known as the "bum of the month club," as promoters held back their better fighters waiting for bigger paydays. The NBA ranked the top heavyweights after Louis (1): the winner of the Tony Galento–Lou Nova bout, (2) Bob Pastor, (3) Johnny Paycheck, and (4) Max Baer. Other rankings put Baer in the top three. Nat Fleischer ranked Joe Louis first, Lou Nova second, Max Baer third, Bob Pastor fourth, Tony Galento fifth, and Maxie Rosenbloom sixth.

Baer was scheduled for an exhibition and then a tune-up in September before he committed to a major fight. At this point Ancil Hoffman was very selective and accepted only high-paying events. So it came as quite a surprise to the press when Baer was offered and accepted $1000 to fight four two-minute rounds with "Big" Ed Murphy at Silver Peak, Nevada, an off-the-map mining camp. Hoffman also scheduled Baer to fight Dave Ritchie in Lubbock, Texas. Texas promoter "Pup" Thomas (often misquoted as "Tuck" Thomas) offered Baer $10,000 win, lose, or draw for a Labor Day fight. The only obstacle to these two bouts was Mrs. Baer. She did not want Max boxing again.

"Big" Ed Murphy, September 4, 1939, Silver Peak, Nevada

Silver Peak was Southern Nevada's most prosperous mining town and residents looked forward to a Labor Day celebration featuring the famous Max Baer and local heavyweight Ed Murphy. Boxing legend Tom Sharkey was selected to referee. "Big" Ed had only boxed once since the previous July 4 celebration, when he was brought out to kayo Dick Bowen in the first round.

The holiday weather was perfect, and out-of-state visitors to Nevada said they enjoyed a place where the "law was not always snooping around."[2] The fight was greatly anticipated. Buddy took his place as Max's second. An official handed the men their exhibition-match 16 oz. gloves.

When the first round began, Murphy came out cautiously. Max swung a big looping right and Ed ducked under and fell into a clinch. Baer broke and hit Murphy with a short left, followed by a right cross to the head. Murphy rushed and landed a hard straight right to Baer's face. Max snarled, laughed, danced back, and then unloaded the kayo punch that ended the bout in one minute, 40 seconds of the first round of four. Referee Sharkey got to the count of "five" when it was evident "Big" Ed wasn't going to get up, and raised Baer's hand in victory.

The next match in Texas would not be an exhibition, but a ten-round main event with 6 oz. gloves. Max flew from Las Vegas to Lubbock.

Babe Ritchie, September 18, 1939, Lubbock, Texas

Willie Murl "Babe" Ritchie, 20, from West Texas, began training for the bout at the Lubbock High School gymnasium two weeks before the battle. His high school football coach Weldon Chapman agreed to serve as his manager. Ritchie's trainer was Tony Herrera, former lightweight turned welterweight from Lubbock. Ritchie hypothesized that Max Baer probably thought he was a pushover, just some big kid from some place in Texas nobody had ever heard of. The husky "redneck" oilfield worker turned professional the year before the Baer fight. Some said he had a total of fifteen professional fights. All that mattered was that the promoter thought he was capable enough, and worth the $10,000 offer to have Baer visit West Texas.

The event was hailed as the most important fight in Lubbock's boxing history. When promoter Thomas went to California in the summer to negotiate the match, Baer had asked him, "Where is Lubbock, Texas?" Thomas requested a globe and tried to point to the exact location, but it was not to be found. Baer responded, "Don't worry, we'll soon have 'er on that globe, kid."[3]

Baer's entourage arrived fashionably. They landed at the airport and were escorted to town by a police brigade with sirens blaring. In the party were manager Ancil Hoffman, Buddy Baer, trainer Izzy Kline, and sparring mate Elza Thompson, all rock stars because they were traveling with Max. Baer requested Kline for his most important battles and brought him in from Chicago for this one. Max needed to make sure the unknown redneck from West Texas didn't do anything foolish to mar his record. Elza Thompson, weighing 250 pounds, had been Max's sparring partner for several years, and was looking for someone to fight him on the same card. Baer also trained with a light-heavyweight making his professional debut in Lubbock, Delmar Koch, from Amarillo. Koch was to fight J.C. Wallace, of Big Spring, Texas, in the four-round preliminary. Buddy was training at the camp, preparing for a fight in Dallas three days after the Lubbock fight.

The group stayed at the Hilton Hotel but worked at an outdoor ring set under trees on the bank of the lower lake of Buffalo Lakes. In addition to his training, Baer made personal appearances, talked on the radio, played golf, attended a luncheon club, took pictures and signed autographs. Most Texans had never seen a group of men that big, and the training camp was inundated with visitors. As a result it was decided that the public would be charged 40 cents for their look at the Baer brothers in action. The charge was meant to discourage gawkers from disrupting training. However, every afternoon at 2 p.m., camp was opened to the public.

Two days before the fight the young "Babe" knocked out one of his sparring partners at the gym and the man had to be taken to the West Texas Hospital for a stay overnight. The KO upped the ante for local interest.

Eleven thousand fans from all over Texas watched Baer kayo Babe Ritchie after one minute and ten seconds of the second round. Young Ritchie, however, did not disappoint. His defensive work in the first round was great. Yet as game as he was throughout, he couldn't fend off Baer's famous right. In the second, Baer rushed in, swung wildly with a rash of rights and lefts and put the boy down. The gate was estimated to be $21,000. Prominent Texans, the land commissioner, state representatives, and minor league baseball heads attended, as well as the lieutenant governor of New Mexico, James M. Murray of Hobbs, whose son was enrolled at Lubbock's Texas Tech.

The only thing that the ever-friendly Max hated about his stay in Texas was having to knock out "a Lubbock boy, and I'm serious about that," he said. "This town has been wonderful to me.... I've been in every state in the union and across the sea to London, Hawaii and a dozen other places and I've never been treated nicer than here in Lubbock.... Well, maybe they did treat me nicer in London," he kidded, "but those guys are perfect gentlemen there all the time."[4]

Buddy Baer left for his match in Dallas, where he kayoed in two rounds Sandy McDonald, who filled in the week before the fight when the promoter needed a last-minute replacement.

Joe Jacobs's Fixed Fights in Philadelphia and New York

In boxing's national picture, big bouts were halted in 1939 until a scandal was investigated regarding fixed fights involving Max Schmeling and Tony Galento.

On January 29, boxer Harry Thomas (whose real name was Herman William Pontius) confessed to two fixed fights—one with Max Schmeling in New York, December 13, 1937, and the other with Tony Galento in Philadelphia, November 14, 1938—in an attempt to build up contenders for Joe Louis. In the bouts in question, Schmeling won on a technical in the eighth and Galento on a technical in the third. Arch Ward broke the story for the *Chicago Tribune* on October 30, 1939, calling it the "biggest swindles in the history of boxing."

Harry Thomas told Ward, "Those fake fights have been worrying me for a long time. I am revealing them now for the sake of younger boxers who may face the same temptations. I'm glad to have the facts printed. For the good of the game, they should have been made known long ago. I knew it was wrong to take part in a fixed fight, but it was the only way I could make any real money. I came up the hard way. I never had a dollar I could call my own until the Schmeling bout. In fact, I was in debt. I'm through with boxing, and it will ease my conscience to have these facts disclosed."[5]

Nate Lewis of Chicago was the manager of Thomas and Joe Jacobs was the manager of both Schmeling (since 1930) and Galento. Thomas said, "I was working for cheap purses. By the time training and incidental expenses were paid and I split my earnings with my manager I had little or nothing left. I was well along in years as fighters go. If I accepted offers to throw bouts to Schmeling and Galento, I would make enough money for a nest egg. If I refused, I wouldn't get a chance to meet opponents who would attract big gates." The gate for the Thomas-Schmeling bout was $63,170 and attendance was 16,000. Thomas cleared $8500. The contract was written on a percentage basis with Schmeling receiving the larger percentage. However, "there was a private side agreement" that pooled a percentage for both fighters to be divided equally after expenses, which increased Thomas's share. That side bet gave him the incentive to keep the matter quiet. With the proceeds, Thomas bought land as his nest egg.[6]

Thomas revealed that Nate Lewis told him before the fight that he had met with Joe Jacobs in New York at the Piccadilly hotel. Jacobs thought a fight with Schmeling would draw $100,000. Thomas was told that he "would get at least 25 percent, but would have to lose in four or five rounds." He agreed to the terms. During the fight, Thomas looked for a way to go down, but Schmeling's punches were not hard enough to cover the fake. Thomas recalled, "In the eighth round I whispered to him to keep throwing punches. I went down six or seven times."[7] Finally, the referee stopped the bout. Thomas was paid a portion of the money after Lewis took $1800 for expenses. Proof of the intention to defraud the public was that Thomas had mailed letters to friends in Minnesota telling them not to bet on the fight.

For the Galento bout, the two managers met in New York to set up the same deal. The fight drew $23,000. Thomas was promised $6,000 but was shortchanged between $600 and $800. Lewis threatened Thomas not to say anything about being shortchanged because the boxing commissioner suspected the fight. Looking back at the *Tribune*'s story of the fight to verify the accusation, reporters noted that Galento downed Thomas with "punches that barely landed," and that Thomas had been counted out after going down five times.[8]

After news broke of the fight fixes, neither Boxing Commission, in Illinois or New York, would issue Joe Jacobs a manager's license.

Baer was fighting his own battles in court. He was called to Superior Court in Sacramento, California, on November 14, 1939, to defend himself against another lawsuit, this time brought by brothers Frank, Anthony, and Rudolph Jacklich and Carl Ahlin for ten percent of his earnings since 1930. The four men alleged that Baer agreed to turn over a percentage of his earnings in exchange for an unpaid $13,500 loan. Baer laughed the matter off, commenting to the press that his $86,000 investment in attorney fees helped him "memorize" the words *incompetent, irrelevant* and *immaterial*. The case was transferred to the Oakland courts and was thrown out on the grounds that Baer had already paid the brothers $15,000 more than the original debt.

With Galento and Jacobs tied up in scandal, every scheduling effort failed for a Baer-Galento fight until former President Herbert Hoover handed an invitation to the promoters on a silver platter.

The Soviet Union had invaded Finland on November 30, 1939. In December, Hoover organized humanitarian relief calling for the United States to aid the Finnish people. Hoover (although the idea could have come from Mike or Joe Jacobs) suggested an activity at Madison Square Garden to support the cause. Mike Jacobs jumped on Hoover's bandwagon, saying he was all for the "Finnish Fund" and would even donate his personal proceeds from a Baer-Galento fight.[9]

Now it seemed the angel-winged Jacobs could appeal to the New York Commission to reinstate the licenses in the name of "charity" so as not to disappoint Herbert Hoover or deprive the hungry Finns. History might have been rewritten on the back of a boxing card had not the New York Commission been so obstinate.

The commission was willing to let promoter Mike Jacobs participate in a relief benefit at the Garden, and Tony Galento could fight for the cause; however, they would not so bless Joe Jacobs with a license. Joe retaliated by sending a message via the newspapers that he would not let Galento fight at all without his being allowed in Tony's corner. The commission would not permit Jacobs to be in the ring until District Attorney Dewey's office officially cleared Jacobs from any complicity in the alleged fake fight between Max Schmeling and Harry Thomas at the Garden in 1937. Although the fraud was not brought to trial for lack of sufficient evidence, the district attorney refused to clear Jacobs's name.

When Joe Jacobs applied for a "second's" license, the commission emphatically refused and steadfastly held to their decision, saying that the subject would be deferred indefinitely. In the meantime, Max told the press that he wanted his proceeds to go to the Finnish Relief Fund and suggested that either Jack Dempsey or Gene Tunney act as Galento's seconds in the ring. But such never happened. The Baer-Galento fight would not occur on March 4 in New York and the Moscow Peace Treaty eventually ended the Finnish conflict and what came to be known as the Winter War.

Meanwhile, the commission approved Mike Jacob's promotion of Joe Louis and Arturo Godoy of Chile at Yankee Stadium. Lou Nova remained the #3 challenger for the heavyweight title, but he was taken out temporarily due to a serious illness.

Nova had been bedridden for three weeks in a Woodland, California, hospital for a mysterious disease that almost killed him. (Some East Coast papers erroneously reported that Buddy Baer was the one afflicted.) Doctors thought that an unhealed scratch on Nova's arm three years earlier caused an infection that had been festering in his system only to roar back with a vengeance. It became so serious that doctors considered amputating his arm. When medicine available at the time didn't kill the infection, doctors injected Nova with the germs of typhoid. After three weeks his condition improved such that the infection was almost "licked." During his hospitalization and with a NO VISITORS sign posted on the door of his hospital room, Max made a surprise visit. After pleasant jabs of mutual kidding, Max Baer pretended to be a doctor holding a stethoscope to Nova's chest to listen to his heart.

The visit turned serious with talk of Baer's upcoming fight with Tony Galento. Nova explained why he had lost his fight with Galento four months earlier in Philadelphia. He did not blame his illness, but it was clear that his performance was unusual. Whitney Martin wrote that Nova was "arm and leg-weary and exhausted as the bout dragged on and on, and looking back on Nova's exhibition of that night it seems he was a slow, clumsy old man in a mental fog."[10] Nova thought the real reason he had lost the fight was that his manager had spent six weeks training him for "infighting." Nova's team thought it best to fight Tony in close by hammering his big belly. But Nova told Baer that the way to beat Galento was to fight him at long range and go directly to the head. He added that Galento couldn't be beaten in a clean fight because he was one of the dirtiest: he stabbed you in the eyes and elbowed and head-butted coming out of a clinch. Before Max left his room, Nova looked at Baer with seriousness, and said, "Max, don't get discouraged. You're the man who can beat Tony Galento."[11]

After Baer left the hospital, he took his young son Max Jr. up above the earth for his first airplane ride.

The only un-eliminated contender for Louis that Mike Jacobs controlled was now Tony Galento, the Jersey Jalopy. Lou Nova and Red "Kayo" Burman were not considered ready to tackle Louis, Baer had already been laid on the canvas by Louis, and Tommy Farr had been beaten by Baer, Braddock, Nova and Burman. The only contender left, after Louis beat Bob Pastor, was Galento, and Mike Jacobs was hesitant to make a Louis-Galento match because Joe Jacobs was still in the New York Boxing Commissions' Neverland, and Mike had to make money on something other than one good fight for the year.

How did such a pug as Anthony Domenico Galento make it to the top and remain in the public eye? In part, ballyhoo. Tony was crazy. He would fight with anyone or anything, including a kangaroo, an octopus, and a grizzly bear. (In 1955, he toured with a bear that had been trained to hulk over Tony's body whenever he went down, and then return to his corner. He did this six nights a week for a total of 150 nights.)

It also helped that Galento had wins over Natie Brown, Abe Feldman, Jorge Brescia, and Lou Nova, and the desire of promoters to match anyone with Joe Louis. In June of 1939, when Louis met the roly-poly barkeep from New Jersey, Tony knocked him down in the second round. Joe eventually won by TKO in the fourth, but the famous knockdown of Louis shot Galento to the top of the ratings, and caused many to believe that Max Baer didn't stand a chance against Two-Ton Tony.

A poll taken among fighters, managers, sportswriters, promoters, and seconds indicated that the number-one match they wanted to see was Max Baer and Tony Galento. Alan Ward said, "Baseball has its Dizzy Dean [whose brother Daffy was also a baseball player], boxing its Max Baer and Tony Galento."[12]

Even though a fight venue outside New York had yet to be determined, it was already being hyped as the comic battle of the bums. The papers quoted manager Joe Jacobs: "My bum will knock that bum out with a couple of punches." On the other hand, many thought it would be a ring epic. Galento had the deadliest left in the business and Baer the deadliest right. And for all his shortcomings, Galento had a ton of courage, which made any of his fights interesting. Lawton Carver said, "It shouldn't be necessary to add that Baer never was great and Galento never was even good ... but both can punch ... and both men will make a brawl of it. In that kind of going there are few better than Galento, especially against a Baer who has been on his way out for three or four years. He probably will be chilled colder this time than ever before."[13]

In January 1940, rains pounded Sacramento, but Max Baer trained religiously, running every morning in the downpour for a match he thought would be in March. He knew that this fight might be his last big marquee event. If he could beat Galento, Louis's #1 challenger, then he would meet Louis. Max needed to show the public that he was not "washed up." Both Buddy and Max spent weeks taking a hoe to two acres of citrus country on Hoffman's ranch to build up arm strength.

In the latter part of January, with Max training hard in California, Mike Jacobs was sent a note saying that Tony needed two more months. He hadn't fought since Nova in September and he felt like he needed more time before facing Baer. Mike was livid. "Why didn't Joe Jacobs notify me about Tony's condition before this—before we had all the trouble with the New York Commission about Joe not getting a manager's license? As far as I'm concerned the Galento-Baer fight is definitely off. I'm sick of monkeying around with it."[14] Both Joe Jacobs and Tony Galento were from Orange, New Jersey, and they pushed for a bout in Philly or Jersey City. By late February, Jersey City's Roosevelt Stadium, a Works Progress Administration (WPA) public project, was selected as the site for the May 28 battle. Newspaper reporters joked that for this particular fight the two boxers could begin getting out of shape!

The New Jersey Commission had no qualms issuing licenses to any of the participants, but the Commission did require an eye exam for Tony Galento since there had been so much talk of his failing eyesight. A complete physical exam by Dr. Louis W. Dodson indicated that Galento was in a fit condition to fight Max Baer.

Then there was a last-minute stipulation. Joe wouldn't sign the Baer contract without a condition in black and white that if Galento won, he would next meet Joe Louis. (This "condition" may have resulted in the $15,000 debt Mike Jacobs later claimed Joe Jacobs owed him, a debt to be subtracted from Galento's earnings from the Baer fight.)

On April 16, Max, Buddy and Ancil Hoffman left California for training camp at Pompton Lakes, New Jersey. Buddy was rapidly approaching contender status in that he had won all of his fights in 1939 with knockouts or technical knockouts. He would be taking on Natie Mann in Madison Square Garden, May 3.

The publicity spigot for Baer-Galento was turned full on. When asked if the fight was going to be a dirty one, Max replied: "If he wants to fight dirty, he'll find a superior in me. I'll stick my thumbs into his pig-eyes until he can't see. I'll cut up his face with my elbows and show him a few tricks he doesn't know."[15] The newspapers said Baer hated Galento. Actually, he thought that Galento violated all ethics of the ring, and he wanted at least one punch at him during his waning career. So in almost every paper came something from Baer like: "I'll hit that loud-mouth everywhere and with everything. He'll get elbows, knees, thumbs, laces and heads. That's what he hands out, so I'll give it to him in a double dose. I was a butcher boy once, and I'll become a butcher boy again."[16]

Actually, it was for another reason that Max was fighting. He really didn't need the money. He could make good money refereeing and doing other odd jobs. He loved being around people; making them happy made him happy. One thing that motivated him for this match specifically was an incident involving his aunt from Omaha.

Aunt Olive had traveled by train out to California from Omaha to see his baby, Max Jr. She rode all night and day sitting upright in coach rather than in a comfortable Pullman. She had packed her lunch because she could not afford to eat in the expensive dining car. When his aunt arrived and Max realized she had only enough money to return home — again in coach — he was determined, in his magnanimous way, to provide for her. "I told my aunt right then that she was going home first class, and live first class from now on. And so are a lot of the others who mean something to me and have been kind to me. Hell — it's a lot easier to take a punch on the jaw when you're 31 than it is to sit up all night in a day coach when you're sixty-five."[17] From the Galento proceeds he planned to give gifts to people who had been kind to him. That was his way of thinking about the fight. He would spend the rest of life giving back to people.

Even cynical sportswriter McLemore was affected, saying that he had seen a "mental peace" about Max Baer that he had never before witnessed. Gone was the playboy, all the swagger and self-interest.

On the evening of April 24, 1940, as Baer spoke to McLemore so seriously about his aunt and his indebtedness to friends, Tony Galento and manager Joe Jacobs were with the movie people making film clips to be used to ballyhoo the upcoming fight. In the process, Joe fell seriously ill and was rushed to a doctor's office, where he suffered a heart attack and died. The cigar-chomping, tough little manager wearing a tipped fedora, and who had grown up in New York's "Hell's Kitchen" (on Tenth Avenue), known as Yussel the Muscle, was only thirteen days short of his 44th birthday. His sudden death was a shock to everyone, especially Tony.

The man who had been such a thorn in everyone's side at the Garden had managed to guide many fighters into prominence. He originally partnered with Billy McCarney to manage Benny Valga, Andre Routis, Johnny Dundee, and Mike McTigue. He later allied himself solely with the heavyweights because, as he said, that was where the "cocoanuts" were. He managed Max Schmeling and Tony Galento. Galento had also been managed before, by Jack Dempsey and Max Waxman, but they had given him up. Jacobs plucked Galento out from boxing's dump heap and turned him into a meal ticket. Jacobs was a regular at all the nightclubs, talking up his men and making deals with anyone who had money for percentages in his fighters. When Galento was called to the doctor's office that night, he was inconsolable. "Come, on Joey," he sobbed, "come back; wake up."[18]

Services for Jacobs were held at Riverside Memorial Chapel and he was laid to rest at Mount Judah Cemetery in Cypress Hills, Ridgewood, New York. Harry Grayson for the *Dunkirk Evening Observer* said the "high-rolling Hebrew from Hell's Kitchen" was a magician. He did the only thing possible with an otherwise comic figure: he made Galento "a throwback to the days when John L. Sullivan cowed barflies.... It remains to be seen how Galento will go without his Svengali."[19] After Jacob's death, Harry Mendel, promoter of bicycle races and a good friend to Joe, stepped in and assumed responsibilities for Galento. Galento's hardscrabble fighting years, like those of the decade, were coming to an end. After Jacobs's death, Tony would take on three more foes before he retired for good.

Joe Jacobs's death was too close to the Baer fight. Tony was in no mental condition to fight anyone and he asked Mike Jacobs for a postponement.

Hoffman, Galento, and Mendel met with Mike Jacobs on May 1 to set a new date. So as not to interfere with his promotion of the rematch of Joe Louis and Arturo Godoy on June 20, Jacobs rescheduled Baer and Galento for July 2. All parties agreed that July 2 was a good omen because on that date Jack Dempsey and George Carpentier drew boxing's first $1 million gate in the same town—Jersey City. Hoffman asked for a $2500 forfeit to make sure the bout was not called off again. Galento fumed at having to shell over good money to assure everyone that he wouldn't run out on the match. Mike Jacobs was supposed to have taken a $15,000 debt repayment off the fight from Joe Jacobs—money that Jacobs or others could have used for muscle on either this fight or another one. With Jacobs gone and a new contract signed, that debt went unpaid or was no longer valid.

Tony Galento, July 2, 1940, Roosevelt Stadium, Union City, New Jersey

With the fight rescheduled, the only reason Hoffman or Max had for remaining in New York was Buddy's bout with Nathan Mann in Madison Square Garden on Friday, May 3, for 12 rounds. The pair stayed and watched Buddy kayo his opponent in the seventh round.

Tony Galento (left) lands an uppercut on Max in their battle July 2, 1940, at Roosevelt Stadium (courtesy David Bergin).

Look magazine called the Baer-Galento fight the "world's heavyweight screwball championship." Describing the bout, the magazine said, "With the possible exception of a jungle fight between two rogue elephants, the Baer-Galento meeting should be the year's roughest exhibition…. Galento, built like a fireplug, will have to punch nearly straight up to do any damage to Baer's profile."[20] The article made it clear that it was a puzzle why these two would want to fight for the honor of meeting Louis again, since both had been given their worst beatings from the champion.

Tony, age 30, was even more motivated to win for his manager Joey, and he wasn't worried about the fight because he was sure that Baer would quit on him. He was building a new bar. He had bought a two-story building and wanted to make it into a "classy joint." "Ain't nobody going to get in without a coat and tie on."[21]

Mrs. Baer did not intend to see the fight. While Baer was training, she and Max Jr. visited her father in Ithaca, New York, for the month. She had never seen a fight before and she didn't plan on seeing this one. She told reporters who followed her every move

Fourteen • The Screwball Championship, Galento, 1940

that she didn't approve of prizefighting, but she understood Max. He liked to spend money and he needed to make big money in order to spend it. "I don't like fights. I hate them, but Max would be lost if he stopped following a career that kept him in the spotlight," she said.[22] She also noted that when Max was anxious or irritable before a fight or even in training, he didn't perform well. When he was calm and confident he did well. Either way, when Max was fighting she preferred to be alone.

On June 22, Mike Jacobs officially announced that Louis would fight the winner of the Baer-Galento fight. Louis spent a day in each camp. He first visited Baer's camp, and had this advice for Max: "Don't try to stiffen him in the first round. That boy's too strong to go out in a hurry. Just stab him like this for a first round. Whenever you see an opening shoot a right cross. Make sure you tie him up in the clinches like this [Joe demonstrated] and watch out for his head ... he's liable to butt your head off your shoulders."[23] Max listened carefully.

Whitey Bimstein would be in Galento's corner as trainer and chief second. In camp, Galento put on a comic show for Louis, Commissioner Abe Green, Mike Jacobs, and one thousand of his closest friends. He pretended to be a feeble old man if the Army recruiter ever came by, and he danced the rhumba and the conga with Madeleine Carroll, Alfred Hitchcock's beautiful actress in *The 39 Steps*. In retort to Baer's calling him a "pig-eye" in the press, he called Baer a "peanut heart." It was a swell show meant to one-up Baer's camp.

In Max's camp, Baer had wrestled with Joe Banovic, who looked more like a sumo wrestler than a sparring partner. They put on a hilarious show of what a go might look like with Tony. Louis remarked that he had never witnessed anything in any training camp like what he had seen in those two days. It was the best show before the show. When asked to pick a winner, Louis declined. "Both," he said, were "powerful funny."[24] He said he wouldn't miss this show for anything.

To the already comic mix of things, Max and Tony agreed to fight without a referee. Abe Greene, New Jersey Commissioner, immediately dismissed the idea and made it clear to the press that the match would have a referee. Jimmy Braddock was considered for the job since he had a New Jersey referee's license, but everyone knew that he disliked Baer. Hoffman wanted Jack Dempsey, but he was ruled out. The referee wasn't revealed until the actual fight. Max said he didn't care who would referee as long as he was someone who could count to ten. But Hoffman wanted it known that all questionable tactics were to be understood by the referee well in advance of the bout. "If any violations go on and are not penalized, I'm going to take Max right off the ring. I guarantee Galento won't get away with the same things he pulled the night he stopped Lou Nova in Philadelphia last fall. Anything went that night and Tony got away with everything but murder. He's going to fight according to the rules this time—or there'll be no fight."[25]

Another dictum issued by New Jersey Commissioner Abe Greene, that made a noticeable difference in the appearance of this fight, was that Max Baer could not wear the Star of David on his boxing trunks. Baer had worn the star on his trunks in all of his heavyweight fights since Max Schmeling. Green said: "At no time should a boxer wear anything emblematic of his religious beliefs, but especially now when the world is torn between conflicting emotions there is no room for any other symbol but of Americanism. A man does not fight as the representative of any religious creed or belief. He performs as a boxer and is entitled to support from the fans only in the measure he can attract it as a fighter and as a sportsman."[26] Baer's use of the symbol, a novelty on professional boxing trunks, had been seen as a promotional means to enhance gate attraction, and it was now denounced for that purpose. Baer would never wear it again in the ring.

The boys down at Jacobs's Beach on 49th Street predicted that Galento had more to gain by this fight than Baer. Galento needed the money; Baer didn't. And no one was really sure that Baer even wanted to fight Louis. The bookmakers picked Galento to win at 2-to-1 odds.

Up to the hour of the fight, the jawboning continued. Max said, "I'm going to work on that fat watermelon right quick. I'm going to cut him up for five or six rounds. Then when he can't see any more, I'll flatten him." Tony said, "I just can't wait till I flatten dat bum Baer, so I kin get another shot at Louis.... If I got as many chances at Louis' chin as that Chilean [Godoy] did, I'd be heavyweight champion today." And about Baer? Galento branded Baer a yellow bum, a good-looking guy for the movies but a cowardly lion in the ring. "The bum has no heart. They know he quit to Braddock 'n' Louis 'n' Nova, and when I hit him on the lug I'll make him fold up like beach chair. Sure, he's a nice looking guy, but you can't get guts in a gymnasium. Ya' gotta be born with 'em. He's a bum, a big bum an' I'll flatten him sure."[27]

Henry McClemore asked the question. What if all they said about each other was true? Why would anyone attend the fight? The answer—to see whose hand would be raised at the end, the hand that would then have to fight Joe Louis, "the one thing that neither Max nor Tony want to happen. And you can't blame them. One trip over Niagara in a canoe is enough for any fellow."[28]

Since Max didn't have a good left hand and Tony didn't have a good right hand, one writer said that together, they offset that with a good backhand. A myriad of labels were assigned to what was otherwise seen as an epic matchup of the Battle of the Bums. The crowd was expected to go over 30,000 and the gate over $150,000, with each man getting 27½ percent of the net receipts.

The first blow of the fight was actually at the official weigh-in the day before. Dr. Max Stern, New Jersey physician, examined both men and pronounced them in fine shape—well, good enough for them. Max weighed 221½ and Tony weighed 244½ pounds. When asked to pose for pictures, Galento stuck out his left fist and Baer swung and knocked it down. Unprintable insults were exchanged, and the handlers jumped between the very big men. Cooler heads came in and told them to knock it off until the next day.

Then each was asked to make final statements for the live radio audience. Baer leaned in and spoke with his usual jocular air, "May the best man win—that's me." Hearing that, Galento rushed at Baer and shouted, "Why you big bum, what happened to you when you fought Nova?"[29] Another fight was about to break out, this time in hearing range of the widespread listening audience.

When everything was calm again, the fighters were given their instructions. Tony objected to the amount of gauze Baer requested. Galento snorted, "You better soak it in plaster if you expect to hurt me." And Baer snapped, "I'll plaster you one right now," as he jumped off his stool and lunged for Tony.[30] Again the handlers had to separate the duo.

Finally, everything was set to go. The combatants had made it through their training, no other manager or party to the fight had died, and the two hadn't killed each other, yet. Everything was good, except for one unfortunate incident, only 24 hours before the fight. Tony was behind the bar attending to the drinking crowd at his Orange lounge when he was hit by a flying beer glass thrown by his 26-year-old brother, Russell. Tony was severely cut on his chin. Russell wanted two tickets for the fight and Tony said, "See me tomorrow."[31] Apparently that wasn't the correct answer. Witnesses told the newspaper that the cut was at least an inch long and deep enough to cancel the fight. But Galento's manager told Mike Jacobs that the cut was only a minor one and the fight would go on. Tony was taken to see Dr. Stern and returned to the bar later that night wearing heavy bandages over three stitches in his lip for a gash that went entirely through the skin.

On the night of the fight, all parties agreed that Tony's cut was simply a "minor abrasion" considering what was about to occur, and it shouldn't stand in the way of a good fight.

Immediately before walking into the ring, Galento was told that Joe Jacobs's brother, Caswell Keppel Jacobs, had served papers on Mike Jacobs attaching Galento's part of the purse on behalf of the Jacobs family.

In the eight-round preliminary, Pat Comiskey of Paterson, New Jersey, stopped Bob Sikes of Pine Bluff, Arkansas, after two minutes, twelve seconds of the first round. Comiskey knocked Sikes down three times (with a left for a nine-count; left for a seven-count; and another left to the jaw for the final knockdown) before the referee called a halt to the fight. This brought Comiskey's record to 29 knockouts in a series of 32 fights. With Tony Galento aging, the 19-year-old Paterson boy was seen as the new star of New Jersey.

In the main event, the fighters greeted each other at ring center: "You bum, I'll make you quit," said Tony. Max replied, "No you won't, fatso. I'll make you quit."[32]

It was a fight of head-butts, slashes with the laces, thumbs, and gouges.

The New Jersey headline the next day pretty much told the story of the fight: "Orange Fatman, With Broken Hand, Takes Only One Round as 'Two Old Men' Slug It Out."[33] It wasn't pretty. Gayle Talbot wrote, "The fat tavern keeper was sitting on his stool, blowing blood like a harpooned whale, when the bell rang to start the eighth round. His handlers wouldn't let him go out." The only thing the bout proved, added Talbot, was that "there isn't a heavyweight in the world today worthy of challenging Joe Louis for the championship."[34]

Max was touted as fighting a "brainy" fight, but spent most of the time snarling, stalking and motioning Galento to come forward.

Galento landed initially in the first round, banging Baer's head twice with left hooks. Baer also went to the head. Then Galento went to the body and Baer followed, ducking under Galento's wild left swings. Tony was warned by Referee Joe Mangold against backhanding. Baer landed a left on the nose, Tony landed a left on the ear. Punches got harder. Tony landed two hard lefts to the face and body. Max was warned by the referee against hitting on the break. Baer had reopened the stitches on Tony's mouth from the bar fight and the new gash was nasty.

The second round would go to Galento, the only round he won soundly. Galento spent the entire round rushing Baer, and Baer tried to avoid Tony's wild swinging left. They rushed and wrestled, and once got into a slugging contest off the ropes. The crowd stood and cheered at the exchange. They both landed dozens of blows with Galento appearing to score more points. Baer ended the round with his nose bleeding.

In the third and fourth rounds, the referee was the hardest-working man in the ring, continually having to break up the clinches. Tony was desperately head-butting and was penalized for it in the fourth. He was not penalized for backhanding in the third. Galento was criticized for his lack of sportsmanship, particularly for his use of backhand, elbow, thumb and head-butt fouls. Even in the sometimes sordid dealings of boxing, there is a line of sportsmanship that participants may not cross. And in the fourth round, Galento crossed that line. During a clinch he brought his head up, with as much power as he could muster, to smash Baer's chin. Baer admitted that the head-butt to the chin that cut his lip was the only real blow that hurt him. The crowd had been with Galento for the initial rounds, but after the fourth, they turned against him.

Between rounds, Galento's handlers worked on his chin. Baer spit blood. In the sixth and seventh, they simply battled away at each other with neither putting up much of a defense. Once, in the seventh, when Tony stumbled to one knee, Baer landed three rights to his head. After the seventh, when Galento failed to come out, the audience yelled for Baer to go over and finish him off at the stool, so tired were they at seeing Tony's foul blows. Whitey Bimstein, Galento's main second, stopped the fight after the seventh. At the end, blood was spurting like a leaking faucet from Galento's mouth and he was babbling incoherently. Everyone thought he had paid for his dirty tactics. Tony had come into the fight wearing three stitches in his face; he left wearing ten.

Nothing was pretty about the fight, but it was a good fight for Max, who needed to reign magnificent again. Some said that Max was not a killer, just a good actor, filling in where Galento failed to show. Others said it was a battle of two old wobble-legs, only one more washed-up than the other at the end.

Joe Louis followed Max back into his dressing room, and photographers snapped pictures of the two sitting next to each other. Max told Joe that he was a credit to his profession and then Max asked if he was going to give him another shot at the title. Joe answered, "Yes." And the photographers snapped more photos. Baer joked to reporters that they had better shake his hand now for free because if he beat Louis, he was going to charge them $5000 each. Max acknowledged the sage advice Louis gave him prior to the fight. Louis grinned, "Yah, Max and me is pals, but I'd like to meet him." Max gave the reporters a final question: "Hey, who quit this time?" The room was silent.[35] Bottom line: Max can still hit.

Attendance was 22,711, and the gate grossed less than expected at $98,000. Max earned $19,821.46. He had expected to earn much more.

Because Galento failed to come out for the eighth, gamblers wanted to know: Did the fight end in the seventh or eighth round? The betting issue had not been settled definitively in 1940. It was noted that Baer had come off his stool ready to fight before the referee called a halt to the battle. In fact, the bell had sounded to start the eighth round. The rules both in New Jersey and from the NBA stated that if a fight was stopped between rounds, the finish was placed officially in the upcoming round. Nevertheless, many were unhappy with that ruling. The official announcement by ring announcer Harry Balogh was, "Galento fails to respond to the bell for the eighth round. The winner by technical knockout is Max Baer."[36] As far as could be ascertained, Broadway bookies paid off only on the eighth round.

Galento's dressing room was funereal. His managers explained that the original stitches in his chin were ripped out in the first round. The wound was expanded, and he had a chipped tooth that snagged yet another opening in his cheek. Blood flowed so extensively that his breathing was affected. Reporters said he was quiet as a mouse, not from his own volition but because he couldn't talk—everything on his face was swollen shut. He had also dislocated a knuckle and fractured a bone in his left hand. He admitted that Baer was a hard hitter. Then he left to go see Dr. Max Stern for repairs. Some 1500 New Jersey fans waited for him back at his saloon. They loved their Tony.

Fourteen • The Screwball Championship, Galento, 1940

Tony Galento and Max Baer at the end of their slugfest.

Max was back on the roller coaster, now at the top and in the good graces of the press, again admired for the finest physique the ring had ever witnessed, the most powerful right hand in punching history, and a rugged ability to absorb punishment. The comeback was seen as remarkable.

He had it all, including money in the bank; and in only a year he could quit boxing and start drawing from his annuity, which now amounted to $1000 a month for life. Max told everyone that it only took one punch to land the title.

Fifteen

The Magnificent's Last Fights, 1940–1941

Old "Doc" Jack Kearns, a throwback to the glory days of Jack Dempsey and Tex Rickard, was standing on Broadway with $6 in his pocket when he was approached by Bill Daley. Daley knew Kearns had roots in California and kept one step ahead of the gossip there. So Daley asked him if he knew how to get in touch with Max Baer. He wanted to arrange a fight for his up-and-coming protégé, Pat Comiskey. Never turning down an opportunity to make a buck, Kearns obliged, but said he needed a thousand big ones for travel expenses.

On August 30, 1940, Jack Kearns visited Sacramento. The next day, two months after the Galento fight, New Jersey Commissioner Abe Greene received word from Ancil Hoffman that he and Max were on their way to New York to sign a formal agreement with manager Bill Daley for a fight with 19-year-old Irish Patrick Edward Comiskey. The Paterson, New Jersey, youth had built up a stout knockout record, yet no one knew what the boy could really do. Max Baer would be that test. But why the rush for Baer to sign? Speculation was that Hoffman was dodging another fight with Joe Louis. Once was enough. And the New Jersey money was good. Kearns billed himself as promoter and offered Baer a $30,000 cash-up-front guarantee.

The money had been collected in ten-thousand-dollar portions from three of Daley's local Paterson business acquaintances. International news editor Lawton Carver admitted that Comiskey was not *yet* connected to the New York mob like his forerunner, Irish Jim Braddock. Carver wrote, "Owen Madden had a piece of Braddock." And Comiskey was not yet tied up to Mike Jacobs simply because he wasn't on the radar—yet. Carver announced, "I think you are looking at the first heavyweight to come out of the ditch and get this far without any business, meaning fixed fights and such."[1] It would not be long before Eddie Brietz reported that "the mobs were trying to chisel in on Comiskey."[2]

Jack Kearns had been a boxing manager, but he saw this bout as a big promotional payday. He expected to make $100,000 on this gate, especially since the Galento fight in the same outdoor stadium grossed $97,000. Over at Jacobs's Beach, Mike scoffed at the idea that Kearns could make such a killing. Jacobs expected a bust. Ticket prices were less than those at the Galento fight. These were dockyard prices, from $1 lowest to $8 highest.

Kearns played the official September 4 signing to the hilt. The Broadway nightclub The Hurricane was packed for the evening's event. Pretty little *hurricanettes* served drinks wearing grass skirts and posed for pictures with celebrities. Kearns, the dinner speaker, repetitiously reminded everyone of just how big this fight was going to be. Really, really big.

Then, it was Hoffman's turn to speak: "I have heard lots of nice talk here, but I haven't seen no money."

Kearns raised his hand, which held an envelope. In a slow, sweeping grand gesture of a bow, the Count of Monte Cristo handed over the money to manager Hoffman.

Hoffman opened the envelope and saw that it contained a check. The silence was matched only by Hoffman's "detached expression," reported sports editor Harry Ferguson.

"What's the matter?" asked Commissioner Abe Green.

"Cash," replied Ancil Hoffman.

"You don't think the check's good?" questioned Green.

"Cash!" repeated Hoffman emphatically.

To which Kearns grabbed the envelope from Hoffman's hands. Then, from inside his coat pocket, Kearns pulled out a wad of bills. He began counting disgustedly, "One hundred, two hundred, three..." until he reached 30 "gees."

"Bingo!" shouted a member of the audience.[3]

All that the invited news-meisters announced the next day was that this was going to be the best fight of the year. The publicity angle was that this fight was going to be announced as the last fight of Baer's career. No one believed that Kearns would hand over $30,000, even if it was others' money, if he didn't have a big publicity stunt lined up. So this was Baer's swan song. Everyone knew he was ancient at 31. He couldn't go on forever. Comiskey was new blood, young, and a knockout artist. If the Clouting Celt could kayo Baer, then he would prove capable of a stab at Joe Louis.

The press took up the now-familiar mantra bad-mouthing Baer: he was not in shape, a high roller, a draw in name only, never much of a fighter, and a quitter when he was in shape.

Pat Comiskey, September 26, 1940, Roosevelt Stadium, Jersey City, New Jersey

Amidst all the bad press, Baer began training for the 15-round bout at the same open-air venue as the Galento fight. Initially, Baer stayed at Tommy Farr's old camp, the West End Casino in Long Branch, New Jersey, and used the dog track there for his exercises. From there, he moved from Long Branch to Meadowbrook in Newark. A postcard sent to George Brignolia of San Leandro, California, on September 6 from the West End Casino (which advertised "Twin Crystal Pools and Ocean Bathing, Dining and Dancing") in Baer's handwriting said, "Well it looks like I should KO the fellow but don't bet on a KO. Bet I win is all. I should. Cheerio for now, best to the Mrs. Always, Max."[4]

Folks in San Leandro took the card to be a tip on how Baer felt about the betting odds. When manager Hoffman discovered that Baer had sent a postcard back home telling people not to wager on a KO, he didn't want that news interpreted as Baer didn't think he could win, or that the fight was a set-up. Hoffman immediately wired his bookmaker Tiny Heller to put $10,000 on Baer for him. He wanted tons of money bet on Baer. In twenty-four hours Heller had covered his bet with even money. Back East, the betting odds were solidly on Baer. Even though this bout paired fighters with one of the greatest differences in ages, Max at 31 and Pat at 19, Baer was still given the odds over his rival, 2 to 1.

Comiskey trained at the Market Street Gymnasium in Newark and then moved to the Hackensack Health center. Comiskey's clouting skill had been honed inside the Jamesburg Reformatory in New Jersey. He had never lost a professional fight in a stellar career of 25 wins, and one draw—until he met Steve Dudas, December 15, 1939. Before Dudas, Comiskey was a big kid with raw talent and a devastating right hand, like Baer's. However, Dudas left Comiskey battered and broken, literally. Comiskey broke his right hand in the battle.

While he waited for his hand to heal, he kept in shape, drilled on footwork, and worked with his left. He came back and met Dudas again and scored a unanimous decision in eight rounds. Two more of his competitors kissed the canvas before his manager declared he was ready for the big time.

When the match was set with Baer, Daley hired Jimmy Braddock to teach the Irishman how to beat Max Baer. The real unknown with Comiskey was that he had never been fully tested against a known talent. And although Baer was a well-known commodity, his performances were always unpredictable. Everyone knew he carried the bomb, but no one ever knew when it was going to explode.

Two weeks before the fight, the NBA ranked the heavyweights, and for the first time, listed Joe Louis as "unchallenged." Listed in order were the contenders: Max Baer, California; Arturo Godoy, Chile; Red Burman, Maryland; Buddy Baer, California; Buddy Walker, Ohio; Pat Comiskey, New Jersey; Bob Pastor, New York; Tony Galento, New Jersey; Lee Savold, Iowa; and Tommy Martin, England. But others said the only person worthy to challenge Louis was his son-to-be. Wife Marva was expecting.

Other, older sportswriters fondly reminisced about the good old days and the "kaleidoscopic career" of old Doc Kearns. Harold Conrad said, "The story of Jack Kearns is always a good one," and this fight "would add at least one more chapter to his colorful career." Kearns's prediction of a $100,000 gate in 1940 sounded like a million-dollar gate in the Dempsey era. "Kearns and Baer," Conrad said, "what a storybook combination."[5] And when Kearns announced that he would ask Jack Dempsey to referee the fight, it was truly a fight to commemorate the Golden Age of Boxing. Kearns knew how to ballyhoo like the old-timers. He held party after party—anything that would make news. He even hosted a barbeque on September 17, at Baer's training camp, with only sportswriters invited for a chance to watch Baer go through his training exercises. Baer showed them a routine of shadowboxing, bag punching and body calisthenics. Jerry Casale, camp manager, cooked a tasty feast for everyone.

The next day Baer began his exercises with sparring partners Charley Ketchuck, Binghamton, New York; Jim Robinson, Philadelphia; and George Hicks, New York. Again, another unfortunate accident happened. Max was warming up by shadowboxing in the ring, and when he went to land an imaginary punch, he leaned into the ropes. The ropes gave way and he was flung out of the ring. His head struck a pole and he was temporarily knocked out. He also hurt his back. Trainer Izzy Kline rushed to his aid. Max took the day to rest, but complained of a backache for the rest of the night. Three hundred people watched the incident from the stands and wondered if Baer would be able to come back from the injury.

Meanwhile, on September 17, Baer had to send a lawyer to Albany, New York, to attend the Appellate Division of the State Supreme Court on the suit involving Frank R.

Fifteen • The Magnificent's Last Fights, 1940–1941

While training at Long Branch, New Jersey, the week before the Pat Comiskey fight, September 26, 1940, Max leaned on a rope while shadow-boxing and fell out of the ring, severely injuring his neck and back. Trainer Izzy Kline came to his rescue.

McKeeby, Binghamton ($20,000) and the late Gertrude Wallace, through husband William Wallace, Rome ($50,000) in the collapse of the grandstand at Baer's 1935 training camp. The result of the action came nine days before the fight—the trial would go forward in Oneida County, ordered Justice Peter Schmuck. Entirely innocent of having anything to do with the grandstand, but out of necessity, Baer paid an out-of-court settlement of $70,000 to have the case dismissed.

Unlike the Baer-Galento fight, there was very little trash talk before or during the fight. Comiskey was a quiet fellow and refused to say anything about Baer. For Baer, this was just another fight, but one that he was confident of winning because of his experience. For this fight he seemed more serious, less prone to clowning. One writer reported that he was a "refreshingly frank and earnest guy, who has been willing to admit he is not the greatest fighter that ever lived."[6] He even said that if he could do something better he would. This was one of the reasons he had so disliked Tony Galento. It was fine for Baer to note his shortcomings, but not acceptable for someone else to call him out as Tony had done. Nevertheless, his behavior did seem to suggest that he was not long for the ring.

On Saturday, September 21, five days before the fight, Dr. Louis W. Dodson, accompanied by Commissioner Abe Greene, examined Comiskey after a heavy workout and declared him in fine condition. Comiskey had sparred two rounds each with Patsy Perroni and Henry Moros. When he unleashed his power in his final two rounds, he knocked out sparring partner Tiger Flowers with a hit to the jaw.

Max was to undergo a similar physical the next day, but he cut his training short due to the extreme heat. It has been said that Max never took his training seriously. But with every Baer fight, writers noted that he had trained harder for that particular fight than any other, which leads one to believe that he was always trained and ready to fight, and that his clowning nature never prevented him from being in good physical condition.

Three days before the fight, when ticket sales were slow (only $15,000 had been sold with $10,000 reserved), headlines read, "May Be Baer's Last Fight." Word had it that "Mrs. Maxie has just about convinced him it's time he hung up the gloves for good."[7] To boost ticket sales it was announced that three distinguished fighters would serve as referees: Jack Dempsey for the main event; Jimmy Braddock for the six-round semifinal between "Fireplug" Joe O'Gatty and Bill Poland; and Mickey Walker for one of the four-round events.

When asked about his strategy for fighting Baer, Comiskey said he would watch Max clown for the ladies because they deserved to see that, but soon afterward he would put him to sleep. And then he would be ready to take on Joe Louis. In the tale of the tape, Comiskey was expected to enter the ring weighing 212 pounds and Baer 217. Pat was 6 foot 4½ inches tall, 2 inches taller than Baer. Pat had an inch and one-half longer reach. Their fists, neck, biceps, forearms, calves, and ankles were essentially the same. The major difference was the age. In earnings, Baer had been given his $30,000 guarantee. Comiskey would earn 15 percent of the gate.

Baer had the experience, and it was probably true: the old warhorse had probably forgotten all that the classy-looking young guy hadn't yet learned. So that made them even. But only hours before the bout, $100,000 betting money on Comiskey appeared and the odds shifted in his favor. Some took the shift to mean that Baer had been paid off.

The fight was on. Max Baer came out from the bell with his fists cocked, ready to battle. Baer landed a barrage of two-fisted blows and they fell into a clinch where they traded hard punches. When Baer pushed him out of the clinch, Comiskey had a red knot over his left eye. In the melee he was able to land a right on Baer's chin. Baer knocked him against the ropes. He would have landed on the canvas had it not been for his chin catching on the top rope and holding him up. After a count of two, he tried to come off the ropes, but sank back into them. Baer went over to finish him off. But as if remembering what he had done to Frankie Campbell so many years earlier, he looked pleadingly at Referee Jack Dempsey. Jack waved Max off. The fight ended after two minutes and 39 seconds of the first round. Together they carried Pat back to his corner.

The bout was over, and so many people were heard saying, "If only Max would fight that way with Joe Louis."[8] Jack Kearns presented Max with a belt for the "White Heavyweight Championship." (It was a title that sprouted up when the early black champions Joe Gans and Jack Johnson held the world titles.) After the fight, Baer stayed in the ring so that any who wanted to take a picture would be able to do so. It seemed to be the general consensus that Comiskey had been rushed into battle too early against such a

Fifteen • The Magnificent's Last Fights, 1940–1941

Measurements of MAX BAER

Age	31
Weight	216 pounds
Height	6 feet 2½ inches
Reach	78 inches
Chest (normal)	44 inches
Chest (expanded)	47½ inches
Neck	17½ inches
Waist	33 inches
Biceps	14½ inches
Forearm	14 inches
Wrist	8 inches
Fist	12¼ inches
Thigh	21½ inches
Calf	15 inches
Ankle	10 inches

Measurements of PAT COMISKEY

Age	19
Weight	209 pounds
Height	6 feet 4½ inches
Reach	79½ inches
Chest (normal)	43 inches
Chest (expanded)	47 inches
Neck	18 inches
Waist	32 inches
Biceps	14¼ inches
Forearm	13½ inches
Wrist	7¾ inches
Fist	12 inches
Thigh	20½ inches
Calf	16 inches
Ankle	10 inches

Baer-Comiskey program, tale of the tape.

ring legend. Unlike today, when contenders are expected to have flawless records, Comiskey's loss to Baer was not expected to set him back, only give him experience and notoriety, which it did.

Attendance was 20,000 with the gross receipts totaling only $68,575. The movie of the fight appeared in theaters the next day in New York. Max was back as the number-one contender for Joe Louis. The decade was almost over, and there did not appear to be any white heavyweight out there that Max could not beat. He was a tiger again.

Everyone wanted to see Max Baer fight Joe Louis. But Mike Jacobs was still not ready to set that one up. It was impossible to estimate what such a gate would generate. Max had lost his title five years earlier, and after losing to Louis, no one had given Baer a fighting chance for a comeback. Where others had failed, Max had succeeded through determination and confidence. Most importantly, Ancil Hoffman had made a wise move when he last left New York. When Mike Jacobs wanted to renew Max's contract, Hoffman stood firm. Hoffman wanted to entertain any and all offers. In stepped Jack Kearns with an offer too good for Baer to turn down, even though his promotion lost money.

Lou Nova's manager Ray Carlen had seen the fight. He believed that Max would never fight Joe Louis. And he wondered, if the Comiskey fight had gone longer than one round, would Baer have lasted? Carlen desperately wanted Baer to fight Nova again. But Hoffman preferred to have Buddy meet Nova.

Max Baer was in demand. He was offered $20,000 to fight Arturo Godoy, $20,000 to fight Red Burman, and $25,000 for Billy Conn. He was also asked to perform in a New York Broadway musical comedy, *Hi-Ya Gentlemen*. He was offered $2500 per week for the theater engagement. Jack Kearns also offered him 4 exhibitions with Jack Dempsey. Kearns was running around telling everyone he could offer Joe Louis $250,000 and Max Baer $100,000 for a fight. But everyone knew that Mike Jacobs was *not* going to let that happen.

America was facing a bigger fight. With war ramping up in Europe, Uncle Sam called on all eligible young American men to register nationwide for the military draft on October 16, 1940. Sign-up day was a patriotic holiday. Businesses closed and hundreds of thousands of citizens volunteered to help with registration at 125,000 centers across the United States. Banners were raised in colorful red, white, and blue. President Roosevelt spoke over the radio: "Democracy is your cause—the cause of youth.... Your act today affirms not only your loyalty to your country, but your will to build your future for yourselves."[9] All professional sports groups were notified: headliners in any sport were not exempt from the lottery or

Publicity photograph taken for Max Baer's first stage performance, *Hi-Ya Gentlemen*.

the draft. Selective service headquarters in Washington estimated that approximately nine million men between the ages of 21 through 35 had registered across the country, over one million every hour that the centers were open. It was expected that within the next four years five million could be drawn for service in the army. During World War I only men between the ages of 21 through 30 registered for the first draft. Ancil Hoffman had been one of those registrants for World War I. He would register again for World War II. The military draft was not expected to take married men. In spite of the fact that they were all married, Joe Louis, Max Baer, and Buddy Baer signed up for the draft in Chicago.

In October, Mike Jacobs started plans for elimination battles to find an acceptable foe for Joe Louis, starting with Billy "the Kid" Conn, who had beaten Lee Savold at Madison Square Garden. He was also considering a rematch of Lou Nova with Max Baer; and a match with Red Burman and Buddy Baer. At one point he thought about setting Max up with Billy Conn. And while Conn was still a light-heavy, he could battle his way around the heavies. No one seemed ready for Joe Louis.

At the end of the year, Eddie Brietz said that of all the boxers, Max Baer did most for the sport this year—"for getting rid of Galento, if nothing else."[10] The New York Boxing Writers, in their annual poll of ratings, named Billy Conn and Max Baer to share the honor of #1 contender for Joe Louis's title. Since they were ranked equally, it seemed a natural to put them together in the ring. But some writers felt that Conn was too light, and "we shudder to think of Max in there with Louis again."[11]

On December 3, Max Baer made his stage debut in Boston in the off–Broadway musical comedy, *Hi-Ya Gentlemen*, about a college campus agent for a horse-race betting syndicate. It was noted that Max's clowning drew more applause on stage than in the boxing ring. The audience enjoyed seeing the ex-heavyweight champ sing and dance, but was especially pleased when he started shedding his clothes in a "strip-tease act" in a scene with Audrey Christie, one of the co-eds, and Sid Silvers, his bodyguard.

Sid Silvers was a veteran vaudevillian, screenwriter, and actor. He recalled an incident with Max Baer. When Baer read his lines for the first time, Silvers complimented him and said, "I'm going to teach you everything I know about show business. Max, I'm going to make you the biggest star on Broadway." "Yeah," Max grunted. "And I'm going to make you the world's heavyweight champ."[12]

When asked if he had the jitters on opening night, he said that he didn't. But he noted, "It's twice as hard as training for a fight. Of course, I just clown through my dances, but my speaking lines are changed almost daily and it's quite a strain up here," he said tapping his forehead.[13] Short-run, experimental stage plays were always in a state of change. And while Baer admitted that he was no John Barrymore, Barrymore probably couldn't do any better on the boxing stage. Paul Zimmerman stated that Baer should change his name to Max Baerymore. The writer noted that it didn't make any difference if the boxer had any real talent for the stage because "Baer is destined to make good newspaper copy even if he can't act or fight a lick."[14] Another writer called his acting "Baerymoronic."

Theater producer Robert Ritchie had hoped to take the musical to Broadway, but after two weeks, the script needed to be overhauled. Baer left with the rest of the cast on Saturday night, December 14. Everyone said that without Max the show would never see Broadway.

It was said that Max had made $100,000 during the year 1940. This was gross and not net, considering expenses. (A federal census report of 1940 shows Baer making $50,000 for the year.) Baer had been in the news for 10 years. It was a rare day during the entire year of 1940 that Max Baer did not appear daily in the news or make the headlines. Looking back on the decade, the *San Anselmo Herald* wrote on October 3, 1940, "The fight racket would have died had it not been for Max Baer. Name any big fight since he won the title, and he was either in it or started it."

The big finale at year's end for Max was not in front of an audience, it was with Mike Jacobs. Mike was pressuring Baer to appear at the Boston fight between Joe Louis and Al McCoy on Monday, December 16, when it would be announced that Max Baer would be Joe Louis's next opponent. Max declined. After his show closed on Saturday night, Baer was on the train the next morning for California. He needed to get home. His wife was sick with the flu, a frightful disease for those remembering the epidemic of 1918, and he wanted to be at her side.

Max did not stay for the Louis fight to see Ray Arcel, Al McCoy's trainer, stop the fight after the fifth. McCoy had been so beaten that his left eye was closed and Arcel felt that if his man took any more punishment from Louis, he might be left blind.

Jacobs was so furious that Max refused to stay and be introduced that an argument ensued. It got so heated that Jacobs told Baer he was now completely out of the plans. Max would never have a fight with Joe Louis.

At ringside after Louis won the fight, Mike Jacobs's press agent Harry Markson handed out a printed statement to the newsmen announcing that Joe Louis would be matched with Billy Conn.

The moment when Baer could have been matched with Joe Louis was now gone. After all of his efforts to attempt to regain the title, Baer would never get his chance. Conn would officially give up his light-heavyweight title and fight Joe Louis in June.

After Baer arrived back in California, he was asked about his ring future. He said he guessed he would have to wait until after the Joe Louis–Billy Conn fight for a chance at the champ. But in six months, June of 1941, when Louis would fight Conn, Max Baer would be out of the ring for good.

On December 27, Nat Fleischer, along with his 168 experts who voted for the annual *Ring* magazine ratings, sharply disagreed with Mike Jacobs in pairing Billy Conn with Joe Louis over Max Baer. By giving Conn the match, it virtually booted out Baer, said Fleischer. *The Ring*'s board and voters said that Max Baer was the No. 1 contender for the heavyweight title for his outstanding victories over Tony Galento and Pat Comiskey. Fleischer called Baer's win over Galento "the thrill of the year."[15] The poll rated Billy Conn No. 2. *The Ring* also named Baer as the best comeback fighter of the year 1940.

Harold Conrad said that it was ironic that everyone wanted a crack at the Brown Bomber, but the one who was in the best position to fight him now didn't want to. Few writers were aware of Baer's falling out with Mike Jacobs. Papers resorted to explanations that Max had never forgotten the beating he took from Louis. Or that Mrs. Baer didn't want him to fight Joe Louis. They couldn't understand why he would take on Comiskey and Galento if he didn't intend to fight Louis. Why did he try so hard to come back? Everyone assumed it must have been all talk. Baer may have looked like he was the number-one contender, but he was called the number-one pretender.

Baer's fighting life seemed such a waste to many. Baer had everything. He could have been another Dempsey, a "killer." After all, he killed Frankie Campbell, he almost killed Max Schmeling, and he cut Primo Carnera to pieces. Then he threw away his title, submitted to Joe Louis, and fought his way back as very few do, only to turn down his chance to fight Louis. "We fear what could have been a great fighting machine has awakened just four years too late," said Harvey Rockwell of the *San Mateo Times*.[16]

By the end of January 1941, New York papers said that Mike Jacobs had seen his error and was trying to promote a rematch between Max Baer and Lou Nova. Why the sudden change in Mike Jacobs's attitude toward Max Baer? Ancil Hoffman answered, "The only reason Buddy Baer is being brought back again to fight Tony Galento is because Mike Jacobs has to use Buddy to get Max!" Art Cohn added, "As if Ancil Hoffman, the Baer Brain Trust, ever overlooked any bets."[17]

At the end of January, it looked like Nova might be ill again and not make the Baer fight scheduled for April. Nova was visiting Madison, Wisconsin, when he got a "touch of influenza." Doctors had his tonsils removed there and sent him on his way, saying he would be fine for the fight.

Baer spent February with his family and made a few appearances. On February 3, Max Baer and Jess Willard opened the annual all-star professional baseball players' match

Left to right: **William Ryan, captain of the (Folsom) Guards, former champion Jess Willard, Former Champ Max Baer, Tony Frietas, pitcher with Cincinnati Reds and the Philadelphia Phillies, February 3, 1941.**

against the Folsom Prison convict league. The final score was 20 to 5 in favor of the all-stars. Dolph Camilli (Frankie Campbell's brother) and Bud Hafey led the professionals in hits.

The Baer brothers left for their training camp in Lakewood, New Jersey, on February 10, and arrived for training February 17. Both brothers had fights, both 12-rounders, with Max and Nova on April 4 and Buddy and Galento on April 8. Max weighed 225 and Buddy 252. Because they were short of sparring partners, Ancil Hoffman allowed them initially to spar with each other. They had not done so for years. Writer Earl McCarney watched Max train and said that he was really "digging in and training more seriously than ever before. Max is so settled it surprises me. And I knew him all through his daffiness days."[18] Max again trained under Izzy Kline. It was said that he got up at 6:30 and jogged. Baer sparred fifteen rounds daily with Elza Thompson and Bob Nestell. Some said that Baer was still leaving himself open to Nestell's punches. He ate only twice a day, at 10:30 and 5:00, and hit the hay at 10:00. But the most important thing was his mental condition. Max thought he was a smarter fighter now, knowing where he made mistakes in the past.

Training camps were as unpredictable for Max as his fights, and this camp was no different. On March 19, while Max and sparring partner Bob Nestell were doing roadwork, a car came speeding around a bend headed straight for the runners. Max dove into a ditch to avoid being hit, but Nestell was not so lucky and was struck by the fender. The driver came to a stop and ran to their assistance. When the frightful event was over, all agreed no one was hurt seriously or permanently.

Again, another unusual event occurred three days before the fight. It wasn't a stray punch that got Baer, it was a wild dog. When Max was doing his early morning run through the woods near the camp he heard the sound of a dog. Max growled and the dog growled back and then came running after Max. Max speeded up, but the dog ran faster, caught up with him, and grabbed onto his left leg. Baer beat him off. Now he could say that he had been bitten by a boxer and a dog during his professional career.

Lou expected to arrive the second week of February for training at Lake Wallenpaupack, Pennsylvania. Nova told writer Pat Robinson that Baer was one of the easiest guys to beat because he never changed his strategy. "He fights the same way all the time. He never changes. It's simple. The formula is stick, step, and duck. You stick a left hand in his face, step to his right and duck his wild roundhouse right. Baer has no left hand to bother about because he only paws with it. You have to step either to his right, as Braddock did, or step inside, as I did against him. It's a mistake ever to pull away from a punch with Baer. If you do, he'll scramble your brains with that long swinging right. Poor old Primo Carnera found that out."[19]

By fight time Nova weighed 207 and Baer was down to 204. Writers stated that Baer was a more formidable fighter at 32 than he was at 26, Nova's age. Baer was confident that he would beat his California rival, and with that kind of confidence, he never lost. In addition, Nova called Baer a quitter, and that infuriated him. Max was a terror when he was mad. In his favor, Max had scored four kayos since they last met. In this fight, Max was avenging his previous loss. Nova was fighting for a shot at Joe Louis. Both expected the fight to end early.

What an era it had been. Max Baer was 32 and rated #1 heavyweight contender. He had been considered an "outstanding boxer" in NBA ratings since the Baer-Braddock title fight in 1935. And Tony Galento, a man who was called "washed up" nine years

Fifteen • The Magnificent's Last Fights, 1940–1941

earlier, was about to fight Buddy Baer. Both older men were still attracting crowds and still posing threats to the youngsters. In 1940, they were training for matches that, if they won, could pop them right back into championship matches. And Louis? No champion had risked his title once a month. He had barred no one. He didn't care where he fought, indoors or out, who refereed, or for what ticket price. He didn't trash talk before or after a fight. What a decade!

Lou Nova, April 4, 1941, Madison Square Garden, New York

In the first round Max Baer and Lou Nova sparred in the middle of the ring, but neither landed. Frustrated, Max waved Lou to come on. Max stood there with his hands on his hips. Then they engaged blows with each landing to the body and chin. Lou hit Baer with a hook on the face that knocked out his mouthpiece. They fought close at the ropes and each thought that the other had hit after the bell. They exchanged words. Nova had drawn first blood by hitting Baer on the nose.

The first and second rounds would be the only rounds Lou won until the seventh.

Baer made a game stand and struck Nova about a dozen times in the early rounds, even knocking him down with his looping overhand right in the fourth for a count of one. At that time Baer looked as though he might be the winner. Baer won the fifth.

Max Baer (left) throws his signature right hand blow at Lou Nova in their second fight, April 4, 1941.

By the sixth, both were tiring, even though Baer was still heaving roundhouse rights and had the better of it. Baer was ahead, surviving Nova's persistent left jabs to the head.

But Nova came back in the seventh and pummeled Baer in the face with his left jab, tearing up his eye, nose, and mouth. Max went into a clinch. In a half-clinch Nova threw three rights to Max's head as Max went to the body. At the end of the round, Max went to the corner with a "mouse" under his eye and his face a bloody mess. Nova had survived to make a comeback.

In the eighth, Baer fired a hard right to Nova's head but he couldn't get out of the way of Nova's jabs. Baer was still bouncing rights off Nova's head when Lou came in with a short right, and Baer was knocked down for a nine count. He then came up, but slipped to the canvas again. His right eye was completely closed. When Referee Arthur Donovan tried to stop the match, Max protested, wanting to continue the battle, but Donovan called it off at 2 minutes, 18 seconds of the eighth, giving Nova the technical win. There was always a question about a Baer match that Donovan refereed. In this one, since Max was ahead on points, did he have enough strength in the eighth to come back and finish off Nova?

Back in his dressing room, Max was amazed at Nova's endurance. "I never saw a guy who could take a punch like that." But Ancil Hoffman told reporters, "A man can't go on forever—Maxie's been fighting nearly 12 years."[20]

In his dressing room, Nova admitted, "I'll say this much for him, though, he still can hit like a ton of brick."[21]

Jack Cuddy summarized the fight: "Lou Nova continued his grave-to-glory comeback tonight by scoring a repeat technical knockout over ancient Maxie Baer in the eighth ... making shorter work of the former champion tonight than he did in 1939 when he stopped Maxie in the 11th round."[22] It was a sellout crowd of 23,000 with a gate of $95,544.17.

The headline for the *Oakland Tribune* read: "Nova Only Real Challenger for Louis: Nova Gets Up to Knock Laugh Out Of Pagliacci of Swing." Jimmy Wood of the *Brooklyn Daily Eagle* said, "At long last we are convinced that there is a heavyweight who really rates the billing of logical contender for Joe Louis' title."

At age 32, Max Baer's career as a top-ranked heavyweight was finally over. As everyone left Max's dressing room that night, writer Harold Conrad said that Max was surely going to miss those lights. But he wouldn't miss the injuries. Two of Max's fingers remained numb two weeks after the fight and he had suffered a cracked vertebra at the base of his neck. Dr. J.B. Harris in Sacramento ordered him to bed. Rumors circulated that Max had died from his injuries.

In the first four months of 1941, Mike Jacobs had grossed $1.5 million from his promotions. Madison Square Garden was averaging $38,000 a fight, with nineteen fights in four months totaling $700,000. Boxing was out of the doldrums, and Mike Jacobs was making more money than ever and still in control.

Nova would fight Joe Louis on September 29, 1941, at the Polo Grounds in New York and lose by a technical knockout in the 6th. After the fight, Nova remarked, "Sure, I respect his punching power. But I can hit pretty good myself. Let me tell you, Joe isn't nearly the killer with one punch that Max Baer was."[23]

Sixteen

You're in the Army Now! 1942 to 1945

For the former champion, chasing his dream in the 1930s to become the first heavyweight to regain the world title was over. It was time to pass the sword. He passed the dream to his brother, and now Max hoped to become one of a pair of brothers who held the heavyweight title. In 1941, the only boxing rings Max Baer actively entered were those where he served as referee.[1]

Brother Buddy stepped into Max's shoes and was given the title shot that Max could have had and that he had long struggled to acquire. Buddy dedicated his fight with Joe Louis, May 23, 1941, at Griffith Stadium, Washington, D.C., to his brother—"the grandest fellow that ever drew on a glove."[2] It would be Joe Louis's 17th title defense and the first heavyweight title bout held in the nation's capital. Expectations were hopeful for Buddy in that Damon Runyon considered him the best of all of the "white hopes."

Even though the 6-foot, 6½-inch Buddy Baer had knocked out 49 of his 60 opponents, he went into the ring with odds against him 10 to 1, including choice of referee. Ancil Hoffman said that he was "forced" to accept Arthur Donovan as the contract stipulated by Louis's management—"take it or leave it." Hoffman objected because he felt Donovan was obligated to or being paid by the Louis camp. All Hoffman told the press was, "The New York official has refereed virtually all of the champion's Eastern bouts and is 'notoriously pro–Louis.'"[3]

For Louis, Buddy was simply another fighter to knock off. The allure of the fight game was gone. "It will be good for him to get away for a year," said manager Julian Black.[4] If Louis's number for the draft did not come up by the fall, he was expected to enlist.

The fight, however, was another bizarre one for the history books.

Buddy Baer vs. Joe Louis, May 23, 1941, Griffith Stadium, Washington, D.C.

Like so many of the Baer fights with Referee Arthur Donovan at the helm, this fight was surrounded by controversy. Buddy threw or knocked the distracted champion out of the ring in the first round. Louis scrambled back into the ring at a count of 4. It was the same spill Dempsey had taken in his fight against Firpo.

In the sixth round, Joe hit Buddy in the mouth and then Buddy opened a cut at the

Buddy Baer fights Joe Louis for the heavyweight title, May 23, 1941. Louis donated his entire purse to Navy relief (Army photograph).

eye with a left and two rights, one of the few times Louis had been cut. Joe replied by dropping Buddy three times with a right, but the last one was after the bell.

Did Louis hit Buddy before, during, or after the bell? Referee Donovan said it was while the bell was sounding. Buddy's seconds, Hoffman and Klein, argued the foul and refused to leave the ring. When the bell rang for the seventh, Hoffman and Klein were still arguing with Donovan that Buddy should be given additional time due to the foul. But Donovan ruled that Buddy failed to come out for the next round.

Donovan told reporters, "I disqualified Baer because his seconds refused to leave the ring. As long as I'm refereeing, I insist that my orders be followed."[5] Hoffman said the blow came three seconds after the bell. Izzy Kline said it came ten seconds after the bell. Buddy said, "I heard the bell then was hit as I was dropping my hands. I'm not taking anything away from Joe Louis, because I believe he's a great champion, but I believe I could have taken him. I took everything he had, and he never hurt me. He was flustered after I knocked him out of the ring in the first, wasn't he?"[6] Louis simply said he didn't hear the bell.

Writer Ferguson argued that Donovan had heard the bell because he was already turned and walking toward a neutral corner. Eighteen other writers at ringside agreed that the punch landed after the bell. The question remained, could Buddy have come back to win the title? Did Donovan allow Louis to foul his way to victory?

Sixteen • You're in the Army Now! 1942 to 1945

The two judges and the timekeeper clearly disagreed with Donovan's action. Judge Jimmy Sullivan commented: "Baer was definitely hit after the bell and should have been given time to recover from the foul blow. [Louis] should have had the round taken from him." Judge Joseph E. Trigg, a noted black physician in D.C., soundly believed that "Baer was hit after the bell which was slightly muffled due to being placed under the ring.... Baer should have been given time to recover." Timekeeper Pat O'Connor: "I told Donovan that Louis had hit Baer after the bell. I'd say about three seconds after it."[7] Hoffman filed an appeal with the District of Columbia Boxing Commission.

It was expected that the commission would, at least, sanction Referee Donovan for failing to give Baer a five-minute rest break for having been fouled.

The District of Columbia Boxing Commission met on May 24 to hear the facts in the complaint that Buddy Baer was "robbed" of the world's heavyweight championship in his fight with Champion Joe Louis. Chairman Claude Owen said that Louis very definitely hit Baer after the bell. The two fight judges and the timekeeper testified that Baer had been hit about three seconds after the bell. The commissioners said they believed that the NBA would recognize Buddy as the titleholder if the Commission ruled that he had won on a foul. However, he explained that according to the rules of D.C., the referee's decision was final. Hoffman also told the board that Louis's friend and personal secretary Fred Guinyard was in Baer's corner the entire time obstructing Baer's seconds from getting in and out of the ring. In addition, Hoffman testified that Donovan was "brought in here to protect the champion."[8] The D.C. Boxing Commission ruled that the fight would go down in the record books as a disqualification against Baer in the seventh round when Ancil Hoffman refused to let Baer answer the bell.

However, Buddy was awarded a rematch for January 9, 1942. It would be Buddy's last professional fight. Some quipped that Joe Louis was now starting his second run of bums. This was, of course, inaccurate. Louis never fought bums. Many of these so-called "bums" were listed as top ten heavyweights. Louis was just that much better than everyone else.

The controversial bout was a popular movie feature and remained in the theaters even after the feature films changed.

The controversy over the Louis-Baer fight was interrupted suddenly with the news of Max Schmeling's death. Jack Cuddy, UP reporter, announced May 29 that Max had died in the Nazi cause. Promoter Mike Jacobs was shocked and said that he knew Schmeling, and he couldn't believe that he died sacrificing his life for a cause in which he didn't believe. A radio broadcast said Schmeling had died in Crete as a parachutist when he broke away from his captives on the besieged Greek island. When Max was told of his death, he was sick. "I hate war and fighting—I mean fighting to kill. I think Schmeling did too.... We were good friends.... His death is a pitiful example of what happens when men bring war to the world. In my racket we can fight and still be friends, but not in war."[9]

The *Los Angeles Times* posted Schmeling's obituary May 29, 1941, highlighting his colorful career. Everyone the press spoke to who knew or fought Schmeling was puzzled and said Max Schmeling was against the Nazi cause. The death brought the European conflict closer to home. Joe Louis announced that he was ready to join the Army.

The next day, the press reported that Max Schmeling was not dead, he was simply injured and in a hospital in Athens for an injury to his knee.

On October 3, 1941, Ancil Hoffman announced that Max was joining the Navy, intending to be a part of the physical education program directed by Gene Tunney. Several weeks after Baer's announcement, Louis went in for his military physical. Louis was ready to fight for the United States and hoped that he would be called.

By the end of October, Buddy had been signed for his rematch with Joe Louis. The 15-round title fight at Madison Square Garden would be for a Navy benefit in January 1942. Little did the boxers know then how useful the championship match would be to the Navy one month later.

December 7, 1941, "A date which will live in infamy"—President Franklin D. Roosevelt

In a surprise attack during the early morning hours over the U.S. Navy Base at Pearl Harbor, Hawaii, more than 300 airplanes from the

Max Schmeling was drafted into the Nazi Wehrmacht during World War II as a paratrooper (Library of Congress, Prints and Photographs [LC-USZ62-135660]).

Imperial Japanese Navy Air Service bombed and torpedoed eight American battleships, three cruisers, three destroyers, and 188 aircraft. Virtually the entire base, power station and shipyard were destroyed. Over 2,400 Americans were killed. During the next seven hours, during a coordinated attack, the Japanese hit other territories held by America and Great Britain—the Philippines, Guam, Wake Island, Malaya, Singapore and Hong Kong. The next day, the United States declared war on Japan. On December 11, Hitler declared war on America, and the United States was fully engaged in World War II.

Only one month prior, on November 13, Rear Admiral Adolphus Andrews, Commandant of the Third Naval District, accepted Joe Louis's offer to give the proceeds from his upcoming fight to the Navy. Buddy donated 10 percent of the challenger's purse to the New York Navy Program. After December 7, the Louis-Baer fight induced not only public appeal but patriotic zeal, as the Navy Relief Society was trying to help 11,000 cases in need.

Never before had a champion donated his ring earnings to a patriotic cause. Louis's loyalty to his country was awe-inspiring, "I'm not risking my title for nothing," he said. "I'm fighting for my country."[10] Whitney Martin said that Buddy Baer was just fighting to make a living. If he "had a viciousness to match his size, he'd be a terror."[11]

The military provided new metaphors for the sportswriters. Jack Singer wrote Buddy

Baer "should be told explicitly what to do in case of an air raid. For he will need this advice when Joe Louis starts firing those high-explosive leather bombs." He said Baer "is so large that the Navy is reported considering converting him into an aircraft carrier."[12]

Joe Louis–Buddy Baer (rematch), January 9, 1942, Madison Square Garden

For the first time, Max Baer was now being introduced as Buddy's older brother. It would take ringsiders and others some time to get used to the reversed roles. Radio announcer Wendell Willkie mistakenly introduced Buddy as Max in the ring for the title fight.

Louis left nothing to chance on that canvas, January 9. After only 2 minutes and 56 seconds of the first round, the fight was over. Buddy was battered down for two nine counts, the first from Louis's smashing rights and the second from a long left. It didn't help that Buddy had been in an auto accident 16 days before the fight, injuring his right arm and shoulder.

The net gate was $180,700.55. The Navy Relief project was given $89,092.01 from Joe Louis's entire profits, along with a portion of Buddy's and Mike Jacobs's profit.

After the Louis fight, Buddy hung up his gloves. He had not made the money that Max had, but he bought a tavern in Sacramento and went into the bar business. He smiled as he told the press, "I'll have to admit that the only way I could be champion is for Joe Louis to retire, and I wouldn't want the title that way."[13]

Max, "a favorite with everyone who knows him," hoped to be used in the Army as an entertainer, to engage personally with the soldiers during the war to help keep the morale up, to keep everyone smiling.[14] He did that and more.

Boxing arenas across the nation were closing due to declining patronage. And with the threat of wartime blackouts, it was not feasible for arenas to stay open.

Champions like Joe Louis, Max Baer, and Jim Braddock, and guest referees like Jackie Fields, Jim Jeffries, Jess Willard, Henry Armstrong and Ceferino Garcia, and Hollywood stars like Bing Crosby, Johnny Weissmuller, and Bob Hope, were all busy raising money in various benefits for the war. By March, Joe Louis had laid another million dollar asset on the Army relief table, this time with Abe Simon.

Before the year was out, the Max Baer family welcomed a second child, James Manny, on August 9, 1942. When asked if four-year old Max Jr. was going to be a fighter or an actor, Max replied, "Neither. He'll be a manager, so he'll get 99 percent of the profits."[15]

Although Japan had begun its attack on China in 1937, the Second World War was not declared a global conflict until Great Britain and France declared war on Germany in 1939. After Hitler's invasion of Poland, nations collapsed as quickly as Louis's opponents in the ring. Economic reasons were partly to blame for the late entrance of the United States into the war, although President Roosevelt had been quietly funneling war equipment to the allies prior to Pearl Harbor.

On December 15, 1942, both Buddy and Max Baer enlisted as buck privates in the U.S. Army Air Force. They were not required to serve; they were both 3-A (with a wife and child). Max had movie offers that could have kept him in Hollywood. But both Baers wanted to help win the war. The brothers sought no higher rank than private. Max explained his new circumstances, in what Oakland journalist Alan Ward called a "Baerism": "I'm being handled by the greatest manager of them all, Uncle Sam."[16]

With right palms raised, the brothers took their oath at McClellan Field, before Captain T.H. Wirak. It was noted that Buddy had to go through piles and piles of clothing and shoes in the quartermaster's corps before he could find something to fit his 6'6" frame and large feet. Eventually, both brothers had custom uniforms made to fit. Then the boys were off for three months of basic training. After training, they returned to the Fourth Air Command Headquarters in Sacramento, where they received their assignments as physical instructors for the Army Air Corps. Ward commented that Max Baer had exchanged his greeting of "Pally" to that of "Sir," while stationed at Camp Tanforan, a race track the Army had converted for Air Force training purposes.[17]

The commanding officers always had good things to say about Max: "He is a good soldier. He does his chores and asks no favors. Every soul here, from private to commanding officer, likes the chap. The same goes for his brother."[18] All of those reporters who said Max would never quit clowning and would never make it in the Army were wrong.

Max called everyone, from privates to majors, "Champ." Whenever he forgot the proper address for superiors, he called them "Champ," and they smiled proudly. Private Baer liked the food. In the military mess halls, he could eat his fill without an overseer. Writer Dan McGuire said he "downed enough GI victuals to keep a Jap battalion going for six months." Now he weighed 230 pounds, 20 over his former fighting weight. McGuire said that "Baer, for all his past sins of omission and commission, is sincere about making good in the army."[19]

At the end of January 1943, Max was sent to Ogden, Utah, to referee a series of boxing matches between fighters at Utah Army bases. When a sports editor suggested a match between Joe Louis against Max Baer and Buddy Baer against Billy Conn, because all four served in the armed forces, Max laughed. The only way he would fight Louis was to have two Baers in the ring at the same time, and he didn't think Louis's management would go for that.

By the end of February, Baer had finished basic training and was assigned to the Sacramento Air Depot Control Area Command at McClellan Field as instructor in physical fitness, boxing and wrestling, and conductor for entertainment and recreation programs at installations in California and Nevada. Many of the boxing shows that Max refereed were between different field units, training centers, and flying schools, competitions used to raise Victory Bond sales for the war effort. Bouts in which he was featured occurred at Camp Merced, April 24; Victorville in May; and Kern County Air Field, June 25 (also appearing were Jim Jeffries and Max Rosenbloom).

Beginning in October of 1943, the brothers began a nationwide tour of military bases where they gave a series of boxing exhibitions, showing techniques that had won them world acclaim. It was in the military that they finally learned how to be in the ring without killing each other. They also gave lectures on physical training for modern warfare. Max said to the men, "I'm all serious in this business. I did enough clowning in my day but we've got a war to win now. It's up to these guys out here and everywhere to get in shape for the big battle."[20] "If I can impress our boys with the necessity for constant physical training in maintaining top fighting condition, I will feel I've done an important job," Max said.[21] He was through with the ring. He had a perforated eardrum and a bad neck. In the military, he was classified as 4-F. He couldn't pass the physical if he wanted to. But he was doing his part.

Sixteen • *You're in the Army Now! 1942 to 1945* 247

Sgt. Max Baer displays his "mighty right" to pilots at Thomasville AAF, Georgia. The lieutenant colonel pilot (third from right) illustrates how young commanding officers were during World War II. November 20, 1943 (U.S. Army photograph).

The tour lasted from October 1943 to April 1944. The Baers made appearances demonstrating their boxing moves in the ring with each other. They went from Oklahoma to Connecticut to Florida to Texas to Idaho, covering 184 locations. As part of his speech, Max joked that he was the one who started the war. "It's this way," he explained, "I knocked out Max Schmeling in 1933 and made Hitler mad. The following year I knocked out Primo Carnera and made Mussolini mad."[22] True enough.

After covering most of the country, Max and Buddy returned to Sacramento, December 29. With their parents gone, Ancil and Maudie Hoffman became their adopted parents, and home was with them in Sacramento.

During their military service, soldiers often commented on how much they enjoyed working with the Baer brothers. It was said that the hour of military calisthenics had, before the Baers showed up, been about as enjoyable as K.P. (kitchen patrol) duty. The Baer brothers always made it interesting and the men enjoyed the skills they learned. And Max didn't shy away from telling everyone that had he been in better physical condition he would have won the battle against Jim Braddock. He never mentioned Joe Louis. But Army experts said that he was in better condition after being in the military than when he was defeated by Louis in 1935.

On May 13, 1943, one of Baer's extended court battles was closed after six years. The California state Supreme Court denied a hearing for a detailed accounting of funds from Baer with regard to the Jacklich brothers of Oakland. They had filed an appeal in their case against Max for 10 percent of his total earnings. Baer testified that he had already paid them off for $33,600. The suit was dismissed.

On June 5, the Baer brothers were promoted to Corporal Max Baer and Corporal "Buddy" Baer, noncommissioned officers. But military duty had taken its toll on the family. By August, Buddy's wife (Mrs. Ralpha Baer) had separated and filed for divorce from her husband. She and 2-year-old daughter Sheila went to live with her parents. The couple had been married for four years.

On March 8, 1944, Max and Mary Ellen welcomed into the family a baby girl, Maudie, named after Ancil Hoffman's wife. Max was in San Antonio but was given leave to return to Sacramento to be with his wife and two sons for the birth.

By March 17, Buddy Baer was back in the hospital in Miami, Florida (he had been treated in January for a neck injury). The problem stemmed from old ring injuries to his neck and legs which recurred during his army service. The military gave many servicemen and women an opportunity to have first-class medical care with expenses paid.

Max said that Buddy had aged considerably, that his "hair had turned almost white."[23] While Buddy was at the Ream General Hospital in Florida where he had been sent to recover, he met a nurse and soon announced his engagement to Ruth Eleanor Boynton Phillips of Palm Beach, Florida. The couple married on September 9, 1944, and made their home in Sacramento while Buddy was still in the service.

In May, after being hospitalized for a month in Florida, Buddy was released on furlough. Two vertebrae had fused in his spine, and he was told that he would never be able to fight again. Ancil Hoffman told Buddy that he had been approached by a Hollywood studio executive telling him that if Buddy was going to be discharged, they had the movie role, Superman, to give him. Buddy was not yet out of the service. The promised film did not make. Neither did his marriage. The couple was divorced on October 2, 1947. (Buddy married a third time, to a former Miss Utah. He was 33 and she was 30. They were married in 1953 and divorced in 1954.)

While Max was in the service, he was scheduled to collect on his annuity, but he postponed the payments.

Max had many boxing awards named in his honor, but one which he was particularly fond of was the "Max Baer Heavyweight Trophy" for the Nevada Golden Gloves.[24]

Joe Louis had also been on tour making speeches and performing for the military. While in London, May 9, at a troop show, he surprised everyone by naming Max Baer as the toughest opponent he ever met.[25] Even sports reporters were surprised at Joe's assessment. Most had thought that Baer had been battered in his fight with Louis and was more afraid of Joe's reputation than he was of fighting him.

Responding to Joe's comments on Baer, sportswriter Whitney Martin said, "But as for quitting while he still had a chance, we can't believe he ever did. No quitter would take the punishment he took. He might get discouraged over his outlook, but there was no fear in him of the fists of an opponent.... It will come as belated satisfaction to him to know his courage has been vindicated by the one man most in a position to be an authority."[26] Martin said that Max took enough punishment in that match with Louis to fell an ox. He added that when Max was down on one knee, yet not out of his senses, you saw the uncertainty behind his bravado, fear not of violence but of public opinion, and the "pathos of a frustrated soul."

Baer was assigned to Kelly Field in San Antonio, Texas, when Joe Louis made his kind remarks. Reporters wanted a comment from Max. They found him at the Kelly

Field Hospital in a bed awaiting routine tests. They told him what his friend Joe Louis had said. He commented that Louis should know what he's talking about. He said he knew, his friends knew, and now that public knew that he never had been a "quitter." "If I wanted to quit, I'm a good enough ham actor to take a punch going away and stay down for the count. Sure, I could have quit and been a hero for it, a 'game loser,' but nobody ever saw Max Baer flat on his back in the ring and they never will." He said he knew that some people thought he had quit to save his own hide, but if that were the case, why did he let Louis hit him so many times before he went down? He said that although he knew he didn't stand a chance against Louis, he was never frightened. "It was a little like a soldier with blank cartridges facing an opponent with live ammunition," he said. He admitted that he "lacked the killer instinct," and added that "it's easy for the fan at the ringside or in the gallery—who doesn't feel a single punch—to be bloodthirsty and yell for the kill, but boxing is supposed to be a sport, not legalized murder." And Baer certainly knew the implications of his statement.[27]

When the results of his tests came back, Max Baer, now a staff sergeant for the Army Air Force, was informed that his training camp accident, when he hit his head on the top of an 85-pound punching bag, had damaged his neck. That injury, in turn, damaged the nerves in his left arm, and as he expressed it, his arm had "dried up and lost its effectiveness."[28] The fall had also damaged his hearing.

September 2, 1944, Max reported to the Fort Logan, Denver, convalescent hospital for treatment for a back injury. By October, Baer was back in San Antonio, and by December his condition became worse. He planned to go to New York for a spinal operation that he hoped would help correct his neck and back problems that had now affected the full use of his legs and one elbow. He was back on the East Coast at Fort Jay Regional Hospital, on Governor's Island in New York Harbor, for observation and treatment, April 19, 1945. He had been in five different Army hospitals over the past 13 months. On May 17, he was cleared for duty at Kelly Field, San Antonio, Texas.

By June 1945, Buddy was also out of the hospital, where he had spent much of the last two years, and on his way to Camp Lee, Virginia, where athletes, singers and actors were trained for Special Services in the Army.

On July 14, in San Antonio, it was announced that Max Baer had received a medical discharge from the Army for injuries he had received in the ring. The news was spread throughout the country. By July 20, 1945, he was home in California on his ranch near Sacramento. With his "youthful exuberance gone," he hoped to get back into the movies. It was reported that he had two boys and one girl, and that his wife Mary Ellen was in the hospital after losing her fourth baby.

On September 23, Buddy Baer was discharged from the army. He had completed two years and nine months in the Special Services Forces. He would return to Sacramento to manage his lounge. He was said to be the tallest bartender in California.

Billy Conn, the pride of Pittsburgh, was also discharged the same day as Buddy and planned to return to the ring for a chance at Joe Louis's title. Conn had been in the service for more than three years. He was said to be managing two service boxers: Tim Dalton from Illinois and Laverne Roach from Texas.

Even though the Baers were dismissed from military service for their disabilities, Mike Jacobs would try to get Conn, Louis, and the Baers back in the ring. Mike tried to entice Baer with a $60,000 guarantee for a fight. Max didn't take the bait. Conn would get his second and last chance at Joe Louis on June 19, 1946. The financial doldrums of the 1930s were over. The bout would be a million-dollar gate ($1,564,791.11). Louis's take was $625,916.44. But he wouldn't clear a dime. After his managers and promoter Jacobs took their cuts, the government started to take its share for Louis's back taxes. (Louis failed to report or pay taxes on his boxing earnings and meager military pay during his service years. After he had donated those large boxing earnings to the Navy, this poor treatment of Louis by the U.S. government angered many boxing and non-boxing fans alike.)

After the fight, Max ran into Jack Benny, who asked Baer if he had seen the last Joe Louis fight picture. In his humorous way, he answered, "Why should I want to see the pictures? I was there the night Joe wrote the original script."[29]

By 1946, Jimmy Johnston moved out (or had been moved out by executives) of Madison Square Garden. He had ruled the Garden's promotions from 1931 to 1937, when Mike Jacobs edged into his territory with Joe Louis promotions.

The war had taken its toll on boxing. Local clubs had not reopened, and the men who had boxed or who had learned to box in the military had left boxing and entered the workforce or gone back to college on the GI Bill. Before the war, California had been a fertile ground for the business. Now, it was noted that two California boxers had to fight each other 25 times in a period of three years. There simply was not the pool of boxers that had existed before the war.

Max Baer's precious boxing earnings that had been saved in an annuity were now worth $225,000.[30] He had earned enough money away from the big rings to support his family and therefore made the decision not to tap into the annuity. He wanted to save it for a rainy day.

Seventeen

Glamour Boy in Hollywood, 1933 to 1958

Until the 1930s, prominent boxers had a financial interest in film recordings of their fights, the sales from which added to their earnings. After 1912, fight films shown in chain movie houses across the nation and elsewhere were illegal if the fights originated outside of the state where they were being shown. A federal law made it a violation of interstate commerce to transport fight films across state lines. However, the mob easily gained access to and control of the distribution of fight films in the 1930s, making lucrative income from the illegal trade. The boxers were cut out of the income. It wasn't until 1940, with the help of Jack Dempsey's testimony to Congress in 1939, that the federal law prohibiting interstate fight film commerce was unanimously repealed.

Film of the big fights appeared as second features in movie theaters until World War II.

Acting became a popular addition to boxers' careers, on stage and in the early cinema. Max Baer's early foray into acting in 1933 had been successful, and he looked to repeat that experience. During the 1930s, audiences wanted adventure and escape from the psychic and physical realities of the crushing American economy. They wanted to see something either better or worse than what they were experiencing. Max Baer gave them the rags-to-riches story of a sailor-turned-boxing contender in the form of a musical comedy in *The Prizefighter and the Lady*.

The Prizefighter and the Lady, *1933*

Hollywood had been circulating a story idea about a sailor and a lady to star Clark Gable and Myrna Loy. But when Gable could not be released from his studio contract, the story was rewritten to showcase a boxer who two-times a beautiful lady. Close at hand to the movie studios, and at the right time, was the California contender Max Baer, who had personality and good looks, and could pass a screen test.

The movie preceded the actual title fight between Baer and Carnera by seven months, and all advertising for the movie was based upon the upcoming title fight, in a See-It-Here-First campaign. The movie was a blend of fact and fiction, using boxers as the star draw. In addition to Max Baer and Primo Carnera, Jack Dempsey starred as the fight promoter. Dan Tobey, an LA ring announcer, played the movie ring announcer. The championship match at the movie's climax was made all the more memorable (and now historic footage) when champions of the ring were introduced before the camera: lightweight Joe Rivers, welter Jackie Fields, middleweight Billy Papke, and heavies Frank Moran, James J. Jeffries, and Jess Willard. Also appearing was heavyweight wrestler Strangler Lewis. Ancil Hoffman was in Max's corner wearing a suit, unusual for the boxer/manager.

The movie also cemented Baer's reputation as a lady's man. Costar Myrna Loy played the "lady," Belle Mercer, a night club singer who leaves her mob boyfriend for her true love, the boxer. After the marriage of the unlikely pair, and a series of wins that inflates the boxer's ego, Champion Steve Morgan becomes a philandering husband with an eye for showgirls. Not until after Morgan's draw with Carnera is everyone reconciled.

In this film, Max demonstrated his talent for dancing and singing, and his 200-pound agility on the gymnastic rings. The ability of such a large man to adapt a boxing work-out to a musical score was an entertaining novelty, proving that good boxers were also light on their toes. The success of this film and Max Baer's acting made it difficult for audiences to separate the fictional playboy from the factual boxing champion.

For this first film, Max had to learn stage protocol. When he heard the sound-stage bell ring for silence for his first take, he started speaking his lines. The director stopped him, "No, no, don't start acting. The bell's just to quiet things down." Maxie replied, "Brother, where I come from, if you don't start acting when the bell rings, you don't act!"[1]

The Hollywood set had never experienced anyone like Max Baer. He loved practical jokes, but his low comedy was a shock to the sensibilities of the movie types who saw themselves as gentlemen and ladies. He greeted prominent stars like Joan Crawford with "Hi, babe." He slapped MGM Producer Irving Thalberg on the back and called him "Pal."[2]

Once at a party at Jean Harlow's, Max pushed her girl-extra, fully dressed, into the pool. After a tongue-lashing, Jean made him buy the girl a new outfit. And when director W.S. Van Dyke gave a party for the publicity staff at his home, Maxie threw reporters into the swimming pool—clothes, notepads and all. When their wives complained, he threw them in too. Max loved to shake things up, and nobody in the make-believe world was going to challenge the real thing.

When the movie was released, the *Los Angeles Times* said, "Max Baer really made a good picture."[3] The Hollywood poster advertised: "Watch your pulse, Girls! A curly haired man is coming into your life. Resist him if you can. Handsome, strong and alive! Hollywood calls him the male 'MAE WEST' with a streamline chassis. Here's a picture for the ladies! A hero who can give it and take it. See Baer vs. Carnera fighting it out in the ring! Nov 24, 1933."[4]

Jack Dempsey said of Max's performance to Jimmy Cannon, "It was as if he were trying to reform [the fight racket] with his jokes, get it to be a nicer business where laughter wasn't considered wrong."[5]

Metro Goldwyn Mayer stated that the English-language version of the film with German subtitles was initially passed by the German censor on January 19. But when the dubbed German version was completed and given to the Film Chamber on March 14, MGM was told that the movie was going to be submitted to the Propaganda Ministry for an official opinion. On March 25, it was suggested that neither the German nor the English version be shown: it would not be "in the spirit of the new Germany because the chief actor is the Jewish boxer Max Baer."[6]

When reached in Lake Tahoe on March 29, 1934, for comment, Baer said, "It's not my loss but the loss of German womanhood, who are deprived of the chance of witnessing a real fighter and a great lover. The real reason is not because I'm a Jew, but because I knocked out Max Schmeling."[7]

Kids on the Cuff, *1935*

The Paramount film was to star Max Baer, Grant Withers, and child actor David Holt. Also signed in August of 1934 was Ancil Hoffman as assistant director in charge of boxing and gymnasium scenes. However, this Damon Runyon script (rewritten by Adela Rogers St. John) began falling apart when director Al Hall left in November of 1934 to direct a picture for Mae West. In January of 1935, Max turned it down for other prospects.[8] Leo Morrison was Baer's Hollywood agent at this time.

Over She Goes, *1938*

In 1937, while Max was in London for his bouts with Tommy Farr and Ben Foord, he was contracted with Associated British Pictures to play the part of Silas Morner, a charming friend turned menace from California, in the film version of the British stage musical comedy, *Over She Goes*. In the story, Silas follows his former girlfriend to London, where she attempts to rekindle an acquaintance with an ex-vaudevillian named Harry, played by John Wood. Harry has inherited the title of "Lord" upon the presumed death of his uncle, Lord Drewsden, but finds it difficult to properly enter society. He calls upon his old vaudeville cronies (played by veteran British stage comedians Laddie Cliff, Syd Walker and Stanley Lupino) for help. His pals become the target of three gold-digging women with their eyes set on a rich marriage. Meanwhile, by the evening of his arrival, Silas soon beds one of the ladies. The plot involves engagements, breaches of promise, and threats of lawsuits, sounding all too familiar to at least one of the actors. All women in the film version were the same stage cast members: Judy Kelly, Claire Luce, Sally Gray and Gina Malo. Max had some shining moments in the film, including impersonating the dead uncle.

Fisticuffs, *1938*

On June 7, 1938, Ancil Hoffman signed both Max and himself for *Fisticuffs*, a short sports film about boxing, directed by David Miller and written by Benny Rubin for MGM. Hoffman was hired to serve as technical advisor and Pete Smith, narrator. Max, the featured star, displayed his boxing techniques (some in slow motion) with sparring partners in the cast: Hank Hankinson, Mickey McAvoy, Al Morro, Jack Roper, and Charles Sullivan.

The McGuerin Series

MGM considered Max Baer the hottest product around. In February of 1942, Max signed a contract with producer Hal Roach to appear in a series of short comedy "four-

Left to right: Grace Bradley, Max Baer as Mr. Samson, and William Bendix, in *The McGuerins from Brooklyn*, 1942, renamed to *Two Mugs from Brooklyn* in 1949 (UA publicity photograph, 1949).

reelers," not quite as long as a regular "B" feature, to be directed by Kurt Neumann. Baer called them "preliminaries." But soon, he said, he would work his way up to third spot, then second, and then the semifinals. He joked, "Then I'll be on top again…. The Champ."[9] The storyline for the series was about the escapades of two taxi-cab drivers in Brooklyn, starring William Bendix as Tim McGuerin and Joe Sawyer as Eddie Corbett. Max Baer played spa owner Mr. Samson.

Filming for *Brooklyn Orchid*, the first in the series, began in June of 1942. While on the set one day, Max Jr. saw his father rip a "breakaway" telephone book in half. Later, when they returned home, little Maxie handed his dad a phonebook and asked him to replay the trick. Max admitted, "Was I in a spot!" He laughed, "I'm now up to the M's."[10]

Max was the lead for *Bridget from Brooklyn*. One problem for the director was that he had to stop the action to give Max a shave. His whiskers grew so fast that the makeup artist was called in during the middle of the day to remove his makeup, give him a shave, and then reapply his makeup. Appearing with Max were William Bendix, Grace Bradley, Marjorie Woodworth and Joe Sawyer.

Another of the short films, *The McGuerins from Brooklyn*, starred William Bendix, Grace Bradley, Arline Judge, Max Baer, Marjorie Woodworth, Joe Sawyer and Marion

Martin. The comedy romance actually premiered at the end of December 1942 and was popular through 1944.

Two Mugs from Brooklyn was remade later as *Two Knights from Brooklyn*, 1949. Max played a major role as Mr. Samson, the owner of Paradise Health Spa resort, where the two mugs, their romantic liaisons, and a mobster end up in a showdown of jealous misunderstandings.

The Navy Comes Through, *1942*

On May 21, 1942, Max signed a contract with Radio Pictures (RKO) for a featured role in *The Navy Comes Through*, directed by A. Edward "Eddie" Sutherland. It made history as the first non-documentary film to be released dealing with American combat in the Atlantic. The movie was a "sea-war picture," a red-blooded melodrama about a Navy gun crew stationed aboard a Merchant Marine freighter. The film was based on a *Saturday Evening Post* story, "Battle Stations," by Borden Chase. The action-packed screenplay, written by Earl Baldwin and John Twist, had all the right elements (both light and serious) of courage, loyalty, sacrifice, and romance. Given the choice between a boxing match with Lee Savold, June 15, in Toledo, Ohio, for $10,000 and a film contract, Max took the movie offer.

The story begins in 1940 when a disgraced Lt. Tom Sands (George Murphy) returns to Navy duty to redeem himself and is assigned to his former commander, Chief Gunner's Mate Mallory (Pat O'Brien). Mallory dislikes Sands because he has a love interest with his sister, nurse Myrna, who is on board to care for wounded crew members. She blames her brother for Sands's disgrace. Their personal conflicts continue as they near a Nazi supply ship and a nest of submarines. The *Sybil Grey* captures the supply ship, but Berringer (Max Baer) dies, refusing to leave his station in a dive-bomber attack. Berringer is covered with the American flag and buried at sea. At the last moment when the flag is removed, Jackie Cooper says, "Seems as though the flag ought to go with him." "No, kid," says Pat O'Brien, "he was here on a rain check. The flag is here to stay."[11]

Max played a serious role in 1942, as a gunner who dies aboard the ship *Sybil Grey* in the movie *The Navy Comes Through*. The movie was the first of its kind during World War II (publicity photograph).

Max said of his last scene, "I've got a scene I love with Jane Wyatt. I hope I can play it. It's dramatic. I die. It's got some wonderful possibilities."[12]

Ordinarily a sea movie would be filmed at sea. But because the Pacific was a war zone at the time, the entire film set, complete with crashing waves and explosive devices, was created from scrap metal for the movie set. The Navy loaned Officer Ben Grotsky, as technical adviser, to train eleven actors how to act like a successful gun crew. Desi Arnaz also starred as a Cuban crew member.

When Max got too close to the tiny sticks of dynamite used to simulate firing of heavy shells, he suffered a powder burn. His arm was dressed and he went back to work. In the scene where Max is killed in an explosion, he was pelted with bits of cement that felt like birdshot. Max complained lightheartedly, "I've hit the canvas more times than I did in the fight with Joe Louis!"[13] He never flinched as he was hit with the bits of flying shrapnel.

For this film, Max refused to wear stage make-up. Director Sutherland argued with him, saying that the make-up was for the benefit of the camera—that everyone knew he was no "powder puff." Max was playing a "tough" and he felt that he didn't need to wear make-up, and he didn't. Max also insisted in his contract that he not be asked to smoke or drink.

When the filming ended, the crew had a party, and Max Baer supplied the meat for the barbeque. After everyone had eaten their fill, they were told that it was not deer meat, but was from a horse. Pat O'Brien said he was certain it was another joke pulled by Max Baer, but some on the set were not convinced.

Max and other actors from the film appeared for the movie's preview October 26, 1942, on the naval base at Treasure Island, San Francisco. The preview proved very popular with its most critical audience—the Navy. The movie officially opened on November 11 at the Pantages in Hollywood. Three days after the film's California premier, it opened in New York theaters on Broadway. It was billed as a picture that paid tribute to the unsung heroic men who guard America's merchant ships and the role they play getting supplies to the fighting forces at sea. The companion feature was *The Big Street*, starring Henry Fonda and Lucille Ball. The cost of a ticket was 36 cents, plus tax.

A review of the movie found Max Baer's appearance to be part of the draw. Critic Sara Davis found him to be "a good showman; his acting is at least adequate; he had made many friends on the Hollywood film lots, and it looks as if he is in pictures to stay."[14] Writing for the *LA Times*, Philip Scheuer said the film had "a mite too much Irish belligerency to suit me, but the voyage has a feeling of technical authenticity about it (despite the overuse of 'process' shots)." He called the delayed-action detonators "original."[15]

Ladies' Day, *1943*

Ladies' Day was an RKO comedy made in 1942 about a relief pitcher for a major league baseball team in a World Series game rocked by the star rookie's romantic encounters. The two stars featured on the marquee were Lupe Velez and Max Baer. Other prominent cast members were Frank Fenton, Eddie Albert, and Patsy Kelly. Four-year-old Max Jr. made his film debut as a mascot of the baseball team.

Baer played the husband of Patsy Kelly. As the catcher, he always managed to do the

Max plays the husband of Patsy Kelly and catcher for the baseball team in *Ladies' Day*, 1943 (RKO publicity photograph).

wrong thing at the right time. The movie opened in 1945 as a second feature to *Hangmen Also Die*, starring Brian Donlevy and Walter Brennan. Cost of the double feature was 25 cents.

The film was not entirely pain-free for Max. In one scene, Patsy Kelly was supposed to kick Max in the shin. Only one leg had a shin-guard and she kicked the wrong leg several times, giving Max a number of large bumps. He enjoyed the fact that the baseball used for the scenes was really a tennis ball stitched to look like a baseball. Max was known to be the first one on set and the last to leave, for this film and others.

By the summer of 1942, Max Baer was well established as a movie actor. The parts were getting better with each picture. He was out of what he had called "the preliminary class."

Buckskin Frontier, *1943*

Baer's next film, announced August 21, 1942, was *Buckskin Empire*. When it premiered May 1, 1943, the name had been changed to *Buckskin Frontier*. It played through 1945 as a second feature. The story was set in the 1860s and was advertised as an epic of the building of the Wild West. The major conflict in the story was the infringement of the railroad on private property. Baer portrayed "Tiny," an Eastern fighter who goes west to become a mule skinner. Other actors included Richard Dix, Albert Dekker, Lola Lane, Joe Sawyer, Jane Wyatt, and Lee J. Cobb. The film was full of fistfights between the Clantons and the railroad workers. In the original script, Max whipped fifteen villains singlehandedly, and then the last villain knocked Max to the floor. Max objected ... the script was rewritten ... and the villain was knocked to the floor.

The Two Maxies in Their Vaudeville Review

Max Baer enlisted in the Army on December 15, 1942, after making *Buckskin Frontier*. When he left the Army in July of 1945, Max was paired in a vaudeville revue with another colorful figure in boxing history, "Slapsie" Maxie Rosenbloom. It was said that the boxers gave up clout for corn, but it was very successful corn. After almost two years on the road, the pair received offers from England, Australia, and Africa.

The vaudeville show first appeared in September 1945, as "Fight for Laughs," at Max Rosenbloom's lounge on Wilshire Boulevard, Los Angeles. It was reported to be a knockout comedy. Rosenbloom played the dopey, rowdy comic to Baer's straight man. The act ran nightly, and Baer was paid $1500 a week. The skit was said to wow the audience, getting big, booming belly-laughs. The comedy was "rough," like Baer's fighting style, but Baer delivered his lines with a smoothness that was quite unexpected of him. Baer's contract ran for ten weeks.

Hedda Hopper, in her column "Looking at Hollywood," said that as an emcee Max had loads of personality, that he "puts over a patter song ... does a baseball skit with Slapsy, Ben Blue and the rest of the gang. He's mellowed and happy."[16]

When the engagement ended, the public wanted more. It seemed that Max Baer had great popular appeal. Said one critic, "The old nerve-grating brashness has been tempered to an amiable, personable spirit of good fellowship which is perfectly suited to Max's new profession."[17]

Reporter Alan Ward said that Baer had "a pleasing singing voice, better than a whole lot of night club ladies with permanent waves and limp wrists." He also mentioned that Baer was getting fat and Rosenbloom getting bald. But unlike other former fighters and champions who became broke and bewildered after their ring careers, "It is gratifying to realize that here are two who not only are doing well financially but are right up in the chips."[18]

The act moved on to Miami Beach, where the pair starred at Kitty Davis's Club. The act followed Milton Berle, and they were paid $5000 a week. Ed Sullivan gave them a great review. He said they were "enormously funny." They were always trying to vie for laughs. One kitchen skit went like this: "So I tell him: Lissen, every act has to have one guy who's the boss, see. I figger I should be the boss, and you figger you ought to be the boss. Well, after this show let's you and me, or you and I, go back in the kitchen with bare hands or gloves and decide once and for all who is the head man." Rosenbloom says he is getting the laughs. Baer chafes at his role as straight man: "So you don't want to be straight man?" Rosenbloom storms, "I seen you one night with Joe Louis, and, brother, you were the straight man that night." "Kid me all you like," Max says, "but I gave Louis a good scare." Rosenbloom agrees: "Yeah, for a while he musta thought he'd killed you."[19]

Then on another occasion at Lowe's in New York, Max goes out on stage and says something entirely unwritten in the script that he thinks is funny. He says, "You now, Slapsy, if you only had my color, what a fighter youda been." "Well," said Slapsie, "That ain't in the act and what's he gettin' poisonal about anyway? So I says to him in answer, 'You know, Max, if you only had my guts what a fighter YOUDA been!' And he gets sore and walks away. I teach him everything I know and now he thinks he knows everything and he don't know nothin.' He gets sore too easy, too."[20]

By September of 1946, the vaudeville show had run in nightclubs for a year. The second year started in Rochester and ran through various cities, including in May 1947, at the Rio Cabana on Broadway. In the fall it was in Boston. The show ran nightly, usually at 8:30 p.m. with a lounge charge of $2.00. The pair always performed an encore. By November 28, 1947, the two partners had gone home to California for the holidays. Slapsie wanted to do a few movies, and then he figured if they went on the road again touring for a year, they could retire comfortably. After the holidays, the pair went back to Tampa, Florida. In June the show ran in Houston.

It was said that whenever Max was asked for an autograph after Rosenbloom had signed, and Max was given the pencil, he would erase the former's name and sign over it. The two were always inventing some prank to top each other.

Tennessee's Partner, *1948*

April 29, 1948, Max signed for producer Harry Sherman's movie *Tennessee's Partner*, starring Joe McCrea. The movie was set to film in January 1949. No surviving copy has been located.

Africa Screams, *1949*

In October 1948, Max was cast in the slapstick comedy, alternately titled *Abbott and Costello's Africa*. Charles Barton directed the 79-minute Nasbro Picture. The female star Hillary Brooke plays a woman obsessed with finding a diamond mine in the heart of Africa. She believes two acquaintances, Abbott and Costello (one named Stanley Livingston), could be useful because they know Africa from their big-game hunts.

Both Max and Buddy Baer had roles, Max as Grappler McCoy and Buddy as Boots Wilson, bodyguards for Hillary Brooke. The characters come face-to-face with lions, alligators, and a huge gorilla. One of the highlights of the movie was Max and Buddy's fistfight with each other, instigated by a troop of monkeys.

The film premiered in New York on May 4, 1949, and showed in other cities through May of 1950.

Love Is Big Business, *1949*

Max Baer starred with Claudette Colbert, Robert Young, and George Brent in the RKO film, produced by Jack H. Skirball and Bruce Manning. Filming began at the end of February 1949.

In the film, Baer portrays a professional wrestler who is thrown out of the ring onto Colbert. She then hires him as her bodyguard.

On the first day of filming, Max was flat on the canvas waiting for lights and director Bill Russell to give instructions. Again, Max refused to wear stage make-up. "I don't like that stuff on my face," he said, adding with characteristic humor, "The only thing that feels natural on my face is resin." Robert Young came back with, "I've seen you in that position many times. In fact, I was among those present one night when a fellow named Joe Louis made you kiss the canvas." Max replied, "Yeah, but every time you saw me like this you will remember that I made sure my face was in the camera, just like it is now." Young whispered to Claudette sitting next to him at ringside, "He likes to clown. He admits he clowned his way right out of the heavyweight title. But his friends will tell you that he was too much of a sentimentalist to hang onto the championship. Baer, his pals still say, lacked the necessary killer instinct."[21] Claudette said to Max, "I should think that with your good looks and talent, by now you would be a great movie star." To which Max replied, "There's still a chance. After all, there's no difference between a prizefighter and an actor—they're both hams at heart."[22]

Max played a wrestler in many of his Hollywood films. This publicity photograph shows Max's incredibly broad shoulders and impressive physique in 1949, at age 40.

Between shoots, Max played gin rummy in his dressing room. A reporter asked him about Joe Louis's career as a promoter (Louis had announced in March 1949 that he was retiring from the ring.) Max replied that he didn't think there were enough big names in the ring now to attract big crowds. "The other day I asked a sports writer to name me 15 of the 25 guys that Joe fought for the title. He couldn't do it. That just shows you."[23] Max Jr. was frequently on the set. The director let him work the boom, raising and lowering the microphone during rehearsals.

The film was banned by the Wrestling Association of America because they said the movie didn't reflect well on the sport.

Riding High, *1949*

In this Paramount movie directed by Frank Capra and starring Bing Crosby, a series of celebrities such as Bob Hope and Ingrid Bergman made guest appearances. Max Baer filmed only one day as the ex-prizefighter who marries Crosby's one-time girlfriend. Max had only one line in the script: "She likes the athletic type of man." And he said, "I only blew the line once."[24]

Robert Young, Claudette Colbert, and Max Baer star in *Bride for Sale*, 1949 (Crest publicity photograph).

Bride for Sale, *1949*

Opening at the Pantages in Los Angeles, December 22, 1949, was the 70-minute Crest Production of *Bride for Sale*, produced by Jack H. Skirball and directed by William Russell. Stars in the comedy were Claudette Colbert as the bride-to-be; Robert Young, who double-crosses her; and George Brent, who double-crosses the double-crosser. Baer portrayed a wrestler in a fixed match, and Gus Shilling portrayed the sailor.

In the film, Nora Shelley (Colbert) works in an accounting office and is looking for a mate the "scientific way," by examining his tax returns. George Brent, her boss, secretly advises Robert Young of her plot and induces him to walk out on her to teach her a lesson. Young takes her to a wrestling match, thus meeting Litka (Max Baer), one of the wrestlers.

2 Roamin' Champs, *1950*

After their long and successful nightclub act, the two Maxies made plans to produce and star in their own picture *Two of a Kind*. That picture later became *2 Roamin' Champs*, released on July 8, 1950.

After successful boxing careers and a vaudeville tour together, the two Maxies made a series of movie comedies. Pictured here are: *left to right,* Max Baer, Hillary Brooke, and Max Rosenbloom in *Skip-Along Rosenbloom,* 1951 (Walter Klein publicity photograph).

Skip-Along Rosenbloom, *1951*

Maxie Rosenbloom played the unlikely sheriff in the starring role in this Western parody written by Eddie Foreman and produced by Wally Kline. Baer played the heavy, "Butcher Baer," a name that referred to his early ring days.

In the movie, Rosenbloom, the "square shootin'" sheriff in Button Hole Bend, shoots square bullets. Hillary Brooke plays the dance-hall queen, and Jacqueline Fontaine, the schoolmarm. The film is full of stock chase scenes on horseback, various scenes searching for the map that locates a gold mine, and shoot-'em-ups by the villain, along with comedic fillers.

During filming of a street brawl, Baer was knocked out for three minutes when he hit his head on a hitching rail. Filming finished November 17, 1950, and the premier was April 18, 1951, in Rochester, New York. A sequel was proposed: *Skip-along Meets Jesse James.*

Comedy Short Subjects

Wine, Women and Bong, *1951*

A series of four comedy shorts (20 minutes) was planned for Max Baer and Max Rosenbloom at Columbia Pictures. They were to be produced by Hugh McCollum, written by Elwood Ullman, and directed by Ed Bernds or Jules White. In the first comedy of the series, the two Maxies told their wives that they would be working late so as to have a fun night on the town. The movie was released on February 22, 1951.

Mental Giants, 1951

Filming started in September of 1951 for this two-reel comedy with the same producer, writer and director as the above. It wrapped on November 7, 1951.

The Champs Step Out, 1951

In this movie, the two ex-prizefighters are hired to guard Professor Bentley's trove of antiquities at his home. Both prizefighters make passes at the professor's secretary who, in reality, is working to rob the place. She laces the men's cocktails, but they wake in time to foil her wicked plot. Shooting wrapped on February 8, 1952.

Rootin' Tootin' Tenderfeet, 1952

The fourth and final of the two-reel episodes for Columbia was written, produced and directed by Jules White. Additional stars were Dick Curtis, Jean Willes and Patricia Joiner.

In the film, the two friends, Max and Maxie, travel to the West to deliver a deed to an heiress. They find her held hostage to a saloonkeeper. The saloonkeeper has his wife accept the deed. After discovering the mistake, the friends spend the remainder of the film trying to reclaim the deed.

1940s and '50s Boxing Documentaries and Docu-dramas

In 1942, MGM produced *Sunday Punch*, a film starring former heavyweight Eddie Simms, the man whose fight with Max Baer injured Baer's hands prior to the title fight with Jimmy Braddock. Simms played Tiger Starky, the prizefighter. Others in the cast were William Lundigan, Dan Dally Jr., Jean Rogers, and a comedian identified as "Rags."

In January 1944 a movie was made about the 35-year-old history of the ring, focusing on the heavyweights from Tommy Burns to Joe Louis. The movie, titled *Kings of the Ring*, used film clips from many of the major and controversial championships and blended them into the documentary film. (Another film by the same name and same format was made in 1995, *Kings of the Ring*, which included heavyweights up to its production date. In the 1995 version, the narrator repeats the theory that Baer's losses were the result of his failure to train properly for fights after his championship.)

In 1946, producer Wally Klein talked about producing a film titled *The Life of Max Baer*, starring Max Baer himself. In 1954 Max flew to New York to sign a deal for a movie version of his life. Instead, he appeared in *The Harder They Fall*. In an interview with Don Page in 1958, Max said of his movies, "I made a lot of movies, corny ones, but they were fun. They're going to make my life story pretty soon."[25] That was September 14, 1958. Baer's life story never materialized.

By the 1950s, public interest in professional boxing grew as a result of televised matches. Erskine Johnson stated, "Women and children, as well as the men, have become excited followers of the regular fight telecasts, and prospects are they will welcome any quality picture with a prize-ring flavor."[26]

Boxers' appearances snipped from fight films and made into docu-dramas were quite popular: *Roar of the Crowd*, 1953; *They Were Champions*, 1954; and *The Joe Louis Story*, 1954. Filmed in 1953 and premiering in 1954, the story of Joe Louis starred Coley Wallace in the title role. Primo Carnera, Max Baer, Max Schmeling, Rocky Marciano, and Jim Braddock appeared in the film via actual fight footage. (*Joe and Max*, about Louis and Schmeling, was made in 2002 with a careful depiction of their two fights, along with their personal relationship and their lifelong struggles.)

In 1956, MGM was ready to start filming *The Leather Saint*, and Paramount, the life of Rocky Graziano based on the best-seller, *Somebody Up There Likes Me*. Also being considered in 1956 was the life story of two boxers, Jack Dempsey and Barney Ross.

The Harder They Fall, *1956*

The movie, based upon the book by Budd Schulberg, is an expose of the prizefight racket which reprised the roles of Max Baer fighting the giant of a man Primo Carnera in the earlier production, *The Prizefighter and the Lady*. Making his final screen appearance, Humphrey Bogart plays the sportswriter who accepts the mob's offer to publicize one of its boxers, in a thinly veiled account of the mobsters and the sportswriters and boxers they own. Bogart was cast as Eddie Willis, bought off by fight manager Nick Benko, played by Rod Steiger. Benko's protégé is a South American giant, a strongman turned boxer, Toro Moreno. The boxer is owned by a powerful syndicate, headed by Benko. The syndicate is able to manipulate their man to the championship through questionable set-ups.

Filming had been originally slated to begin in February 1949, by RKO. In December of 1949, Buddy Baer asked for the role of the giant prizefighter. By the time the movie was made by Columbia Pictures, Mike Lane had been selected for the role. Max, however, was selected to play the champion Buddy Brannen, who beats the Argentine. Jersey Joe Walcott played an equally starring role as George, the giant's trainer. John Indrisano, former welterweight, staged the realistic fight scene.

Even before the movie was filmed, the thin disguise of the title fight between Max Baer and Primo Carnera came under fire. Movie studio executives found themselves up against the wrath of the International Boxing Club run by James D. Norris, the syndicate that had taken control of Madison Square Garden. The movie was supposed to be filmed at authentic locations: Madison Square Garden, Stillman's Gym, and the Chicago Stadium. But because of the movie's unflattering look at the powerful New York syndicate, the IBC nixed those plans. The studio claimed "that the tentacles of the IBC have reached out to other fields."[27] The studio was forced to build two massive sets, dubbed "Madison Square Ranch," that would hold the boxing ring and 500 extras as spectators. When Humphrey Bogart was asked if he feared for his life because of the mob, he said that he was not worried because he was surrounded by real fighters Jersey Joe Walcott and Max Baer.

Director Mark Robson expertly created the boxing scenes. When original fight sounds were found to be inadequate, Columbia's sound man, Lambert Day, came up with the idea of hanging a ham struck by a boxer next to a sensitive mike. The film seemed

The 1956 movie *The Harder They Fall* took a critical look at boxing. Humphrey Bogart starred (in his last film) as the sportswriter; Max Baer played himself; Mike Lane, the Argentine of the Andes; Jersey Joe Walcott played Toro's trainer George; and Pat Comiskey played Dundee, the character based on Ernie Schaaf. *Left to right:* Max Baer, Humphrey Bogart, and Jersey Joe Walcott (MGM publicity photograph).

so realistic that initial audiences had to be reminded that it was "fiction." It took makeup expert Bob Schiffer eleven hours to apply chocolate syrup, berry stain and glycerine to make the Argentine look like he had slashes, cuts and bruises across his face and a broken jaw.

Bogart fearlessly commented on the social impact of the film, saying that he realized "a lot of fight fans are as interested as I am in seeing the bad elements in boxing cleaned up."[28]

When the movie opened in theaters in 1956, Primo Carnera sued Columbia Pictures and the book's author Budd Schulberg for $1.5 million, charging that both products were an invasion of privacy causing him scorn and ridicule and the loss of respect. The suit claimed that the caricature of Carnera was identified by his unusually large build and was characterized as stupid and unable to conduct his own business affairs.

When asked to comment on the film, Jersey Joe Walcott said, "It took my two fists and 20 years of hard work to cash in…. Maybe this movie will be able to clear out some of boxing's bad." The final message of the movie was: "Boxing in the U.S. must be cleaned up, even if it takes an act of Congress to do it."[29] It was profitably advertised as "The Picture They Tried To Stop!"

The movie was a bookend to Baer's very popular initial film, *The Prizefighter and the Lady*, in that both films captured the unsavory aspects of boxing that he and others had to deal with during their careers. Both movies appealed to audiences larger than boxing fans.

The fictional portrayal of Max Baer as a psychopathic, proud ring killer of Gus Dundee (Frankie Campbell) in this movie would be the one adopted for the movie about the famous Baer-Braddock fight, *Cinderella Man*, made in 2005.

Utah Blaine, 1957

After *The Harder They Fall*, Max was signed to star with Rory Calhoun in the Katzman production of *Utah Blaine* directed by Fred F. Sears for Columbia Pictures, July 1956. The movie premiered in April 1957. Max played Gus Ortman, the town strongman and owner of the dry goods store. Ortman is tested in a fistfight with Blaine and then joins forces with Blaine to save the 46 Connected Ranch from a land-hungry gang of thieves. Ortman is shot, and while recovering he tries to save the ranch-owner's daughter and is shot again and killed. One character says, "If he couldn't use his fists he was beat." This was a good performance by Baer in a classic Western of the period three years before he died.

Once Upon a Horse, 1958

This Western comedy written, directed, and produced by Hal Kanter stars Dan Rowan and Dick Martin as two incompetent rustlers who try to ply their trade in Empty Cup, Colorado. Max plays Ben, and Buddy Baer has a role as Beulah's brother.

The Syndicate, 1968

By October 2, 1958, Max had signed for one of the leads in *The Syndicate* for the King Brothers. "I play one of the brains in this story of the underworld."[30] Unfortunately, Max died before the movie was eventually made. It premiered ten years later, in 1968.

Cinderella Man, 2005

Ron Howard directed this Universal Pictures historical drama about the story of Irish James Braddock, played by Russell Crowe. In the film, Braddock is considered a "washed-up" boxer, struggling to feed his family during the Depression, when he returns to the ring to beat the champion Max Baer. Baer is played by Craig Bierko, who looks remarkably like the dark, curly-headed champion in his younger days. Renée Zellweger co-stars as Mae Braddock; Paul Giamatti plays Joe Gould, and Bruce McGill is Jimmy Johnston.

Boxing historians have never recovered from the character assassination of Max Baer in this movie portrayal. Max first appears in a scene at a hotel room, not with one woman but with two, where he verbally abuses his consorts, yelling, "Shut up!" Back at his MSG office, matchmaker Johnston shows Braddock film footage of a dying Frankie Campbell and warns Braddock not to accept the fight with the brutish killer, Max Baer. Later, at a luncheon at MSG, a surly Max confronts the Braddocks and warns Mae, disrespectfully, "You're too pretty to be a widow. Maybe I can comfort you after he's gone."

While the film deservedly remains in the list of all-time best boxing films, the complications of the real story are hinted at in the movie, but missed in its conclusion. Prior to the Lasky fight, Joe Gould suggests to Jimmy Johnston that should Braddock happen to win, Johnston could make a killing. A suspenseful pause occurs in the movie while ring spectators wait for the results of the Lasky-Braddock fight. Johnston smiles knowingly (implying a set-up) when it is announced that the "decision" goes to the scorecards, and it is "unanimous" for Braddock. (For most viewers, this backstory is entirely missed.) Unlike *The Harder They Fall*, the "killings" made by the racketeers of the era are not directly examined in the film. But the brutish character of Baer, who is decidedly proud of his "killer" reputation, is taken from the earlier film. The final fight scene emphasizes Braddock's broken ribs, but nothing is said of Baer's bum hands. It is, after all, an underdog story about James Braddock.

Television

During the early years of the 1950s, television was a novelty and a luxury in homes. Like the radio broadcasts, shows were both national and local; locally produced programs featured local people and local news. The broadcasts were in black and white and went off the air at midnight with the national anthem. Shows resumed at 6 a.m. Saturday kid shows featured cartoons and locally produced shows for children, many times inviting local children on set. Television broadcasting was an experiment, initially operated by the large radio networks and frequently called "radio pictures."

Max said about television that he wished it had been in general household use when he was fighting his way to the championship. He said that if television had been around he would have had the presence of mind "to mention my sport's product while taking a count!" "He knows he'd have been a TV sensation. He's so right," said Alan Ward, sports editor in 1952.[31]

Max Baer starred, hosted, and made many guest appearances on television during the last decade of his life:

Milton Berle Show, NBC, October 31, 1950, and October 4, 1958.
Texaco Star Theater (which ran from 1948 to 1956). Baer starred in 1 episode in 1950. (Over the course of the broadcast, only three sports figures appeared on the show: Jack Dempsey, Jackie Robinson, and Max Baer.)
You Asked for It, September 20, 1951.
Dennis Day Show, Sacramento, February 20, 1952.
Abbott and Costello Show, *Killer King* or *Killer's Wife*, 1953.
Perry Como Show, January 7, 1956.
Arthur Murray Party (dance teacher), June 21, 1956, a dance competition among four boxers: Max Baer, Maxie Rosenbloom, Rocky Graziano, and Jake LaMotta.
So This Is Hollywood, February 5, 1956, Los Angeles, Baer appears with Art Aragon and Johnny Indrisano.

Sheena, Queen of the Jungle (25 episodes made for TV by ABC, 1955–1956, shot in Mexico City, starring Irish McCalla). Max was a white hunter in 3 episodes.

Kendall, signed for 2 episodes, producer William Nassour.

Playhouse 90, a series of 90 plays written by Rod Serling for CBS. *Requiem For a Heavyweight*, October 11, 1956, starring Jack Palance, Keenan Wynn, Kim Hunter, Max Baer, Maxie Rosenbloom and Ed Wynn. Palance played the role of the broken-down prizefighter who is nearly destroyed by his loyalty to his manager. When Max was in New York for a photo shoot for the picture, his hulking frame dwarfed those of his co-stars. The photographer asked Baer to kneel in front of the group. He said, "The last time I was in this position I was in Madison Square Garden and got $200,000 for it."[32] (Made into a feature film in 1962 starring Anthony Quinn.)

Make Room for Daddy, aka *The Danny Thomas Show* (TV series starring Danny Thomas, 1953–1965). Max Baer starred February 3, 1958 (Episode 18), in "Rusty the Bully." Max teaches Rusty to box, but when Rusty becomes the bully, father Danny and Max have to find a way to teach Rusty how not to fight.

Max Baer Show, an hour-long variety show airing daily from 11:00 pm. to midnight from Los Angeles on KHJ, Ch. 9. The show premiered September 1, 1958, on the same channel as *The Ed Sullivan Show*. Max talked about his ring wars and interviewed sports figures. Written into his contract, "My first guest will be the loser of the Patterson-Harris fight—him I KNOW I can get."[33] Max said about the show, "I want to say nice things about people. I want to find out what they like, what they want to do in life, nice things. I'm not going to be like some of these other guys who insult people; anybody can do that."[34] Some of his guests were Jack Dempsey, singers Billy Daniels and Kitty White, actors Caesar Romero and Jimmy Durante, and Gov. Goodwin Knight. The show ran three months before it was canceled January 15, 1959, and replaced with an 11 o'clock nightly rerun of a filmed bowling series.

Baer's Bar or *Maxie's Bar*, a CBS pilot made beginning December 2, 1958, with Arline Judge (glamour girl of the 1930s making her comeback in TV). The show was rated second in the lineup for 1959. The story consisted of these two older kids (Maxie and Arline) who run a soda fountain for teenagers. They interact and follow the stories of the teenagers. (The TV series projected an early model for the very successful TV comedy series, *Happy Days*.) This was Baer's last pilot.

The Untouchables (1959–1963). March 31, 1960, *The Doreen Maney Story*, Max played a boxer; aired after his death.

Sports on TV

Wrestling: the first wrestling bouts on TV, Valley Garden Arena, Los Angeles, February 7, 1953, Max refereed.

Boxing: nationally televised in New Orleans, January 2, 1955, Max refereed Cisco Andrade vs. Ralph Dupas.

- Televised November 18, 1959, in Phoenix on ABC, Max refereed Zora Folley and Alonzo Johnson.
- Gillette Cavalcade of Sports (1 episode, 1959).

Livestock auction: Because of his early knowledge of cattle, Max served as emcee and auctioneer for the nation's largest sale of registered beef bulls, February 9, 1957, televised live from the Cliff House in San Francisco.

Radio

Max broadcast several radio shows from his training camps, such as *Taxi*, 1934, and *Lucky Smith*, 1935.

He also appeared on various radio shows, such as the *Hall of Fame*, June 23, 1934; the *Al Jolson* show, April 6, 1935; and the *Eddie Cantor Show*, Nov. 13, 1947.

Max broadcast two radio shows on Sacramento stations in 1951 and 1952. Both were broadcast live from various restaurants in the Sacramento and San Francisco areas. *The Max Baer Show* aired daily over KFBK, an affiliate of the American Broadcasting Company. His show *Sunday Breakfast* aired live on Sunday mornings. His broadcasts went to seven Western states, Hawaii and Canada.[35]

Max Baer in his last entertainment publicity shot, 1956.

Stage

Hi-Ya Gentlemen, 1940

Stage debut, December 3, 1940. Max sang and danced in the musical about a college campus agent for a horse-race betting syndicate. The off–Broadway play ran for two weeks in Boston.

Casey at the Bat, 1952

August 29, 1952, Stockton, California. Max played the role of the mighty Mudville slugger who struck out. The play opened in Stockton because it was once called Mudville, and Stocktonites claim that a baseball game played there was what inspired Ernest L. Thayer (an *Examiner* reporter) to write his famous poem. The poem was published in *The (San Francisco) Daily Examiner*, June 3, 1888.[36]

Eighteen

Maximilian's Last Act

Max's reputation seemed to loom larger with each passing year. "Gene Tunney, Jim Braddock and Jack Sharkey," reported Alan Ward, "could walk down the street and be identified by only a few passersby. Not Baer, Dempsey or Louis."[1] By 1955, only two decades after he lost the championship to Braddock, one newspaper incorrectly reported that Max had defended his title 48 times.[2]

To children Max stood 12 feet tall. He loved kids. "I like to work for the youth of America who'll be running this country in the future, and I hope better than we are."[3] Ancil Hoffman remarked that Max was always "doing that which is closest to his heart—helping young people."[4]

Once in 1933, a kid reporter, thinking he was a young Grantland Rice, interviewed Max. Max gave him the entire afternoon. "Where do you live?" asked the prizefighter.

"Brooklyn," the boy replied.

"Rudy," Max directed, "Give 'im five dollars for a cab."

The kid declined. He had a nickel for the subway. The kid was Red Smith, who later became a sports reporter for the *New York Tribune*.[5] He never forgot Max's kindness.

Max was always boxing's star on the invited guest list. He rode in untold numbers of parades, and was the featured speaker at a myriad of luncheons, testimonial dinners, and 2-bit breakfasts. He played golf for any number of charities: for the Crippled Children, the Hard of Hearing Society, the Damon Runyon Cancer Tournament, and the March of Dimes. He emceed a TV marathon, setting a financial record in 1953 for the Cerebral Palsy Foundation. He hosted talent shows and beauty pageants, performed skits at baseball games, emceed fashion shows, opened shopping malls, danced the rumba for a dance club, sold ice cream "as a breakfast food" for the National Association of Retail Ice Cream Manufactures at their 1957 convention, and even starred at halftime in front of 10,000 fans at the first Copper Bowl football game in Tempe, Arizona, with old-time greats of the gridiron, December 20, 1958.

He refereed professional boxing and wrestling matches: for Gene Fullmer, Willie Pep, Zora Folley, Rocky Marciano, Archie Moore, and numerous professional wrestlers, such as Tony Rocca. He refereed fights for Golden Gloves, police departments, fire departments, the Navy, and numerous charitable organizations. He always wanted to show his audience that he was still athletically nimble, and, in his signature move, he would exit the ring by jumping over the ropes.

Max didn't touch his annuity because he was making enough money to support his family by refereeing and doing other miscellaneous activities. Baer even had a little money

Max loved sporty convertible automobiles and appeared in countless parades. Max Jr. (in sunglasses) and Jimmy in back seat in Orangevale (bordered by Hoffman's property), 1949.

to invest in the Texas oilfield business. He purchased an interest in a 15-well operation in Archer County, 35 miles from Wichita Falls—the same ranchland where Tex Rickard had lived, started on trail drives, and served as sheriff. (Had Rickard known of the Texas-sized gold-strikes in oil in his own back yard, he might not have gone fortune-seeking in Alaska.) Nine miles from Baer's drilling operation, Jack Dempsey and Gene Autry made strikes.

On April 18, 1950, doctors told Max that his years in the ring had set up a condition called "an athletic heart." He was told to take it easy—to curtail his activities and "walk slowly and keep from climbing stairs"—or he would not live to see another day.[6] He was only 41 years old.

For the next few months, Max went home to Sacramento and took it easy. Max Jr. had a paper route, and Max decided to deliver

Referee Max Baer awarded light-heavyweight champion Archie Moore a technical knockout in the fifth round over Sonny Andrews (of Los Angeles) in Sacramento, March 3, 1953. Coleman Studio.

papers with him six evenings a week from the easy chair of his convertible's driver's seat. It was just another example of his humorous way of addressing life.

Then he thought about wrestling. He went to sports doctor Vincent Nardiello, who checked him over and said he was "the finest physical specimen he ever jabbed with a stethoscope."[7] But one unnamed source said that when Baer tried to work out, he became winded and couldn't go on. After ten minutes of headlocks and flying tackles, he gave up the idea of a wrestling career, saying, "This ain't for me!"[8]

Nevertheless, on September 8, 1952, eighteen years after their original title-transferring battle, Max Baer met Primo Carnera in a four-round boxing match, billed as the "Exhibition of the Century," at the Wilmington Bowl, Long Beach, California. Their first battle made $428,000; this one was not expected to gross more than $4280. Both men looked in good shape, and both appeared to do more clowning than fighting, in 16-oz. gloves. Referee Reggie Gilmore called the exhibition bout a draw.

Max continued to referee wrestling matches, including one between Primo Carnera and Warren Bockwinkel in California. He refereed bouts in Canada as well as the Western part of the United States.

It must have been a bit of slap in the face when it was announced that Joe Louis had signed to make a movie of his life, *The Joe Louis Story*, in 1952, when for so many years the topic of a life story of Max Baer had been toyed with in Hollywood but never made.

By the early '50s, other giants of boxing had opened successful bars in New York: Jack Dempsey's Restaurant at 8th Ave. and 50th St., Braddock's Inn at 157 West 49th St.; and Mickey Walker's Bar and Grill at 8th Ave. and 49th St., all near the Garden.

While Buddy was comfortable running a bar, Max Baer was more of an entertainer. He had a daily job as a disc jockey in Sacramento. His radio job, along with refereeing wrestling matches and various nightclub work, earned him $25,000 per year. One day when he was leaving his radio station, he walked outside where a small crowd had gathered. Among the group was William R. Mattox, a Republican candidate for Congress. The politician called Max an unprintable name. Max never liked arguments. He tried to stop them. But if someone tried to take him on, they were going to lose.

"I wish you wouldn't call me names," Max said.

"You told the newspapers I was a liar," said Mattox.

"If I did, I'm sorry, but I don't think I did."

The politician dropped his briefcase and put up his dukes, ready for a fight.

Max picked up the briefcase and flung it into the man's chest. "Don't swing on me because if you do you might run into something that wouldn't be my fault, would it?"

About that time, Police Captain Walter Sked approached and asked the men to leave, saying they were attracting a crowd. Max replied to his friend the policeman, "I like a crowd. I never liked to work before an empty house." Max was the master of all comebacks.[9]

Alan Ward said, "To walk down the street with the 250-pounder is to hear dozens of greetings from men, women and kids. Every 10 feet the big fellow pauses to shake hands and exchange pleasantries. Max probably doesn't know the name of one person in 100 who greets him, but his response is booming and friendly. He calls all men 'Champ.' Most men salute him the same way.... He has a genuine love of people, and will go far out of his way to demonstrate that affection. His effusiveness at times has been mistaken for juvenility. It isn't. He's a good business man, a solid citizen."[10]

When he couldn't box or wrestle, he played baseball. In 1958, he toured six Southwestern cities playing celebrity baseball matches.

Ever the prankster, Max Baer (center) puts "devil horns" behind Tony Galento's head (left) and his hand on Joe Louis's shoulder (right) as the boxing greats pose for a serious picture ringside at the Rocky Marciano–Archie Moore fight, September 21, 1955.

He lived a mile a minute. "To retire is to deteriorate," he told writer Aline Mosby.[11] "Yeah, the champ life has been good to Ol' Max."[12]

His fan mail came from all over the world, some of it addressed simply, "Max Baer, the Champ, U.S.A."[13]

Max was approaching 50; his hair had grayed and he weighed 255 pounds. He was still married and financially sound, about to draw on his annuity that he had let grow. He would finally draw $2500 a month at his next birthday. He was mellow and pensive. Money wasn't what made him a rich man. He said, "I sit down in my room at home and look at all the pictures of the people I knew and loved. There's Al Jolson—he introduced me to Ancil Hoffman—and Marie Dressler, and Fannie Brice and F.D.R. They're all gone now—but in this room they're still with me. I'm a rich man for having known them, for having the sincerity of my friends and the health of my loved ones."[14]

Maxie was advertising for his friend Larry Cameron's car agency in Sacramento and was about to launch a television show of his own from Los Angeles, called *The Max Baer Show*.

Frequently, his memory failed him. Whenever he would run into a celebrity he would greet them with, "God love ya, Champ." Then he would ask, "Who was that?" About his terrible memory he would reply, "I was lucky. I was strong and could take a good punch to the head." But he always came back with a wisecrack, "Me punchy? I'll tell you this, I walk around carefully so I won't bump my head. If I ever knock myself conscious I'll starve to death."[15]

Toward the end of his life he said, "Some people had me wrong. I never harmed anyone outside of the ring. I loved people." Another thing he said that he was proud of: "When I got married, people said it would never last. Well, I've been married 25 years."[16]

On Tuesday, October 28, 1958, London's Harringay Arena was scheduled to close after its last fight. It was if it had seen the last of a great era. The main event was British lightweight champion Dave Charnley against Carlos Ortiz of New York. Celebrities scheduled to bid farewell ringside were Gus Lesnevich (former light-heavyweight champ), Max Baer, and Henry Armstrong (feather, light, and welter champ turned Baptist minister). Anyone who had ever fought there was invited to "be on hand for the fistic funeral."[17] The poor economy had claimed the famous stadium. It was only 22 years old, and had seen over 600 fights.

On Sunday, January 25, 1959, on his way to Denver to referee Zora Folley (third-ranked challenger to Floyd Patterson) vs. Alex Miteff in a ten-round bout, Maxie's flight was delayed due to a snowstorm in Reno. As he waited in the airport for the weather to clear, he lost some coins in a slot machine. He picked up the entire machine, shook it, and then set it back down. Some kids, wide-eyed, watched the man with such strength. He smiled and tossed them his remaining quarters. His parting threat to the slot machine: "I'll be back through Saturday!"[18] After Denver, he went to Phoenix to referee the L.C. Morgan–Joe Miceli ten-round.

While in Phoenix, Max missed his son's first boxing match. At California's Santa Clara University, Max Jr. had taken up boxing and had signed for his first match with Stanford's Trev Grimm, February 9, 1959. Max Sr. had no idea his son was boxing. When he heard that Max was knocked out, he sent orders to him to "knock it off." He didn't want him boxing.[19] The next week, Max Jr. beat Tom McNamara from the University of San Francisco, when his opponent failed to come out for the third round.

A dinner celebrating Max's life was planned for late in the year 1959, like the dinner at the Waldorf-Astoria honoring the life of Jack Dempsey. In charge of planning the grand fete was former Canadian rodeo rider Robert "Larry" Cameron, "Calgary Red," the Sacramento car dealer. Two thousand plates were planned for celebrities and friends: former boxing champions, other sports figures, motion picture and TV stars, and others. For reasons unknown, the testimonial dinner was postponed to June 1960. It would be too late.

On the afternoon of Tuesday, November 17, 1959, Max returned to Phoenix to referee the nationally televised bout between Zora Folley and Alonzo Johnson. Max was the heaviest he had been, at 261. Because the event was a formal affair to raise money for the Cystic Fibrosis Foundation, Max was asked to wear a tuxedo on November 18. He asked playfully if the contestants were also going to wear tuxedos.[20]

The day of the bout, Max thought he had a "flu bug," so he took a long nap in the afternoon. That night, he was his typical "jovial self." Folley won a unanimous decision.

After everyone shook hands, Max jumped over the ropes. While a bit portly, he seemed in fine form. Max scored the fight 99–96 Foley. Jimmy Cannon said, "Those ten rounds didn't help that heart which was always in the wrong body."[21]

The last picture Max took outside the ring was with a child in a wheelchair at the Phoenix airport. Max returned to California and checked into the Hollywood Roosevelt Hotel, Thursday, November 19. Newspapers reported that he was in Los Angeles to make a commercial.

One-time sparring mate and sportswriter Curley Owen, from Garden Grove, California, reported an additional reason for Max's being in Los Angeles. He said that when his son Ronnie was five, Max told him that he would give him a car when he turned eighteen. On Friday night, November 20, Ronnie was playing in his high-school football game. Max appeared before the game with a foreign-built sports car and presented it to the eighteen-year-old. Baer stayed to watch the game. Max's friends that night said that he was suffering from a cold and had mentioned that he had experienced two mild heart attacks recently.

Early Saturday morning, November 21, Max called the hotel switchboard to ask for a physician, saying that he thought he had suffered a heart attack.[22] Dr. Edward S. Koziol went to Baer's room at 8:15 a.m. and found him sitting on the bed. An ambulance was called.

By 9 a.m. the doctor wanted Max to go to the hospital, but Max declined, saying that he had had these minor attacks before and he needed to get to a phone to cancel his television appearance. There were no jokes told that morning. The doctor gave him medication, and a fire department rescue team arrived within minutes and administered oxygen. Baer complained of severe chest pain as the doctor was talking to him. Then, he uttered his last words: "Oh, God, here I go." He slumped on his left side, turned blue, and lapsed into unconsciousness. Max Baer was dead in a matter of minutes. The cause of death: a coronary thrombosis.

Headline news that Maxie Baer had died was reported worldwide. He was 50. Max Jr. was 21, James was 17, and Maudie was 15.

Ancil Hoffman was now a Sacramento County Supervisor, still living on his property at Fair Oaks. When he was notified of Baer's death he remarked, "He was so generous and good to everybody. I used to tell him he was his own worst enemy, but he just kept going the way he always did. I guess there was no changing him."[23]

The last photograph taken of Max Baer, four days before he died after refereeing the Zora Folley fight, 1959. He knelt on one knee to talk to a child sitting like a king in his wheelchair. Max was 50.

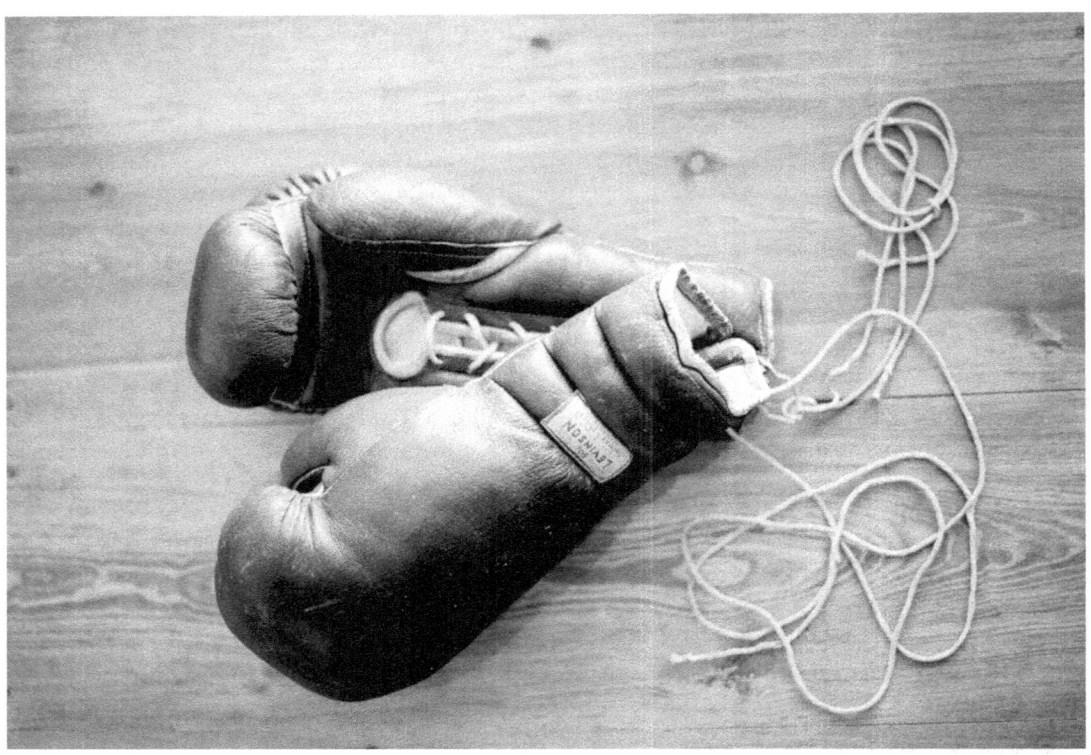

Max Baer gave both pairs of the Sol Levinson sparring gloves to Ike Aycock (photograph by Jori Turpin).

The body was taken to Edwards & Cummings Mortuary in Pasadena and later placed on a private plane to Sacramento. His funeral was set for Tuesday, November 24.

Max Baer was given military honors. His funeral service was at 2 p.m. at the Culjis Mortuary, followed by a graveside service at St. Mary's Cemetery. Attendance was the largest number ever gathered in Sacramento for a funeral. Jack Dempsey, Joe Louis, and Henry Armstrong, many aging boxers, and 1500 of his friends attended. The Rev. Patrick McHugh, pastor of the Holy Spirit Roman Catholic Church, read a brief service in the chapel and again at the Catholic Mausoleum. There was no eulogy. Baer was not Catholic, but his wife and children were.

The graveside service was conducted by the Veterans of Sacramento. An honor guard presented Mrs. Baer with the flag from his bronze coffin. There was a salute from a military rifle squad and then a lone bugle played taps.

Buddy was on a film location in Germany and could not be there. When notified of his brother's death, he "wept like a baby."[24] When it was all over, Baer's sparring partner and publicist Curley Owen "wept as he took down Max's gloves from a huge white floral piece."[25]

No testimonial dinner was given Baer and no film of his life was made. He never touched the boxing earnings that he had socked away in that famous annuity for his future, but it took care of his family.

Jimmy Cannon said, "It isn't because he was a famous pug who once was heavyweight champion of the world that we should cherish his memory. We should honor him because he delighted us with his personality."[26]

His jokes were his gifts. And for the people whose lives he tried to make better, he was the jolly St. Nick, to be remembered not for his short life but for his generous heart: in the twenty-dollar bills he so frequently handed to the down-and-outers, in the palatial mansion and its luxury furnishings he gave to his parents, in the expensive foreign car that he bought for an eighteen-year-old son of a lifelong friend, and in the expensive boxing gloves he handed to his "Old pal."

Postscript

Buddy Baer became an actor, appearing in television series and epic-scaled movies, like *Quo Vadis*. Until his death, July 18, 1986, at age 71, he believed his world title had been stolen by referee Arthur Donovan. He is buried at Sierra Hills Memorial Park in Sacramento.

Mary Ellen Baer never moved from Sacramento. She died on April 30, 1978, and is buried at St. Mary's Catholic Cemetery and mausoleum.

Children: The year after Max's death, Max Jr. signed an acting contract with Warner Brothers. At age 21, he was 6'5" weighed 218 pounds. He became a successful actor and director, and is perhaps best remembered for his role as Jethro in the TV series *The Beverly Hillbillies* (1962–1971). At the time of this writing, Max lived in Reno and Maudie in Sacramento. Brother Jimmy died in 2009, one month before turning 67. He is buried at St. Mary's in Sacramento.

J. Hamilton Lorimer, the "Millionaire Kid," Max Baer's early manager, died after a long illness at his home in Oakland on November 3, 1941. It was said the stress of managing Baer and negotiating with promoters was too much for him. He was 46.

Ancil Hoffman retired from the boxing business to become a gentleman farmer on his Fair Oaks property. He served on various school boards and city councils in the Sacramento area and lived to be 91.

Mary K. Brown's greatest notoriety was being Max Baer's girlfriend in 1935. After Max's death, she went into seclusion and died of a "heart attack" one year later in her New York Park Avenue hotel room at the Delmonico. She was 45.

James J. Braddock retired to his home in North Bergen, New Jersey, the home that he bought with the money earned from the Baer fight. He died on November 29, 1974, at the age of 68.

Joe Gould served the Army in 1944 at Camp Shanks, New York, as the facilities director. He was court-martialed for defrauding the government of military equipment. He was sentenced to three years in prison and fined $12,000. He died in 1952, at the age of 53.

"Uncle Mike" Jacobs suffered a stroke in 1946; retired in 1949, at the age of 66; and died in 1953, at the age of 73.

Joe Louis joined the forces of James Norris at Madison Square Garden after Mike Jacobs retired. Louis died of a heart attack in 1981, one month before turning 67. He is buried at Arlington National Cemetery.

Sportswriter **Art Cohn** of Oakland, whose writing style was to "call a spade a steam shovel," was generally disliked by the boxers. After his bout with Max, Les Kennedy came to Cohn's office to "punch Cohn in the nose." Cohn died in 1958 in a plane crash near Grants, New Mexico, that also took the life of Mike Todd (married to Elizabeth Taylor). Writer and film producer Todd had been in Albuquerque promoting *Around the World in 80 Days*. Cohn was 49.

Appendix: Ring Record

E (exhibition), E-A (Army exhibition), W (win), L (loss), KO (knockout), TKO (technical), D (draw), ND (no-decision), DQ (disqualification), Dec (Decision)

Date	Opponent	Location	Result
1929			
May 16	Chief Caribou	Stockton, CA	W KO 2
June 6	Sailor Leeds	Stockton, CA	W KO 1
July 4	Tillie Taverna	Stockton, CA	W KO 1
July 18	Al Red Ledford	Stockton CA	W KO 1
July 24	Benny Hill	Oakland, CA	W Dec 4
July 31	Benny Hill	Oakland, CA	W Dec 4
Aug. 28	Al Red Ledford	Oakland, CA	W KO 2
Sep. 1	Joe Simoni	Oakland, CA	E
Sep. 4	Jack McCarthy	Oakland, CA	L DQ 3
Sep. 25	Frank Rudzenski	Oakland, CA	W KO 3
Oct. 2	George Carroll	Oakland, CA	W TKO 1
Oct. 16	Chief Caribou	Oakland, CA	W TKO 1
Oct. 30	Alex Rowe	Oakland, CA	W KO 1
Nov. 6	Natie Brown	Oakland, CA	W Dec 6
Nov. 20	Tillie Taverna	Oakland, CA	W KO 2
Dec. 4	Chet Shandel	Oakland, CA	W KO 2
Dec. 30	Tony Fuente	Oakland, CA	W KO 1
1930			
Jan. 15	Tiny Abbott	Oakland, CA	L DQ 3
Jan. 29	Tiny Abbott	Oakland, CA	W KO 6
Apr. 9	Jack Stewart	Oakland, CA	W KO 2
Apr. 22	Ernie Owens	Los Angeles, CA	W Dec 10
May 7	Tom Toner	Oakland, CA	W TKO 6
May 28	Jack Linkhorn	Oakland, CA	W KO 1
Jun. 11	Buck Weaver	Oakland, CA	W KO 1
Jun. 25	Ernie Owens	Oakland, CA	W KO 5
July 15	Les Kennedy	Los Angeles, CA	L Dec 10
Aug. 11	KO Christner	Emeryville, CA	W KO 2
Aug. 25	Frankie Campbell	San Francisco, CA	W TKO 5
Dec. 19	Ernie Schaaf	New York, NY	L Dec 10
1931			
Jan. 16	Tom Heeney	New York, NY	W KO 3
Feb. 6	Tommy Loughran	New York, NY	L Dec 10
Apr. 7	Ernie Owens	Portland, OR	W KO 2
May 5	Johnny Risko	Cleveland, OH	L Dec 10
July 4	Paulino Uzcudun	Reno, NV	L Dec 20

Date	Opponent	Location	Result
Aug. 9	Buddy Baer	Neptune Beach, CA	E ND 1
Aug. 9	Abel Fererro	Neptune Beach, CA	E ND 2
Aug. 9	Eddie Jorge	Neptune Beach, CA	E ND 2
Sep. 23	Jack Van Noy	Oakland, CA	W TKO 8
Oct. 21	Jose Santa	Oakland, CA	W KO 10
Nov. 09	Johnny Risko	San Francisco, CA	W Dec 10
Nov. 23	Les Kennedy	Oakland, CA	W KO 3
Dec. 30	Arthur De Kuh	Oakland, CA	W Dec 10

1932

Date	Opponent	Location	Result
Jan. 29	King Levinsky	New York, NY	W Dec 10
Feb. 22	Tom Heeney	San Francisco, CA	W Dec 10
Apr. 26	Paul Swiderski	Los Angeles, CA	W TKO 7
May 11	Walter Cobb	Oakland, CA	W TKO 4
Jul. 4	King Levinsky	Reno, NV	W Dec 20
Aug. 31	Ernie Schaaf	Chicago, IL	W Dec 10
Sep. 26	Tuffy Griffiths	Chicago, IL	W TKO 7

1933

Date	Opponent	Location	Result
Apr. 5	Sam Greer	Denver, CO	E KO 2
Apr. 5	Wee Willi Medivitch	Denver, CO	E KO 2
Apr. 7	Ed Willis	Chicago, IL	W KO 1
June 8	Max Schmeling	Bronx, NY	W TKO 10
June 16	Cecil Harris	Pittsburg, PA	E W 3
June 19	Pete Wistort	Buffalo, NY	E W 4
June 20	Pete Wistort	Louisville, KY	E W Dec 3
June 21	Cecil Harris	Cincinnati, OH	E ND 2
June 21	Pete Wistort	Cincinnati, OH	E ND 2
June 22	Cecil Harris	St. Paul, MN	E WD 3
June 23	Cecil Harris	Duluth, MN	E WD 3
June 26	Pete Wistort	Atlanta, GA	E ND 3
June 27	Pete Wistort	New Orleans, LA	E ND 3

1934

Date	Opponent	Location	Result
Apr. 16	Babe Hunt	Tulsa, OK	E ND 2
Apr. 16	Buddy Baer	Tulsa, OK	E ND 2
Apr. 19	Buddy Baer	Kansas City, MO	E ND 2
Apr. 19	Babe Hunt	Kansas City, MO	E ND 2
Apr. 19	Max Brown	Kansas City, MO	E ND 2
Apr. 25	Buddy Baer	Jefferson City, MO	E ND 2
Apr. 25	Max Brown	Jefferson City, MO	E ND 2
Jun. 14	Primo Carnera	Queens, NY	W TKO 11 World Heavyweight Title
Dec. 14	Les Kennedy	Kansas City, MO	E ND 4
Dec. 28	King Levinsky	Chicago, IL	W KO 2

1935

Date	Opponent	Location	Result
Jan. 4	Babe Hunt	Detroit, MI	E ND 4
Jan. 10	Dick Madden	Boston, MA	E W D 4
Jan. 21	Tony Cancela	Tampa, FL	E ND 4
Jan. 28	Jim Maloney	Miami, FL	E ND 4
Feb.16	Stanley Poreda	San Francisco, CA	W KO 4
Apr. 23	Eddie Simms	Cleveland, OH	ND 4
Apr. 26	Babe Hunt	St. Louis, MO	E ND 4
June 13	James Braddock	Queens, NY	L Dec 15 World Heavyweight Title
Sep. 24	Joe Louis	Bronx, NY	L KO 4

Date	Opponent	Location	Result
1936			
June 15	Tony Souza	Salt Lake City, UT	W Dec 6
June 17	Bob Fraser	Boise, ID	W TKO 2
June 19	Harold Murphy	Pocatello, ID	W Dec 6
June 23	George Brown	Tyler, TX	W TKO 3
June 24	Wilson Dunn	San Antonio, TX	W TKO 3
July 2	Buck Rogers	Dallas, TX	W KO 3
July 13	James Merriott	Tinker AAF, Oklahoma City, OK	W KO 2
July 16	Junior Munsell	Tulsa, OK	W KO 5
July 17	Cecil Smith	Ada, OK	W Dec 4
July 24	Bob Williams	Ogden, UT	W KO 1
Aug. 15	Trent Fair	Eureka, CA	E ND 3
Aug. 19	James J. Walsh	Vancouver, Canada	E W KO 1
Aug. 19	Buddy Baer	Vancouver, Canada	E ND 2
Aug. 19	Sonny Buston	Vancouver, Canada	E ND 2
Aug. 24	Nails Gorman	Marshfield, OR	W TKO 2
Aug. 25	Cecil Myart	Portland, OR	W Dec 6
Aug. 29	Al Frankco	Lewiston, ID	W KO 2
Aug. 31	Don Baxter	Coeur d'Alene, ID	W KO 1
Sep. 2	Al Gaynor	Twin Falls, ID	W KO 1
Sep. 3	Soldier Eddie Franks	Provo, UT	W KO 3
Sep. 4	Cyclone Lynch	Rock Springs, WY	W KO 3
Sep. 7	Sammy Evans	Casper, WY	W KO 3
Sep. 14	Bearcat Wright	Des Moines, IA	W Dec 6
Sep. 19	Willie Davis	Cedar Rapids, IA	E ND
Sep. 22	Andy "Kid" Miller	Sheldon, IA	E ND 6
Sep. 24	Willie Davis	Ottumwa, IA	E ND 6
Sep. 30	Babe Davis	Keokuk, IA	E ND 4
Oct. 6	Tim Charles	Evansville, IN	W KO 4
Oct. 7	Willie Davis	Evansville, IN	W KO 3
Oct. 8	Willie Davis	Platteville, WI	L Dec 6
Oct. 19	Dutch Weimer	Toronto, Canada	W KO 2
1937			
Apr. 15	Tommy Farr	London, UK	L Dec 12
May 27	Ben Foord	London, UK	W TKO 9
July 30	Al Rovay	San Francisco, CA	E ND 4
Oct. 6	Nash Garrison	Oakland, CA	E ND 4
1938			
Mar. 11	Tommy Farr	MSG, New York, NY	W Dec 15
Sep. 30	Buddy Baer	San Diego, CA	E ND 2
Sep. 30	O'Dell Polee	San Diego, CA	E ND 2
Oct. 22	Andre Adoree	Honolulu, HI	E ND 4
Oct. 26	Hank Hankinson	Honolulu, HI	W KO 1
Oct. 26	Al Baffert	Honolulu, HI	E ND 4
Oct. 28	Andre Adoree	Lihue, HI	E ND 4
1939			
June 1	Lou Nova	Bronx, NY	L TKO 11
Sep. 4	Big Ed Murphy	Silver Peak, NV	W KO 1
Sep. 18	Babe Ritchie	Lubbock, TX	W KO 2
1940			
July 2	Tony Galento	Union City, NJ	W TKO 8
Sep. 26	Pat Comiskey	Union City, NJ	W TKO 1

Date	Opponent	Location	Result
1941			
Apr. 4	Lou Nova	New York, NY	L TKO 8
1943			
Jan. 30	Harry Williams	Ogden, UT	E ND 4
Feb. 11	Vic Lindskog	Palo Alto, CA	E ND
Oct. 22	Buddy Baer	Tinker AAF, Oklahoma City, OK	E-A
Nov. 8	Buddy Baer	Mitchell AAF, NY	E-A
Nov. 9	Buddy Baer	Bradley AAF, CT	E-A
Nov. 11	Buddy Baer	Camp Springs, MD	E-A
Nov. 13	Buddy Baer	Richmond AAF, VA	E-A
Nov. 14	Jimmy Jones	Langley AAF, VA	E-A, L TKO 1
Nov. 18	Buddy Baer	Charleston AAF, SC	E-A
Nov. 19	Buddy Baer	Atlanta AAF, Atlanta, GA	E-A
Nov. 20	Buddy Baer	Thomasville AAF, GA	E-A
Dec. 8	Buddy Baer	Lincoln AAF, Lincoln, NE	E-A, ND 3
Dec. 8	Buddy Baer	Sioux City, IA	E-A
Dec. 10	Buddy Baer	Dalhart AAF, Dalhart, TX	E-A, ND 3
Dec. 12	Buddy Baer	Pocatello AAF, Pocatello, ID	E-A, ND 3
Dec. 15	Buddy Baer	Casper AAF, Casper, WY	E-A
1944			
Jan. 15	Buddy Baer	Ardmore AAF, Ardmore, OK	E-A
Jan. 19	Sgt. Phil Romano	San Antonio, TX	E L Dec
Jan. 22	Buddy Baer	Page AAF, Ft. Myers, FL	E-A, ND 4
Jan. 26	Buddy Baer	Homestead AAF, Tampa, FL	E-A
Jan. 26	Buddy Baer	Pinellas AAF, FL	E-A, ND 4
Jan. 26	Buddy Baer	Dale Mabry AAF, FL	E-A, ND 4
1952			
Sep. 8	Primo Carnera	Long Beach, CA	E ND 4

Chapter Notes

Chapter One

1. Ernest Barcella, *Oakland Tribune*, May 19, 1941.
2. "Cauliflower Report," *Asbury Park Press*, Sept. 25, 1940.
3. "Bill Corum Says," *San Bernardino County Sun*, May 23, 1939.
4. Henry McLemore, "Baer Braddock Feud Nothing to Fret About," *Santa Ana Register*, May 18, 1939.
5. Grantland Rice, Jan. 21, 1939.
6. "Max Baer Fine Specimen, His Doctor Declares," *Daily Independent Journal*, Jan. 17, 1951.
7. "Sport Postscripts," *Los Angeles Times*, July 30, 1942.
8. S. Brumbelow, *Buddy Baer Autobiography*, p. 22. (This book states that it is a compilation of memories of various members of the Baer family and news clippings from the *Oakland Tribune*. One source (William Pettite) told C. Aycock that Joseph Brumbelow was a relative of Buddy Baer's fourth wife. The book was not published until 2003. Buddy Baer, Max Baer's brother, died in 1986, so the authorship is unclear. The cover of the book awkwardly indicates Buddy "was 5 feet 18½ inches tall, and 285 pounds." Two-thirds of the book discusses Max Baer and the remainder Buddy Baer. Some of the facts appear erroneously reported or questionable.) As author, I selected the spelling "Achill" for this book in that it was the spelling used in Achill Baer's final will probated on May 16, 1921, and the spelling used on his gravestone. Achill Baer died on August 29, 1900, at age 69. Various spellings of his first name appeared in city directories and census reports as: "Achille" in 1870, "Aschiell in 1892, "Achschell" in 1900, and Aschill in 1904. It is possible that the family's reference to names of the Tribes of Israel may have denoted Achill's brothers rather than his sons in that "Asher" was the name of a Hebrew tribal leader. Any siblings of Achill are unknown at this time. One Civil War record indicates that an Achielle Baer served for one month in an Ohio unit. Jacob Baer indicated in census reports that his mother Fanny (also spelled "Fannie") was born in Germany (some records say Austria) and his father in France. Modern equivalents of the name "Achill" may have been Asher or Herschel.
9. Edward Burns, "Max Baer—The Fighting Clown," *Chicago Tribune*, June 18, 1934; John Lardner, "Jake Trained Boxing Greats," *Los Angeles Times*, June 17, 1934.
10. Red Smith, "Views of Sport," *Oakland Tribune*, May 17, 1950. It is possible that this competition actually refers to the championship held in Chicago in 1902.
11. "Disillusioned Baer Quits Path of Brother for That of Father," *Santa Ana Register*, Jan. 21, 1942.
12. "Last Rites Held for Ex-Fighter," *Arizona Republic*, Jan. 7, 1945.
13. Brumbelow, p. 25.
14. John Lardner, "Jake Trained Boxing Greats," *Los Angeles Times*, June 17, 1934. Brother Ben was a lawman in Denver.
15. Red Smith, "Views of Sport," *Oakland Tribune*, May 17, 1950.
16. The reason this part of the Baer family history was lost is that references during members' lifetimes incorrectly identified the location as *Kaylor* and *Moehler*. The coal mine at Koehler supplied the St. Louis, Rocky Mountain and Pacific railroad with 31 million tons of coal before it closed in 1924 when miners left for other camps, and Koehler became a ghost town. Buddy Baer's autobiography incorrectly identifies the town as "Kaylor," which is understandable in that the misspelling indicates how the name was pronounced. An article in 1934 incorrectly identified Koehler as "Moehler": "Old-timers say that Max Baer once lived at the Moehler mining camp" ("New Mexico Has Claim on Maxie," *Oakland Tribune*, June 16, 1934). Remains of the town today exist on Ted Turner's Vermejo Park Ranch, which covers a large expanse of Northern New Mexico and is closed to the public.
17. James and Barbara Sherman, *Ghost Towns and Mining Camps of New Mexico*, p. 129.
18. Brumbelow, pp. 36–39.
19. By 1923 the Baer family was living in Oakland (at 9434 Plymouth). By 1925 they had moved to Hayward, California (at 369 C, Street). At this time, sister Fanny, who was 20, worked as a telephone operator for Pacific Telephone and Telegraph.
20. Arthur Daley, "The Big, Bad Baer," *New York Times*, Nov. 25, 1959.
21. *Oakland Tribune*, Jan. 19, 1939.

22. Max Baer, "Unkissed and 'Yellow' at 19," *American Journal*, June 18, 1934. Official records at the time considered school completed at grade 8 unless a person "completed high school," which comprised 11 grades. Thus, many records only show Max Baer "completing" grade 8, a stark contrast to Mary Ellen Baer, who completed college (comprised of 3 years).
23. Dan Parker, "Killer Instinct Would Have Made Baer Greatest," *The Mirror*, Nov. 24, 1959.
24. Daley, "The Big, Bad Baer."
25. Lee Dunbar, "On the Level," *Oakland Tribune*, Aug. 13, 1944.
26. Baer, "Unkissed and 'Yellow' at 19."
27. *Ibid.*
28. *Ibid.*
29. *Ibid.*
30. *Ibid.*
31. Harry Grayson, "Book on Etiquet [sic] Floored Baer," *San Bernardino Sun*, June 23, 1934.
32. "Had First fight on Father's Ranch When He K.O.'d 'Hand,'" *Press and Sun Bulletin*, June 13, 1933.
33. Eddie Murphy, "Grist from the Sport Mill," *Oakland Tribune*, Oct. 18, 1932.
34. Henry McLemore, "McLemore Says," *Oakland Tribune*, Sept. 27, 1940.
35. "Max Baer Rises from Laborer to Big Time Boxing Circles in Ten Months," *Democrat and Chronicle*, Jan. 5, 1931.
36. "John Lorimer Funeral Set," *Oakland Tribune*, Oct. 28 1947.
37. "Record House Expected to See Big Boys Fight," *Oakland Tribune*, May 28, 1930.
38. "Man Who Once Managed Max Baer," *Oakland Tribune*, Nov. 3, 1941.
39. "Daily Knave," *Oakland Tribune*, Dec. 18, 1951.
40. Colleen Aycock and Mark Scott, *Tex Rickard*, p. 129.
41. "Fred Morrison Is First in Earnings," *San Mateo Times*, Jan. 29, 1932.
42. "Big Leaguers Signing Up for 1931," *Daily Messenger* (Canandaigua, NY), Feb. 2, 1931.
43. "Gordon to Meet O'Leary Tuesday," *Healdsburg Tribune*, March 28, 1927.
44. Nat Fleischer, *Max Baer*, p. 8.
45. Gans fought Harry Lewis and thought highly of the young fighter. Lewis needed a manager, and as historian Harry Boonin noted, Lewis came around the next day without a manager and said, "What's wrong with Al here?" So Lippe took on Lewis.
46. Damon Runyon, "Al Lippe, One of Ring's Old Guard Returning Home," *Times-Union* (Albany, NY), March 31, 1933.
47. Fleischer, p. 9.
48. It appears he fought Harvey Kohinka repeatedly. Scoop Beal, "Around Our Town," *Times Standard*, April 8, 1953.
49. "Lively Card Provided at Arcadia Pavilion by Parente," *Hayward Daily Review*, July 24, 1929.
50. Russ Allen, "Negro Battler Beats Red Uhland in Arcadia Bout," *Hayward Daily Review*, July 25, 1929.
51. *Ibid.*
52. "Max Baer Wins Oakland Fight" *Livermore Journal*, Aug 29, 1929. The only reason to mention Ledford's race is that the press said Baer never fought, and his mother forbad him to fight, a black man. Such was never the case. He fought all fighters.
53. "Max Baer Will Perform in Ring at Home Town," *Oakland Tribune*, Jan. 10, 1930.
54. Russ Allen, "Men O'War Will Scramble in Arena Wednesday Night," *Hayward Daily Review*, Sept. 25, 1929.

Chapter Two

1. Bob Shand, "Grist from the Sport Mill," *Oakland Tribune*, December 31, 1929. Antonio de la Fuente had been boxing the likes of Benny Hill, George Godfrey, Leon Bombo Chevalier, Jack De Mave, and Young Stribling for 9 years before he took on Baer.
2. "Baer 'Carried' Foe Is Charge," *Hayward Review*, Feb. 4, 1930.
3. "Referees Put on Pan," *Los Angeles Times*, Nov. 15, 1930.
4. *Ibid.*
5. Leonard Lyons, "Mathematical Dub," *Long Beach Independent*, June 28, 1956.
6. Bob Shand, "Carnera Can Really Fight but Has Not Been Called to Meet Real Opponent," *Oakland Tribune*, April 13, 1930.
7. "Local Boxing Men Prepare for Carnera," *Oakland Tribune*, March 31, 1930.
8. *The Harder They Fall*, Columbia Pictures, 1956. Benko is played by Rod Steiger.
9. Bob Shand, "Frame-Up Charged as Carnera Wins Fight," *Oakland Tribune*, April 15, 1930.
10. "Death Threats Produce Big Sensation at Investigation of Chevalier Fight Fiasco," *Oakland Tribune*, April 21, 1930.
11. "Primo Carnera Banned from State Rings," *Oakland Tribune*, April 15, 1930.
12. "Ripley's Believe It or Not!" *Albuquerque Journal*, April 23, 2017.
13. "Paul Lowry, "An Underpaid Pasting," *Los Angeles Times*, April 24, 1930.
14. "Baer Beats Toner but Fails to Show Champ Calibre," *Hayward Review*, May 9, 1930.
15. Ross Allen "Seven Heavy Bouts Set for Arcadia Wed. Night" *Hayward Daily Review*, Aug. 27, 1929.
16. Bob Shand, "Jack Linkhorn Is Still Riding on Street Cars," *Oakland Tribune*, May 21, 1930.
17. Bob Shand, "Record Crowd Sees Snappy Knock-Out at Auditorium, Linkhorn Downed 3 Times." *Oakland Tribune*, May 29, 1930.
18. *Ibid.*
19. Bob Shand, "With the Knights of the Gloves," *Oakland Tribune*, June 3, 1930.
20. Bob Shand, "Buck Weaver Puts Francis to Sleep," *Oakland Tribune*, June 10, 1930.
21. "Trying to Match Baer for Two Contests," *Livermore Journal*, June 5, 1930.

22. Bob Shand, "Livermore Leveler Takes Owen's Best Blows," *Oakland Tribune*, June 26, 1930.
23. "Livermore Names Horse for Max Baer," *Oakland Tribune*, July 3, 1930.
24. Two other losses came from disqualifications. One, when Baer struck his opponent while his opponent was being given the count. The second, on September 4, 1929, when Baer suffered his first loss in a six-round fight with Jack McCarthy. Max was disqualified in the third round.
25. Referee Jack Kennedy was not related to the father of the former U.S. president. Ref. Kennedy was said to have established the first rules for scoring fights by one-point rounds.
26. Bob Shand said as much in the *Oakland Tribune* on July 17. The same sentiment came from the *Livermore Journal*, also on July 17, 1930.
27. "Fans' Attitude Is Puzzle to Heavyweight Boxer," *Oakland Tribune*, July 17, 1930.
28. *Ibid.*
29. "Baer Kayoes Christner," *Los Angeles Times*, Aug. 12, 1930.
30. Robert Edgren, "But for Campbell's Death, Livermore Boy Would Rank Near Top," *San Francisco Chronicle*, September 14, 1930.
31. Le Pacini, "The Fight That Changed "Maxie the Killer" into "Maxie the Clown," *Boxing Illustrated* (Aug. 1970): pp. 28–54.
32. "Frankie Campbell Dies Following Bout with Baer Monday Night," *Livermore Journal*, Aug. 28, 1930; "Terrific Ring Blow Injures Brain Tissue," *San Bernardino Sun*, Aug. 27, 1930.
33. "Referee of Bout Faces Criticism," *San Bernardino Sun*, Aug. 27, 1930.
34. Joseph R. Svinth, "Death Under the Spotlight," The Manuel Velazquez Collection, most recent update, Oct. 2011.
35. Allan T. Baum, sportswriter for the *San Francisco Examiner*, is republished in "Frankie Campbell Dies Following Bout with Baer Monday Night," *Livermore Journal*, Aug. 28, 1930.
36. Parker, "Killer Instinct Would Have Made Baer Greatest."
37. "Charges That Fight Racketeers Took $10,000 Toll from Slain Boxer During Last Year," *San Bernardino Sun*, Sept. 14, 1930.
38. *Ibid.*
39. "Rumors of Betting on Ring Bouts Disclosed: Secretary of State Commission Testifies Before Boxing Probers," *Oakland Tribune*, Nov. 14, 1930; "Referees Put on Pan," *Los Angeles Times*, Nov. 15, 1930.
40. *Ibid.*
41. "Traung's Life Threatened: State Inquiry into Prize Fight Fixing Reveals Commissioner's Peril," *Oakland Tribune*, Nov. 13, 1930.
42. *Ibid.*
43. "Baer Refused State Permit," *Livermore Journal*, Feb. 5, 1931.

Chapter Three

1. Sir Walter Scott's epic poem *Marmion: A Tale of Flodden Field*, a stirring poem of heroic Scottish valor set in 1513, was published in 1838. It comprises 1174 lines. Quoted here are 313–318. Manuscript eprinted in 2015 without a named publisher, p. 89. The Battle of Flodden was the last medieval battle in England. It was fought between the Scottish, led by King James IV (who died in battle), and the English king, Henry VIII, with the English winning.
2. "Suit Decision Tuesday," *Bakersfield Californian*, Feb. 16, 1935.
3. There were different types of saloons in the cities in those days, high-class and the working man's. I am indebted to Judge William Pettite for the many conversations we have had beginning on February 11, 2014.
4. By 1938 Ancil Hoffman still owned the Espanol restaurant and hotel, built originally by D.O. Mills in the west end of Sacramento, considered the old part of town.
5. Judge William Pettite, phone interview, April 9, 2017.
6. Rudy Hickey, "Ancil Hoffman Met Fame with the Baer Brothers," *Fresno Bee: The Republican*, July 13, 1941.
7. J.G. Newlands "Max Baer Sees Fights at Labor Day Meet," *Nevada State Journal*, Sept. 1, 1930.
8. In 1931 the residency requirement for a divorce changed to six weeks.
9. Third-generation descendent of Thomas Bucklin Wells, "Pancho" Frank Wells very kindly informed me in 2016 about the Wells family and (Uncle) Tommy Wells II, and Wells's marriage to Dorothy Dunbar.
10. "Dorothy Dunbar Seeks Divorce," *Reno Evening Gazette*, Nov. 6, 1930.
11. Baer, "Unkissed and 'Yellow' at 19."
12. "Reputed Movie Actress Freed," *Reno Evening Gazette*, Jan. 28, 1931.
13. Harry Grayson, "Book on Etiquet [sic] Floored Baer," *San Bernardino County Sun*, June 23, 1934.
14. L.S. Cameron, "Baer Secures Big Time Test in Tom Heeney," *San Bernardino County Sun*, Jan. 16, 1931.
15. Bob Shand, "Expressmen Happy as Max Baer and Managers Depart for the 'Big Time,'" *Oakland Tribune*, Nov. 29, 1930.
16. Bob Shand, "Baer's Departure Delayed Until All His Managers Can Be Gathered Together," *Oakland Tribune*, Nov. 27, 1930.
17. "Baer Talking for Big Title," *San Bernardino County Sun*, Dec. 6, 1930.
18. *Ibid.*
19. Grantland Rice, "The Sportlights" *Syracuse Herald*, Dec. 16, 1930.
20. *Ibid.*
21. "Baer Talking for Big Title," *San Bernardino County Sun*, Dec. 6, 1930.
22. "Heavyweight of Lot of Promise Is Baer," *Daily Messenger*, Dec. 15, 1930.

23. Jack Gallagher, "Well-Dressed Pubs Praise Needle Hobby," *Oakland Tribune*, Feb. 21, 1950.
24. "Max Buys Auto but Is Asked Not to Drive," *Oakland Tribune*, Dec. 12, 1930.
25. Edward J. Neil (for AP), "Ernie Schaff Punches Out Hard Fought Triumph Over Baer, California Battler; Decision Meets with Many Boos," *Bluefield Daily Telegraph*, Dec. 20, 1930.
26. Max Baer, "Boxing Lessons from Loughran in Ring and at Luncheon Described by New Champ," *New York Journal American*, June 25, 1934.
27. Dan Parker, "Killer Instinct Would Have Made Baer Greatest," *Mirror*, Nov. 24, 1959.
28. "Critics Say Mike Walker Best Fighter; 62 Sports Writers Decide Middleweight Champ All-Around Ace," according to *New York Evening Sun*, Dec. 27, reported in *Syracuse Herald* Dec. 28, 1930.
29. "Hooks and Slides," *Syracuse Herald*, Dec. 20, 1930.
30. "Stribling Ranked as Leading Heavy in United States" as published in the *New York Sun*, Dec. 27, *Syracuse Herald*, Dec. 27, 1930.
31. "Boxing Association Has Listed Ratings for Fight Divisions," *Bakersfield Californian*, Jan. 5, 1931.
32. Grantland Rice, "Jack Sharkey's Angle," *Syracuse Herald*, Dec. 22, 1930.
33. Grantland Rice, "The Sportlight," *Syracuse Herald*, Jan. 6, 1931.
34. Copeland C. Burg, International News Service sportswriter, "Losers Proving Winners," *Olean Evening Times*, Jan. 12, 1931.
35. Frank Graham, "Graham's Corner," *New York Journal American*, Nov. 12, 1959.
36. Max Baer, "Boxing Lessons from Loughran in Ring and at Luncheon Described by New Champ," *New York Journal*, June 25, 1934. The dialogue that follows is from this article.
37. "Problem of Weight Confronts Max Baer," *Syracuse Herald*, Jan. 14, 1931.
38. Henry McLemore, United Press, "Max A. Baer Will Battle Tom Heeney," *Olean Evening Times*, Jan. 16, 1931.
39. The semi-final bout for the Baer-Heeney card was between Paul Swiderski and Marty Gallagher, 10 rounds. Also on the undercard was a 10-round match between Stanley Poreda (future contender) and Tony Starr.
40. L.S. Cameron, United Press, "Max Baer Credited with Knockout for Freak Heeney Bout," *Bakersfield Californian*, Jan. 17, 1931.
41. Max Baer, "Boxing Lessons from Loughran in Ring and at Luncheon Described by New Champ," *New York Journal*, June 25, 1934. Dialogue comes from this article.
42. *Ibid*.
43. "Tommy Loughran Beats Max Baer," *Canandaigua Daily Messenger*, Feb. 7 1931.
44. Max Baer, "Boxing Lessons from Loughran in Ring and at Luncheon Described by New Champ," *New York Journal*, June 25, 1934.
45. Al Abrams, "Sidelights on Sports," *Pittsburgh Post-Gazette*, Jan. 26, 1945.
46. *Ibid*.
47. Frank Graham, "Graham's Corner: On Seeing Max Baer Again," *Journal American*, May 25, 1955.
48. Bob Shand, "Manager of Baer Says He's Through," *Oakland Tribune*, Feb. 7, 1931.
49. *Ibid*.
50. *Ibid*.
51. Max Baer, "Boxing Lessons from Loughran in Ring and at Luncheon Described by New Champ," *New York Journal*, June 25, 1934.
52. The following list of boxing tips from Jack Dempsey, in Grantland Rice, "Jack Dempsey Offers Max Baer Expert Advice on How to Box," *Oakland Tribune*, March 22, 1931. (Baer would later show these methods to his sparring partners, like my father Ike Aycock, who in turn enjoyed showing others, especially how that same hip movement translated into a golf swing. These were also tips that this author used when fencing in college—movements that seemed to come naturally as a result of these basic boxing lessons at home.)
53. *Ibid*.
54. Don Page, "Mellowed Max Baer Loves Everybody on Own Flourishing Television Show," *Los Angeles Times*, Sept. 14, 1958.
55. Grantland Rice, "The Sportlight," *Syracuse Herald*, Feb. 11, 1931.
56. *Ibid*. Dempsey's advice.
57. *Ibid*.
58. The following situation is described by Max Baer in "Boxing Lessons from Loughran in Ring and at Luncheon Described by New Champ," *New York Journal*, June 25, 1934, in a series posted for several days, beginning on the 25th.
59. Bob Shand, "With the Knights of the Gloves," *Oakland Tribune*, Feb. 18, 1931.
60. The "Prodigal Son" is a Biblical parable about greed, foolishness, discontent and willful disobedience. The son spends his father's money recklessly and when his wealth is gone, so are his friends. He is forced to work (in a loathsome activity for the Jews) feeding the pigs. Undoubtedly, the minister thought this an appropriate lesson for Max.
61. Russ Allen, "Portuguese Battler to Face Grosso; Max Baer Sent Back West by Risko," *Hayward Daily Review*, May 6, 1931.
62. Bob Shand, "With the Knights of the Gloves," *Oakland Tribune*, May 13, 1931.

Chapter Four

1. "Nevada at Work on Sporting Plant for Boxing and Racing; Finish Fight Are Part of Program Planned by Dempsey," *Bakersfield Californian*, May 8, 1931; "Baer, Uzcudun Purse Figure Is Estimated," *Nevada State Journal*, July 1, 1931. The "finish fight" in the gloved ring in Rickard's 1906 promotion was 45 rounds. (That fight between Gans and Nelson went 42

rounds.) For Dempsey in 1931, it was either 20 or 25 rounds. In other words, both promoters wanted the men to be able to finish the fight, even if it took more rounds than what was normally allowed at the time. Even though Dempsey called his fight a "finish fight" it would not go longer than 20 rounds—longer than the normal title fight 15 rounds. Nevada had no limit on the number of rounds. But, to be clear, "finish fights" were *not* limitless rounds after 1900.

2. "Max Baer Arrives as Bout Arranged," *Nevada State Journal*, May 15, 1931.

3. "Dempsey's Father Will Take Bride," *Bakersfield Californian*, March 6, 1931.

4. "Baer, Uzcudun Purse Figure Is Estimated," *Nevada State Journal*, July 1, 1931. To put those general $3 ticket prices in perspective: in 1931, 20 pounds of laundry could be cleaned for $1, and that included pick-up and delivery; the price of a reserved seat would buy a pair of men's leather shoes that sold anywhere from $5 to $10.

5. "Dempsey Declines Cleveland Offer of $750,000 for 'Comeback' There," *Nevada State Journal*, July 1, 1931.

6. "Max Baer Is Deprived of Car, Driver," *Oakland Tribune*, June 12, 1931.

7. "Dempsey Letter Brings Retort from Max Baer," *Nevada State Journal*, June 13, 1931.

8. Alan Ward, "On Second Thought: Boy, Wotta Night!" *Oakland Tribune*, Jan. 28, 1949.

9. "Reno Swept by U.S. Prohibition Raids," *Nevada State Journal*, Reno, July 1, 1931.

10. George Scherck, *Oakland Tribune*, March 4, 1941; Fried, *Corner Men*, p. 194.

11. Fried, *Corner Men*, p. 194–5.

12. "Uzcudun Says Baer Butted During Fight," *Nevada State Journal*, July 5, 1931.

13. "Baer's Kin to Miss Wedding," *Los Angeles Times*, July 8, 1931.

14. "Max Baer to Take Bride in Reno Today," *Oakland Tribune*, July 8, 1931.

15. "Baer to Wed on Wednesday," *Hayward Daily Review*, July 4, 1931.

16. This number comes from Edward Burns, *Chicago Tribune*, June 19, 1934.

17. "Max's Manager Plans Robust Fight Program," *Nevada State Journal*, July 9, 1931.

18. Bob Shand, "Max Starts Over Come-Back Trail Against Hard Hitting Heavyweight from the South," *Oakland Tribune*, Sept. 22, 1931. On the undercard was Paul Drake vs. Eddie McGovern, Frankie Limas vs. Bob Newton, Walter Fields vs. Red Brockley, and Joe Gruell vs. Jimmy Lynch.

19. *Ibid.*

20. *Ibid.*

21. Bob Shand, "Grist from the Sport Mill," *Oakland Tribune*, Sept. 24, 1931.

22. "Baer's Showing Is Poor in Victory Over J. Van Noy," *Santa Cruz Evening News*, Sept. 24, 1931.

23. "Mrs. Max Baer Seeks Lorimer's Share of Cash," *Petaluma Argus-Courier*, Sept. 25, 1931.

24. Bob Shand, "Commission May Settle Row Over Max; Wife's Move for Management Turned Down," *Oakland Tribune*, Sept. 26, 1931.

25. "Jose Santa," *Bakersfield Californian*, Oct. 21, 1931.

26. Bob Shand, "Max Pummels Joe Almost to Pulp," *Oakland Tribune*, Oct. 22, 1931.

27. *Ibid.*

28. Bob Shand, "'I'll Beat Max,' Says Kennedy," *Oakland Tribune*, Nov. 21, 1931.

29. The Oak Knoll Country Club would go bankrupt in the Depression and would be purchased by the Navy for a hospital. The facility would close in 1996.

30. Bob Shand, "Max Rescinds His Lawyer's Demand," *Oakland Tribune*, Jan. 1, 1932.

Chapter Five

1. George Kirksey, UP, "Dempsey to Meet Winner of Schmeling-Sharkey Bout," *San Mateo Times*, Jan. 29, 1932.

2. B. Bennison, "The Man-Eater from Chicago Is Here," *Illustrated Sporting and Dramatic News*, March 26, 1937, p. 632.

3. Frank Graham, "Graham's Corner: On Seeing Max Baer Again," *Journal American*, May 25, 1955.

4. "Max Baer Wins in Easy Battle," *Bakersfield Californian*, Feb. 23, 1932.

5. Kay Owe, "Max Baer Heavyweights in Limelight: Big Fellows Collide in Top Spot Here This Week: Pole Made Reputation When He Floored Walker," *Los Angeles Times*, April 24, 1932.

6. *Ibid.* In the preliminaries, Swede Berglund and Tom Jeffries battled six rounds to a draw, and Ray Impelletiere defeated Chief White Horse in a three-round exhibition. Swiderski's giant stablemate, Ray Impelletiere, was 6-foot-7 and weighed 260 pounds.

7. *Oakland Tribune*, April 30, 1932.

8. Bob Shand, "Cobb Stopped in Fourth by Baer: Manager of Loser Protests, Inspector Takes License," *Oakland Tribune*, May 12, 1932.

9. "Fighter in Reno on Dual Errand," *Los Angeles Times*, May 31, 1932.

10. "Mrs. Max Baer Sues for Divorce," *Modesto News-Herald*, June 4, 1932.

11. "Max Baer and Wife Make Up," *Oakland Tribune*, June 19, 1932.

12. "Max Baer Pounds Out Victory on King Levinsky's Ribs Before 9000 Reno Fight Enthusiasts," *Reno Gazette-Journal*, July 5, 1932.

13. Alan Ward, "On Second Thought," *Oakland Tribune*, Jan. 23, 1949.

14. Al W. Moe, *Roots of Reno*, pp. 88–89.

15. *Ibid.*

16. Charles Vackner, "Joe Promises Wife Gift—Win Over Lee," *Brooklyn Daily Eagle*, May 25, 1932.

17. "Max Baer Preparing for Important Boxing Match Goes Through Strenuous Workouts for Battle with Ernie Schaaf," *Freeport Journal Standard*, Aug. 23, 1932.

18. "Max Baer Gains Decision Over Ernie Schaff Last Night," *Freeport Journal-Standard*, Sept. 1, 1932.
19. "Ernie Schaaf Is Outpointed by Winston," *Fitchburg Sentinel*, Oct. 21, 1932.
20. "Max Baer's Ring Record Best in Modern Times," *Chicago Tribune*, Sept. 25, 1932.
21. "Baer-Griffith at Stadium Monday Eve," *Brookfield Magnet*, Sept. 22, 1932.
22. Westbrook Pegler, "Kearns Halts Bout at End of Eighth Round," *Chicago Tribune*, Sept. 27, 1932.
23. *Ibid.*
24. "Baer-Carnera Match Rumor Denied," *Oakland Tribune*, Oct. 18, 1932.
25. "Maxie's Pilot Says Sharkey Bout Is Off," *Syracuse Herald*, Oct. 20, 1932.
26. *Pittsburg Press*, Oct. 21, 1932.
27. Ed Hughes, "Ed Hughes' Column," *Brooklyn Daily Eagle*, Oct. 21, 1932.
28. "Dempsey Signs Schmeling and Baer for 15-Rounder to be Staged Next June," *Daily Messenger*, Dec. 23, 1932.
29. *New York Sun*, Dec. 28, 1932. Honorable mention: Tommy Loughran, Larry Gains, Steve Hamas, Unknown Winston, Charlie Retzlaff, Lee Ramage, Paulina Uzcudun, Tuffy Griffith, Arthur Huttick.
30. *Ibid.*

Chapter Six

1. Grantland Rice, part of the column, "The Sportlight," *Syracuse Herald*, June 19, 1933.
2. Jimmy Donahue, "Jack Dempsey Steals Show on Broadway," *Syracuse Herald*, Jan. 1933.
3. George Kirksey, "Schaaf Favorite Over Baer Tonight," *San Mateo Times*, Aug. 31, 1932.
4. Judge William Pettite, interview, February 11, 2014.
5. "Memories of Muldoon by Laufer," *Syracuse Herald*, June 8, 1933. William Muldoon was said to have invented the portable "shower-bath" during his service in the Civil War—a crude bucket with holes poked in the bottom, hung on a pole above the head. He was also said to have invented the medicine ball. He hated cigarettes, calling them "coffin nails," and he refused to give any reporter who smoked them an interview.
6. Grantland Rice, "Jack Dempsey—1919–1933," *Syracuse Herald*, April 8, 1933.
7. *Ibid.*
8. "Schmeling Is Rich Man Out to Get Title," *Press and Sun Bulletin*, July 1, 1936.
9. "Schmeling in U.S. for Bout with Baer," *Syracuse Herald*, April 14, 1933.
10. Grantland Rice, "The Sportlight," *Syracuse Herald*, May 1, 1933.
11. Ken Blady, *The Jewish Boxers' Hall of Fame*, 1988, p. 207.
12. Ken Blady, "Introduction," by Hank Kaplan, pp. xiv–xv.
13. Lester Bromber, pp. 314–315.
14. *Desert Sun* (Palm Springs), Feb. 26, 1953.
15. On the back of the photo taken March 31, 1951, Ralph Dohme wrote "Max Baer recites Chapter III from St. Luke to Curley Owen."
16. Ken Blady, p. 209.
17. Henry McLemore, "McLemore Comments," *Oakland Tribune*, May 22, 1938.
18. Bill Henry, "Jewish Fans May Boycott Schmeling Baer Fight Due to Hitler," *Los Angeles Times*, May 30, 1933.
19. Henry McLemore, "McLemore Comments," *Oakland Tribune*, May 22, 1938.
20. Dan Parker, "Killer Instinct Would Have Made Baer Greatest," *New York Mirror*, Nov. 24, 1959.
21. Bill Corum, "Sports," *New York Journal*, June 13, 1935.
22. "Things They Ask the Tribune," *Oakland Tribune*, March 26, 1930.
23. "Schmeling Improved, Declares Lou Barba," *Canandaigua Daily Messenger*, June 3, 1933.
24. Max Baer was a good golfer. So was Babe Ruth, who shot only a few stokes above par at this time.
25. Matt Jackson, "Conditioned by Bimstein—An Old Ritual," *Democrat and Chronicle*, Dec. 28, 1936.
26. Associated Press, "Best Fight Since Firpo-Dempsey Is Expectation of Fans," *Syracuse Herald*, June 4, 1933.
27. Alan Ward, "Max to Be at Ringside for Title Bout," *Oakland Tribune*, June 27, 1933.
28. *Ibid.*
29. Donald Red Barry, Washington vs. Tony Galento, Orange, New Jersey, eight rounds; Abe Feldman, New York vs. Charley Massera, Pittsburgh, eight; Marty Fox, New York vs. Jack Redman, South Bend, Indiana, six; Jack Van Noy, California vs. Phil Cohen, New York, four; Georgie Simpson, California vs. Joe Mach, New York, four.
30. Henry McLemore, "Real Battle Would Help Sport but a Daisy-Chain Party Would Cause Its Downfall." *Syracuse Herald*, June 8, 1933.
31. *Ibid.*
32. Paul Harrison, "New York," *Poughkeepsie Eagle News*, June 17, 1933.
33. "Baer on Harris' Chances: 'Didn't Braddock Beat Me!'" *Press and Sun-Bulletin*, July 31, 1958.
34. "Grantland Rice, The Sportlight," *Syracuse Herald*, June 15, 1933.
35. *Ibid.*
36. Henry McLemore, "Baby Son, Home Troubles Change Baer's Outlook," *San Mateo Times*, Dec. 15, 1937.
37. Ronald Wagoner, "Baer Climbs Rapidly After Levinsky and Schaaf Fights," *San Mateo Times*, June 20, 1934.
38. *Ibid.*
39. "Baer Batters Big German to Win Sensational Bout on Technical Knock-Out," *Daily Messenger*, June 9, 1933.
40. *Ibid.*
41. Henry McLemore, "Baer, New Dempsey, to Lead Boxing to Its Old Popularity," *Syracuse Herald*

June 9, 1933; Grantland Rice, "The Sportlight," *Syracuse Herald*, June 15, 1933.
42. Jack Dempsey, "Dempsey Pays Winner High Compliment," *Oakland Tribune*, June 9, 1933.
43. Hype Igoe, "Schmeling's Blows Light, Says Victor," *New York Evening Journal*, June 9, 1933.
44. Alan Ward, "Max to Be at Ringside for Title Bout," *Oakland Tribune*, June 27, 1933.
45. "Does He Play Tag?" *Santa Ana Register*, July 17, 1933.
46. "Schmeling Going Home to Marry," *Syracuse Herald*, June 13, 1933; "Two Maxes Meet at Dempsey's Banquet," *Santa Anna Register*, June 13, 1933.
47. Grantland Rice, "The Ups and Downs," "The Sportlight," *Press and Sun Bulletin*, Oct. 14, 1936.
48. Henry McLemore, "Baer Just a Chump, I'd Like Crack at Him, Says Boastful Sharkey; Boston Sailor Is Same Old Blushing Violet as He Compares Self to Californian," *Syracuse Herald*, June 10, 1933.
49. *Ibid.*

Chapter Seven

1. For a thorough look at his career, see Joseph Page's *Primo Carnera: The Life and Career of the Heavyweight Boxing Champion*.
2. Comment to the author.
3. For a thorough look at his career, see James Curl's *Jack Sharkey: A Heavyweight Champion's Untold Story*.
4. "Odds Drop Under Flood of Wagering on Carnera," AP, *Syracuse Herald*, June 29, 1933.
5. "Secret Punch Turned Trick," *Poughkeepsie Eagle News*, June 30, 1933.
6. "Max Baer's Wedding to End in Divorce," *Canandaigua Daily Messenger*, Sept. 28, 1933.
7. "Shhh!!! Max Baer Agrees to Lose to Carnera," *Syracuse Herald*, Aug. 11, 1933.
8. "Baer, Ready to Start Work on Film, Tells Views on Movies," *San Bernardino County Sun*, Aug. 15, 1933.
9. Movie, *The Prizefighter and The Lady*, by Metro-Goldwyn-Mayer, 1933.
10. "Motion-Picture Career Awaits Champion Baer," *Los Angeles Times*, June 15, 1934.
11. Jack Dempsey, "Baer Must Pick Ring or Stage," *New York Evening Journal*, Jan. 12, 1934.
12. Ronald Wagner, "Maxie All a Flutter in Social Whirl," *Fresno Bee*, Nov. 19, 1933.
13. The Benny Franklin promotions were: Beny Schwartz-Pancho Villa, flyweight; Harry Greb-Fay Keiser, middleweight; and Andre Routis-Buster Brown, featherweight.
14. Grantland Rice, "The Sportlight," *Syracuse Herald*, Dec. 7, 1933.
15. "Levinsky Is Likely to Get Carnera Bout," *Syracuse Herald*, Jan. 19, 1934.
16. "Carnera Whips Loughran, Hopes for Max Baer Next," *Kingston Daily Freeman*, March 2, 1934.
17. Biddy Bishop, "Max Popping Off in Oakland, Riled Jack Says New Yorker," in "Ringside Blasts from the Northwest," *Sports Redhead Weekly*, June 17, 1935.
18. *Ibid.*
19. Jo Ranson, "Radio Dial-Log," *Brooklyn Daily Eagle*, June 4, 1934.
20. "Radio Dial-Log," *Brooklyn Daily Eagle*, May 21, 1934.
21. George H. Beale, "Film Beauties Desert Baer," *Santa Ana Daily Register*, June 13, 1934.
22. "Miss Dunbar Raps Baer 'Life Story,'" *Santa Ana Register*, July 5, 1934.
23. Alan Gould, "No Laughing Matter," *Kingston Daily Freeman*, July 24, 1933.
24. Jack Dempsey, "Baer to Win by Knockout, Says Dempsey," *Santa Ana Register*, June 13, 1934.
25. *Ibid.*
26. "Doctors Say Baer Is Fit for Battle with Carnera," *Tennessean*, June 9, 1934.
27. *Ibid.*
28. "Maxie Appears in Better Shape for Bout Than Primo," *Tennessean*, June 13, 1934.
29. The preliminaries included: Al Ettore, Philadelphia vs. Charley Massera, Pittsburgh (staged after the main event); Corn Griffin, Ft. Benning, Georgia (from the Carnera camp) vs. James J. Braddock, Jersey City (former light-heavy champion); Dynamite Jackson, Los Angeles (from Baer's camp) vs. Willie McGee, Tampa; Al White, Brooklyn vs. Lon Poster, Pottsville, Pennsylvania; Eddie Hogan, Waterbury, Connecticut vs. Chester Matan, Brooklyn (one of Primo's sparring partners); Don Petrin, Newark vs. Ed Karolak, Schenectady.
30. Joseph S. Page, *The Life and Career of the Heavyweight Boxing Champion: Primo Carnera*, p. 147.
31. Dan Parker, "Killer Instinct Would Have Made Baer Greatest," *The Mirror*, Nov. 24, 1959.
32. Frank Graham, "Graham's Corner: On Seeing Max Baer Again," *Journal American*, May 25, 1955.
33. *Ibid.*
34. Art Cohn, "Cohn-ing Tower" *Oakland Tribune*, Sept. 28, 1941.
35. "Boxer Raises Bar on Man Who Handled 2 Title Bouts," *Syracuse Herald*, June 11, 1935.
36. James P. Dawson, "Crowd of 56,000 Sees Baer Win Title by Knocking Out Carnera in Eleventh," *New York Times*, June 15, 1934.
37. H. Allen Smith, "Dempsey Says Fight Greatest Ever," *Los Angeles Times*, June 15, 1934.
38. John Lardner, "Donovan Forgives Baer for Pre-Bout Remarks," *Los Angeles Times*, June 15, 1934.
39. Ronald Wagoner, "Max Baer's Life," *Oakland Tribune*, June 22, 1934.
40. Judge William Pettite, conversation, Feb. 11, 2014, for details of the scorecard incident. In 1935, one reporter said the scorecards from the New York Commission indicated only Judge Lynch gave the fight to Carnera, Judge Shortell to Baer, and Arthur Donovan gave Baer 6 rounds. This goes against other documents that said he gave the fight to Carnera. Ancil Hoffman brought the matter before the commission prior to the Braddock fight, and Donovan may have turned in a different scorecard to the Commission after Baer won by knockout.

41. James P. Dawson, *New York Times*, June 15, 1934.
42. "Baer Praises Carnera for Good Fight, Jeers Brown," *San Bernardino Daily Sun*, June 15, 1934.
43. *Ibid.*
44. "Beaten Champion Weeps Like Child," *New York Times*, June 15, 1934.
45. "Carnera's Right Ankle Was Broken in Fight," *Tennessean*, June 17, 1934.
46. "Jeffries Lauds New Champion," *San Bernardino County Sun*, June 15, 1934.
47. "Baer, Carnera 'Cheese' Champs," *San Bernardino County Sun*, June 15, 1934.
48. "Baer's Ma Listens In: Cries When It's Over," *Poughkeepsie Eagle News*, June 14, 1934.
49. Emily Belser, "Picture Recalls Carnera Received $47.07 for Fight," *Corsicana Daily Sun*, Dec. 30, 1955.
50. "Motion-Picture Career Awaits Champion Baer," *Los Angeles Times*, June 15, 1934.
51. For numbering, see Ronald Wagoner, UP, "Max Baer's Life," *Oakland Tribune*, June 19, 1934.
52. Robert Edgren, "Sports Through Edgren's Eyes," *Kingston Daily Freeman*, July 21, 1934.
53. Edward Burns, "Max to Give Up His Beer—for Champagne," *Chicago Tribune*, June 18, 1934.
54. *Ibid.*
55. "Max Plays with Primo's Toes on Visit to Fallen Champion," *Democrat and Chronicle*, June 23, 1934.
56. *Ibid.*
57. John Lardner, "Champion Baer Prizes His Wardrobe Highly," *Los Angeles Times*, June 20, 1934.

Chapter Eight

1. Edith Dietz, *Screen and Radio Weekly*, Dec. 2, 1934.
2. Norman "Ike" Aycock and his older brother Tom were left to make ends meet on their own when they were 14 and 16 years old, after their large family left the Rio Grande Valley and moved to Kenedy, Texas. The family's moves were timed with the rent—when the rent was due and they couldn't pay, they picked up and moved. The Depression made survival very difficult for poor families. Girls could be placed in orphanages, but boys could not remain there after age 14. At one point, Ike needed shoes and he stepped into a street corner boxing ring where men had thrown coins hoping to attract challengers. He won his first match, collected $5, and bought a nice pair of leather shoes. Such was the driving force of many men during the Depression.
3. Neil Elder appeared in his flight helmet, walking among a group of sailors next to heavy shells, in the first photo taken aboard an American ship in the Pacific conflict published in *Life* magazine, Jan. 5, 1942, p. 16.
4. Ronald K. Fried, *Corner Men*, p. 328.
5. William Weekes, AP, "Newspapermen to Render Decision in Event Bout at Chicago Goes Limit," *Oakland Tribune*, Dec. 28, 1934.
6. Edward Burns, "Levinsky Goes Down Under Right Smashes," *Chicago Tribune*, Dec. 29, 1934.
7. W.W. Edgar, "The Second Guess ... Max Baer Explains," *Detroit Free Press*, Jan. 6, 1935.
8. *Ibid.* Slave bracelet: a popular West African bracelet with chained links attached to a ring.
9. Edward Burns, "Levinsky Goes Down Under Right Smashes," *Chicago Tribune*, Dec. 29, 1934. On the undercard were Frank Battaglia of Chicago and Kid Leonard of East Moline, Ill.
10. "Max Baer K.O.'s Levinsky in Film at State Theater," *Oakland Tribune*, Jan. 7. The theater also showed Max's 19-year-old brother Buddy in his win over Gene Stanton. Those films played along with *The Last Gentleman* when Baer appeared in Boston.
11. W.W. Edgar, "The Second Guess ... Max Baer Explains," *Detroit Free Press*, Jan. 6, 1935.
12. *Ibid.*
13. *Ibid.*
14. *Ibid.*
15. Charles P. Ward, "Max Charges Card-Stacking in Primo Fight," *Detroit Free Press*, Jan. 6, 1935.
16. *Ibid.*
17. "Louis Would Like to Meet Baer in March," *Oakland Tribune*, Jan. 9, 1935.
18. "Bares Baer Boys' Feud: Max and Buddy Jealous of Each Other's Ability, Says Hoffman," *New York Journal American*, March 3, 1938.
19. "World Champ to Battle in 4 Rounder," *Oakland Tribune*, Feb. 15, 1934.
20. Ralph Bell, "Mrs. Campbell and Baer Meet," *San Mateo Times*, Feb. 16, 1934.
21. "Baer Benefit Nets $11,000 for Mrs. Frankie Campbell," *San Mateo Times*, Feb. 15, 1935.
22. Newspapers variously reported $10,000, $10,500, and under $15,000 for the Campbell benefit.
23. Al Lamb, "Spinning the Sports Top," *Press and Sun-Bulletin*, June 15, 1935.
24. "Baer Gives Merry Ha! Ha! to the Boxing Commission," *Kingston Daily Freeman*, March 27, 1935.
25. "Baer Faces Simms in Non-Title Bout," *Akron Beacon Journal*, April 19, 1935.
26. George Kreker, "Fans' Fare," *Decatur Herald*, Sept. 15, 1936.
27. "Baer Starts Training Tomorrow for Braddock," *Los Angeles Times*, April 29, 1935.

Chapter Nine

1. Frank Eck, "Many Champions to Be Crowned in Big September Sports Month," *Ithaca Journal*, Aug. 29, 1946.
2. Dan Parker, "Killer Instinct Would Have Made Baer Greatest," *The Mirror*, Nov. 24, 1959.
3. Paul Zimmerman, *Los Angeles Times*, July 30, 1942.
4. Grantland Rice, "The Sportlight," *Syracuse Herald*, May 2, 1935.
5. *Ibid.*
6. "Max Baer Is Perky After Chest Accident,"

Kingston Daily Freeman, May 10, 1935; *San Bernardino Sun*, May 10, 1935.
    7. *Time* magazine, July 15, 1935, p. 41.
    8. "Braddock Turns State Trooper," *Canandaigua Daily Messenger*, June 4, 1935.
    9. Matt Jackson, "Conditioned by Bimstein—An Old Ritual," *Democrat and Chronicle*, Dec. 28, 1936.
    10. "Mike Cantwell, Former Trainer of Baer, Files Prediction Challenger Will Win Thursday's Bout After Watching Drill," *Syracuse Herald*, June 9, 1935.
    11. "Baer Burlesques Training Stunts; Maxie Again Clowns Way About Camp as Bout Nears," *Syracuse Herald*, June 6, 1935.
    12. *Ibid.*
    13. Grantland Rice, "Max Baer's Condition," *Syracuse Herald*, June 11, 1935.
    14. *Ibid.*
    15. Bob Ray, "The Sports X-Ray," *Los Angeles Times*, May 31, 1935.
    16. "Titleholder Is Disturbed by Actions of Manager," *Syracuse Herald*, June 7, 1934.
    17. "Dr. Walker Says Baer's Hands May Bother Him in Braddock Battle," June 8, *Syracuse Herald*, June 9, 1935.
    18. "Aftermaths of Title Battle," *Oakland Tribune*, June 15, 1935.
    19. Conversations from the meeting were reported in Henry McLemore, "Art Donovan," *Dunkirk Evening Observer*, June 12, 1935, and Ed Frayne, "Baer Braddock? Ducks Forfeit," *New York American*, June 21, 1954.
    20. Davis J. Walsh, "Claim Baer's Hands Were Bandaged Poorly," *Times, Hammond*, June 20 and 21, 1935.
    21. *Ibid.*
    22. *Ibid.* Leo Friede was also a noted sportsman: an international decked-canoe sailing champion, from 1913 to 1933 and on an Olympic committee for sailing. J. O'Brien was also a good friend of Max. He was a wealthy insurance agent, the Chairman of the American Olympic bobsled committee, and also owned a penthouse in New York. He would serve as best man at Max's wedding to Mary Ellen Sullivan.
    23. Dan Parker, "Killer Instinct Would Have Made Baer Greatest," *Mirror*, Nov. 24, 1959.
    24. Davis J. Walsh, "Pilot Says 'Someone' Got Baer," *New York Evening Journal*, June 20, 1935.
    25. "Baer-Braddock Fight on NBC Chains Tonight," *Syracuse Herald*, June 13, 1935. Also on the show was Kate Smith, singing with the glee club from the New York State Penitentiary at Newburgh, and the Coronation of the King and Queen of the Annual Rhododendron Festival at Asheville, North Carolina.
    26. Transcript of the radio broadcast by Colleen Aycock, "The Voice of Boxing: A Brief History of American Broadcasting Ringside," 2014.
    27. Bond explains that the radios are "complete with antennae valued at $125.50 each." "They receive foreign and domestic, police calls, aviation and amateur signals, all with the clearness and faithfulness of reproduction that will amaze you. You'll be proud to have one in your home." Also given as prizes "every week from June 17 to July 22. The Gillette safety Razor Company will award for the 10 best names received from consumers, 10 of these writers for the next 40 names each week will each receive a Gillette aristocrat one-piece razor. On July 22 a Grand Prize of $1000 in cash will be awarded to the first in sending in the name judged to be the most appropriately submitted during the entire contest." Then he explained how to "enclose your name, in an empty blue-blade package, addressed to Gillette Safety Razor Company, with the name and address of your dealer from whom you purchased the blades. We ask you to send the name of the dealer because if you win one, your dealer will also win one and you wouldn't want to see him lose out, would you? Mail your entrees to Box 20, Boston, Mass. Winners will be announced every Monday night on the Gillette radio program starring Max Baer in the big mystery thriller, Lucky Smith."
    28. Colleen Aycock, radio transcript.
    29. Dan Cuoco, discussions with the author.
    30. Grantland Rice, "The Sportlight," *Press and Sun Bulletin*, May 10, 1939.
    31. Colleen Aycock, radio transcript.
    32. Dan Parker, "Killer Instinct Would Have Made Baer Greatest," *Mirror*, Nov. 24, 1959.
    33. Nat Fleischer, *Glamour Boy of the Ring*, pg. 33.
    34. James P. Dawson, "Braddock Outpoints Baer to Win World Ring Title," *New York Times*, June 15, 1935.
    35. Al Lamb, "Spinning the Sports Top," *Press and Sun Bulletin*, June 15, 1935.
    36. Ed Hughes, "Ed Hughes' Column," *Brooklyn Daily Eagle*, June 15, 1935.
    37. *Ibid.*
    38. Paul Gallico "How It Feels," *Democrat and Chronicle*, June 16, 1935.
    39. Grantland Rice, "Baer Has No Excuse for Defeat; He Fought Poorly and Lost Title," *Syracuse Herald*, June 14, 1935.
    40. Joe Williams, "Sports Roundup," *Syracuse Herald*, June 14, 1935.
    41. Damon Runyon, "Braddock Defeats Baer to Win Heavyweight Title," *New York American*, June 14, 1935.
    42. Art Cohn, "Cohn-ing Tower," *Oakland Tribune*, Sept. 28, 1941.
    43. Walter Winchell, "On Broadway," *Wilkes-Barre Times Leader, Evening News*, Pennsylvania, June 17, 1935.
    44. Joe Williams, "Sports Roundup," *Syracuse Herald*, June 14, 1935.
    45. James P. Dawson, "Braddock Outpoints Baer to Win World Ring Title," *New York Times*, June 14, 1935.
    46. William Weer, "Cries of Racketeering Greet Victory of Braddock," *Brooklyn Daily Eagle*, June 14, 1935.
    47. "Phelan Denies 'Fix,'" *Kingston Daily Freeman*, June 14, 1935.
    48. "No Phoney, Cries Baer to Charges," *Los Angeles Times*, June 15, 1935.
    49. "Both Max's Hands Broken, X-Rays Disclose," *New York Evening Journal*, June 14, 1935.

50. Eddie Brietz, "Braddock Gets Offers That May Pay Total of 150 Grand," *Democrat and Chronicle*, June 16, 1935.
51. "German No Longer Interested in Elimination Fight with Baer and Wants Direct Chance at Title," *New York Times*, June 15, 1935.
52. Joseph C. Nichols, "Check for $31,244 Paid to Braddock," *New York Times*, June 15, 1935.
53. "Former Champion Takes Mary Ellen Sullivan of Ithaca as Second Wife," *Syracuse Herald*, June 30, 1935.
54. "Baer Reveals He May Become Roman Catholic," *New York Evening Journal*, July 1, 1935.
55. *Ibid.*
56. "Vatican Officials Would Accept Baer," *San Bernardino County Sun*, July 5, 1935.
57. Bill Farnsworth, "Mitt Solons Rule Schmeling No. 1 Title Challenger," *New York Evening Journal*, July 21, 1935.
58. "Hoffman Set Friday for Surgery," *Oakland Tribune*, July 9, 1935.
59. "Baer Returns to Cottage; Hands O.K.," *Oakland Tribune*, July 11, 1935.
60. Harvey Woodruff, "Braddock Paid $31,244; Louis, Carnera Are Out," *Chicago Daily Tribune*, June 15, 1935.

Chapter Ten

1. *Kingston Daily Freeman*, Sept. 24, 1940.
2. Ronald K. Fried, *Corner Men*, p. 132.
3. Frank Graham, "Graham's Corner, Max Baer," *New York Journal American*, March 30, 1964.
4. Grantland Rice, "The Sportlight," *Syracuse Herald*, July 11, 1934.
5. "Baer Training with Much Pep," *The Daily Messenger*, Aug. 20, 1935.
6. Al Wolf, "Sportraits," *Los Angeles Times*, Feb. 9, 1944.
7. "Fists of Black Bomber Usher in New 'White Hope' Epoch," *Times Herald*, Olean, NY Sept. 25, 1935.
8. "Louis, Baer Site Selected," *Los Angeles Times*, Aug. 23, 1935.
9. "Bares Baer Boys' Feud," *New York Journal American*, March 3, 1938.
10. Grantland Rice, "The Sportlight," *Press and Sun-Bulletin*, Aug. 27, 1935.
11. *Ibid.*
12. Paul Gallico, "In Whose Lap," *Democrat and Chronicle Sun*, Sept. 22, 1935.
13. "Jim Braddock Picks Max Baer," *Oakland Tribune*, Aug. 30, 1936.
14. Ed Hughes' Column, *Brooklyn Daily Eagle*, Sept. 24, 1935.
15. George Dixon in the late 1800s demanded seats for black patrons who wanted to see his fights, and they were allowed to buy seats in a segregated section in the upper decks.
16. Red Smith, "Max Baer," *New York Journal American* (University of Texas Clippings File, exact day unreadable), Nov. (23?) 1959.
17. "Fists of Black Bomber Usher in New 'White Hope' Epoch," *Times Herald* (Olean, New York), Sept. 25, 1935.
18. Louis was said to have made $5 million during his lifetime, but after having spent lavishly and having his earnings siphoned off by managers, promoters, even James Braddock, he would end up penniless and spend the last half of his life owing the United States government for back taxes. For Baer's take of $150,000, see Henry Super, "Baer Sells Shares, Loses Thousands," *Oakland Tribune*, Sept. 26, 1935.
19. "Bomber Unmarked After Battle, Says Beaten Rival 'Certainly Has Tough Chin.'" *New York Times*, Sept. 25, 1935.
20. Joe Louis, *Joe Louis: My Life*, p. 73.
21. "Swell Fighter, Is Max's Tribute to Victor—Will be Cattle Rancher in Livermore," *New York Times*, Sept. 25, 1935.
22. Jack Dempsey, "Dempsey, Praising Louis Highly, Doubtful Whether Any Fighter Can Cope with Him," *New York Times*, Sept. 25, 1935; *Petaluma Argus-Courier*, Oct. 1, 1935.
23. Joe Williams, "Louis Calls Baer Toughest Opponent but Fight Was Not Hardest Champion Has Had," *Press and Sun-Bulletin*, May 19, 1944.
24. "Ex-Mrs. Max Baer Says He's 'Too Kind Hearted to Fight,'" *Oakland Tribune*, Nov. 8, 1935.
25. Alan Ward, "Champ Seeking Bout with Negro," *Oakland Tribune*, Nov. 21, 1935.
26. Untitled. *Los Angeles Times*, Dec. 6, 1935.
27. Roger Treat, "A Bellyful of Bums," *New Yorker* (Sept. 1939): p. 35.
28. O.O. McIntyre, *San Bernardino County Sun*, Jan. 19, 1936.
29. Charles McMurtry, "Maxie Baer Takes Another Crack at Movies," *Poughkeepsie Eagle-News*, June 24, 1942.
30. Paul Zimmerman, "Sport Postscripts," *Los Angeles Times*, July 30, 1942.
31. Ernest Hemingway, "Million-dollar Fright: A New York Letter," *Esquire* (Dec. 1936). http://archive.esquire.com/issue/19351201, accessed February 8, 2017. Ernest Hemingway loved sport, particularly boxing, fishing, hunting and bullfighting. He used those subjects memorably in his fiction. But using his fictional tools to depict the nonfiction event did a great injustice to Max Baer.
32. *Ibid.*
33. "Max Baer Voted Greatest Sport Disappointment in '35," *Dunkirk Evening Observer*, Jan. 6, 1936.
34. "Louis Lists Victims of Boxing Ring," *San Bernardino County Sun*, Dec. 15, 1935.
35. George E. Helmer, "Baer Would Fight Joe Louis on 'Winner Take All' Basis," *San Mateo Times*, Dec. 31, 1935.

Chapter Eleven

1. Edward Burns, "Max Baer—The Fighting Clown," *Chicago Tribune*, June 19, 1934.

2. "Max Must Pay, Says Hoffman," *Oakland Tribune*, Jan. 24, 1936.

3. George Helmer, "Mat Promoter Seeks to Sign Former Champ," *San Bernardino County Sun*, Jan. 14, 1936.

4. George E. Helmer, "Mary, Wife of Mr. Max Baer Disapproves of Wrestling," *Petaluma Argus Courier*, Jan. 14, 1936.

5. Henry McLemore, "Hank in Favor of Saving Public from Baer Comeback," *Oakland Tribune*, Feb. 24, 1936.

6. "Bud Baer Meets Phil, No Damage," *The Times*, Feb. 19, 1936.

7. Lee Dunbar, "Max Offered $25,000 for 'Comeback,'" *Oakland Tribune*, Feb. 17, 1936; "Max Vows to End Clowning," *Santa Ana Register*, Feb. 17, 1936.

8. *Ibid.*

9. *Ibid.*

10. "Ramey Still Rated No. 1 for Canzoneri," *Democrat and Chronicle*, April 1, 1936.

11. Max paid $55.22 for the license plate for his large sedan in Roseville, California. "Maxie Baer Pays Heavy for Big Car," *San Bernardino County Sun*, Feb. 7, 1936.

12. Russ J. Newland, "Baer Ready to Fight His Way Back to Top," *Santa Cruz Evening News*, June 19, 1936.

13. *Santa Cruz Evening News*, June 19, 1936.

14. "Baer Joyous Over Victory of Big Uhland," *Salt Lake Tribune*, June 20, 1936.

15. "Max Baer Offers $200,000 to Get Braddock in Ring," *Miami Daily News-Record*, June 23, 1936.

16. "Baer Offered Schmeling Contest," *San Antonio Light*, June 25, 1936.

17. Ed Hughes, "Ed Hughes Column," *New York Daily Eagle*, June 25, 1936.

18. Henry McLemore, "Some More Predictions," *Times Herald*, June 27, 1936.

19. "Baer Leaves with Boos Ringing in Ears," *San Antonio Light*, June 25, 1936; "Max Baer Routed by Booes of Fans San Antonio Bout," *Corsicana Daily Sun*, June 25, 1935.

20. "Baer Has Several Irons in the Fire but None Getting Hot," *Pampa Daily News*, July 5, 1936.

21. "Bomber to Ask for Max Baer: Jacobs Urged to Capture Californian for Bout at Soldier Field," *Poughkeepsie Eagle News*, July 17, 1936.

22. "Baer Choice for Joe's Comeback," *Democrat and Chronicle* (Rochester, NY), July 20, 1936.

23. "Heavyweight Ex-Champs Clutter Fistiana's Broadway," *Democrat and Chronicle*, July 26, 1936. Now the picture was nothing but ex-champions on comeback tours.

24. Felix R. McKnight, "Sports Talk," *Denton Record Chronicle*, July 6, 1936.

25. "Will Joke with an Ex-Great," *Brooklyn Daily Eagle*, July 31, 1936.

26. "Max Saves 'Papa' Baer from Death," *Oakland Tribune*, July 28, 1936.

27. "Sport Tabloid," *The Bend Bulletin*, Oregon, Aug. 25, 1936.

28. "Critic Due for Razzing, Says Max," *Evening Herald*, Aug. 24, 1936.

29. "Baer May Fight in Garden Soon," *Idaho Falls Post-Register*, Sept. 3, 1936.

30. *Times Herald* (Olean, NY), Sept. 19, 1936.

31. "Serious Baer Drills at 'Y,'" *Des Moines Register*, Sept. 11, 1936.

32. "Buddy Baer Stops Rival," *Des Moines Register*, Sept. 19, 1936.

33. "Baer Clowns Through Bout as Suckers Yell," *Mason City Glove-Gazette*, Oct. 1, 1936.

34. "Max Baer Floors Someone by the Name of Charles," *Daily Chronicle* (DeKalb, IL), Oct. 7, 1936.

35. "Chicago Negro Outpoints Baer," *Rhinelander Daily News* (Wisconsin), Oct. 9, 1936.

36. "Max Baer's Comeback Tour Ends Suddenly—'Homesick,'" *Democrat and Chronicle*, Oct. 23, 1936.

37. Grantland Rice, "Max and Buddy," *Press and Sun Bulletin*, Oct. 14, 1936.

Chapter Twelve

1. "Baer in Demand," *New York American*, July 8, 1936.

2. Joe Louis had expected to go over in May, but after negotiating a deal with manager Joe Gould, Louis was offered the title fight in June with Jimmy Braddock.

3. "Max Baer Aims at Comeback," *Ithaca Journal*, Oct. 29, 1936; "Max Baer Will Fight in London Next February," *Press and Sun-Bulletin*, Oct. 29, 1936.

4. "Max Baer Outlines Plans for Return Bout with Louis," *Los Angeles Times*, Jan. 4, 1937.

5. Art Cohn, "Cohn-ing Tower," *Oakland Tribune*, Jan. 31, 1937.

6. Art Cohn, "Fire Gives Max Baer Long Count—100: Baer Raids Outfitters for Raiment," *Oakland Tribune*, Jan. 19, 1937.

7. "Buying Sox for Max Baer Tough Task," *Los Angeles Times*, Feb. 2, 1937.

8. Art Cohn, "Cohn-ing Tower," *Oakland Tribune*, Feb. 3, 1937.

9. "Braddock Signs with Jacobs for Two Exhibitions," *Chicago Tribune*, Feb. 3, 1937.

10. We know that Johnston's job was at stake because Garden executives were making inquiries with other managers and promoters. Ancil Hoffman said he had been approached by the Garden to take over fight promotions. Mike Jacobs was also approached to lease the Garden for his fights.

11. Gould and Braddock would get (through promoter Mike Jacobs) 10 percent of all of Joe Louis's title fight earnings for the next 10 years.

12. "Art Cohn "Cohn-ing Tower," *Oakland Tribune*, Feb. 4, 1937.

13. *New York Journal American*, Feb. 24, 1937.

14. Art Cohn, "Cohn-ing Tower," *Oakland Tribune*, Feb. 25, 1937.

15. "Mitt Solons Grant Baer License," *Journal American*, Feb. 29, 1937.

16. "Schmeling to Arrive Today to Prepare to Meet Champion in June," *Daily Messenger*, March 2, 1937.
17. "Schmeling to Arrive Today to Prepare to Meet Champion in June," *Daily Messenger*, March 2, 1937.
18. "Heavyweight Situation Appears to Be Muddled," *Daily Messenger*, March 3, 1937.
19. *Ibid*.
20. "Madcap Maxie Baer Dodges Law, Press, Women; Sails for Merry England," *Democrat and Chronicle* (Rochester, NY), March 4, 1937.
21. *Hartlespool Northern Daily Mail* (Durham, England), March 10, 1937; "Max Smacks One," *Santa Cruz Evening News*, April 6, 1937.
22. Jack Singer, "Louis Warns Armstrong to Avoid Pedro Montanez," *Los Angeles Times*, April 5, 1937.
23. Frank Piccassi moved to Phoenix, Arizona. He had been in the boxing business for 20 years and had worked with Baer, Carnera, and Jack Dempsey. He was frequently found in Max's corner for his exhibitions and was expected to attend Max in exhibitions when he returned to the United States. (On July 30, 1937, he was back in San Francisco attending a four-round exhibition with Al Rovay of San Jose. Max received the newspaper decision.)
24. Farr's son Gene gives his birth year as 1913; however, numerous sources give the year as 1914. The source for his boxing record of 83 won (23 KO), 34 lost (6 KO), and 17 drawn, comes from *Man of Courage: The Life and Career of Tommy Farr* by Bob Lonkhurst. The record should note that he fought many more battles than what has been recorded. He was cremated at Worthing.
25. "Tommy Farr Beats Max Baer," *Nottingham Post* (England), April 16, 1937.
26. "Farr Decisively Outpoints Baer," *New York Times*, April 16, 1937.
27. Gayle Talbott, "Farr Seeking Schmeling Battle," *Oakland Tribune*, April 16, 1937.
28. "Max Training to Become 'Papa' Baer," *Los Angeles Times*, Aug. 2, 1937.
29. Al Wolf, "Sportraits," *Los Angeles Times*, Feb. 9, 1944. Farr's bout with Braddock was Braddock's last fight before he retired, and only his second fight (excluding exhibitions) since winning the title from Max Baer in 1935.
30. "Baer 'Foords' Oblivion River in Comeback," *Brooklyn Daily Eagle*, May 28, 1937.
31. Harry Grayson, "The Payoff," *Santa Ana Register*, June 16, 1937.
32. *Ibid*.
33. Helliwell, p. 19.
34. Helliwell, p. 20.
35. Helliwell, p. 21.
36. "Max Baer 'Best'!" *Brooklyn Daily Eagle*, Dec. 11, 1938.
37. Ed Brennan, "Braddock-Baer 30th Anniversary: New Disclosure by Braddock on His Climb to Title," *The Ring* (Feb. 1965): p. 56; Peter Heller, *In This Corner!*, p. 176.
38. "Order Arrest of Baer on Non-Appearance Charge," *San Bernardino County Sun*, Aug. 31, 1937.
39. "Max Baer," *Journal American*, Aug. 29, 1937.
40. "Judge Assails Maxie Baer as Nuisance," *Journal American*, Aug. 31, 1937. It is unknown at this writing if Max ever posed for the judge.
41. "Buddy Baer Set for Big Campaign," *Los Angeles Times*, July 16, 1937.
42. "Max Baer Father of 8-pound Boy," *Democrat and Chronicle* (Rochester, NY), Dec. 5, 1937.
43. Henry McLemore, "Baby Son, Home Troubles Change Baer's Outlook," *San Mateo Times*, CA, Dec. 15, 1937.
44. *Ibid*.
45. "Bud Baer Wants Braddock Next Because He Beat Brother Max," *Brooklyn Daily Eagle*, Dec. 18, 1937.
46. Gayle Talbot, "Sweet-Tempered Farr Wants Max Baer after Braddock," *Oakland Tribune*, Jan. 18, 1938.
47. Art Cohn, "Cohn-ing Tower," *Oakland Tribune*, Jan. 24, 1938.
48. *Ibid*.
49. "Gould Rules Out Baer but Wants Louis," *Santa Ana Register*, Jan. 24, 1938.
50. "Baer-Farr Bout Due for March 11," *Oakland Tribune*, Feb. 1, 1938.
51. "Girl Suing Max Baer Wants 'Vindication,'" *American Journal*, Dec. 19, 1937; "Suit Settled by Max Baer: $2000 Balm Paid Out of Court to N.Y. Showgirl," *Oakland Tribune*, Feb. 9, 1938.
52. Gayle Talbot, "Buddy Baer to Meet Gunnar Barlund," *Petaluma Argus Courier*, March 2, 1938. Gayle Talbot, "Secret of Baer's Success Revealed," *San Bernardino County Sun*, March 3, 1938.
53. "Gunnar Barlund Blasts Predictions of Experts and Baer's Title Chance," *Times Herald* (Olean, NY), March 5, 1938.
54. "Maxie Baer Harder Puncher Than Louis," *Oakland Tribune*, Feb. 5, 1943.
55. "Predicts Max Win Over Louis," *Petaluma Argus-Courier*, April 19, 1938.
56. "Referee Donovan Clears Baer's Name," *Oakland Tribune*, April 1, 1938.

Chapter Thirteen

1. "Louis Laughs After Victory," *Los Angeles Times*, June 23, 1938.
2. Alan Ward, "Baer Scores Champ's Win," *Oakland Tribune*, July 13, 1938.
3. *Ibid*.
4. *Ibid*.
5. "Max Schmeling's Hip Bone Broken," *Los Angeles Times*, June 23, 1938.
6. *Ibid*.
7. Eddie Brietz, "Baer Next for Bomber Luis: Max Schmeling Continues to Improve at N.Y. Hospital from Fight Injury," *San Bernardino County Sun*, June 25, 1938.
8. "Joe Denies Retirement Form Ring," *Santa Cruz Sentinel*, June 25, 1938.

9. "Louis-Baer Bout Next September," *Kingston Daily Freeman*, July 14, 1938.
10. Harry Grayson, "The Payoff," *Santa Ana Register* Aug. 8, 1938.
11. Art Cohn, "The Cohn-ing Tower," *Oakland Tribune*, Aug. 7, 1938.
12. Alan Ward, "On Second Thought," *Oakland Tribune*, Aug. 9, 1938. The same day as Dora's death, her brother-in-law (Max's uncle) Benjamin Baer, a police officer in Denver, was in court and sentenced to pay $2500 in damages to Mr. F.A. Piper, who claimed that Ben Baer beat him up after their automobiles collided. The Baers had a prideful love of cars.
13. Henry Super, "Baer's Future Mixed Up in Lou Nova Battle Tomorrow," *Bakersfield Californian*, Dec. 15, 1938.
14. Jack Cuddy, "Cuddy Says Nova Would Stop Louis," *Los Angeles Times*, Dec. 20, 1938.
15. "Cowboy Max Baer Seeks Ring Work," *Ithaca Journal*, Jan. 11, 1939; "Heigh Ho, Maxie! Baer's in Movies," *Democrat and Chronicle*, Jan. 11, 1939.
16. "Max Baer Wants Nova or Galento," *Kingston Daily Freeman*, Jan. 11, 1939.
17. Bill Corum, "Bill Corum Says...," *San Bernardino County Sun*, Jan. 11, 1939.
18. "Galento and Baer Exchange 'Pleasantries,'" *Santa Ana Register*, Jan. 12, 1939.
19. "Farr May Get 2nd Title Shot," *Middletown Times Herald*, Jan. 12, 1939.
20. Henry McLemore, "Henry McLemore Says," *Oakland Tribune*, Jan. 20, 1939.
21. Dan Parker, "No Excuse for Nova-Baer Fight, Parker Says," *Democrat and Chronicle* (Rochester, NY), Jan. 18, 1939.
22. "Galento Stops Jorge Brescia," *Oakland Tribune*, Jan. 20, 1939.
23. "Baer to Face Lou Nova on May 25," *Los Angeles Times*, Jan. 15, 1939.
24. Art Cohn, "Cohn-ing Tower," *Oakland Tribune*, Jan. 23, 1939.
25. Compare: "Baer Admits Nova Fighter," *Oakland Tribune*, Jan. 24, 1939; "Maxie Wants Crack at the Title," *Albuquerque Journal*, Jan. 24, 1939.
26. Bill Corum, "Bill Corum Says..., Max Baer Present," *San Bernardino County Sun*, Jan. 17, 1939.
27. Harvey Rockwell, "Canzoneri Picks Baer Over Nova," *San Mateo Times*, Feb. 2, 1939.
28. Art Cohn, "Galento Beaten Only 24 Times," *Oakland Tribune*, Feb. 29, 1939.
29. "Louis to Gun for Quick Win," *Los Angeles Times*, March 9, 1939.
30. *Brooklyn Daily Eagle*, March 15, 1939.
31. Frank Finch, "Lou Nova Confident He'll Defeat Max Baer and Louis," *Los Angeles Times*, March 19, 1939.
32. Braven Dyer, "The Sports Parade," *Los Angeles Times*, April 3, 1939.
33. Eddie Brietz, "Sports Roundup," *Ithaca Journal*, May 4, 1939.
34. "Sweet Charity Move Just Headache, They Find," *Democrat and Chronicle* (Rochester, NY), Jan. 18, 1939.
35. "Max Baer Heads East: Ex-Champ Confident He'll Beat Nova and Then Regain Title," *Los Angeles Times*, April 3, 1939.
36. "Lou Faces Task of Throwing Off Cold Before Bout," *Kingsport Times*, May 24, 1939.
37. "Nova to Train at Swank Camp: Exclusive Club has Elephants, Tigers, Teacher of Yogi," *Oakland Tribune*, March 30, 1939; "The Place to Train!" *Brooklyn Daily Eagle*, March 30, 1939.
38. Henry L. McLemore, "Braddock to Give Nova Notes on Baer Taken in Slow Fight," *Press and Sun*, May 10, 1939.
39. Gayle Talbot, "Nova Cinch—Braddock," *Oakland Tribune*, May 16, 1939.
40. Al Wolf, "Baer Ready to Supply 'Oomph' for Movie and Fight Industries," *Los Angeles Times*, Aug. 1, 1939.
41. "Ed Hughes' Column," *Brooklyn Daily Eagle*, June 2, 1939.
42. Bill Potts, *Los Angeles*, Sports Weekly, September 23, 1939.
43. Art Cohn, "Louis-Roper Outdrew Baer-Nova," *Oakland Tribune*, June 2, 1939.
44. Henry McLemore, "Mrs. Baer Tells Why Max Fought Again," *Santa Ana Register*, June 3, 1939.
45. "Baer Pleased Braddock Won," *Oakland Tribune*, Jan. 23, 1938.
46. Alan Ward, "On Second Thought," *Oakland Tribune*, June 4, 1939.

Chapter Fourteen

1. Hype Igoe, "Art Donovan Philly Referee," *Press and Sun Bulletin*, July 19, 1939.
2. "Hundreds Enjoy Thrilling Bouts," *Goldfield News*, Sept. 8, 1939.
3. "Maxie, Buddy Baer, Hoffman Hit City!" *Lubbock Morning Avalanche*, Sept. 12, 1939.
4. Collier Parris, "Baer's Famous Right Kayoes," *Lubbock Morning Avalanche*, Sept. 19, 1939.
5. Arch Ward, *Chicago Tribune*, Oct. 30, 1939. Boxer Harry Thomas had taken the name of his first trainer in Los Angeles, Dan Thomas. While working for the Southern Pacific rail lines in Los Angeles, he turned to boxing. He was raised in poverty and never owned anything but pants and a sweater. After a year with Thomas, Jack Dempsey took over his contract for 3 fights until Thomas got blood poisoning in his arm and had to retire and go back to the railroad. Chicago promoter Jim Mullen brought him from Los Angeles to Chicago, where Jack Hurley took over his affairs. After Hurley had a falling-out with Mullen, Nate Lewis took over his contract.
6. Arch Ward, "Thomas Admits Fakes; 28,000 Fans Swindled," *Chicago Tribune*, Dec. 30, 1939.
7. *Ibid.*
8. *Ibid.*
9. "Galento Vs. Baer Heads Finnish Relief Program," *San Bernardino County Sun*, Jan. 5, 1940.

10. Whitney Martin, "Maxie Baer Claims Ready to Meet Louis Again and This Time Get Title; So Did Nova," *Santa Cruz Sentinel Sun*, Feb. 18, 1940.
11. Whitney Martin, "Ancil Hoffman Believes Baer Wants to Fight," *Santa Cruz Sentinel*, Feb. 24, 1940.
12. Alan Ward, *Oakland Tribune*, April 18, 1941.
13. Lawton Carver, "Baer, Galento Should Stage No. 1 Brawl," *Fresno Bee, The Republican*, Jan. 14, 1940.
14. "Jacobs Gives Up His Galento-Baer Match," *Santa Ana Register*, Jan. 19, 1940.
15. "Baer Open Verbal Tiff with Tony," *Los Angeles Times*, April 23, 1940.
16. *Ibid.*
17. "McLemore Says," *Dunkirk Evening Observer*, April 24, 1940.
18. "Joe Jacobs, Tony Galento's Manager, Dies in New York," *Oakland Tribune*, April 25, 1940.
19. Harry Grayson, "Two-Ton Must Beat Baer Sans Aid of Jacobs, Who Performed Greatest of Managerial Feats," *Dunkirk Evening Observer*, May 7, 1940.
20. "Fugitives from Squirrel Case, Baer and Galento Decide Screwball Honors," *Santa Cruz Sentinel*, May 8, 1940, from *Look* magazine, May 7, 1940.
21. Henry McLemore, "McLemore Says," *Dunkirk Evening Observer*, May 28, 1940.
22. "Max Baer to Stay in Ring, Says Wife," *Democrat and Chronicle*, May 31, 1940.
23. Pat Robinson, "'Before Tenth Round'-Champ," *Santa Ana Register*, June 24, 1940.
24. "Tony-Max Buildup Reaches Comic Peak," *San Bernardino County Sun*, June 24, 1940.
25. "Braddock Seen Referee for Baer-Galento Tussle," *Poughkeepsie Eagle News*, June 27, 1940.
26. "Baer Cannot Wear Star of David on Trunks," *Petaluma Argus Courier*, June 27, 1940.
27. Harold Conrad, "Dat Louis Has Slowed Up Galento Tells Constituents," *Brooklyn Daily Eagle*, June 27, 1940.
28. Henry McLemore, "Worst Fight in History Set Tuesday," *Bakersfield Californian*, June 27, 1940.
29. Harry Ferguson, "Baer Hits Galento at Weigh-In," *Oakland Tribune*, July 2, 1940.
30. *Ibid.*
31. "Galento's Face Cut in Brawl, Injury Will Not Delay Fight," *Asbury Park Press*, July 1, 1940.
32. Arthur Daley, *New York Times*, Nov. 25, 1959.
33. Gayle Talbot, "Galento Still Popular with New Jersey Fans," *Asbury Park Press*, July 3, 1940.
34. *Ibid.*
35. "Maxie Eyes Bout with Louis," *Los Angeles Times*, July 3, 1940.
36. "Baer, Galento Drew $97,254," *Oakland Tribune*, July 3, 1940.

Chapter Fifteen

1. Lawton Carver, "Believe Young Irish Fighter Next Champ," *Santa Ana Register*, Sept. 20, 1940.
2. Eddie Brietz, *Courier-News*, Sept. 18, 1940.
3. Harry Ferguson, UP Sports Editor, "'Cash' Says Hoffman and Kearns Produces," *Santa Ana Register*, Sept. 5, 1940.
4. Photocopy of the postcard stamped Long Branch, Sept. 6, 4–6 p.m. Brignolia was the apothecary in San Leandro.
5. Harold Conrad, "It's 'Color, Inc.' with Max Baer in Doc's Venture," *Brooklyn Daily Eagle*, Sept. 18, 1940.
6. *Brooklyn Daily Eagle*, Sept. 17, 1940.
7. "May Be Baer's Last Fight," *Asbury Park Press*, Sept. 22, 1940.
8. Henry McLemore, "McLemore Says," *Oakland Tribune*, Sept. 27, 1940; Joseph C. Nichols, "20,000 See Baer Win from Comiskey by Knockout in First," *New York Times*, Sept. 27, 1940.
9. "Millions of Young Men Register in Mass for U.S. Military Service," *Petaluma Argus Courier*, Oct. 16, 1940.
10. Eddie Brietz, "Roundup of Sports by Brietz," *Petaluma Argus Courier*, Dec. 4, 1940.
11. Jimmy Wood, *Brooklyn Daily Eagle*, Dec. 11, 1940.
12. Leonard Lyons, "Broadway Medley," *San Mateo Times*, Dec. 26, 1945.
13. "Baer Well Received in Hub Stage Debut," *Brooklyn Daily Eagle*, Dec. 4, 1940.
14. Paul Zimmerman, "Max Baerymore," *Los Angeles Times*, Dec. 5, 1940.
15. Jack Cuddy, "Max Baer Is Rated Ranking Contender for Heavy Title," *Bakersfield Californian*, Dec. 27, 1940.
16. Harvey Rockwell, "Sports Slants," *San Mateo Times*, Dec. 28, 1940.
17. Art Cohn, "Cohn-ing Tower," *Oakland Tribune*, Feb. 3, 1941.
18. "Beginning to Have Its Effect," *Dunkirk Evening Observer*, March 12, 1941.
19. Pat Robinson, "Nova Will Use 'Stick, Step, Duck' Formula on Baer," *Fresno Bee*, March 28, 1941.
20. Jack Cuddy, "Baer Beaten by Nova," *Los Angeles Times*, April 5, 1941.
21. *Ibid.*
22. *Ibid.*
23. Sid Feder, "Nova Plans to Outpunch Louis in Yankee Stadium Title Battle," *Democrat and Chronicle*, Aug. 12, 1941.

Chapter Sixteen

1. On April 29, 1941, in Santa Rosa he refereed a bout of welterweights, George Duke and Manuel Gonzales. On May 10, he was inducted into the Santa Barbara Los Rancheros Visitadores after a grand rodeo with a performance by Monte Montana. On May 18, Max was the Grand Marshall of the Hayward Rodeo parade.
2. "Buddy Baer to Beat Louis for Maxie—He Says," *San Bernardino County Sun*, May 19, 1941.
3. Jack Cuddy, "Manager Contends Louis' Blow Landed After Bell," *Oakland Tribune*, May 24, 1941.
4. "Bomber Sees No Early KO," *New York Journal American*, May 23, 1941.
5. "Ancil Shouts 'Robbery' in Dressing Room," *Oakland Tribune*, May 24, 1941.

6. *Ibid.*
7. "Officials Agree Buddy Was Hit After Bell Rang," *Brooklyn Daily Eagle*, May 24, 1941.
8. "Boxing Commissioners Convinced at Hearing Baer Was Hit Illegally," *Press and Sun-Bulletin*, May 26, 1941; "Bout 'Won in 7' for Records," *New York Journal American*, May 24, 1941.
9. "Max Baer Speaks on Schmeling Death," *Dunkirk Evening Observer*, May 29, 1941.
10. Harold Conrad, "Louis Is 5 to 1 Over Buddy in Navy Relief Fund Battle," *Brooklyn Daily Eagle*, Jan. 9, 1942.
11. Whiney Martin, "Joe Should Stop King-Sized Baer," *Poughkeepsie Eagle-News*, Jan. 3, 1942.
12. Jack Singer "Buddy Sees KO Finish: Doesn't Fear Joe; Blames Referee for Earlier Defeat," *New York Journal American*, Jan. 7, 1942.
13. Harry Grayson, "Disillusioned Baer Quits Path of Brother for That of Father," *Santa Ana Register*, Jan. 21, 1942.
14. "Maxie Baer Definitely to Be in Santa Rosa for Big Army Benefit Boxing Card," *Press Democrat* (Santa Rosa), Jan. 28, 1942; and "Battle Royal," same paper, next day.
15. "Not So Dumb," *Los Angeles Times*, June 9, 1942.
16. Alan Ward, "Baer, Ex-Playboy of Ring, Is Rated as 'Good Soldier,'" *Oakland Tribune*, Jan. 29, 1943.
17. *Ibid.*
18. *Ibid.*
19. Dan McGuire, "Max Baer Praises New Manager, Uncle Sam," *San Mateo Times*, Feb. 1, 1943. (I believe that McGuire's reference to "omission and commission" points to the day before Baer's title defense with Braddock.)
20. Walt Dobbins, "Former Heavy King, Max Baer Says Fitness Great Asset to Men," *Nebraska State Journal*, Dec. 10, 1943.
21. "Max and Buddy Baer Visit San Bernardino Air Field," *San Bernardino County Sun*, Sept. 16, 1943.
22. Oscar Fraley, "Max Baer Blames War on His Ring Conquests," *Democrat and Chronicle*, Nov. 9, 1943. The tour began at Tinker AAF OK and went to San Bernardino Air Field CA and then to Utah and on to Patterson Field, Dayton, Ohio. After that, the tour went to the East Coast: Mitchell AAF NY, Bradley AAF CT, Camp Springs MD, Richmond AAF VA, Langley AAF VA, Charleston AAF SC, Atlanta AAF GA, Thomasville AAF GA, Lincoln AAF NE, Sioux City AAF IA, Dalhart AAF TX, Pocatello AAF ID, Casper AAF WY, San Antonio TX, Page AAF FL, Dale Mabry AAF, Hillsborough AAF FL, Pinellas AAF FL, Greenville AAF NC, Esler AAF LA, Key AAF MS, and William Northern AAF TN. Max and Buddy boxed exhibitions at every base until Buddy was hospitalized in February 1944 for old boxing injuries. Then there were no more boxing exhibitions. Through January 1944, newspaper articles exist for 16 boxing exhibitions on the tour. If half of the locations were visited by the end of January, then the actual number of boxing exhibitions was far more than 16, and maybe as high as

90. Max told the *Oakland Tribune* on Dec. 30, 1943, "To fulfill the itinerary [we] had to catch two camps a day every once and a while, and that hardly allowed time for changing clothes. Train, bus, plane, private car—all [were] employed in the cross-country tour."
23. "Sgt. Bud Baer May Receive Discharge," *Petaluma Argus-Courier*, Mar. 17, 1944.
24. Winner of the Max Baer Trophy in 1943 was Pvt. Robert Radish. He was part of the Hawthorne Marines in the Battle for the Marshall Islands in 1944. He was wounded in the arm in battle. Winner of the same heavyweight trophy in 1944 was E.W. Bailey, Navy.
25. "Joe Louis Labels Max Baer 'Toughest Opponent,'" *Democrat and Chronicle*, May 10, 1944. Louis named Billy Conn as the smartest and also the fastest; Lee Ramey as most courageous; Arturo Godoy as most troublesome; Bob Pastor as fastest retreater; Johnny Paycheck as easiest opponent; and Al Delaney as landing the hardest punch to his chin, 1934. On the other hand, he said the hardest punch he ever landed was on Paulino Uzcudun, 1935.
26. Whitney Martin, "Maxie Given Verbal Pat on Back by Champion Joe Louis," *Abilene Reporter-News*, May 15, 1944.
27. "Max Baer Tells World He's Glad He Never Was 'Quitter,'" *Troy Record*, May 22, 1944.
28. "Max Baer Quits Due to Injury," *Press Democrat*, July 4, 1944.
29. Jack Lait, Jr. "Hollywood," *Brooklyn Daily Eagle*, Jan. 5, 1947.
30. Ben Gould, *Brooklyn Daily Eagle*, May 9, 1946.

Chapter Seventeen

1. Hedda Hopper, "Looking at Hollywood," *Los Angeles Times*, Jan. 8, 1946.
2. Henry Sutherland, "Filmland Aghast at Baer's Movie Cowboy Ambitions," *San Bernardino County Sun*, Feb. 17, 1936.
3. "Braddock in Town for Bout," *Los Angeles Times*, Nov. 26, 1935.
4. *Syracuse Herald*, Nov. 24, 1933.
5. Jimmy Cannon, "Sports Today: A Laughing Man," *New York Journal American*, Nov. 22, 1959.
6. "Objection to Jewish Performer," *The Times* (London), March 31, 1934.
7. "Baer Movie Ban 'Tough on Women,'" *Oakland Tribune*, March 29, 1934.
8. Louella O. Parsons, "Prison Break Will Be Pictured in Movie," *Fresno Bee*, Jan. 18, 1935.
9. Charles McMurtry, "Maxie Baer Takes Another Crack at Movies," *Poughkeepsie Eagle-News*, June 24, 1942.
10. Harrison Carroll, "Behind the Scenes in Hollywood," *Press Democrat*, April 21, 1942.
11. Erskine Johnson, "Harrison in Hollywood," *Dunkirk Evening Observer*, Oct. 17, 1942.
12. Charles McMurtry, "Ham as Actor, Laughs Baer," *Democrat and Chronicle*, Aug. 2, 1942.

13. Paul Harrison, "Harrison in Hollywood," *Dunkirk Evening Observer*, July 7, 1942.
14. "Sara Davis' Reviews of Previews," *Fresno Bee*, Nov. 15, 1942.
15. Philip K. Scheuer, "Big Street Real Surprise," *Los Angeles Times*, Nov. 19, 1942.
16. Hedda Hopper, "Looking at Hollywood," *Los Angeles Times*, Oct. 15, 1945.
17. John H. Whoric, "Sportorials," *Daily Courier* (Connellsville, Pennsylvania), Jan. 12, 1946.
18. Alan Ward, "On Second Thought," *Oakland Tribune*, Nov. 11, 1946.
19. Ed Sullivan, "Little Old New York," *Morning Herald* (Uniontown, Pennsylvania), March 6, 1946.
20. Dick Hyland, "The Hyland Fling," *Los Angeles Times*, Jan. 5, 1948.
21. "Used to Kissing Canvas," *Democrat and Chronicle*, April 8, 1949.
22. Frank Neill, "In Hollywood," *Bakersfield Californian*, March 2, 1949.
23. Bob Thomas, "Ex-Champ Max Baer Finds Acting in Movies Is Softest Racket Yet." *Press and Sun-Bulletin*, March 17, 1949.
24. Patricia Clary, "Hollywood Film Shop," *Bakersfield Californian*, June 15, 1949.
25. Don Page, "Mellowed Max Baer Loves Everybody on Own Flourishing Television Show," *Los Angeles Times*, Sept. 14, 1958.
26. Erskine Johnson, "Prize Fight Films Are Latest Craze," *Corpus Christi Caller-Times*, Jan. 31, 1956.
27. Vernon Scott, "Bogart in Bitter Battle with Big Boxing Leaders," *Waco News-Tribune*, Nov. 19, 1955.
28. *Ibid.*
29. "Walcott, Boxing Disagree on Movie Role," *Arizona Republic*, May 10, 1956.
30. *Democrat and Chronicle*, Oct. 2, 1958.
31. Alan Ward, "On Second Thought," *Oakland Tribune*, May 25, 1952.
32. Leonard Lyons, "The Lyons Den," *Post-Standard*, Oct. 13, 1956.
33. Mike Connolly, "Gotta Buy Tickets," *Desert Sun*, Aug. 30, 1958.
34. Don Page, "Mellowed Max Baer Loves Everybody on Own Flourishing Television Show," *Los Angeles Times*, Sept. 14, 1958.
35. Recordings of Max Baer's radio programs can be located at the Center for Sacramento History Online Archive of California (oac.cdib.org), Max Baer Recordings, Series 3, completed 2016.
36. Also in the Stockton cast were Monte Pearson, former New York Yankee, playing the role of the pitcher who struck out Casey; Eddie Mulligan, president of the Sacramento Solons, as Blake on second; and Bobby Doerr, formerly of the Boston Red Sox, as Flynn on third. Mulligan and Doerr wore their original Mudville uniforms. The umpire was Jake Powell, of the Pacific Coast League umpires, and the catcher was Jerry Donovan. The play drew 2,235 spectators.

Chapter Eighteen

1. Alan Ward, "On Second Thought," *Oakland Tribune*, May 25, 1952.
2. Emily Belsar, "Picture Recalls Carnera Received $47.07 for Fight," *Corsicana Daily Sun*, Dec. 30, 1955. Those were the days before IBRO and Boxrec.com.
3. "Madcap Maxie Faster in Business Than in the Ring," *Arizona Republic*, June 14, 1959.
4. "Baer Is New Director of Moose Membership," *Fresno Bee,* Jan. 18, 1949.
5. Red Smith, "Prizefighter and the Kid," *New York Tribune*, Nov. 22, 1959.
6. Whitney Bolton, "Hemingway to Pen 'Bullfighter Ballet,'" *News-Press*, April 18, 1950.
7. "Max Baer Fine Specimen His Doctor Declares," *Daily Independent Journal*, Jan. 17, 1951.
8. Alan Ward, "On Second Thought," *Oakland Tribune*, Aug. 12, 1951.
9. "Broken Up by Police," *Oakland Tribune*, Feb. 15, 1952.
10. Alan Ward, "On Second Thought," *Oakland Tribune*, May 25, 1952.
11. Aline Mosby, "Maxie Baer Trades Gloves," *Brownsville Herald*, Oct. 4, 1955.
12. Norman Ritter, "Heavies Today Are Stinkers Says Max Baer," *Odessa American*, Feb. 24, 1954.
13. "For Pith Helmet in TV," *Brownsville Herald*, Oct. 4, 1955.
14. Bill Furlong, "Maxie the Exception: Ex-Fighter with Dough," *Press and Sun-Bulletin*, Aug. 17, 1958.
15. Vernon Scott, "Maxie Baer Playing Poor Man's Levant," *Press and Sun-Bulletin*, Sept. 13, 1958.
16. Don Page, "Mellowed Max Baer Loves Everybody on Own Flourishing Television Show," *Los Angeles Times*, Sept. 14, 1958.
17. *Journal News* (White Plains), Oct. 25, 1958; "Old Time Champs Fete Harringay's Last Bout," *Arizona Republic*, Oct. 28, 1958. Harringay Arena was bought for a grocery warehouse.
18. Rollan Melton, "Nevada Sports," *Reno Gazette-Journal*, Jan. 26, 1959.
19. Art Rosenbaum, "Quit Ring, Max Baer Tells Son," *Los Angeles Times*, Feb. 17, 1959.
20. "Ticket Sales Spurt After TV Blackout," *Arizona Republic*, Nov. 16, 1959.
21. Jimmy Cannon, "Sports Today: A Laughing Man," *New York Journal American*, Nov. 22, 1959.
22. Comments by Harry Markson (publicity director for Mike Jacobs and later the IBC) have become a part of the lore of Max Baer's death. Markson said that when Max called the hotel operator to send the doctor to his room, she asked, "Do you want the house doctor?" Max was said to have replied, "No, a people doctor!" This was a line from his comedy act. None of the writers who covered the original details of Max's death told this story.
23. "Ex-Heavyweight Champ Max Baer Dies in California of Heart Attack," *Ogden Standard-Examiner*, Nov. 21, 1959; "Max Baer Dies Here of Heart Attack

at 50," *Los Angeles Times*, Nov. 22, 1959; "Ex-Ring Champ Max Baer Dies After Heart Attacks," *Arizona Republic*, Nov. 22, 1959. Some believe that a woman was in Max's room before he died because expensive items of Max's jewelry went missing from the scene. Perhaps these are two different matters. Max was very ill, thinking he had the flu, and arrived very late at the hotel from the drive after a late evening at the football game. Any woman would have been nursing a very sick man.

24. Al Warden, "The Sports Highway," *Ogden Standard*, Nov. 24, 1959.

25. "1500 Attend Max Baer's Funeral," *Times Record*, Nov. 25, 1959.

26. Jimmy Cannon, "Sports Today: A Laughing Man," *New York Journal American*, Nov. 22, 1959.

Bibliography

Aycock, Colleen. "The Voice of Boxing: A Brief History of American Broadcasting Ringside," 2014.

Aycock, Colleen, and Mark Scott. *Tex Rickard: Boxing's Greatest Promoter*. Jefferson, NC: McFarland, 2012.

Barrow, Joe Louis, Jr., and Barbara Munder. *Joe Louis: 50 Years an American Hero*. New York: McGraw-Hill, 1988.

Blady, Ken. *Jewish Boxers' Hall of Fame: A Who's Who of Jewish Boxers*. New York: Shapolsky, 1988.

Brumbelow, Joseph S. *Buddy Baer Autobiography*. Panama, S.A.: Rhino, 2003.

Clifton, Guy, *Dempsey in Nevada*. Reno: Jack Bacon, 2007.

Curl, James. *Jack Sharkey: A Heavyweight Champion's Untold Story*. Iowa City: Win By KO, 2015.

DeLisa, Michael C. *Cinderella Man: The James J. Braddock Story*. Wrea Green, UK: Milo, 2005.

Fitch, Jerry. *Johnny Risko: The Cleveland Rubber Man*. Tora, 2016.

Fleischer, Nat. *Max Baer: The Glamour Boy of the Ring*. New York: C.J. O'Brien, 1941.

Fried, Ronald K. *Corner Men: Great Boxing Trainers*. New York: Four Walls Eight Windows, 1991.

Hague, Jim. *Braddock: The Rise of the Cinderella Man*. New York: Chamberlain Bros., 2005.

Heller, Peter. *In This Corner! 42 World Champions Tell Their Stories*. New York: De Capo, 1994.

Helliwell, Arthur. *The Private Lives of Famous Fighters*. London: Cedric Day, 1942.

Hemingway, Ernest. "Million-dollar Fright: a New York Letter," *Esquire*, Dec. 1936.

Kofoed, Jack. "Box-Office Champ: The Life-Story of Max Baer." *Jack Dempsey's Fight Magazine* (August 1934): 75–90.

Lonkhurst, Bob. *Man of Courage: The Life and Career of Tommy Farr*. Lewes: Book Guild, 1997.

Louis, Joe, with Edna and Art Rust, Jr. *Joe Louis: My Life*. New York: Harcourt Brace Jovanovich, 1978.

Margolick, David. *Beyond Glory: Joe Louis vs. Max Schmeling, and a World on the Brink*. New York: Vintage Books, 2006.

Max Baer Collection (Documents of his radio programs) [2000/189], Center for Sacramento History.

Moe, Al. *The Roots of Reno: Northern Nevada's Early Casinos and the Sins It Took to Build Them*. Self-published, 2008.

Page, Joseph S. *Primo Carnera: The Life and Career of the Heavyweight Boxing Champion*. Jefferson, NC: McFarland, 2011.

Roberts, Randy. *Joe Louis: Hard Times Man*. New Haven: Yale University Press, 2010.

Schaap, Jeremy. *Cinderella Man: James J. Braddock, Max Baer, and the Greatest Upset in Boxing History*. Boston: Houghton Mifflin, 2005.

Schulberg, Budd. *The Harder They Fall*. Chicago: Ivan R. Dee, 1996 reprint, orig. 1947.

Scott, Walter. "Marmion: A Tale of Flodden Field," 1833. Unknown pub., 2015.

Sherman, James E., and Barbara H. Sherman. *Ghost Towns and Mining Camps of New Mexico*. Norman: University of Oklahoma, 1975.

Silver, Mike. *Stars in the Ring: Jewish Champions in the Golden Age of Boxing*. Guilford, CT: LP, 2016.

Sussman, Jeffrey. *Max Baer and Barney Ross: Jewish Heroes of Boxing*. Lanham, MD: Rowman & Littlefield, 2017.

Newspapers

Abilene Reporter-News, Texas
Akron Beacon Journal, Ohio
Albuquerque Journal, New Mexico
Appeal Democrat, Marysville, California
Arizona Republic, Phoenix
Asbury Park Press, New Jersey
Bakersfield Californian, California
Bend Bulletin, Oregon
Bluefield Daily Telegraph, West Virginia
Brooklyn Daily Eagle, New York
Brownsville Herald, Texas
Canandaigua Daily Messenger, New York
Chicago Tribune, Illinois

Chino Champion, California
Corpus Christi Caller-Times, Texas
Corsicana Daily Sun, Texas
Courier-News, Bridgewater, New Jersey
Daily Chronicle, De Kalb, Illinois
Daily Courier, Connellsville, Pennsylvania
Daily Independent Journal, San Rafael, California
Daily Review, Hayward, California
Democrat and Chronicle, Rochester, New York
Denton Record-Chronicle, Texas
Desert Sun, Palm Springs, California
Des Moines Register, Iowa
Detroit Free Press, Michigan
Dundee Courier, Angus, Scotland
Dunkirk Evening Observer, New York
Durango Democrat, Colorado
Feather River Bulletin, Quincy, California
Fitchburg Sentinel, Massachusetts
Freeport Journal-Standard, Texas
Fresno Bee, The Republican, California
Goldfield News and Weekly Tribune, Nevada
Harrisburg Telegraph, Pennsylvania
Hayward Daily Review, California
Healdsburg Tribune, California
Illustrated Sporting and Dramatic News, London
Ithaca Journal, New York
Journal News, White Plains, New York
Kingsport Times, Tennessee
Kingston Daily Freeman, New York
Livermore Journal, California
Long Beach Independent, California
Los Angeles Sports Weekly, California
Los Angeles Times, California
Lubbock Morning Avalanche, Texas
Mason City Glove-Gazette, Iowa
Miami Daily News, Florida
Middletown Times Herald, New York
Minneapolis Star, Minnesota
Mirror, New York
Morning Herald, Uniontown, Pennsylvania
Nebraska State Journal, Lincoln
Nevada State Journal, Reno
New York Age
New York American
New York Evening Journal
New York Evening Sun
New York Times
New York Tribune
News-Press, Fort Myers, Florida
Northern Whig, Antrim, Northern Ireland
Nottingham Evening Post, England
Nottingham Journal, England
Oakland Tribune, California
Odessa American, Texas
Ogden Standard-Examiner, Utah
Oneonta Star, New York
Pampa Daily News, Texas
Petaluma Argus Courier, California
Philadelphia Inquirer, Pennsylvania
Pittsburgh Post-Gazette, Pennsylvania
Poughkeepsie Eagle News, New York
Post-Register, Idaho Falls, Idaho
Press and Sun-Bulletin, Binghamton, New York
Press Democrat, Santa Rosa, California
Reno Gazette-Journal, Nevada
Rhinelander Daily News, Wisconsin
Salt Lake Tribune, Utah
San Antonio Light, Texas
San Bernardino County Sun, California
San Francisco Chronicle
San Francisco Examiner, California
Santa Ana Register, California
Santa Cruz Evening News, California
Syracuse Herald, New York
The Tennessean, Nashville
The Times, Hammond, Indiana
The Times, London
The Times, San Mateo, California
Times Herald, Olean, New York
Times Standard, Eureka, California
Times-Union, Albany, New York
Troy Record, later *Times Record*, New York
Waco News-Tribune, Texas
Woodland Daily Democrat, California

Index

Numbers in ***bold italics*** indicate pages with illustrations

Abbott, Milton "Tiny" 18–19, 31, 280
Abbott & Costello 259, 267
Adamick, Jimmy 192
Adoree, Andre 203, 282
Africa Screams 259
Ahlin, Carl 217 282
All Quiet on the Western Front 206
Allen, Russ 16, 52
Allison, Wiler 154
Anderson, Johnny 29
Andrews, Rear Adm. Adolphus 244
Andrews, Sonny ***271***
annuity 35, 95, 167, 176, 227, 248, 250, 270, 273, 276
Apostoli, Fred 38
Arcel, Ray 88
Arizona, Northern 10
Armstrong, Henry 245, 274
Army Air Force: boxing 246–247; enlistments 245–246; hospitals 248–249
Associated British Pictures 253
Attell, Abe 13, 87, 103
autographs 83, 96, 112, 156, 163, 166, 183, 216, 251
automobiles 10, 19, ***21***, 38, 52, 111, 168, 197, 271, 294ch11n11
Autry, Gene 271
Aycock, C. Norman "Ike" 113–***114***, ***276***, 277, 291n2

Baer, Achill (grandfather) 6–7, 87–88, 284n8
Baer, Benjamin (Ben) Franklin (uncle) 6, 91, 96, 296n12
Baer, Bernice Jeanette (sister) 9, 197
Baer, Charles (uncle) 6, 8–9
Baer, Dora (Bales; mother) 8, 10, 32, 87, 108, 110, ***121***, 130, 197, 202
Baer, Edward (uncle) 6, 8–9
Baer, Frances (Fanny) Fischel (grandmother) 6
Baer, Frances (Fanny) May (sister) ***8***–9, 8, 11, 147, 197
Baer, Jacob (Jake; father) 6–10, 12, 23, 36, 58, 87, 91, 95, 109, ***121***, 130, 173, 185, 190, 192, 197, 284n19; boxer 7
Baer, Jacob, Jr. (Buddy; brother): autobiography 284n9; boxing 1, 5, 7, 56, 111, 113, 115–124, ***116***, ***121***, 141, 146–147, 151–152, 157, 163, 165–169, 171, 173–179, 185–186, ***189***, 190–194, 197, 202, 215–216, 218–221, 230, 234–235, 237–239, ***242***, 249, ***271***, 280, 281; business 272; entertainment 133, 163, 187, 259, 264, 266, 276; family 5–7, 9, 120, 190, 197, 202, 206, 248, 276; vs. Louis 241–242, 245; military 245–249
Baer, James (Jimmy) Manny (son) 245, ***271***
Baer, Joseph (uncle) 6
Baer, Marx M. (uncle) 6
Baer, Mary Ellen (Sullivan; 2nd wife) 87, 147, ***148***, 151, 154, 167, 179, 186, 191, 197, 211, 236, 248–249 279
Baer, Matilda (Tillie; aunt) 6
Baer, Maudie (daughter) 248, 275, 279
Baer, Max, Jr. (son) 3, 191, 197, 211, 219–220, 222, 245 260, 271, 275; boxer 274; movies 254, 256, 279
Baer, Minnie (aunt) 6
Baer, Olive (aunt) 220
Baer, Phillip (uncle) 6
Baer, Ralpha Pearl (1st wife of Buddy Baer) 206, 248
Baer, Ruth Eleanor (Boynton Phillips; 2nd wife of Buddy) 248
Baer, May (Mann; 3rd wife of Buddy) 248
Baer, Sheila (daughter of Buddy and Ralpha) 248
Baer, Vicki (last wife of Buddy) 279
Baffert, Al 203, 282
Bales, John H. 8, 87, 202
Ball, Lucille 256
Balogh, Harry 226
Banovic, Joe 223
Barcella, Ernest 5
Barlund, Gunnar 194
Barry, Patrick Michael 177
Barrymore, John 235
Barton, Charles 259
baseball: performing at 270; played 10, ***237***, 238, 272
Basque 54, 56–57
Bass, Benny 87
Battle Stations 255
Baum, Allan T. 29
Baxter, Don 174, 282
Beal, (Scoop) 14
Beaudry, Thomas 7
Beck, Olive 35, 81
Belasco, David 58
Belcastro, Pete 191
Bench, "Cyclone" 175
Bendix, William ***254***
Bennison, B 66
Benny, Jack 187, 250
Berengaria 181, 190
Berg, Jackie "Kid" 41
Bergin, David 33, 55, 73, 94, 100, 112, 120, 136, 144, 155, 184, 186, 189, 212, 222
Berglund, Swede 288n6
Bergman, Ingrid 260
Berlenbach, Paul 61
Bernard, Dr. Pierre 207
Bernds, Ed 263
Bernal, Joe 34
Berry, Wallace 71
Beyer, Morris 105
Bierko, Craig 3, 266
The Big Fight 58
The Big Street 256
Bimstein, Whitey 57–58, 90, 129, ***144***, 223, 226
Birkie, Hans 55
Black, Alton 122
Black, Julian 153
Blackburn, Jack 13, 151, 153, 162, 183
Blady, Ken 88
Blake, George 71, 131
Blyttner, "Tiny Tiger" 176

Bockwinkel, Warren 272
Bogart, Humphrey 19, 264–265
Bond, Ford 133–135, 137, 140
Bookman, Bayard 157
Borgman, Clarence R. *see* Gorman, Nails
Bowen, Dick 215
boxing documentaries and docudramas 263–264
boxing gloves 81, 91, 113–116, 121, 124, 134, 156, 175, 215, *276*
Braddock, James 36, 41, 89, 92, 105, 117–118, 123–127, 149–152, 154, 156, 158, 163–172, 180–183, 187–193, 201, 208, 211, 219, 223–224, 228, 230, 232, 238, 245, 247, 263–264, 266–267, 270, 272, 281; vs. Baer 128–147, *144*
Bradley, Grace *254*
Braven, Dyer 207
Brennan, Ed 190
Brennan, Dr. Robert Emery 201
Brennan, Walter 257
Brent, George 259
Brescia, Jorge 203
Brice, Fanny 273
Bride for Sale 261
Brietz, Eddie 207
Brignolia, George 229
British Board of Boxing Control 183
British Broadcasting Corporation (BBC) 20, 185
British Columbia 173
Britt, James (Jimmy) 12
Briz, Lou 55
Brockley, Red 288*n*18
Broderick, Louie 70
Bromber's, Lester 87
Bronner, Milton 187
Brooke, Hillary 259, *262*
Broom, Harold Algernon 203
brother boxers 103
Brown, George 171, 282
Brown, Mary Kirk 100, 126, *127*, 143, 146, 279
Brown, Max 281
Brown, Natie 16, 280
Brown, William J. 105, 109, 123, 130, 133–134, 141, 147, 156, 168, 181, 207
Bruner, Judge A. W. 202
Buckley, Johnny 37
Buckley, Johnny "Puggy" 51
Buckskin Frontier 257–258
Buick 158
Burman, Red "Kayo" 205, 219, 230, 234–235
Burns, Edward 111, 117
Burns, Frankie 27, 36, 50–5, 63
Burns, Tommy 2, 104, 106, 263
Buxton (Buston), Sonny 174, 282

California: Beverly Hills 68; Needles 10; Perkins 33; Sacramento 16, 23, 26, 33–34, 80, 179, 203, 206, 217, 219, 228, 240, 245–249, 267, 269, 271–276; San Francisco 10, 12–15, 19, 23–24, 26, 29–30, 34, 37, 48, 51, 61, *62*, 65, 68, 114, 120, 153, 156, 163, 167, 169, 179, 190, 256, 269; Stockton 14–15, 269
California Athletic (Boxing) Commission 18–19, 25, 27, 29–31, 36, 41, 44–45, 47–48, 50, 52, 58, 60, 62, 66, 69–70
California boxing venues: Arcadia Pavilion, Oakland 16, 18; Broadway (Eureka) 14; Dreamland Auditorium, SF 121; Oakland 20, 60, 70; Olympic Auditorium, LA 17, 20, 24, 60, 68, 70; Seals Stadium, SF 60–61, 68
California gyms: Dolph Thomas 190; Duffy's 59, 63, 149, 167, 180, 190, 193, 197, 203; Imperial 12; Yosemite Gym 43, 51, 59, 63
Callahan, Mushy 87
Calvary Cancer Hospital 83
Cameron, Robert Larry "Calgary Red" 273, 274
Camilli, Dolph 26, 238
Camp Funston, Kansas 14
Campbell, Elsie 30, 54
Campbell, (Camilli) Frankie 2, 19, 23–24, *25*, 26–32, *28*, 36, 47, 280
Campolo, Victorio 17, 41, 52, 54, 60
Cancela, Tony 153, 281
Cannon, Jimmy 252, 272
Cantor, Eddie 54, 267
Cantwell, Mike 109, 129
Canzoneri, Tony 41, 134, 206
Capra, Frank 260
Carey, William F. 38
Caribou, Chief 14, 16, 280
Carlen, Ray 27, 36, 203, 205–206, 214, 234
Carnera, Primo 1, 2, 16, 26, 36, 41, 44, 56, 63, 66, 72, 76, 78, 80–81, 83, 85, 87, 90, 92–93, 95–113, 118–119, 121–124, 126, 129–131, 134, 141–142, 145–147, 149–150, 153–154, 156, 158, 162–163, 165, 167, 169, 175, 188, 195, 201, 236, 238, 247, 251–252, 264–265, 272; CA suspension 19–20; vs. Baer 180, 281
Carpentier, Georges 154, 221
Carroll, George 280
Carroll, Madeleine: *The 39 Steps* 223
Casale, Jerry 129, 230
Casey at the Bat 269, 299*n*36
Casper, Jack 173
Cavalier, Paul 153
Cavanaugh, Billy 194
CBS radio network 185
Cerebral Palsy Foundation 270
Cermak, Anton 82
The Champs Step Out 263
Chapman, Hanna, H. 54
Chapman, Weldon 215
charisma 14; "it factor" 187–188; news copy 2, 36–37, 204
Charles, Tim 176, 282
Charnley, Dave 274

Chase, Borden 255
Chevalier, Leon "Bomba" 19–20
Chicago Stockyards 6, 164; Stadium 73–74, 264
Chicago Tribune 75–76, 111, 216
Chick, Due 191
Chocolate, "Kid" 101
Christie, Audry 235
Christner, "K.O." *25*, 26, 65–66, 280
Churchill, Frank 19
Cinderella Man 3, 5, 143, 145, 193, 266–267
Cliff, Laddie 253
Cobb, Lee J. 258
Cobb, Walter 79; vs. Baer 69–70, 281
Coffroth, Jim "Sunny" 14, 110
Cohan, Morrie 197
Cohn, Art: *Oakland Tribune* 108, 143, 179–181, 193, 202, 206, 211, 237, 279
Colbert, Claudette 112, 259, *261*
Collins, Phil 75–7
Colorado: boxing 6–7; Denver 6–9, 50, 83, 91, 106, 110, 249, 274; Durango 9; Elyria-Swansea 6–7; influenza epidemic 9, 81, 236–237, 274; Jack Dempsey 9; Riverside Cemetery 6, 9
Comiskey, Patrick Edward "Irish" 5, 151, 225, 228–232, *233*, 236, 265, 282
Conn, Billy 234–236, 246, 249, 103
Conrad, Harold 230, 236, 240
Conroy, Jack 174
Copper Bowl (football) 270
Corbett, Eddie 254
Corbett, "Gentleman" Jim 48, 104, 110, 127
Corbett, Tom 59
Corbett, Young 7, 71
Corum, Bill 5, 89, 204, 206
Crawford, Joan 101, 252
Crippled Children Foundation 270
Critchley, Brig. Gen. A.C. 178, 183–189, 274
Crosby, Bing 245, 260
Crowe, Russell 3, 302
Cuddy, Jack: *UP* 243
Cunard White Star Liner *see Berengaria*
Cunningham, Bob 135
Cuoco, Dan 138
Curtis, Dick 263
Cystic Fibrosis Foundation 274

Daley, Arthur 10, 228, 230
Daley, Bill 228, 230
Dally, Dan, Jr. 263
Dalton, Tim 249
Damaski, Paul 194
Daro, Lou 167
Davies, William (Willie) 176, 282
Davis, Babe 176, 282
Davis, Sara 256
Dawson, James, *NY Times* 145

Index

Dean, Bobby 153
Dean, Daffy 219
Dean, Dizzy 219
de Garcon, Jaime 35
Dekker, Albert 258
De Kuh, Arthur 63, 281
De La Fuente, Tony 18–19, 60,, 280, 285*n*1
DeLisa, Michael 3
DeMave, Jack "Golden Boy" 17
Dempsey, Elsie 54
Dempsey, Hiram 54
Dempsey, Jack 2, 9–10, 12–13, 17, 20, 23–24, 26–27, 29, 32, 36–37, 42, 44–49, 52–59, 65, 68, 70–71, 75, 77–80, 82–87, 89–92, 95, 98, 100–101, 103–106, 109–111, 116–119, 130, 149–151, 154–155, 157–158, 160, 162–163, 174–176, 178, 186, 188, 191, 200, 204, 211, 218, 221, 223, 228, 230, 232, 234, 236, 241, 251–252, 264, 267–268, 270–272, 274, 276; vs. Carpentier 85; Dempsey Bowl, Reno 54–58, 70–72; vs. Firpo 44; horse racing 54; vs. Levinsky 68; vs. Tunney 75; vs. Willard 1, 83
Denning, Jack 76
Depression 1, 3, 53, 64–65, 89, 98, 114, 150, 160, 266; sports writing 5
Deverer, Bill 174
Dickerson, Ed 131
District of Columbia Boxing Commission 243
Dix, Richard 258
Dixon, George 293*n*15
Dodson, Dr. Louis W. 232
Dohme, Ralph 87
Donahue, Jimmy 80
Donlevy, Brian 257
Donovan, Arthur 44, 81, 92, 94, 98, 107–110, 131, 151, 160–161, 169, 176, 180, 187, 195–196, 198, 199–201, 214, 240–243
Dougherty, Rowen 154
Doyle, Pat 55
draft *see* military draft
Drake, Paul 288*n*18
Dressler, Marie 273
Dudas, Steve 230
Dunbar, Dorothy 35–36, 42, 49–50, 58, 66–**67**, 71, 81, 98, 100, 104, 163
Dundee, Johnny 158, 103
Dunn, William 66, 171, 282

earnings, ring 111, 176–177, 235–236, 272–273
Ebbets Field 97
Eddie Cantor Show 269
Edgren, Robert 27, 50–52, 59, 110
Edwards & Cummings Mortuary 276
Eichner, Eddie 70
Elder, Neil 115, 291*n*3
Elks Club 202–203
entertainment *see* movies; radio shows; stage plays; television shows
Epsom Downs, England 104
Escobar, Madame Senora Conchita 104
Ettore, Al 172, 290*n*29
Evans, Sammy "Cowboy" 175, 282
Exhibition of the Century 272
exhibition tours: Army Air Force tour, listed 298*n*22; Championship tour 115–124; "E" on Fight Record 280–283, Madcap Comeback tour 166–177

Fair, William Trenton 282
Farnsworth, Bill, *New York Journal* 149
Farr, Tommy "Tonypandy Terror": 5, 178, 183–187, 190–196, 202–204, 206, 208, 219, 229, 253, 295*n*24; vs. Baer 183–187, 194–**195**, 282; vs. Foord 183; vs. Louis 191
FBI 54
Feldman, Abe 152, 157, 219
Fenton, Frank 256
Fererro, Abel 280
Fields, Irwin 170
Fields, Jackie 87, 245, 252
Fields, Walter 288*n*18
Fields, William Claude (Dukenfield) "W. C." 54
Fine, Mr. and Mrs. Harry 38
Fine's Gymnasium, NYC 38
finish fight 53, 71, 287*n*1
Finland (Finish Fund) 217–218
Finnazzo brothers 103
Firpo, Luis Angel 44, 49, 68, 91, 241
Fisticuffs 253
Fitzsimmons, Bob 12, 27, 110, 119, 142
Fleischer, Nat 3, 88, 141, 150, 214, 236
Flowers, Lew "Tiger" 153, 232
Folley, Zora 268, 270, 274, **275**
Folsom Prison **237**, 238
Fonda, Henry 256
Foord, Ben 175, 178, 181, 183, **184**, 185, 187–189, 194, 253; vs. Baer 187–189
Ford, Henry 82
Foreman, Eddie 262
Frankco, Al 174, 282
Franklin, Benny 101
Franks, Eddie "Soldier" 174, 282
Fraser, (Frazier) Bob 169, 281
Frayne, Edward J.: *New York American* 149
Frazen, Al 134
Frazier, Bob 122, 281
Free Milk Fund for Babies 110
Friede, Leo 132, 143, 146, 292*n*22
Friedman, "Goodtime" Walter 106
Frietas, Tony **237**
Fritz, Judge A.J. 30
Fullam, Frank 210
Fullmer, Gene 270
Futch, Eddie 115

Gable, Clark 251
Galento, Anthony Domenico (Tony) 5, 192–193, 202–206, 210, 214–**227**, 228–230, 235–238; vs. Buddy Baer 238; Max Baer-Galento 221–227, **273**, 282
Gallagher, Marty 287*n*39
Gallico, Paul 142, 153–154
Gans, Joe 12–14, 68, 151, 153, 232
Gans, (Allentown) Joe 13
Garcia, Ceferino 245
Garrison, Nash 191
Gastanaga, Isadore 167
Gaynor, Al 282
Genshlea, Joseph 31
Giamatti, Paul 3, 266
Gibbons, Mike 14, 103
Gillette: dog contest 124, **128**, 131, 292*n*27; *Cavalcade of Sports* 268; fight sponsor 133–134 143; *Lucky Smith* radio show 129, 133–134, 143
Gilmore, Reggie 272
Glenn, Judge Malcolm C. 166
gloves *see* boxing gloves
Godfrey, George 41, 61, 97, 119
Godoy, Arturo 218, 221, 224, 230, 234
Golden Age of Boxing 230; heavyweights 6
Golden Gloves 177, 248, 270; Max Baer Heavyweight Trophy 248
Golden Jubilee, Vancouver 173
Goldstein, Abe 87
Gorman, Nails 174, 282
Graham, Frank: *New York Journal-American* 42 107, 151
Graham, William 53
Graney, Ed 14
Gray, Sally 253
Grayson, Harry 35, 190, 202, 221
Graziano, Rocky 264, 267
Greene, Abe 223, 228, 232
Greenlee, Gus 202
Greer, Sam 83, 281
Griffin, H.A. "Spider" 12, 105, 126
Griffin, John Charles "Corn" 105, 126, 290*n*29
Griffiths, (Griffith) Gerald Ambrose "Tuffy" 41–42, 66; vs. Baer 74–**75**, 281
Grimm, Trev 274
Griswold, Morley 71
Grotsky, Ben 256
Gruell, Joe 288*n*18
Guinard, Fred 243
gym fees 43

Hackensack Health Center 230
Hafey, Bud 238
Hague, Jim 3
Hall, Al 253
Hall of Fame 112, 269
Hamas, Steve 106, 119
Hangmen Also Die 357
Hankinson, Hank 197, 203, 253, 282
Hard of Hearing Society 270
The Harder They Fall 19, 110, 163, 264–266

Hardles, Charles R. 204
Harlow, Jean 100, 104, 113, 252
Harringay Arena, London 178, 183–185, 187–**188**, 274
Harris, Cecil (Ceil) 103, 153, 281
Harris, Dr. J.B. 240
Harris, Sam 13
Hart, Jac 187
Hays, Teddy 69
Healey, Dr. W.V. 147, 210
Heeney, Tom: 42–47, 49–50, 52, 56, 60–61, 68, 79; vs. Baer **43**–47, 68, 280, 281
Heller, Peter 190
Heller, Tiny 229
Helliwell, Arthur 188
Hell's Kitchen 221
Helmer, George 164
Hemingway, Ernest 161, 164, 206, 293*n*31
Henry, Bill 87
Herman, Tillie **25**, 26
Herrera, Tony 215
Hi-Ya Gentlemen **234**–235, 269
Hicks, George 230
Higgins, Chuck 175
Hill, Benny 15–16, 280
Hill, Edwin 157
Hitchcock, Alfred 223
Hitler, Adolf 81–82, 85, 88–89, 92, 180, 190, 197, 201, 244–245, 247
Hoffman, Ancil: boxer **34**; business 33–34, 279; Fair Oaks ranch 34, 51, 80, 178, 275; manager-promoter 2, **3**, 23–24, 29–36, 38, 40–43, 45–51, 54–55, 58–61, 66, 68–70, 72, 76–82, **78**, 89–90, 92–93, 95, 103, 105, 108–113, 119–123, 130–134, 143–147, **149**, 151–153, 156–157, 162, 164–167, 169–175, 177–182, 186, 192–194, 196–197, 202–204, 208, 214–215, 219–223, 228–229, 234–235, 237–238, 240–243, 247–248, 252–253, 265, 270–271, 273, 275, 294*ch*12*n*10
Hoffman, Maudie 80–82, 130, 247
Hogan, Eddie 192, 290*n*29
Hollywood, CA 10, 12, 92, 98–99, 101, 104–105, 110, 143, 166, 190, 245, 248, 251–253, 256, 258, **260**, 267, 272, 275
Holt, David 253
Holy Spirit Roman Catholic Church, Sacramento 276
Hoover, Pres. Herbert 217–218
Hoover, J. Edgar 54
Hope, Bob 187, 245, 260
Hope, Dave 10
Hopper, Hedda 258
Hornblower, William 30
"house doctor" story 299*ch*18*n*22
Howard, Ron 266
Hughes, Ed 77, 142, 154, 170, 195
Hulls, Sydney 181
Humphreys, Joe 92, **94**, 106, 134–135, 157
Humphries, Alden 36

Hunt, Alvin Earl "Babe" 69, 117–118, 120, 124–125, 175, 281
Hurley, Jack 104
Hurricane Club 228

Igoe, hype 95
Illinois State Athletic Commission 116, 176, 180
Impelletiere, Ray 106, 123, 288*n*6
influenza epidemic 9, 81, 236–237, 274
International Boxing Research Organization (IBRO) 45, 62, 75, 175, 188, 195, 210
Irwin, Toby 20, 23, **25**, 27, 29, 68, 70
Italian Boxing Federation 112

Jacklich, Anthony 23, 36, 217, 247
Jacklich, Frank 23, 36, 217, 247
Jacklich, Rudolph 23, 36, 217, 247
Jackson, Dynamite 63, 65, 103, 290*n*29
Jacobs, Caswell Keppel 225
Jacobs, Joe 41, 65, 76–77, 80, 82, **84**, 85, 92, 95, 118–119, 202, 216–221, 225; Hell's Kitchen 221
Jacobs, Mike 50, 65, 123–124, 130, 147, **149**–151, 154, 156, 158, 168, 170, 172, 175, 180, 190–193, 197, 200–202, 203, 205, 207, 210–211, 214, 218–221, 223–225, 228, 234–237, 240, 243, 245, 249–250, 294*ch*12*n*10
Jacob's Beach 224, 228
Jamesburg Reformatory NJ 230
Japanese Imperial Air Service 244
Jeanette, Joe, trainer 72, 81
Jeffries, James J. (Jim) 7, 12, 27, 53, 90, 110, 142, 150–151 158, 245–246, 252
Jeffries, Tom 288*n*6
Jerricki, Fay 173
Jewish Boxers Hall of Fame 87, 88
Jewish boxing fans 85, 89–92
Jewish Sports Hall of Fame, Israel 87
Jewish War Veterans 87
Jews in Hall of Fame 87
Johnson, Alonzo 268, 274
Johnson, Erskine 264
Johnson, Jack 7, 53, 106, 150–151, 153, 158, 191, 198, 232; Jeffries-Johnson 53
Johnson, Larry 153
Johnson, Lester 48
Johnston, Charles 77
Johnston, Jimmy 36, 65, 76–77, 80, 83, 92, 98–**99**, 103, 111–113, **116**, 118–119, 123, 132, 143, 145, 147, 149–150, 155, 167, 170, 172, 180, 182, 195, 207, 250, 266–267
Joiner, Patricia 263
Jolson, Al 92, 124, 269, 273
Jorge, Eddie 280
Joshua, Anthony 97

Kaofed, Jack 3
Kaplan, Hank 87
Kaplan, Hymie 89

Karolak, Ed 290*n*29
Kearns, Jack "Doc" 20–21, 27, 41, 69, 76, 228–229, 230, 232, 234
Keaton, Buster 54
Kelly, Chaplin 51–52
Kelly, George P. 66, 139, 141–142
Kelly, Judy 253
Kelly, Patsy 256, **257**
Kennedy, Jack 131, 286*n*25
Kennedy, Les 17, 24, 26, 59, 63, 69, 97, 115, 117, 131, 279; Kennedy-Baer 63, 280, 281
Kennedy, Pat 7
Kenworthy, Jess 131
Ketchuck, Charley 230
Kids on the Cuff 253
killer instinct 3, 6, 10, 11, 26–31, 36, 38, 40, 47, 63, 93–95, 106, 109, 114–115, 151, 154, 160, 165, 199, 206, 236, 240, 243, 246, 249, 260, 266–267
Kilpatrick, Col. John Reed **99**, 181
Kirk, Jack 35
Kirksey, George 158
Kitty Davis' Club, Miami Beach, FL 258
Klatt, Oscar 61
Klein, Ed 74
Klein, Wally 263
Klick, Frankie 203
Kline, Izzy 87, **116**, **162**, 183, 208, 215, 230, **231**, 238
Kline, Walley 262
Klitschko, Wladmir 97; brothers 168
Knight, Goodwin 268
Knight, June 100, 117
Koch, Delmar 215
Koziol, Dr. Edward S. 275

Labarba, Fidel 41
Ladies' Day 256, 257
Lamb, Al 123, 141, 264
LaMotta, Jake 267
Land of My Father 185
Langford, Sam 14, 151
Lardner, John 7, 101, 111
Lasky, Art 72, 87, 97, 118–119, 122, 123, 126, 130, 143, 145, 149, 267
Latzo, Pete 69
lawsuits 19, 32, 63, 81, 101, 109, 111, 122, 166, 182, 186, 190, 194, 204, 217, 230–231, 247, 265
Lawton Springs, NV 55, 71
Ledford, Al "Red" 16, 280
Lee, George Washington "Yellow Peril" 34
Leeds, Sailor 15
Lennon, Tom E. **25**
Leonard, Benny 106, 158
Leoncavallo's *Paglicacci* 193
Lesnevich, Gus 274
Letts, F. Dickinson 147
Levinsky, Kingfish "Battling" (Harris Krakow): 14, 52, 61, 70–72, 78, 79, 85, 87, 96, 103, 109, 113–118, 127, 151, 153–154, 163, 172; vs. Baer 65–68, 71–**72**, 281; vs. Bennison 66

Levinson, Sol 115, **276**
Levy, "Leaping Levy" Krakow 66
Lewis, John Henry 126, 186, 202–204
Lewis, Nate 74–75, 130, 216–217; Harry Thomas contract 296*n*5
Lewis, Strangler 252
Limas, Frankie 288*n*18
Lindskog, Vic 283
Linkhorn, Jack 15–16, 21–23, 280
Lippe, Al 13–14, 19, 27, 30, 285*n*45
Livermore, CA 6, 10–12, 16, 18, 21, 24–25, 38, 52, 72, 78, 85, 111, 121, **128**, 154, 162–163
Lochinvar 32, 37, 58
Lomski, Leo 13
London, Jack 186
London, Jackie 167
Long Branch, NJ 130, 229, **231**
Long Island Bowl 76, 98
Lorimer, J. Hamilton "Millionaire Kid" 12, 14, 20–**21**, 23, **25**, 29–30, 32, 36, 43, 45, 47, 50, 58–64, 66, 69–70, 74, 95, 122, 166–167, 203
Lorimer, John W. 12; Diesel Engine Co. 12, 14
Los Angeles, CA **21**, 23–24, 26, 30, 59, 63, 68–69, 71, 126, 167, 174, 197, 206–207, 211, 243, 252, 258, 261, 267–268, 274–275
Loughran, Tommy 37–38, 41, 49–50, 52, 54, 58, 60–61, 65–66, 75, 81, 85, 97, 103, 105, 106, 121, 134, 187; vs. Baer 45–47, 280
Louis, Joe: 2, 5, 8, 13, 66, 71–72, 89–90, 92, 115, 118–119, 123–124, 130, 145–147, 149–207, 211, 214, 219–224, 226, 229–230, 232, 234–250, 258, 260, 263–264, 270, 272–273, 276, 279; vs. Buddy Baer 241–243; vs. Conn 236; *Joe Louis Story* 272; Marva Trotter, wife 156, **157**, 230; vs. Max Bear 151, **155**, **161**, 281; vs. Schmeling 169
Louttit, Tom 51
Love Is Big Business 259–260
Lovell, Alberto 192
Lowe's, New York 258
Loy, Myrna 100, 251, 252
Luce, Claire 253
Lundigan, William 263
Lupino, Stanley 253
Lurine liner 203
Lynch, Charles 135, 141
Lynch, Cyclone 282
Lynch, Jimmy 288*n*18
Lynch, Joe 210

Machon, Max 84, 96, 170, 200
Madden, Dick 120, 281
Madden, Owen (Owney) 106, 132, 145–146, 228
Madison Square Garden 14, 36, 38, 41–46, 49, 53, 65–66, 76–77, 79, 81, 83, 95, 97–100, 103, 111, 119, 123–124, **132**, 133, 135, 149–150, 165, 167, 180–181, 183, 192–195, 206, 217, 220–221, 235, 239–240, 244–245, 250, 264, 268, 279
Malcewicz, Joe 167
Malo, Gina 253
Maloney, Jim (Jimmy) 41, 54, 97, 281
Maloney, Tom "Greaseball" 27, 30
Mangold, Joe 225
Mann, Nathan (Natie) 192–193, 220–221
Manning, Bruce 259
Mara, Tim 77
March of Dimes 270
Marciano, Rocky 264, 270, **273**
Margolick, David 3
Market Street Gymnasium, Newark, NJ 230
Markson, Harry 299*ch*18*n*22
Marmion: Sir Walter Scott 32, 286*n*1
Martin, Marian 254–255
Martin, Tommy 230
Martin, Whitney 218, 244, 248
The Mask and the Face 80
Massera, Charley 103, 290*n*29
Mattan, Chester 290*n*29
Mattox, William R. 272
Marx, brothers 54
The Max Baer Show 269
McAllister, Bob 14–15, 18–19, 51, 59–64, 70, 80
McArdle, Tom 40
McAvoy, John 131
McAvoy, Mickey 253
McCarney, Billy 142, 221
McCarney, Earl 238
McCarthy, Clem 157
McCarthy, Jack 16, 133, 280
McCarty, Luther 142
McCarty, Pat 55
McCollum Hugh 262
McCoy, Al 236
McCrea, Joe 259
McDonald, Sandy 216
McGee, Willie **152**, 290*n*29
McGovern, Eddie 288*n*28
McGovern, Terry 13
The McGuerin Series 253
McGuire, Dan 246
McHugh, the Rev. Patrick 276
McKay, James 53
McKeeby, Frank R. 230–231
McLarnin, Jimmy (Jimmie) 30, 41, 101, 106, 134
McLemore, Henry, UP 12, 43, 92, 95–96, 167, 170, 191, 205, 208, 220
McNamee, Graham 106, 133–134, 137–141
McNamara, Tom 274
McTigue, Mike 14, 221
meat packing (slaughterhouses) see packing companies
Medivitch, Wee Willie 83, 281
Mendel, Henry 221
Mental Giants 263
Merriott, James (Jimmy) 172, 282
Merritt Hospital CA 66
Metro Golden Mayer (MGM) 252, 253, 254, 263, 264, 265

Miceli, Joe 274
Michel, Dr. Leo L. 145, 146
Michigan, Red Jacket (Calumet) 6
military: boxing exhibition tours 298*n*22; discharges 249; draft 234–235; enlistments 246; honors 276; Max Bear Trophy 298*n*24
The Milky Way 11
Miller, Andy "Kid" 302, 292
Miller, David 253
Millerick, Jack, rodeo 24
Missouri Athletic Commission 174
Mittef, Alex 274
Mix, Tom 10, 71
Monroe, Al 154
Moore, Archie 270, **271**
Moran, Frank 252
Morgan, L.C. 274
Morgan, Steve **100**, 106, 108, 134, **144**, 157, 252
Moros, Henry 232
Morrison, Larry 26
Morrison, Leo 253
Morro, Al 253
Mosby, Aline 273
Mountain View Cemetery, San Leandro, CA 197, 202
Muldoon, William 6, 83, 97, 289*n*5
Multnomah Stadium, Portland OR 174
Munsell, Rollie Thurman "Junior" 172, 282
Murphy, "Big" Ed 214–215, 282
Murphy, George 255
Murphy, Harold "Millionaire" 169, 282
Murray, Arthur 267
Murray, "Fighting" Billy 14, 34
Murray, James M. 216
Mussolini, Benito 112, 197
Myart, Cecil 174

Nardiello, Dr, Vincent 5, 105, 272
National Boxing Association (NBA) 41, 122, 211, 214, 226, 230, 238, 243
National Broadcasting Company (NBC) 106, 129, 133, 267
National Sporting Club, London 178
The Navy Comes Through 255–256
Navy Relief **242**, 244, 245
Nazi 82, 88–89, 92, 180–182, 198, 201, 243–244, 255; Propaganda Ministry 252
Nebraska Douglas 8; Omaha 8, 175, 220
Neil, Edward J., AP 40
Nelson, Battling 10, 14, 151
Nestell, Bob 238
Neumann, Kurt 254
Neusel, Walter 178
Nevada: Goldfield 13; Lawton Springs 55; Silver Peak 214; Steamboat Springs 54

New Jersey: Jersey City 220; Roosevelt Station 220; *see also* training camps
New Jersey Boxing Commission 220, 223, 228
New Mexico: Albuquerque 203; Koehler **8**, 9, 284*n*16
New York Athletic (Boxing) Commission 41, 45, 48, 83, 91, 97, 100, 108, 122–123, 130–131, 134, 141, 152–153, 156, 168, 172, 180–181, 194, 207–8, 217–219
New York Athletic Club 85
New York Times 5, 108, 145, 158, 162, 201
New York Tribune 37, 270
New York World Telegram 84, 90, 161
New York Yankees 91
Newton, Bob 288*n*18
Niagara Falls 224
nicknames for Max 6, 32, 38, 78, 87, 111, 169
Nokin, Albert 42
Nolan, Sylvester 55
Norfolk, Kid 13
Nova, Lou: 36, 197, 203–214, 218–219, 223–224, 234–235, 237–240; vs. Baer 211–208, **239**–240, 282; vs. Louis 240

Oak Knoll Country Club, Oakland, CA 64
Oakland, CA 1, 10, 12–13, **15**, 15–16, 18, 23–24, 26, 31, 35–36, 43, 47, 51–52, 56, 59–61, 63, 68, 80–81, 90, 95, 108, 111, 121–122, 149, 163, 167, 173, 179–180, 190–191, 193, 197, 199, 203, 207, **212**, 217, 240, 246–247
O'Brien, Jay 132, 147, 292*n*22
O'Brien, Pat 256
O'Conner, Pat 243
O'Gatty, Joe "Fireplug" 232
oil field business 271
Oklahoma: Ada 172; Oklahoma City 172
Olin, Bob 126
Oliva, August R. (Gus) 19, 30
Olympia Stadium, Detroit 117
Once Upon a Horse 266
Ortiz, Carlos 274
Ortiz, Manuel 38
Osborne, Livingston 74
Over She Goes 253
Owen, Claude 243
Owen, Leo "Curley" **55**, 87, 275–276
Owen, Ronnie 275
Owens, Ernie 20, 23, 51, 69, 280

Paccassi (Piccassi), Frank 122, 168, 171, 178, 183, 186, 295*n*23
packing companies 5, 8, 9, 10
Page, Joseph 97, 106
Palzer, Al 142
Panama Canal 49–50
Pantages Theater 256, 261
Papke, Billy 252

Paramount 37, 253, 260, 264
Parente, Louie 14, 16, 19, 23, 26, 58–61, 70, 95, 122
Parker, Dan 30, 40, 89, 106, 126, 132–133, 141, 205
Parker, "Kid Hats" 15, 21
Pastor, Bob 180, 190, 192, 207, 214, 219, 230
Patterson, Floyd 274
Paul, Tommy 122
Paycheck, Johnny 214
Pearl Harbor 244
Pegler, Westbrook 2
Pelkey, Ray 13, 117
Pep, Willie 270
Perroni, Patsy 232
Perry, Bob 20
Peterson, Jack 171, 181
Petrin, Don 290*n*29
Pettite, William 33, 82, 89, 109
Petty, Fred 154
Phelan, John J. 131, 145, 181, 208
Poland, Bill 232
Polee, Odell 197, 282
Polo Grounds 77, 240
Poreda, Stanley 74, 120–121, 281, 287*n*39
Porst, Otto Von 17
Porter, Mr. & Mrs. Vernon 156
Poster, Lon 290*n*29
The Prizefighter and the Lady 87, 100, 106, 129, 251, 264
The Prodigal Son 51, 287*n*60
professional golf (PGA) 3, 13, 201
Prohibition 34, 56
Putnam, George 61, 68

Quinn, Anthony 268
Quinn, William J. 29

racketeers: 18–19, 34, 72, 106, 120, 142, 228; arson 179; Broadway friends 132; at Carnera-Baer 109; clubs 132, 146, 206, 228; deals 18–19, 180; fixed fights 19–20, 216–218, 123; movie rights 169, 251; New Orleans 114; protection 72; referees 31; Reno 53–54
rankings 1, 240; (1930) 41; (1932) 78–79; (1934) 112; (1935) 164; (1937) 192; (1939) 211; (1940) 214, 230, 236, 238
Ray, Bob 130
Ream General Hospital, Army 248
refereeing: boxing 176, 202, 220, 241, 246, 270, 271, 270, 274, 275; wrestling 167, 172, 196, 268, 270, 272
Rejenski (Rudzenski), Frank 16, 280
Rice, Grantland 37–38, 41–42, 47–49, 56, 65, 80, 83, 85, 93, 96, 102, 126, 130, 138, 142, 151, 153, 176, 200, 270
Rickard, Tex 1, 13–14, 53–54, 65, 77, 83, 100, 105, 124, 147, 150–151, 228, 271
Riding High 260

Rienhoff, Dr, William F., Jr. 147
Riggi, Frankie 122
Rio Cabana, Broadway club, NYC 259
Risko, Johnny 37, 41, 44, 49, 51–52, 54, **55**, 56, 58, 65–66, 72, 78, 81, 85, 117; vs. Baer 61–63, 281
Ritchie, Dave 214
Ritchie, Robert 235
Ritchie, Willie Mur "Babe" 106, 215–216, 282
Rivers, Joe 252
Riverside Cemetery, Denver 6
RKO (Radio Pictures, Inc.) 163, 255–259, 264
Roach, Hal 253
Roach, Lavern 249
Roaring Twenties 13
Robinson, Jackie 267
Robinson, Jim 230
Robinson, Pat 238
Robinson, Sugar Ray 5
Rocca, Tony 270
Rockwell, Harvey 237
Rodenberg, Gus 90
rodeos: Hayward 297*ch*16*n*1; Livermore 24; Los Rancheros Visitadores 297*ch*16*n*1; "Max Baer" horse 24; Ogden Pioneer Days 173
Roger, Jean 263
Rogers, Buck 282
Romano, Phil 283
Roosevelt, Franklin 82, 150, 174, 234, 244–245, 273
Roosevelt, Theodore, Jr. 158
Roosevelt Hotel, Hollywood 275
Roosevelt Stadium 220–221, 222, 229
Root, Jack 106
Rootin' Tootin' Tenderfeet 263
Roper, Jack 253
Rosenbloom, Max 69, 87, 192, 214, 246, 258–259, **262**, 267–268, vs. Olin 126
Ross, Barney 87, 264
Roth, Abe 69
Rothenburg, Walter 133, 146
Routis, Andre 221
Rovay, Al 190, 295*n*23
Rowe, Alex 16, 280
Rowe, Billy 154
Roxborough, John 150, 153–154, 202
Rubin, Benny 253
Ruehl, Red 29
Ruggirello, Salvatore 176
Runyon, Damon 6, 13, 32, 95, 143, 149, 241, 253, 270
Russell, William (Bill) 260
Ruth, Babe 13, 112, 158
Ryan, William **237**

Sacks, Leonard **55**, 65, 70
Sacramento Athletic Club 34
Sacramento Community Players 80
St. John, Adela Rogers 253
St. Mary's Cemetery 276, 279

saloons 7, 10, 33, 34, 82, 173, 226, 263, 286n3
Salvold, Lee 230, 235, 255
Santa, Jose (Santa Camarao) 97; Santo-Baer 60–63, 281
Santa Fe Chief 206
Sarazen, Gene 13
Saturday Evening Post 255
Sawyer, Joe 254, 258
Schaaf, Ernie: 37–42, 44, 47, 49–50, 52, 54, 61, 65–68, 75–76, 78–79, 81–85, 95, 97–98, 107, 121, 154, *265*; vs. Baer 38–41, 72–74, 280, 281; vs. Braddock 41; death 81; vs. Uzcudun 65
Schapp, Jeremy 3
Schenone ranch 10
Scheuer, Phillip 256
Schmeling, Maximillian Siegfried Adolph Otto (Max) "Black Uhlan": vs. Baer 77–96, 281; boxer 1–3, 17, 23, 25–26, 37–38, 40–42, 52, 54, 56, 61, 65, 68–69, 72, 75–76, 97–98, 101, 103, 118, 122–123, 127, 129–131, 145–146, 149, 153–154, 164–165, 168–172, 178, 180–183, 186, 188, 190–193, 195–201, 216–218, 221, 223, 236, 247, 253, 264; German paratrooper 243–*244*; vs. Walker 69
Schmuck, Peter 231
Schwartz, Billy 42
Schwartz, Izzy 87
Scott, Phil 17
Scott, Sir Walter 32; *see also Marmion*
Scozza, Lou 153
Shand, Bob: *Oakland Tribune* 22–23, 36, 47, 59
Shandel, Chet 16, 18–19, 280
Sharkey, Jack: 1–2, 17, 23, 25, 37–38, 40–41, 52, 56, 61, 63, 65–66, 68–69, 72, 75–79, 80, 83, 85, 90–98, 106, 119, 158, 165, 170–172, 191, 196, 200–201, 270; vs. Carnera 40; vs. Schmeling 65
Sharkey, Tom 7, 27, 215
Shaw, Jack 90
Sheeline, Harry 58
Sherman, Harry 259
Shilling, Gus 261
Ship and Bottle, Reno Casino 72
Shufflin' Sam 5
Shultz, Fred 175
Sikes, Bob 225
Silva, August (Augie) 10, 197
Silver, Mike 3, 28, 51, 86
Silver, Syd 235
Simms, Eddie 124, 145, 263, 281
Simms, Frankie 69
Simon, Abe 87
Simoni, Joe 16, 280
Simpson, Charles 174
Simpson, Tommy 51
Simpson, Mrs. Wally 179
Sixth Avenue Pub 87
Sjoberg, Elvy 24
Sked, Walter 272
Skip-Along Rosenbloom 262

Skirball, Jack H. 259
slaughterhouses *see* packing companies
Smalley, Garrett L. 174
Smith, Cecil 282
Smith, Gunboat 14, 26, 66
Smith, Harry B.: *San Francisco Chronicle* 68, 107
Smith, Kate 292n25
Smith, Pete 253
Smith, Red: *New York Tribune* 270
Snailham, Billy 16
Soresi, Louis 110
Souza, Tony 169, 173, 281
Soviet Union 217–218
Spanish flu *see* influenza
Spiletti, Henry 55
Stanton, Gene *116*, 117; vs. Buddy Baer film 291n10
Star of David 3, 86–89, 92, 95, 223
Starr, Bee 101
Starr, Tony 287n39
Stein, Sammy *212*
Stern, Dr. Max 224
Stine, T.M. *102*
Stork Club *see* racketeering clubs
Stribling, Ma 66
Stribling, W.L. (Young) 17, 37, 40–41, 54, 63, 66, 78, 97
Strickland, Maurice 177
Strongfort, Lionel 82
Stummie, Henry 59
Sullivan, Charles 253
Sullivan. John L. 221
Sullivan, Mary Ellen *see* Baer, Mary Ellen
Sunday Breakfast 269
Sussman, Jeffery 3
Swiderski, Paul 68–69, 79, 281, 287n39, 288n6
Sybil Grey 255

Taverna, Tillie 15, 16, 280
Taxi 104, 269
Taylor, Estelle 54
television shows 267–269
Ten Greatest Jewish American Boxers 87
Tendler, Lew 87
Tennessee's Partner 259
Thalberg, Irving 252
The 39 Steps 223
Thomas, Dolph 109, *144*
Thomas, Harry (Herman William Pontius) 216–218, 296n5
Thomas, Pup 214
Thomas, Tommy 74
Thompson, Elza 215, 238
Three Mile House, Denver 7
Tobey, Dan 251
Toler, Roscoe 192
Toner, Tom 20, 280
Trafton's Gym, Chicago 156
training camps: Ace of Spades, England 183; Asbury Park NJ 103, 109, 126–9, 146; Clarkstown Country Club, Nyack, NY 207; Grossinger's Country Club Lake, the Catskills, NY 208;

Lake Swannanoa, NJ 90; Lake Wallenpaupack, PA 238; Lakewood, NJ 191–194, 238; Loch Sheldrake, Catskills, NY 126; Long Branch, NJ 190, 229, *231*; Meadowbrook, Newark, NJ 229; Pompton Lakes, NJ 105, 153, 220; Steamboat Springs, NV 55; Wilson's, Orangeburg, NJ 38, 66
trains: motion picture 54; Overland Limited 36; Pullman cars 54
Traung, Charles F. 20, 25, 30–31
Treat, Roger 163
Trickle, Vern 176
Trotter, Marva *see* Louis, Joe
Trotter, the Rev. Paul 156
Trulmans, Al 122
Tully, Jim 71
Tunney, Gene 12, 16, 43, 52, 61, 65, 75, 83, 98, 105–106, 131, 147, 150–154, 158, 173, 188, 191, 196, 201, 204, 218, 244, 270
Turner, George 152, 157
Twentieth Century Athletic Club 50; *see also* Jacobs, Mike
The Two Maxies in Their Vaudeville Review 258–259
2 Roamin' Champs 261

Ullman, Elwood 263
United Press 37, 43, 147
Utah Blaine 266
Uzcudun, Paulino (Paolino) 23, 26, 41, 44, 65–68, 75, 97–98, 123; vs. Baer 54–61, 280

Vackner, Charles 73
Valga, Benny 221
Valhalla, New York 83
Vallee, Rudy 133
Vanderbilt Hotel 153
Van Dyke, W. S. 252
Van Noy, Jack 59–60, 63, 281
Velez, Lupe Weismuller 101, 104, *256*
Veterans of Sacramento 276
Villa, Pancho 30, 34
Vinson, Helen 154

Wagoner, Ronald 109
Wainwright, Bill 183
Walcott, Jersey Joe 264–*265*
Waldorf-Astoria 274
Walker, Buddy 230
Walker, Mickey 21, 41, 61, 69, 72, 75–76, 78, 175, 232, 272
Walker, Syd 253
Walker, Dr. William 105, 130–131, 152, 156, 181, 208
Wallace, Coley 264
Wallace, Gertrud 231
Wallace, J.C. 215
Wallace, William 231
Walsh, Davis J., *INS* 131–132
Walsh, James J. 173, 282
Walton, Scotty *116*
Ward, Alan 56, 163, 202, 211, 219, 246, 258, 267, 270, 272

Ward, Arch 216
Ward, Charles 118–119
Ward, Jem 103
Ward, Nick 103
Washington, Chester 154
Waterman, Joe 167
Waxman, Max 221
Wear, Dr. Walker 181
Weaver, Buck 23, 280
Wedge, Hugh 167
Weer, William 145
Weimer, Dutch 176, 282
Weissmuller, Johnny 101
Wells, Thomas Bucklin, II 35
Wembley Stadium 185
West, Mae 113, 252–253
Western Union 197
White, Al 290*n*29
White, Jules 263
White Heavyweight Champion 232
"white hope(s)" 7, 151, 158, 204, 241
Wignall, Trevor 178, 187
Wilde, Jim 185
Willard, Jess 9, 56, 200, *237*, 245, 252
Willard Hotel, Washington D.C. 147
Willes, Jean 263
Williams, Bob 173, 282
Williams, Hannah 98
Williams, Harry 283
Williams, Joe 143, 163
Willis, Ed 83, 281
Willkie, Wendell 245
Wills, Harry 14, 175
Wilson, Gus 43
Winchell, Walter 143
Wine, Women and Bong 262
Wingfield, Mayor 71; Wingfield's Riverside Hotel, Reno 53
Winston, Eddie (Unknown) 74
Winter, Max 71
Winter War, 1939 217–218
Wirak, T.H. 246
Wistort, Pete 281
Withers, Grant 253
women 6, 54–56, 82, 167, 182, 190, 198, 248, 264, 272
Wood, Jimmy 240
Wood, John 253
Woodworth, Marjorie 254
Work Progress Administration (WPA) 220
Working, Cal 26, 30
World War I 9, 12, 14, 235
World War II 3, 4, 38, 115, 124, 235, *244*, *247*, 255, 302; boxing 250; movies 251, *255*
world's fair 78, 82
Wotanski, Frank 146
Wrestling Association of America 260
Wright, Ed "Bearcat" *175*, 282
Wyatt, Jane 256, 258

Yankee Stadium 77–78, 80, 91, *94*, 146, 150, 156, 158, 170, 172, 175, 191, 200, 205, 208, 218
Young, C.C. 30
Young, Robert 259, *261*
Youssef, Georgie 208

Zellweger, Renée 3, 266
Zimmerman, Paul 5, 126, 164, 235
Zivic brothers 103

www.ingramcontent.com/pod-product-compliance
Lightning Source LLC
Chambersburg PA
CBHW081539300426
44116CB00015B/2689